TEN MOVIES AT A TIME

Books by John DiLeo

Ten Movies at a Time:
A 350-Film Journey Through
Hollywood and America, 1930-1970 (2017)

Screen Savers II:
My Grab Bag of Classic Movies (2012)

Tennessee Williams and Company:
His Essential Screen Actors (2010)

Screen Savers:
40 Remarkable Movies Awaiting Rediscovery (2007)

100 Great Film Performances You Should Remember—
But Probably Don't (2002)

And You Thought You Knew Classic Movies:
200 Quizzes for Golden Age Movie Lovers (1999, 2013)

TEN MOVIES AT A TIME

A 350-Film Journey Through

Hollywood and America

1930-1970

John DiLeo

HANSEN PUBLISHING GROUP

21 20 19 18 17   11 10 9 8 7 6 5 4 3 2

ISBN   978-1-60182-652-7 (paperback)
         978-1-60182-653-4 (ebook)

Cover photograph: Gene Kelly in *It's Always Fair Weather* (1955)

All photographs courtesy of Photofest.

Hansen Publishing Group, LLC
302 Ryders Lane
East Brunswick, NJ 08816
http://hansenpublishing.com

For Earl

Contents

Photographs

Preface

Ten movies at a time: that is both the format and the content of this book. Yes, each chapter addresses ten movies as examples of a particular subject, but the "at a time" factor also signifies the era of each grouping of ten, their distinct moment in movie history, which may be a few years or perhaps a whole decade. Within each chapter, the films are presented chronologically, including those from the same year, taking into account the month (or even week) of each film's release. Essentially, the book covers the period from *Little Caesar* to *Little Big Man,* from the dawn of the talkies to the inception of the ratings system.

Any story of American movies is automatically a story of America, a reflection of what was happening at any given time, or of how the country seemed to see itself, including such things as codes of behavior regarding love, sex, and marriage, and the national mood during hard times or good times, wartime or peacetime. From the anti-war grief of early-'30s WWI movies to the depictions of society's comforts and constrictions within Eisenhower's America, Hollywood is on the record—sometimes bravely, sometimes skittishly. In addition to reacting to contemporary US history (the Depression, World War II, the Cold War, etc.), Hollywood has, along the way, had its own history to absorb (the sound revolution, the enforcement of the Production Code, the end of black and white, etc.). Naturally, the impact of these forces— those from both outside and within the industry—are inextricably linked, their boundaries blurred.

Some stars, such as Bette Davis and Fredric March, are present for this book's duration, carving out space for themselves through changing times and styles, aging through a range of roles. There are also frequent appearances by the likes of Claudette Colbert, Clark Gable, Barbara Stanwyck, Tyrone Power, Susan Hayward, James Stewart, and Natalie Wood, all of whom shared an ability to adapt, to grow, and to continue to connect with audiences.

In three of the chapters, including the opener, the focus is on one individual, someone whose resounding appeal forged a unique career arc and legacy. For the most part, the emphasis is on the *kinds* of movies, the subject matter: genres and sub-genres; trends and cultural shifts; emerging concepts and tried-and-true conventions. If you wonder why I overlook a certain film or mention it only in passing, perhaps I've covered it in a previous book and chose, instead, to examine films I haven't tackled before. Whether good or bad, classic or obscure, popular or dismissed, important or minor, each of these 350 movies reveals something of valued interest to the Hollywood story of 1930 to 1970.

J.D.

TEN MOVIES AT A TIME

Our Jazzy Joan: Silent Sensation Turns Sound Superstar (1930-1932)

The *Jazz Singer* famously changed the course of movie history when it premiered on October 6, 1927, signaling the inevitable demise of the silent era (even though the film was only a partial talkie). Clearly, there would be no turning back. It was somewhat ironic, and certainly bittersweet, that 1928 proved to be the silent era's greatest year, with one artistic triumph after another coming from Hollywood: *The Man Who Laughs, The Crowd, The Circus, The Cameraman, A Woman of Affairs, The Wind, Street Angel, The Last Command, Show People, Steamboat Bill, Jr.,* etc. The subliminal message seemed to be, "It's okay to move on to sound; we've pretty much taken the art of silent cinema as far as it can go." It was in 1929 that the sound era officially got rolling, quite emphatically with the February release of *The Broadway Melody,* which gleefully extolled the virtues of "All Talking! All Singing! All Dancing!"

An interesting thing happened just five months before *Broadway Melody* opened: the emergence of Joan Crawford, a late-breaking silent star. Oh, she'd been kicking around MGM since 1925, with a career already touched by the stuff of legends: as Lucille LeSueur, she was magically plucked from a New York chorus line for a screen test, followed by a Hollywood contract, then christened "Joan Crawford" thanks to a movie-magazine name-the-star contest. The grooming process at MGM included teaming her, with increasing importance, opposite the full roster of the studio's male assets: John Gilbert, Ramon Novarro, William Haines, Tim McCoy, James Murray, and Lon Chaney. She was gaining in confidence and growing more striking (those enormous eyes!) with each successive assignment.

The film that changed everything was *Our Dancing Daughters,* released in September of 1928, almost a full year after Al Jolson in *The Jazz Singer* had rung a death knell for the silents. Crawford became a full-fledged stand-alone movie star directly between Jolson's "You Ain't Heard Nothin' Yet" and the stock market crash in October of 1929. She was the last great star created in the silent era, the final major representation of the Roaring Twenties female, whether you call her a flapper, a jazz baby, a modern, or a flaming youth. She was *all* that, right before it was to be no more. Crawford was the girl of the moment (the way Julia Roberts was after *Pretty Woman* opened in 1990), the idol of millions, a zesty mix of sweetness and naughtiness, charm and exuberance. Considering the hardness of Crawford's middle-aged image, it can be quite a surprise to be confronted with the youthful radiance of her star-making persona. *Our Dancing Daughters* pedaled the well-worn but surefire tract of wild doings tempered by old-fashioned morality, a world of "good girls" and "bad girls" (who pay the price). Crawford plays a rich girl in a high-sheen black-and-white Art Deco paradise, decked out in shimmering fringed costumes and furred capes, her hair a short bob (and lighter than usual). The plot is soapy drivel, with fun-loving Crawford a good girl pretending to be a bad one, calling herself "Diana the Dangerous" but really just a dancing-fool virgin. Basically, it covers the perils of catching a husband in this modern age. Laughable as drama, it luxuriates in divine production values, buoyant spirits, and its undeniably magnetic young star (and not only when she's cutting loose with a Charleston). In its splendid opening, Crawford's feet can't stop dancing while she dresses, perfectly setting the tone of youthful abandon. Alongside sound effects, meat-loaf leading man Johnny Mack Brown, and Anita Page and Dorothy Sebastian as the other "daughters," it's Crawford's show all the way.

After two more silents, *Dream of Love* (1928) and *The Duke Steps Out* (1929), Crawford made an auspicious talkie debut (along with nearly every other star on the lot) in the musical variety extravaganza *The Hollywood Revue of 1929*. Her moment, singing and dancing "Got a Feelin' for You," notably revived in *That's Entertainment!* (1974) long after it had been forgotten, shows Crawford's obvious limitations as a musical star, mostly elbows and knees, yet her freshness and enthusiasm surpass the clumping choreography and her unrefined skills. There would be one more silent, *Our Modern Maidens* (1929), not a sequel but definitely aimed at the *Dancing Daughters* audience, with Anita Page ("hot" after *The Broadway Melody*) back at Crawford's side. It's another romance-magazine trifle, with Crawford again playing a rich girl, another modern who's really just an old-fashioned gal. She's engaged to Douglas Fairbanks, Jr. (whom she married in real life that year), but she falls for Rod La Rocque. Satisfying fans' expectations of their Charleston-mad star, she dances again, though this time in a more serious and dramatic sequence. A pre-crash hit during the fall of 1929, *Our Modern Maidens* is one of the final gasps of true Roaring Twenties cinema.

Crawford made her dramatic talkie debut in *Untamed*, released in late 1929, a month after the crash. Despite depicting a world that was suddenly over, *Untamed* was a positive harbinger for Crawford's future in talkies. (It was her first of six movies with Robert Montgomery, a bright newcomer ready to secure his place among MGM's talking personalities.) Following the formula of her previous hits, *Untamed* is about clothes, hair, parties, and lavish interiors, even though it begins, rather bizarrely, in South America with Crawford having been raised by her oilman father in a primitive world. She sings and dances, with her customary abandon, to "Chant of the Jungle." (Hard to imagine now, but Crawford's fans continued to expect her to sing and dance.) Though wealthy when she moves to New York, she's also feisty and naively uncivilized. About halfway through the picture she becomes Joan Crawford, the party girl in beautiful dresses. Thus far, and continuing into the '30s, Crawford's vehicles didn't aim very high, content to satisfy a public who merely wanted romantic adventures and pretty accessories, happy enough just to be in Crawford's vibrant company. *Untamed* is relentlessly silly, but you might call it fun, if you're inclined to be won over by Crawford's allure. She was peddling Hollywood glamour and was by now a feminine ideal whom young females wanted to emulate. Greta Garbo was decidedly not a mere mortal, but Joan Crawford was a screen queen whose fabulousness just might be attainable.

   With the Depression about to be the new reality, how exactly was Joan Crawford, the newest star of '20s glitter and frivolity, going to fare in a darker landscape? Might she go the way of "It Girl" Clara Bow and soon be a distant memory of a madcap era? And what of all those silent leading men who helped groom Crawford? They would all soon be gone, either dead or washed up or retired or relegated to B pictures. Among MGM's ladies, only Garbo and Norma Shearer would accompany Crawford to greater heights in the '30s. By refashioning herself to fit the times, Crawford quickly became one of the talkies' biggest stars, occasionally still playing rich girls but more importantly becoming the quintessential shopgirl, a Depression-era working gal whose beauty and ambition catapulted her into chic romantic fantasies (vicariously devoured by young women across America). In 1932, she was ranked number three among box-office stars (behind Marie Dressler and Janet Gaynor). I use Crawford here to look at the formation of the Golden Age of Hollywood through the prism of one career. The silents had been her training ground and springboard, but here's Crawford in her first ten movies of the 1930s, making the most of her assets, triumphing over threadbare material, refining her image, personality, and talents, becoming one of the more iconic movie stars of an illustrious decade.

Grand Hotel (1932): John Barrymore and Joan Crawford

Montana Moon **(1930)** – The first Crawford movie of the new decade, released in March, was unsurprisingly very much a pre-crash vehicle, an *Our Dancing Daughters*-type picture with Crawford as a carefree rich girl running around with a loose, useless crowd. She's over animated and playfully coy in the Norma Shearer manner (all that posing and attitudinizing in such a tiresomely self-conscious way). She becomes smitten with cowboy Johnny Mack Brown (still eminently resistible) who works on a ranch owned by her father. Billed solo above the title, Crawford is clearly a movie star, looking swell in her Adrian-designed fashions, but you wouldn't ever mistake her for an actress. Call her a green, enthusiastic amateur. Movie musicals were the new craze, and *Montana Moon* is a partial, halfhearted example, with Crawford again singing quite acceptably, backed by a cowboy chorus. This time her dance is a tango, with the unctuous Ricardo Cortez. It's an entirely forgettable, throwaway picture, mostly of interest for its pre-crash vestiges, before Hollywood had figured out how to handle America's new reality. *Montana Moon* gives Crawford minimal support, unfortunately proving how little MGM felt it had to exert itself to please Crawford's fan base. If she were to continue being popular, her formula would have to be retooled for less frivolous times.

Our Blushing Brides (1930) – The *Our Dancing Daughters* trio is back, but what a difference two years makes. It's Crawford's first Depression picture, introducing the Crawford shopgirl formula. If she could no longer be a devil-may-care debutante, well, she'd represent the typical working girl (whose atypical beauty opens doors to a world of splendor, including expensive clothes and handsome suitors). Call *Our Blushing Brides* Depression escapism, a get-rich (yet moralistic) fantasy. Crawford is a NYC department-store model making $22.50 a week, with Anita Page and Dorothy Sebastian her roommates and co-workers. Crawford is the good girl who believes in love, unwilling to settle for a sugar daddy, while the other two gals provide cautionary tales: Page meets a bad end after becoming the mistress of the boss' son; Sebastian marries a rich guy who turns out to be a criminal. Crawford wards off the advances of Robert Montgomery, the boss' other son, but she also likes him. As with many an early Crawford picture, the target audience seems to be teenage girls daydreaming about their romantic options (with the helpful bonus of seeing how easily it can all go *bad*). No surprise that the movie includes two fashion shows, one focused solely on lingerie while the other, the film's colossal centerpiece, is an orgy of Adrian clothes presented at Montgomery's Oyster Bay estate. He also has an Art Deco treehouse with a sunken living room. (Only in the movies!) After heaps of melodrama, the good and patient smart girl wins the rich boy, with Crawford's own career soaring in the process. But Ms. Page, a no-talent, vanished amid the emergence of Jean Harlow, and Ms. Sebastian would soon be gone too. Montgomery continued his easygoing rise to stardom while Crawford, still showing only mild glimmers of talent, was dominating her films through sheer force of looks and presence.

Paid (1930) – Audiences had already known and liked the flapper Crawford and the shopgirl Crawford, but *Paid* delivered another popular, dependable persona: hard, no-nonsense Crawford. Like many early talkies, Crawford's movies took outdated melodramas and embroidered them with enough modern trappings to make them seem new again. Nonetheless, *Paid* is creaky, overlong crime fare, based on the 1912 play *Within the Law*. More than anything else, it seems to be carried by the transfixing intensity of Crawford's eyes. Though innocent, she's convicted of grand larceny at the workplace, another department store. She serves three years, vowing revenge on the boss who accused her and conveniently studying law books during her incarceration. Prison pal Marie Prevost hooks her up with crook Robert Armstrong, which leads to big bucks in the blackmail racket. Crawford pursues Kent Douglass, her old boss' son, and she marries him! But, you guessed it, she really falls in love with him. And he adores her no matter what. There's plenty of rubbish concerning Crawford's attempts to stop Armstrong's shenanigans. She works herself into frenzies of emotion, but she's more overheated than effective. It's a stagy picture, a genuine relic, the kind in which a Japanese servant can be referred to as "you yellow peril." In this loose era (pre-enforcement of Production Code censorship), *Paid* shows Crawford getting a leer from an older female at the prison shower.

Dance, Fools, Dance (1931) – Crawford gets to have it all here, starting as her onetime flapper self and then becoming just another working girl (two Crawfords for the price of one!). Despite its intriguing fall-and-rise arc, the film's only claim to fame is as the first of Crawford's eight movies with Clark Gable (here billed sixth, while she's billed solo above the title). Things get off to a racy start on a yacht with a crowd of young people, including Crawford, stripping down to their undies and diving into the water. She is also sleeping with boyfriend Lester Vail, believing in "trying love out." Then the stock market crashes, her dad drops dead, and she and brother William Bakewell are left with nothing. However, she adapts, thriving at a newspaper job, while he sinks. She's really too wonderful and brave and hardworking for words, soon preferring her more useful life to her once pampered one (a pandering attempt to make the Depression audience feel good). Bakewell goes to work for bootlegger Gable. In his villain phase (not unlike Humphrey Bogart's dues-paying days), Gable was also nasty that year to Norma Shearer (*A Free Soul*) and Barbara Stanwyck (*Night Nurse*). Continuing to work every Crawford trick into the mix, the film has her going undercover as a dancer in Gable's club, doing a number similar to her *Hollywood Revue* routine, sexy and free but mostly about showing off her legs. If you know Crawford best as Mildred Pierce, it's truly hard to fathom just how often she danced in her early '30s movies. (She also does a ballroom number on the yacht.) Investigating a killer, she has no idea that it's her brother she's pursuing. Gable and Crawford don't meet until an hour into this increasingly ridiculous movie. He actually tells her, "We're gonna take you for a pleasant little ride." Gable was making his name by always being the most natural actor in any scene in which he appeared, often making those around him look hopelessly phony. It didn't hurt that he threatened sex with every glance. Crawford had at last met her match in star power, someone with whom she could not only develop a sizzling chemistry but who could also raise her game as an actress.

Laughing Sinners (1931) – Gable is back but Crawford is still solo above the title. Again, MGM wasn't choosing her vehicles with great care. Here's another assembly-line product, utilizing the Crawford personality but doing nothing to nurture her or expand her potential, playing more with her hair color than her acting range. In a particularly crummy, shopworn plot, she goes from bad girl to good girl to bad girl, before finally settling on being a good girl. First seen as a restaurant entertainer, she's dumped by her traveling-salesman lover (Neil Hamilton, billed above Gable), devastated when he marries his boss' daughter. Gable, of the Salvation Army, rescues Crawford from a suicide attempt on a bridge, and she joins up! He plays the drum; she plays the tambourine. Of course, Hamilton returns, practically twirling his mustache, hoping to set her up somewhere as his mistress. She succumbs to him, then hates herself in the morning. As the two men fight for her soul, there are no surprises, and certainly no nuances. Early in the film, she has two numbers, a comic dance in which she morphs from bearded hillbilly to jazz baby, and a torch song atop a piano. Her dancing remains uninhibited, though it's hard to believe she would have danced as often as she did if Eleanor Powell had arrived at MGM a few years earlier, showing what a real dancer could do. (Moviegoers hadn't yet seen Fred Astaire either, not until his 1933 debut in *Dancing Lady,* partnering Crawford!) Gable has a thankless good-guy role (a reformed ex-con), though at least he punches out Hamilton. And underused Marjorie Rambeau, here as Crawford's pal and fellow performer, later played her mother in *Torch Song* (1953). How bizarre that *Laughing Sinners* is based on a play called *Torch Song.*

This Modern Age (1931) – The most persuasive element here is how fetching Crawford looks as a blonde. This Paris-set soap has her reuniting with her long-estranged mother (Pauline Frederick) after the death of her father. Mother and daughter become very close, but Ms. Frederick keeps secret the fact that she's been a kept woman for the last seven years. Neil Hamilton is back, as a rich Harvard lad who becomes Crawford's love interest. (Really, MGM, couldn't you do better for your glowing star than Neil Hamilton?) Still able to be cast as nineteen, Crawford is a spirited "good girl," well-matched to Frederick, with whom she shares a definite physical resemblance. Their relationship is warm and appealing, with Crawford revealing acting promise in their shared sensitivity. She eventually hopes to reform Frederick, and so there's some bumpy melodrama on the way to a happy ending. More than Mr. Hamilton, Crawford's main romance is with her Adrian wardrobe, the major reason to see this film.

Possessed (1931) – Here's the quintessential pre-Code Crawford vehicle, elegantly directed by Clarence Brown. You can feel all the forces of MGM glamour fusing triumphantly, not just the Adrian clothes but also the decor and the black-and-white cinematography. Unexceptional as drama, it's an intoxicatingly crafted poor-girl Crawford fantasy, charting her rise from small-town factory worker to mistress of a wealthy lawyer (Gable). It begins in 1928 when she goes to NYC and meets him, then cuts to 1931, after her transformation into a sophisticated hostess (posing as a divorcee) kept by Gable in her own apartment. They're madly in love, but he won't marry her because of lingering bitterness over his divorce from a cheating wife. In addition to being at the peak of her beauty, Crawford comes through with her best performance to date, her fullest and most confident. Though Gable had risen considerably over the course of their three 1931 films, his role here isn't much. Crawford is still billed solo above the title, still commanding the show. (It wasn't until their next one, 1933's *Dancing Lady,* that they were on equal footing, following his 1932 *Red Dust* smash with Jean Harlow.) The most memorable sequence comes early when the poor Crawford gazes into the windows of a slowly passing train, observing rich people and their servants, palpably yearning for this slide show of splendors—it's a peerless Depression-era movie moment. The melodrama becomes florid when Crawford turns noble, trying to disappear from Gable's life so he can run for governor without scandal. Pretending she doesn't love him (so he'll dump her), she valiantly plays a *Camille* scene. He slaps her and calls her a "little tramp." (Men are often stupid in women's pictures.) Nonetheless, this is a richly sensual movie, including a sexy scene in which our stars are late for their own party, detained by lovemaking. No dancing in this one, but Crawford, at the piano, sings in English, French, and German.

Grand Hotel (1932) – After the all-around success of *Possessed,* Crawford was ready to hold her own in this all-star Oscar-winning Best Picture, one of MGM's crowning achievements of the 1930s, a movie endlessly imitated, iconic in the clichés it introduced (including Greta Garbo's line, "But why am I telling you all this? Last night I didn't know you at all"). It remains expert, vastly entertaining, and emotionally affecting. It's the granddaddy of big-name ensemble pictures, beautifully directed by Edmund Goulding, boasting a script of remarkably efficient, intertwined storytelling. Add top-notch production values, lustrous photography, and the percolating confinement of two days set entirely on the hotel premises in Berlin. Within are Garbo as a Russian ballerina and tortured artist, and John Barrymore as a broke baron and hotel thief, both stirringly transformed by their sudden romance. Garbo is an iridescent, hypnotic force, beyond mere acting, while Barrymore is the picture's warm heart, subtler than Garbo but no less devastating. Crawford is the stenographer, a temp hired by industrial magnate Wallace Beery, and Lionel Barrymore, in the performance of his career, is the dying man ready to spend his savings. (Though his role would seem to play into his penchant for hamminess, his acting is unguardedly exposed and intensely moving.) Unfortunately, the ladies share no screen time, but Crawford, in dire need of talented co-stars beyond Gable and Montgomery, scores with both Barrymores, forging touching friendships and honest rapports. Though used and bruised (and willing to prostitute herself to Beery), she's never self-pitying. Crawford had surpassed herself two pictures in a row, exuding smarts, inner strength, and vulnerability as never before. It's Beery who is the movie's weak link. Does he seem so phony because he's the only one using a German accent? *Grand Hotel* is the sole film to win Best Picture without receiving a single other Oscar nomination (not even for either of the Barrymores). Crawford, billed third (after Garbo and John Barrymore), had at last added some integrity and class to her movie career, seeming right at home alongside giants.

Letty Lynton (1932) – It's famous as the movie with the Adrian gown (white organdy with ruffled shoulders) that Macy's copied and sold like hotcakes, a testament to Hollywood's infinite impact on fashion trends and tastes. Its other claim to fame is as the Crawford movie that's been out of circulation since 1936, thanks to a plagiarism suit, still available only in bootleg copies. As for the film itself, it's a disappointing setback for Crawford after *Possessed* and *Grand Hotel,* a junky vehicle that, yes, melds fabulous clothes with overblown melodrama, but in no way takes advantage of her recent strides. This time she's a rich girl gone bad, but when she wants to be good again, she can't shake her past. The age-old story! It begins in Montevideo, with Crawford in a sexual relationship with slithery Nils Asther. She leaves him, sails to NYC and meets rich boy Robert Montgomery aboard ship. They fall in love, as if in a romantic comedy, but Asther, evoking a dastardly nineteenth-century villain, isn't letting her go. Why not just tell Montgomery the truth? That'd be too easy. Plus there are those incriminating love letters. It all leads to poison and a mickey, just like real life! Despite being directed by Clarence Brown (*Possessed*), Crawford isn't at all relaxed, seeming extremely self-conscious, mostly about maintaining her affected MGM speech (which never suits her). She was always best when playing poor strivers (see *The Women*), which was something she actually knew about. *Letty Lynton* presents Crawford purely as a visual object, all eyes and hair and Adrian. (Another white gown, with a dark bit of fabric hanging from her belly, is positively obscene.) Montgomery, by now a star in his own right, deserved better than a service role in a Crawford ritual. Her fans, still willing to watch her in just about anything, came to see their glamour-drenched idol, then stopped at Macy's to try to emulate her.

Rain (1932) – Crawford and Norma Shearer were side by side, both becoming stars in the second half of the '20s, both smoothly adapting to talkies and reigning as MGM queens of the early '30s. They were modestly talented and highly ambitious, but not quite on equal footing. Shearer was married to Irving Thalberg, the studio's "supervisor of production" (its artistic director), thus getting first dibs on the more prestigious scripts (*Private Lives, Strange Interlude, Smilin' Through*), alternating those films with more commercial melodramas (*A Free Soul, Strangers May Kiss*), the kind that were Crawford's bread and butter. It was on loan to United Artists where Crawford got the kind of challenge she craved, working for the great Lewis Milestone (*All Quiet on the Western Front*) on the first sound version of the sensational 1922 stage success *Rain*, which, based on a W. Somerset Maugham story, had made Jeanne Eagels an acting legend. Gloria Swanson had already gotten an Oscar nomination for the 1928 silent version titled *Sadie Thompson*. And now it was Crawford's turn for all that prestige, with a screenplay by no less than playwright Maxwell Anderson. Despite her admirable attempt, she got slammed for her effort. Sure, she tends to be rather obvious in her effects, but she's every bit as good or bad as Gloria Swanson was. Besides, the material is impossibly hoary, incessantly verging on camp, a cliché melodrama with lead characters in no way plausible. In spite of Milestone's attempts to open things up, plus his use of quick cuts, striking lighting, and the inventive cinematography of Oliver Marsh, the film remains stagy. But Crawford does have a great entrance: we see one wrist, then the other, one ankle, then the other, and finally that face! Playing a prostitute, she is overly made up, eyes blazing. You know she's a tramp because "St. Louis Blues" can be heard; that's the song that *always* told moviegoers when a woman was "like that." In Pago Pago, while waiting for a boat during interminable rain, Crawford's Sadie is harassed by Walter Huston's Mr. Davidson, a reformer. (Huston gives a rare disappointing performance, sorely lacking variety.) Crawford's transition to being "saved" is unconvincing (as it is in Swanson's film and in Rita Hayworth's 1953 *Miss Sadie Thompson*), with the material coming across as nothing more than masochistic trash, albeit reliably enlivened by its whore with a heart of gold and its sexually repressed holy man. Her transition back, after Huston rapes her, also feels abrupt, mere switches going on and off. (The best acting comes from William Gargan as the marine enamored with Crawford.) After all her Adrian fashion parades, Crawford has just two costumes here, the whore get-up and a dark robe. That's how you know she's a serious actress! No, *Rain* didn't do for Crawford what she had hoped. She returned to MGM and continued her box-office supremacy in lighter material, playing the usual Crawford formulas until they were all tired out and she was no longer young enough to put them over. For the next three decades, despite slumps, she was the screen's deftest master of reinvention, even adding a *Mildred Pierce* (1945) Oscar to her mantle. But, in that first gasp of the sound era, when the talkies were finding their way, when Hollywood was consolidating its resources and creating a golden era, there were few movie stars more dependably transporting than Joan Crawford.

On Speaking Terms: The Talking Breed of Movie Star (1930-1933)

As Joan Crawford sauntered painlessly into the talkies, she was a member of a rather select group of silent players. Joining her were Ronald Colman and John Barrymore, at last able to show off their vocal resonance and finesse, as well as Crawford's MGM studio-mates Norma Shearer and Greta Garbo, neither an obvious shoo-in for sound-era success thanks to Shearer's erratic acting skills and Garbo's Swedish accent. The most recent silent stars, such as Gary Cooper and Janet Gaynor (and Crawford herself) were new enough not to have been *too* imprinted by the silent era, still fresh enough to be refitted without undue stress. While audiences and critics embraced all the aforementioned stars, the casualty list grew ever longer. Unlike Garbo's husky purr, a strong accent appears to have been the chief reason why Hungarian Vilma Banky and German Emil Jannings (the first-ever Best Actor Oscar winner) opted out of Hollywood, while some native-born stars, including Norma Talmadge and Mae Murray, dipped a toe into talkies, then quickly bolted. Superstar Mary Pickford hung around long enough to win an Oscar for the talking *Coquette* (1928)—bad movie, bad performance—allowing her to exit with her dignity intact, making only four more talkies, while Lillian Gish, unimpressed with the new medium, made two lackluster attempts before refocusing her career toward the stage. Others were more determined to conquer the beast, remaining as long as possible, until it was blatantly clear that their silent magic simply wasn't translating. Maybe "It" girl Clara Bow and animated juvenile William Haines were too associated with pre-crash America to assimilate into a Depression-era landscape. He-man Richard Dix was among those valiantly trudging forward, finding major (if undeserved) success with *Cimarron* (1931) but soon was relegated to B pictures, while the more sensitive Richard Barthelmess, still above the title in his early-'30s Warner Brothers vehicles, saw his stardom trounced by exciting newcomers. Ramon Novarro tried singing his way into the talkies but was challenged by his thick Mexican accent and was eventually rejected as both leading man and musical star. (Accents could also enhance a star's career—look at Marlene Dietrich and Charles Boyer—but it was a perilous adjustment when an accent had to contend with a stardom built in silence.) Only Gloria Swanson's first of six talkies, *The Trespasser* (1929), was a hit, leaving her to abandon films after the musical *Music in the Air* (1934), but of course, she'd be back, while Marion Davies' career limped along until

1937, with not even William Randolph Hearst powerful enough to keep her stardom afloat. True, no one was getting any younger, and quite a few silent stars, including swashbuckling Douglas Fairbanks, were simply too old to continue doing the things that had made them stars in the first place. Perhaps the two saddest stories, both at MGM, were the declines of John Gilbert and Buster Keaton. Gilbert, unfairly tagged as having a career-shattering voice, steadily crumbled and was dead in 1936, while Keaton lost artistic control and was thoroughly mishandled, a situation worsened by alcoholism.

If talkers were now needed—talkers who could act—isn't that exactly what the legitimate theater is all about? Only people with trained, aurally pleasing voices need apply, those knowing how to deliver a line, how to use vocal inflection to get a laugh or wring a tear, not to mention people who could really sing. (With microphone-limited camera mobility, many early talkies were going to look like filmed theater anyway.) However, just as silent stars didn't necessarily have proper voices, stage stars didn't automatically have screen presence. Several Broadway giants took their stabs at the talkies and didn't "click." Consider musical star Marilyn Miller, sophisticated comedienne Ina Claire, and the team of Alfred Lunt and Lynn Fontanne (despite their respectful Oscar nominations for *The Guardsman* [1931]). Or how about Tallulah Bankhead, who wouldn't score in movies until *Lifeboat* (1944)? Even Helen Hayes, an Oscar winner for *The Sin of Madelon Claudet* (1931) and star of a classic, *A Farewell to Arms* (1932), had no staying power and was gone by 1935 after a string of flops, not returning until middle-aged. There was no way to assume who would succeed and who wouldn't, the outcomes dictated only by ticket buyers.

The early sound era was a great time for up-and-comers with stage backgrounds, those who had shown theatrical promise without yet becoming theatrical fixtures, suggesting that they might be highly adaptable at fine-tuning their stageworthy skills for the newest variation of a relatively new art form. Some of the earliest of these stars would rank among the screen's most enduring legends, instantly distinct from their silent precursors because of what they had to say and, more specifically, *how* they said it: Barbara Stanwyck with her streetwise Brooklynese, Edward G. Robinson's snarling nasality, James Cagney's rat-tat-tat delivery, Katharine Hepburn's Bryn Mawr affectations, and Mae West's sly moans between quips. This new breed staked their claim not only to be watched but to be *heard*.

Morocco (1930): Gary Cooper and Marlene Dietrich

Ladies of Leisure (1930) – When director Frank Capra is mentioned, it's common to think first of James Stewart or Gary Cooper, yet it was Barbara Stanwyck who made five movies with Capra, including this one, their first together and her fourth overall. It's also the movie that made her a star. She was a Broadway actress who had a personal success in the play *Burlesque* (1927), which became the film *The Dance of Life* (1929) starring Nancy Carroll. Columbia's *Ladies of Leisure* proved to showcase all the things audiences would love about Stanwyck for decades to come: naturalness, a likable toughness, and bruised vulnerability. The script and its situations are thin, tired, and obvious, but Capra is clearly a talented young filmmaker providing visual verve, the better to highlight the gifts of a young star he clearly admires. She's a self-proclaimed party girl, more accurately a call girl. Rich-boy painter Ralph Graves (a zero) asks her to pose for his masterpiece titled "Hope," wanting to capture the *real* her. Stanwyck may be a feisty wisecracker but she also evokes, unsentimentally, a child's innocence. She falls for Graves, even though he's engaged. There's a lovely sleep-over moment when Graves approaches, and she, assuming he's going to force himself on her, is instead thrilled when he covers her with a blanket. When he falls for her, too, and is threatened with disownment, we're in soap territory with his mother begging her to give him up. Luckily, Capra tempers the melodrama with a tender, delicate fade-out. Despite shortcomings, *Ladies of Leisure* retains the charge of seeing a star and a director persuasively declaring themselves, with Stanwyck already sculpting a career-sized persona.

Morocco (1930) – Marlene Dietrich was riding a wave of attention from the German release (April 1930) of Josef von Sternberg's *The Blue Angel*. Directed next by von Sternberg for her US debut in *Morocco,* she seduced the American audience when it opened in November of 1930, one month before *The Blue Angel*'s US premiere. Dietrich plays self-possessed cabaret performers in both films, but in Paramount's *Morocco* she has a more interesting arc to play, and she's no longer in support of another character. (*The Blue Angel* is mostly about Emil Jannings' masochistic self-destruction.) *Morocco* introduces her as a genuine figure of mystery—emotionally neutral, unfazed by anything— with the self-protective cover of a woman who, susceptible to love, has lost all faith in men. Her moody languor is perfectly attuned to von Sternberg's hazy glamour, his aura of divine decadence. Stunningly photographed by Lee Garmes, amid studio-bound exotica, *Morocco* has Dietrich exquisitely costumed (far from her *Blue Angel* seediness). Clad in top hat, white tie, and tails, she wows a crowd with a French song, then, in a daring, uninhibited attention-grabber, she kisses a female patron on the mouth. For "What Am I Bid for My Apples?" she's in a short black costume with a boa, displaying the famed Dietrich gams. Gary Cooper, a private in the French Foreign Legion, as well as a cocky womanizer, unsettles her composure. Both are running from unspecified pasts. They have a steamy chemistry of beautiful opposites, his American energy versus her European repose. They don't really share any happy times together but recognize their mutual love as undeniable fact. It becomes triangular with rich, kind, and patient Adolphe Menjou (unusually good) who offers Dietrich material splendors. As plot, *Morocco* is hopeless, dreary stuff, and many will find its pace slow-going. However, as a treatise on romantic love, it's an unrivaled intoxication. Because of von Sternberg's visionary control over all aspects, *Morocco* plays as a mood piece, a visual poem. Once her passion is ignited, Dietrich is no longer the jaded, in-control woman. There's a key moment at a fancy dinner when she hears the approach of the legion, thus anticipating Cooper's return; this snaps her out of Menjou's world, causing her accidentally to break the string of pearls he just gave her, a perfect metaphor for the end of any future with him, the end of anything that doesn't involve Cooper. In a positively transcendent ending—profoundly absurd and masochistic or devastatingly moving and hypnotic, depending on your outlook—Dietrich impulsively chooses pure love, making it feel as if no other choice is possible. We're not meant to imagine what comes next, just to feel the force of her gesture, to luxuriate in a heightened romantic cinema. She kicks off her shoes in the sand and follows love, as if having found her true purpose. There's nothing real about it, except Dietrich herself, devoid of melodrama. Ever-modern and subtle in her emotional gradations, she makes *you* go to *her*. In her only Oscar-nominated performance, Dietrich is a marvel, moving from cool detachment to amorous unrest, exposing a soft romantic yearning that seems even to surprise herself.

Min and Bill (1930) – Marlene Dietrich lost the Oscar to someone as unlike her as can be imagined. Whereas Dietrich withheld and suggested, Marie Dressler let it all hang out, shamelessly courting audience love and winning it handily. This blowsy sexagenarian became a surprise box-office powerhouse with an in-your-face mix of toughness and sentimentality. Her acting was broad—some might call it mugging—but it usually worked because she was so damned likable, exuding such fondness for her fans. After a lifetime in the theater and silent movies, Dressler enjoyed movie superstardom in the last four years of her life, winning the Best Actress Oscar for this waterfront *Stella Dallas*, an immodest piece of surefire manipulation, a hoary tale of sacrificial motherlove. Though it came from MGM, you'll find no glamour here! Director George Hill gave it a salty West Coast dockside ambiance, the location of Dressler's lowdown hotel for fishermen, including Wallace Beery, her drinking buddy and sort-of love interest. Though his role is decidedly secondary to hers, this film might also be called his star-maker, coming soon after his Oscar-nominated turn in *The Big House* (1930). He's in his dopey-lug mode, amusingly no match for her formidability, especially in the scene where she beats him up, which climaxes with Dressler actually wielding an axe! The *Stella Dallas* stuff involves Dressler raising Dorothy Jordan, a waif abandoned by tramp-boozer Marjorie Rambeau. The irresistible trick of Dressler's performance is her brusque treatment of the now-teenage Jordan, the kind of put-on harshness that never for a moment lets you doubt how much the old bag adores the kid. Dressler increasingly hurts the girl's feelings for her own good, sending her to a fancy school, *nobly* driving her away from the waterfront. Trouble comes with the return of Rambeau, but, don't worry, Dressler will secure Jordan's future with whatever it takes. The happy-sad ending further endeared Dressler to audiences (and Academy members), and her comic antics and affectionate camaraderie with Beery led to *Tugboat Annie* (1933), a popular reteaming. *Min and Bill* is minor, including a terrible slapstick sequence involving a runaway speedboat, but Dressler truly delivers, knowing exactly how to make an audience smile (and sniffle).

Little Caesar (1931) – After a string of Broadway credits, it didn't take Edward G. Robinson long to become one of the talkies' more commanding new stars. His breakthrough was Warner Brothers' *Little Caesar,* the textbook rise-and-fall gangster picture, filled with situations and dialogue to be imitated ever after. If it now seems like an antiquated milestone, that doesn't negate director Mervyn LeRoy's fierce and fluid filmmaking, including a superbly edited New Year's Eve hold-up, or Robinson's towering work as a nobody who's ambitious to be a somebody. He and pal Douglas Fairbanks, Jr. start out together but go in different directions, with Fairbanks becoming half of a ballroom-dance team with Glenda Farrell. Within a world of Italian gangsters, Robinson's Rico is ruthless with a gun and violent without guilt, but he never touches liquor or apparently women. Fairbanks is the only person he cares about, suggesting that "Little Caesar," so determined to be the toughest tough guy, is overcompensating for the fact that he's in love with his best pal. (Robinson never has a girlfriend, not even a single date.) He tells Fairbanks, "Who else have I got to give a hang about?" In a major moment, Robinson intends to shoot Fairbanks but can't. There's a riveting close-up of him unable to kill the thing he loves, undone by this one and only vulnerability, those homoerotic feelings of which he isn't consciously aware. On the run, he says to an underling, "This is what I get for liking a guy too much." I'm hardly the first to have noticed this, and yet Little Caesar still hasn't been generally acknowledged as a closet case, perhaps too threatening a notion within such a hyper-masculine genre. Robinson is also terrific whenever strutting with pleasure, as when buying ten copies of a newspaper splashing his photo. The flip side of his preening arrogance is the childlike insecurity fueling it, leading to those sharply funny show-off tendencies, the hunger for spiffy clothes and jewelry, all part of his inferiority-driven ego and hubris. With his primal grunts and growls, Robinson is an operatic presence, dominating the screen despite his diminutive size, a case of personality over square footage. Like a Roman Candle, his Little Caesar has a flashiness fated to be fleeting. If the performance now suggests a Robinson impersonation, well, it's a caricature that retains much of its initial zest.

The Public Enemy (1931) – About four months after their smashing success with *Little Caesar,* Warner Brothers released another instant classic of the genre, doing for Irish hoodlums what they had just done for Italians. William A. Wellman's *The Public Enemy* took another New York talent, James Cagney, in his fourth film, and made him as dazzling and explosive a star as Edward G. Robinson, a charismatic individual of white-hot self-assurance and volatile unpredictability. Excitingly modulated by Wellman, *Public Enemy* has many memorable spurts of nasty humor and violence, with Cagney seeming to enjoy batting around both men and women, including that famous grapefruit impulsively smashed into Mae Clarke's kisser. He rises during Prohibition, often in the role of "muscle," thriving in a beer racket that brings him clothes, cars, and dames. (Unlike Robinson's Rico, Cagney's Tom is a ladies' man.) For all his pugnacious charm, Cagney is plainly believable as a cold-blooded killer. At the climax, in a downpour, and with a gun in each hand, he gleefully anticipates the revenge he's about to take (off-screen) on the mob who killed his best friend. The ending, as grisly today as it was in 1931, packs a disturbing wallop. Unfortunately, the family scenes, involving Cagney's good-boy brother Donald Cook and sickeningly jovial mother Beryl Mercer, do not hold up as well as the mobster elements. Though movie buffs remember Ms. Clarke and her citrus-pummeled cheek, do they recall that she and Cagney are living together unmarried? Jean Harlow and Joan Blondell are also featured, but the other female to watch is Mia Marvin who sleeps with Cagney when he's drunk. Hung over the next morning, he has no memory of it until she reminds him. He slaps her, not so much for taking advantage of him, but for temporarily, and unforgivably, wresting his power away from him. What's even more unforgivable is that neither Cagney nor Robinson got Oscar nominations for their extraordinary bursts into gangster stardom.

A Free Soul (1931) – In 1931, newcomer Clark Gable appeared onscreen with Joan Crawford, Barbara Stanwyck, Greta Garbo, Jean Harlow, and Norma Shearer. Is it any wonder that so many illustrious ladies quickly realized the benefits of sharing the screen with its future King? He'd been on Broadway and had done extra work in silents, but the talkies were clearly his destiny, and MGM's *A Free Soul,* among his dozen of 1931 films, is probably the one that most firmly declared his potential. Though a vehicle for Norma Shearer (billed solo above the title), and despite Lionel Barrymore winning the Best Actor Oscar for it, *A Free Soul* is seized by Gable; he remains its most enduringly modern element. Hardly a good movie, call it a juicy pre-Code provocation. Director Clarence Brown is unable to prevent Shearer from overacting any chance she gets, yet she does have one great moment, the look on her face at first seeing Gable—instant arousal. When she and the film are relaxed and offhand, things crackle, but as it all becomes too "dramatic," beware. Shearer is the upper-class daughter of an alcoholic lawyer (Barrymore); they're black sheep of a stodgy society family. She becomes caught between a dull, adoring fiancé (Leslie Howard) and a sexy gambler-mobster (Gable). Eight years before Vivien Leigh, Shearer ponders the choice between Ashley Wilkes and Rhett Butler, which, come on, is never much of a contest. (Cast to type, Howard is an insufferable wet-noodle, while Gable is a walking erection; the *GWTW* boys share three scenes.) Shearer plays a thrill-seeking free thinker, slumming by enjoying sex with bad-boy Gable. He'll become a more brutish threat, continuing the Robinson-Cagney tradition by having his most attractive and unattractive qualities swirl together, like a soft-serve ice-cream twist. It's all leading to the broken-down Barrymore back in a courtroom, making it possible for him to win that Oscar. (Though he's good at making his thirst for alcohol feel genuine, he succumbs to the overblown bait of the climax.) Tolerate all the melodramatic creaking so you can savor the stylish Art Deco packaging of sin, plus the effortless eroticism of young Clark Gable.

Frankenstein **(1931)** – When Lon Chaney died at forty-seven in 1930, it wasn't only the loss of a major film artist but the potential loss of an entire genre. Who was now going to haunt moviegoers' nightmares? Universal presented Bela Lugosi in *Dracula* (1931), soon followed by Boris Karloff in *Frankenstein,* with Karloff topping Lugosi as the screen's premier scare-maker by virtue of his versatility, a big talent who just happened to intersect indelibly with the horror genre. James Whale's *Frankenstein* is probably Hollywood's all-time great horror movie, a seminal mega-classic; it's impossible to imagine pop culture without its iconic imagery. Colin Clive is the actual star, and as Dr. Frankenstein, he's perfection, the quintessential mad scientist, so rapturously obsessed and nearly always on the verge of becoming hysterical. (If you're going to play God, you should probably try calming down.) Karloff doesn't enter for a half hour, but what an entrance, lumbering backward toward the camera, turning slowly to reveal *that face* and its hooded stare. How astonishing, the amount of "acting" Karloff is able to achieve behind the makeup. Vocally and physically, his work is original and ingenious, conveying an aching humanity from within a cobbled-together creature. The Monster is a sublime contradiction: an innocent, fearful psyche trapped inside an outwardly destructive hulk. Karloff physicalizes this conflict through astounding pantomime, the lurching unsteadiness offset by his poetically expressive hands. Despite the monstrous growl, the sudden anger, and a strength beyond his awareness, Karloff creates a profound portrait of unendurable loneliness all the way to his harrowing panic at the fiery climax. When he meets the little girl (Marilyn Harris), he connects on a child's level, smiling at making a friend, uttering staccato emissions of pleasure. He's only a monster when he's reminded that he is. I have to ask: how come Dr. Frankenstein doesn't notice the "Abnormal" label on the brain's jar? Why trust Fritz (Dwight Frye) to take care of something as vitally important as that? The biggest question is this: what might have happened if Boris Karloff had not been available to play the Monster and put his stamp on the genre? Now that's horrifying.

Dr. Jekyll and Mr. Hyde (1931) – Fredric March shared the Best Actor Oscar for this dual title role, famously tying with Wallace Beery for *The Champ.* However, *Jekyll's* success seems every bit as—if not more—reliant on the performance of Miriam Hopkins as Ivy, the unfortunate Cockney music-hall gal, the abused plaything of Mr. Hyde. Both stars, Broadway veterans, were solidified as full-blown film stars thanks to *Jekyll,* assisted by Rouben Mamoulian's consistently imaginative direction, including split screens, P.O.V. shots, and the magnificent start of the first transformation (involving only makeup and lighting). As drama, it's pretty crude, even rather absurd. The story is certainly provocative—a supernatural metaphor on the hypocrisies of Victorian repression—but the treatment feels like silly mad-scientist fare. March is a caring London doctor named "Jeekyl" who is interested in separating man's good and evil natures, idealistically and naively treading in God's domain. (This Jekyll isn't very sympathetic, nor does he seem especially bright.) After March rescues Hopkins from a brute, she's aggressively flirty, rolling down her garters and flinging them at him, getting into bed naked, and lunging for a kiss. (He'll remember her when he becomes Hyde.) After nearly a half hour, March achieves the transformation, but I can't help wishing it was only his personality that changed. Why must he become such an ape-like monster, with wide nostrils, horrid teeth, and actual fangs? The effect is almost comical. Of far more interest is Hopkins' Ivy, trapped by Hyde's pursuit. The beatings, whippings, and sexual degradation happen off-screen, yet Hopkins suggests every horror endured; she's no longer the slinky minx first introduced. Shouldn't Jekyll show some initial pleasure in the fact of his id-releasing life as Hyde? Though a monster, Hyde is also capable of behaving rationally, making murky the overall conception. March isn't afforded depth and isn't asked to expose complexities. As Jekyll, he comes off as stagy, in a matinee-idol way (without being English enough); as Hyde, he's too buried under prosthetics. He got his Oscar for the role's showiness, getting to play Dr. Frankenstein *and* the Monster, yet he can't compete with Hopkins' agonizing fear and touching desperation.

A Bill of Divorcement (1932) – Following her Broadway success in *The Warrior's Husband* in early 1932, Katharine Hepburn was cast as John Barrymore's daughter in this George Cukor-directed film version of a 1921 Clemence Dane play. The movie's claim to fame is Hepburn's screen debut (in a role created onstage by Katharine Cornell), not its hopelessly dated theatrics, which often play like a spoof of a 1920s melodrama, with plenty of masochism and self-sacrifice to go around. Hepburn's performance was hardly a harbinger for the brilliant career ahead—she's even inauspiciously billed as "Katherine" in the end credits—but it did serve as an introduction to an unusually striking young woman, angular and lovely, classy and fashionable. Her mix of poise and sensitivity is enticing, and she has a swell look-at-me entrance, swooping down a staircase and into David Manners' arms for a dance, an enchanting leap into a movie career. Barrymore, billed solo above the title, has gentle, affecting moments as a talented composer who has been in an asylum for the last fifteen years due to a latent insanity aroused by shellshock in WWI. He can get a bit flagrant in his acting, which is also true of Billie Burke as his ex-wife, though she, too, has tenderly drawn moments. In yet another *Enoch Arden* variation, Burke is about to remarry when her ex-husband returns unexpectedly and is still in love with her. *A Bill of Divorcement* must have seemed modern in its sympathetic treatment of divorce, allowing Burke out of her "sentence" to the hospitalized Barrymore. The crux of the plot—set in England over the Christmas holiday—is the revelation that insanity runs in the family, leaving Hepburn's plans to marry Mr. Manners in disarray (which, considering his appeal, is not the worst thing in the world). A warming bond develops between Hepburn (who has no memory of her father) and

Barrymore (who still has that sonata to finish!). Cukor and Hepburn would next make *Little Women* (1933), a peak achievement for both of them, with *A Bill of Divorcement* merely their tantalizing teaser for the soon-to-be great Kate.

She Done Him Wrong (1933) – With just her second film, Mae West skyrocketed to movie stardom and became a signature (and shapely) figure of the pre-Code era of casual morals. Set against a gay-nineties NYC and based on West's 1928 play *Diamond Lil, She Done Him Wrong* establishes West's winning formula: she's a loose-living woman but she's honest, she loves jewelry and fabulous gowns, and she drives men wild. Her unique persona suggests a female playing a drag queen playing a female. Three middle-aged lugs vie for her, but she's got eyes for two lookers: crook Gilbert Roland and mission worker Cary Grant. Forgettable as a crime melodrama, *She Done Him Wrong* provides just enough plot to permit Mae to strut her stuff and toss those suggestive one-liners. She enters only after much talk about how beautiful she is. Who could possibly be disappointed once she opens her mouth, holding forth with such pearls as "When women go wrong, men go right after them," or calling Roland "warm, dark, and handsome," and the great "Come up some time…see me" sequence with boy-toy Grant. At the end, when Grant says, "You bad girl," she replies, "You'll find out." She also makes time to sing three songs! All these years later, West remains a daring diva, a sinful delight, a first-rate comedienne and presence, making it easy to see why Depression audiences were so entranced by her chutzpah. Like all the stars in this chapter, Mae West grabbed her opportunity and announced herself as someone worth watching, and it's been true ever since.

Interrupted Melody: The Birth and Near-Death of the Movie Musical (1930-1933)

Perhaps the most abundant gift of talking pictures was the dawn of a new genre—the movie musical. Performers had always been able to dance on the screen, with young Joan Crawford recently reaching stardom with the help of her Charleston, but no one had ever been able to become a movie star by singing, not until Al Jolson delivered "Dirty Hands, Dirty Face" in Warner Brothers' *The Jazz Singer* (1927), capping it with "You ain't heard nothin' yet." Only a partial talkie, *The Jazz Singer* paved the way for the first hundred-percent movie musical, MGM's *The Broadway Melody*, released in February of 1929 and riding its popularity and innovation all the way to the second-ever Best Picture Oscar, the first for a talkie. Seen today, *The Broadway Melody* looks like it was made in the Stone Age, not just a flat early talkie but a musical with unimpressive talent, clumsily executed numbers, and too much dressing-room hysteria. As a backstage musical, it spawned hundreds of similarly plotted affairs, yet its three stars quickly vanished from the screen: feisty Bessie Love, colorless Charles King, and the dreadful Anita Page, a real-life Lina Lamont hampered by her New Yawk accent (even though her character is new to the city). Ms. Love's sass survives, and some of the tunes remain winners, but this dumb movie, carried far by its novelty, would soon look laughably archaic. However, a craze had begun, and a slew of musicals followed. The transition to talkies was enlivened by this thrilling new genre.

On the heels of *The Broadway Melody* came a number of notable 1929 musical efforts: *On with the Show,* of interest as a forerunner to *42nd Street* (1933) in its plotting, and for its treasurable musical turns by Ethel Waters and Joe E. Brown; *Say It with Songs,* Jolson's first all-sound picture, mired in schmaltz; and *Sunnyside Up,* in which silent romantic favorites Janet Gaynor and Charles Farrell, both musically deficient, somehow scored (helped by the movie's catchy title tune). Then there were variety shows—MGM's *The Hollywood Revue of 1929* and Warner Brothers' *The Show of Shows*—built as showcases for studio contract players (whether or not they could sing or dance), with both films featuring sequences in two-strip Technicolor. *The Hollywood Revue,* which introduced "Singin' in the Rain," has to be the only movie that mentions the film (*The Broadway Melody*) which eventually beat it for the Best Picture Oscar! These 1929 musicals, once *so* state of the art, are priceless historical artifacts, though deadly as entertainment. Most of them seem to have been made *before* sufficient performing talent had arrived in

Hollywood and before audiences and studio heads knew any better, a time when it was still enough for "musical" performers to look good, carry a tune a little, and shake to the music. Choreography mostly meant kick lines, marching in formation, or simply gyrating madly.

The best of the 1929 group is Ernst Lubitsch's *The Love Parade* which stars two actual musical talents—Maurice Chevalier and Jeanette MacDonald. Not a backstage musical nor a vaudeville show, it cast Chevalier as a womanizing count and military attaché who becomes prince consort to queen MacDonald but soon tires of being her royal plaything. It's a role-reversal sex comedy, a tickling charmer with a melodious score and an attractive, extravagant production. With Lubitsch confidently dispensing his flair for amorous sophistication, and his charismatic stars decidedly seen to advantage, *The Love Parade* became another Best Picture Oscar nominee. No one would have a better run of musicals in the early '30s than Chevalier. Some of them were minor—*The Big Pond* (1930) and two more for Lubitsch, *The Smiling Lieutenant* (1931) and *One Hour with You* (1932)—but two of them were extraordinary—Rouben Mamoulian's *Love Me Tonight* (1932), the first *great* movie musical, and finally Lubitsch's *The Merry Widow* (1934), both co-starring MacDonald (as did *One Hour with You*). Maurice and Jeanette were the genre's most important and distinguished team until Fred and Ginger came along (and before Jeanette switched to Nelson Eddy).

Talent wasn't always enough. Broadway troupers Marilyn Miller and Helen Morgan and opera stars Lawrence Tibbett and Grace Moore appeared in movie musicals fleetingly (though Moore did return and find success mid-decade). No one could predict who would click and who wouldn't. Jeanette MacDonald surely wasn't the world's greatest soprano, but she had onscreen qualities that better singers didn't necessarily have: beauty, charm, humor, and sensuality. The early days of musicals are strewn with skilled professionals taking a stab at Hollywood, given their shot at stardom, then *gone,* discarded in the ongoing quest to find the next MacDonald, Chevalier, or Jolson. Anyone remember early movie-musical names such as Lawrence Gray, Winnie Lightner, Nick Lucas, Claudia Dell, Alexander Gray, Bernice Claire, Stanley Smith, or Marion Harris? Probably not, but to the rescue came the next wave of musical stars. Fred Astaire, Eleanor Powell, Dick Powell, Judy Garland, and Alice Faye were among the genre's soon-to-be legends, light years from what had passed for talent in *The Broadway Melody* a mere half-decade ago. Yet the genre almost didn't survive the early 1930s.

It was after the big successes of 1929 that movie musicals got out of control and too many productions glutted the market. Even worse was the fact that most of them were terrible, and moviegoers had figured this out! With the novelty of musicals fading fast, was the genre merely a fad that had run its course? Had it been too hot not to cool down? Lubitsch and Chevalier continued to thrive artistically, but they were among the very few inspired by the movie musical's potential. Responding to the genre's relentless mediocrity and the onslaught of repetitive fare, the 1930 audience essentially stayed home. Most of the initial affection afforded musicals had been wiped out as sharply and decisively as the recent stock-market crash. The proof lies in the numbers: after roughly seventy-five musicals released in 1930, there were only about ten apiece produced in 1931 and 1932. Ouch! It wasn't until Warner Brothers released *42nd Street* in March of 1933 that the genre was commercially recharged. With its Depression-era mix of cynicism and corn, iconic casting, and those glorious Harry Warren-Al Dubin songs, *42nd Street* remains a landmark, and much of the credit belongs to the breathless wizardry of Busby Berkeley's production numbers, which firmly declared that the movie musical had boundless possibilities. Berkeley's spectacles, conceived for a series of backstage musicals at Warners, dazzled and transported moviegoers, bursting well beyond the limiting confines of proscenium theatres (where these numbers were supposedly, and impossibly, taking place). Thus began a more than two-decade golden age for the Hollywood musical, both creatively and financially.

But, before that happy ending, before the decade found its way to *Top Hat* (1935), *Show Boat* (1936), *On the Avenue* (1937), *Maytime* (1937), and, of course, *The Wizard of Oz* (1939), let's consider that briefly treacherous period for the movie musical, from the beginning of 1930 to the beginning of 1933. There were occasional triumphs within those years, but it's mostly a fascinatingly fumbling time and virtually forgotten once the genre found its footing. In these examples, you can still feel the growing pains, the fits and starts. It's a genre in infancy, and yes, it looks rather primitive. Pioneering work is never easy.

Monte Carlo (1930): Jeanette MacDonald

They Learned About Women **(1930)** – For about five minutes, Bessie Love, Oscar-nominated for her work in *The Broadway Melody,* was MGM's biggest musical star, a precursor to the stardom of Joan Blondell (at Warners). Right after she was reteamed with her *Broadway Melody* co-star Charles King in the thrown-together *Chasing Rainbows* (which at least gave us "Happy Days Are Here Again"), Ms. Love appeared in *They Learned About Women,* a forerunner to *Take Me Out to the Ball Game* (1949), another musical combining vaudeville with baseball. Instead of Gene Kelly and Frank Sinatra, it's the team of Gus Van and Joe Schenck, with Van the baritone-catcher and Schenck the tenor-pitcher. Not exactly Kelly and Sinatra, they look more like Lon Chaney (Van) and Jack Haley (Schenck). It's clear that they just don't have whatever it takes to make it as film personalities because they're too committed to recreating rather than adapting their vaudeville technique, plus they further distance themselves today by their moldy ethnic-humored specialty material (like their "Wop" song). While it was certainly logical to approach the new genre as filmed stage entertainment, the results risked looking stiff and uninspired as they do here. (One has to admit, though, that in this pre-lip-synching era, it can be quite pleasant to hear people genuinely break into song.) Ms. Love mostly pines for Mr. Schenck, and yes, the boys win their World Series. There's a big "Harlem Madness" tap number for an African-American ensemble, but the most memorable and eyebrow-raising musical sequence is a generously fleshy "spiritual" performed in the locker room and showers. Later the same year, Ms. Love starred in the first film version of *Good News,* but she'd soon be gone from MGM. Her usefulness had apparently expired. So much for having scored in the talkies!

In Gay Madrid (1930) – If you're intrigued by seeing gay Ramon Novarro in a gay Madrid, you're going to be disappointed—and not just because it's only the first few minutes that are set in Madrid. One of MGM's prime silent assets, Novarro was hoping to parlay his trained singing voice into movie-musical success. He'd already had a hit with the Napoleonic *Devil-May-Care* (1929), which came early enough in the musical cycle to seem fresh, even though it's a creaky mix of historical fiction and comic operetta. Novarro certainly could sing, but his light, thin voice was hardly first-rate. A bigger problem was the thickness of his Mexican accent which can make his English challenging; his singing is more pleasing than his speaking. *In Gay Madrid* rehashes Novarro's title role in Ernst Lubitsch's sterling silent *The Student Prince in Old Heidelberg* (1927), giving the old plot a half-hearted Latino makeover. Son of a marques, Novarro is sent to college outside the city after some wild behavior in Madrid. It's a college musical and a Latin Lover picture with Novarro romancing Dorothy Jordan (his *Devil-May-Care* leading lady), though it appears that it's her brother who's in love with classmate Novarro. (I thought it was in Madrid where things were gay.) This is a pretty slight vehicle for such a big star, but Novarro seems fairly relaxed, assured, and humorous (though his once-extraordinary beauty has somewhat faded). When the plot becomes heavy and overheated, you'll yearn for things to go back to being so dismissively slight. The songs aren't bad, but try though he might, Novarro would never make it as a musical star, giving up for good in 1935, surrendering to Bing Crosby, Dick Powell, and Nelson Eddy. Few even remember that this great silent star, Ben-Hur himself, had ever even dabbled in the genre.

Monte Carlo (**1930**) – One of the better 1930 musicals, it's silly but tuneful, and it has Ernst Lubitsch as director and Jeanette MacDonald as leading lady. She's lovely and spirited, but where, oh where, is Maurice Chevalier? Instead, there's Scottish song-and-dance man Jack Buchanan, later so brilliant as the "genius" director, opposite Fred Astaire, in *The Band Wagon* (1953), one of the genre's almighty peaks. However, back in 1930, Buchanan seems an odd choice as a leading man, a skillful performer but not sexy or attractive and *not* loved by the camera. He never dances here; he does sing, but rather nasally. *Monte Carlo* is lesser Lubitsch, but it still offers intermittent wit and charm and some inventive touches. It opens with a wedding marred by pouring rain, as drenched well-wishers race across an outdoor carpet, a harbinger of doom. Cut to the feet of a girl stepping onto a moving train, the runaway bride (MacDonald, in just a fur coat and a slip). On board she sings the movie's big song, "Beyond the Blue Horizon," with train sounds providing percussive accompaniment. It's an early small-scale "Atchison, Topeka" kind of number, though it's derailed by all those happy singing peasants outside her window. As a penniless countess, MacDonald hopes to score in Monte Carlo, while Buchanan is a smitten count, posing as a hairdresser so he can be in her employ, an unfortunate twist because Buchanan's masculinity is already in question. His casting was a pre-Astaire attempt at creating an Astaire-like star, including top hat, white tie, and tails, but it fizzled. Again, the genre was figuring out what worked and what didn't, while alienating audiences in the process.

Big Boy (**1930**) – Al Jolson had topped his *Jazz Singer* success with another boffo partial talkie, *The Singing Fool* (1928), a slobbering slab of masochistic hokum complete with blackface, with Jolson working *extremely* hard to please moviegoers. ("Sonny Boy" was its big tune, sung to kid Davey Lee.) *Say It with Songs* (1929), Jolson's first all-talkie, is even worse, with "Little Pal" the "Sonny Boy" wannabe, and Davey Lee again playing Jolson's son, leading to ever-moldier manipulations. After *Mammy* (1930) came *Big Boy*, an adaptation of Jolson's 1925 stage hit, with its title role for a horse. Not only does Jolson don blackface yet again, but he is actually playing a black man! It's something you'll never get over, as if you were in the audience at *Springtime for Hitler*. You will stare in stupefied, open-mouthed wonder. Directed by *The Jazz Singer's* Alan Crosland, *Big Boy* is a horse-racing musical melodrama with gamblers, frame-ups, and sabotage, with Jolson working in the stables of a vast Southern estate. Of course, he overemotes in his big crying scene with Big Boy, later winning the Kentucky Derby atop him. There's an extended flashback to 1870, more appalling than the 1930 scenes, with Jolson leading a rendition of "Let My People Go." There are lots of songs, *all of them* performed by Jolson, all of them forgettable. In the finale, he appears as himself, on a stage with the full cast, as if we have just watched a stage performance. Along with *Say It with Songs, Big Boy* ends with a ham joke.

Bright Lights (1930) – Like *On with the Show* (1929), this one is set during a stage performance, onstage and off, in this case a Broadway closing night. Dorothy Mackaill is the show's star and is retiring to marry a millionaire, even though she and co-star Frank Fay are clearly in love. The casting is problematic, with stage star Fay (later the original Elwood P. Dowd in *Harvey*) so unappealing and so lacking in screen presence, while the attractive Mackaill is obviously not a true singer-dancer. James Murray (from the 1928 silent classic *The Crowd*) and Inez Courtney are the secondary couple, and Frank McHugh, as a reporter, is already doing his drunk act (repeated in countless other Warner Brothers movies). The director, Michael Curtiz (*Yankee Doodle Dandy*), was not yet at home in the genre, offering an elaborate but static musical, and all in just sixty-eight minutes! Its plot eventually descends into ludicrous backstage melodrama, with a gunshot death and a murder investigation. It surely is odd to see a big production number titled "Wall Street" in a movie released in the fall of 1930! But the main reason to catch *Bright Lights* is for its connection to *Singin' in the Rain* (1952), specifically to its "dignity, always dignity" sequence, when silent-star Gene Kelly lies about his humble past to radio listeners while we enjoy contrasting visuals: flashbacks of the unembroidered truth. Here, Ms. Mackaill, behaving grandly with the press, speaks of being raised on an English farm while we view the grungy reality of her scantily clad "Congo" dance in a dive. As she talks about her fashionable girls' school on the Hudson, we see her as a hooch dancer in a cheap carnival. It's the same device used by the *Singin' in the Rain* writers, Betty Comden and Adolph Green, but who can say if they ever even saw this movie? And what of the similarities between the plots of *Bright Lights* and *Kiss Me Kate*? In both, a leading lady is about to retire and marry well, though she's really in love with her co-star, and it's all playing out mid-performance. Also, Mackaill's top hat, white tie, and tails number got to the screen a few months before Marlene Dietrich's in *Morocco*. None of this makes *Bright Lights* any good, but it surely makes it interesting.

Follow Thru (**1930**) – An adaptation of a 1929 Broadway hit, this one is a honey. Recently restored to its two-strip Technicolor glory, it's beguiling proof of the striking and rapturously pretty possibilities of that limited early-color process. A musical about golf, *Follow Thru* is pure fluff, preserving the spirit of late '20s musical comedy, an invaluable record of a typical show of that time. The innocence and the goofiness remain likable, the frivolous plot still fun and romantic. It may be drawn-out for something so feathery, but it's carried by a swell DeSylva, Brown, and Henderson (*Good News*) score, with additional songs by other contributors, and a cast led by Nancy Carroll. With her red hair, slightly puffy cheeks, and gorgeous clothes, you can't take your eyes off her. A late-breaking silent star, Carroll was a radiant personality, a good actress, and a fresh beauty. She was also one of the best things to happen to early talkies, with her pleasantly fluty speaking voice and appealing song-and-dance skills. Charles "Buddy" Rogers, a star of *Wings* (1927), is another looker who can sing. He and Ms. Carroll do well by the love song, "A Peach of a Pair," which sounds like something from *Dames at Sea*. It's reprised on a phonograph record as the lovers gaze into each other's eyes, *feeling* the lyrics as they're sung by another—it's a lovely moment. The central comic duo is Jack Haley and Zelma O'Neal, repeating their Broadway roles and performing "Button Up Your Overcoat," a zesty delight. O'Neal's "I Want to Be Bad" production number, complete with fire and angels, is a charmingly silly and outrageous sequence, and Ms. O'Neal is dynamite. Nine years away from screen immortality as the Tin Man, Haley is funny in his broad role, twitching whenever he's around females. There's a third couple, teenagers Don Tomkins and Margaret Lee, also from the Broadway cast, also quite winning. Usual for the time, the clunky choreography is sometimes eccentric but more often heavy and slap-happy. In addition to being a valentine to Ms. Carroll's short-lasting stardom, the heavenly hokum of *Follow Thru* stands as a testament to the joys of the musical-comedy conventions of its Broadway era. Seeing it feels like time-machine travel to a great seat at a hot show on a glittering New York evening of ninety years ago.

Just Imagine (**1930**) – It sounds so promising, a 1930 musical set in 1980, yet it does almost nothing with the concept. Short on charm and wit, it moves at a dreary pace and won't even make you laugh. This time, a DeSylva, Brown, and Henderson score proves unmemorable, with numbers that have too little to do with the central conceit. These songs could be from almost any '20s-style musical. The opener is a paean to old-fashioned girls (of 1930), but wouldn't it be more fun to embrace 1980? And with most of the movie's hair and clothes screaming 1930, why even bother? The NYC of the future, looking like an attempted copy of Fritz Lang's *Metropolis* (1927), has citizens with names like J-21; they use picture phones and have meals in pill form. Unfunny El Brendel is top-billed as a 1930 man resurrected from his lightning death, predating the basic idea of Woody Allen's *Sleeper* (1973). A childlike, Betty Boop-looking Maureen O'Sullivan is the ingénue; she sings a little. A bland, stagy Englishman, John Garrick, is the male lead, with support from secondary couple Frank Albertson and Marjorie White. Albertson is the film's most engaging participant; Ms. White clearly wants no part of his restraint. With its dearth of inspiration, *Just Imagine* soon gets bored with its futuristic New York and sends its three male leads on a mission to Mars, where, on arrival, the movie worsens. Mars is inhabited by half-naked chorines, cavemen types, and a mad, metallically glitzy queen (Joyzelle Joyner, later of Cecil B. DeMille's 1932 *Sign of the Cross*); she's ridiculous camp. There's plenty of awful, writhing "dancing," further proving that *Just Imagine* is beyond idiotic. It wastes all of your initial good will toward its premise, leaving you glum about the future (including the future of movie musicals).

Delicious **(1931)** – Though the silent romantic team of Janet Gaynor and Charles Farrell continued their popularity in the sound era, it's hard to know why. Their 1929 musical *Sunnyside Up* was a hit, even though it would be difficult to say anything nice about their work in it (whereas you have to be made of stone not to be enraptured by them in 1927's *7th Heaven*). In talkies, Gaynor is a cloying actress with a helium-overdosed voice; Farrell is a lackluster presence with a high, toneless voice. So much for bad voices halting careers! Farrell's popularity did soon wane, but Gaynor's soldiered on, notably in *State Fair* (1933) and *A Star Is Born* (1937), before she wisely opted to retire. Though musicals were endangered by 1931, *Delicious* had its two big stars to help sell it, plus a score by George and Ira Gershwin which has to be among their worst. The title tune informs us that "Delicious" is pronounced in four syllables, as "De-li-*shi*-ous." Doesn't that make you hate this movie already? Unerringly trite, the plot follows a Scottish lass (Gaynor, with an abominable accent) who comes to the US in steerage and is turned away on arrival. (Can you blame them?) She acts like a grown-up version of Shirley Temple, coy and infantilized, while Farrell, as a wealthy polo player she meets aboard ship, barely figures at all (handsome but little else). Gaynor escapes immigration officials and, wanted by the police, is hidden by some Russians who put her in their club act. Raul Roulien, as a Russian composer who falls in love with her, sings the dreaded title tune; Gaynor butchers a ballad, "Somebody from Somewhere." Directed by David Butler, *Delicious* isn't a bit tasty, yet the team of Gaynor and Farrell, never able to compete with their silent selves, still managed to make movies together until 1934.

The Kid from Spain (1932) – As the fortunes of the movie musical were dwindling, Eddie Cantor, another Broadway veteran, appeared unaffected. After *Whoopee* (1930) and *Palmy Days* (1931), he remained popular, with *The Kid from Spain* the movie-musical hit of its under-producing year. I suspect that was because audiences liked Cantor as a funnyman even if they had, by then, decided that they hated musicals. *The Kid from Spain* is, in fact, no more than a labored, scattered, and tedious experience. It's rather astonishing that it was made by some of the same contributors—director Leo McCarey, songwriters Kalmar and Ruby—who would deliver the Marx Brothers' *Duck Soup* (1933), one of the funniest comedies with music, as well as one of the greatest of *all* movies. This time there was no inspiration and therefore no hilarity. (An in-your-face entertainer, Cantor was more like Jolson than Groucho, as this movie's unfortunate blackface number will attest.) There are a few pre-*42ⁿᵈ Street* numbers from Busby Berkeley, with the opener the real eye-catcher, a festival of college-dorm cleavage in which girls wake up, rise from their satiny beds, and eventually plunge into an Esther Williams-type pool number. (Berkeley later worked with Williams on three MGM musicals.) The tunes are serviceable as the plot moves nonsensically from college to a bank robbery to Mexico (where Cantor poses as a great bullfighter). Robert Young, of all people, plays a mustachioed Mexican! Then there's Paulette Goddard as one of the Goldwyn Girls. But the first face you see in this movie belongs to teenager Betty Grable, introducing the dorm number, in the grandest dorm in college history.

Hallelujah I'm a Bum (1933) – Al Jolson's first movie since *Big Boy*, this Depression-era whimsy was a flop, yet it's one of the best of early musicals, a one-of-a-kind entry of true charm, warmth, and feeling. Expertly directed by Lewis Milestone (*All Quiet on the Western Front*), it's beautifully photographed by Lucien Andriot, featuring fresh outdoor locations and lively editing. Unusual in its use of rhymed dialogue, and its odd score of song fragments (plus some great full-out songs), it's a work by Richard Rodgers and Lorenz Hart, following their masterpiece *Love Me Tonight*. (Rodgers can be seen here as a photographer's assistant, while Hart is a bank teller with two lines, both "No.") This musical is a rather bizarre celebration of dropping out, of being a happy hobo, and of the freedom of having nothing, with Jolson the "mayor" of Central Park. After all the rotten things I've said about Jolson's hammy theatrics, here he is relaxed as I've never seen him—easy, tender, and human. His peak moment is the title tune, a breezy, infectious explanation of his lifestyle. A surprisingly elegant and good-looking Frank Morgan plays the actual mayor of NYC, and he and Jolson share an offbeat friendship. (It's amusing when Morgan, future Wizard of Oz, says to Jolson that "there's no place like home.") Though clearly influenced by the cinematic fluidity and sparkling wit of Lubitsch, Mamoulian, and Rene Clair, *Hallelujah I'm a Bum* feels unlike any other musical. Not for all tastes, it's an enchanting curiosity. The plot is filled with huge coincidences, yet the movie continues to accumulate in emotional depth, especially once it becomes a wistful romantic triangle. Lovely Madge Evans is Morgan's lover, but he loses her thanks to his unfounded jealousies. After her drowning suicide attempt and rescue by Jolson, she wakes with amnesia. Changed by his love for her, Jolson gets her an apartment and goes to work (in a bank). She's smitten with him, too, as well as being on the receiving end of his rendition of the great ballad "You Are Too Beautiful," another high point of early musicals. Ms. Evans just has to look good, but Morgan's heartfelt honesty and Jolson's unexpected simplicity add immeasurably to this risky and bittersweet fairy-tale musical. A month after its disappointing release came *42nd Street,* coincidentally starring Jolson's wife, Ruby Keeler. Hollywood soon put those perilous early years of the genre behind them. Yet that trial-and-error period was an essential part of a creative process that led directly to the movie musical's eventual status as one of the greatest things to happen to twentieth-century American culture.

"Lost Generation" Found: Making Peace with World War I (1930-1933)

World War One was the USA's first major international conflict after the emergence of movies, a time when Hollywood realized its role in something bigger than itself, including the potential to influence national opinion. America entered the European war (which had begun in 1914) in April of 1917 and fought all the way to the armistice of November 1918, allowing sufficient time for movie people to learn how important a function they could play. Stepping outside their realm of make-believe, silent-era superstars, including Mary Pickford and Charlie Chaplin, publicly raised money at war-bond rallies to show their support for the cause and even brought the war into their work. Look at Pickford's drama *The Little American* (1917) or Chaplin's comedy *Shoulder Arms* (1918), two war-related movies released during the American involvement, both informing public perception about what was happening abroad. It was all a warm-up for more elaborate and longer-lasting duties during World War II when the industry unwaveringly saw itself as an essential tool of the war effort. Until then, though, WWI was the main war-movie subject, a case of recent history delivered with passion and immediacy.

Silent WWI-themed successes of the 1920s offered variety: *The White Sister* (1923), a romantic soap starring Lillian Gish and Ronald Colman; *What Price Glory* (1926), director Raoul Walsh's raucous marine picture with Victor McLaglen and Edmund Lowe; and *Four Sons* (1928), a cross-continental family melodrama from John Ford. The best of the bunch was King Vidor's *The Big Parade* (1925), the *Gone With the Wind* of WWI movies, a heady blend of the personal and the epic, featuring a career-best John Gilbert as a rich, spoiled American forever altered (and exceedingly humanized) by wartime love and suffering. With its devastating 40-minute combat sequence, which includes a chilling trek through a sniper-infested forest, *The Big Parade* anchors its intoxicating romance (between Gilbert and French peasant Renée Adorée) to the sanity-shaking world of modern warfare, a prestige picture decidedly pro-love and anti-war.

In 1927 two WWI classics were released, both of them deified by the brand-new Academy Awards: *Wings,* the first-ever Best Picture, and *7th Heaven,* which nabbed Best Director and Best Actress. William A. Wellman's *Wings*—soon followed by the notable flying pictures *The Dawn Patrol* and *Hell's Angels* of 1930—remains outstanding when airborne, merely routine on land. Technically phenomenal with its still-dazzling aerial photography, *Wings* has boundless size and a soaring flexibility. What it lacks is *The Big Parade*'s emotional depth and historical-cultural heft; instead it's satisfied to present the war as little more than an opportunity for glory and adventure, a chance to rule the skies. *The Big Parade* and *Wings* represent a fundamental dichotomy of WWI movies made during the fifteen years after 1918: those trying to make sense of the war and those using it as an excuse for lofty sagas of romanticized heroism.

As for *7ᵗʰ Heaven,* it was in the *White Sister* sub-genre of female-driven wartime gushers, a lovely melodrama directed with poignant grace and detailed intimacies by Oscar-winning Frank Borzage. It stars Janet Gaynor (an actress better in silents than talkies) who merited her Oscar for a luminous yet understated performance as a Parisian unfortunate, complemented by a handsome, never-better Charles Farrell, her perennial co-star. The plot concerns love in a garret between a waif and a sewer worker (promoted to street washer). Old-fashioned in its manipulations but infused with the wonder of its seventh-floor heaven, this buoyant romance swells with sentimental power, especially when the lovers try to sustain their bond's intensity once Farrell is called to the front. Selling optimism on a grand scale, *7ᵗʰ Heaven,* like *Wings,* was part of Hollywood's mythologizing of WWI, the former in romantic terms, the latter literally in the clouds.

After Ernest Hemingway's 1926 novel *The Sun Also Rises* solidified the concept of a war-scarred "Lost Generation" (which happened to be concurrent with the arrival of talkies), Hollywood began to probe WWI as never before (or ever again). With an audience who had been affected first-hand, and a decade or so for reflection, objectivity, and post-war adjustments, WWI movies of the early 1930s prodded the subject with some penetrating agendas. Quite a few of these movies may be described as anti-war, and of course, nothing says anti-war like peacetime! By the mid-'30s—as Hitler's intentions began worrying people across the globe, with world war once again looming—the tolerance for anti-war stories began to fade. Hollywood was on its way to accepting unprecedented responsibility as the nation's chief morale builder. Most ironically, early-'40s Hollywood used WWI as flag-waving inspiration for some of its earliest WWII-minded propaganda, including such smash hits as *Sergeant York* (1941), *Yankee Doodle Dandy* (1942), and *For Me and My Gal* (1942). Each of these movies took WWI, often previously depicted as a subject of unrelieved pain and moral skepticism, and turned it into a promotional tool and rallying cry. When WWII ended and it was time to examine it in more realistic and painstaking detail, Hollywood never lagged in its interest, maintaining WWII as the movies' war of choice. How could WWI—historically so much harder to explain, and with its less iconic enemies—possibly compete? Occasionally, there would be a major WWI picture, such as *Paths of Glory* (1957), but ever since the attack on Pearl Harbor, a war movie mostly signifies WWII.

Despite its early-'30s immersion in WWI's agonies and their aftermath, Hollywood hadn't abandoned the subject's potential as romantic-action-sentimental pulp. Consider *Waterloo Bridge* (1931), which rigged the war as backdrop to a touching and doomed love story, or *Mata Hari* (1931), an occasion for some exotic, glamorized Greta Garbo nonsense, or *Today We Live* (1933), which proved that WWI could even be fodder for the Joan Crawford formula. Among the more offbeat war-themed movies is *Men Must Fight* (1933), a fascinating curiosity that begins in WWI but is mostly set in 1940. It pessimistically predicts WWII while offering pacifist arguments and anti-pacifist warnings, which means it bites off more than it can possibly chew in seventy-two minutes. *Ever in My Heart* (1933), starring Barbara Stanwyck, broaches the toxic anti-German sentiment here at home, which leads to the unraveling of one happy American family. Most relevant of all were the films confronting the fates of the veterans, including the colossal *I Am a Fugitive from a Chain Gang* (1932), in which decorated Paul Muni watches his post-war life destroyed by cruel, incessant injustice. By the later '30s, assisted by the enforcement of the whitewashing Production Code, a softening shift in WWI movies was apparent, with the Jean Harlow vehicle *Suzy* (1936) a quintessential piece of melodramatic idiocy. Two good 1938 remakes, of *The Shopworn Angel* (1928) and *The Dawn Patrol* (1930), were among the last American movies (for some time to come) with any shred of the anti-war expression exhibited in films from not so long ago. Of the features highlighted here, several share an enduringly grim outlook while others aim to be more conventional war-based melodramas, yet they are all connected by their proximity to the actual event, the best of them revealing some illumination, even if it was only fleetingly absorbed into the culture.

All Quiet on the Western Front (1930): Lew Ayres

***All Quiet on the Western Front* (1930)** – Like *Wings,* it won a Best Picture
Oscar, but any similarity ends there. Based on Erich Maria Remarque's 1929
novel and adapted by heavyweights Maxwell Anderson and George Abbott, it
remains one of the greatest of anti-war films, ingeniously crafted by director
Lewis Milestone and cinematographer Arthur Edeson. In light of just how
early a talkie it is, its level of technical virtuosity in its staging and its sound
effects is awe-inspiring. The central battle sequence is a stunner, especially
when assuming the vantage point of a machine gun as it kills in assembly-
line fashion. The most obvious flaw is a crudeness in much of the acting, yet
the amateur quality of some of the young men seems apt, augmenting the
heartbreaking impact of their innocence colliding with untimely death. With
his own awkward lack of polish, Lew Ayres is sweetly affecting as the main
boy. *All Quiet* is told from a German perspective, with all these green young

soldiers representing our so-called recent enemies. That American audiences could so willingly empathize with their German counterparts says much about the film's ability to reduce war to its shared horrors, no matter which side you're on. The superb opening features a schoolmaster rousing naive male students to enlist, inciting fantasies of glory; the scene ends with an emptied-out classroom. Then comes the reality of the front, the awful conditions, the lack of food, with everything seeming ever more pointless. There's some wonderful respite from the terror, a sex scene instigated by four skinny-dipping (and ass-flashing) soldiers excited by the prospect of three available French girls. It's the more sobering moments that can't be shaken: a pair of boots being passed from man to man, as each dies off; Ayres stabbing a French soldier in a foxhole, then watching him die a slow death; Ayres' return to his classroom, speaking truths about the war that no one wants to hear. With its brilliant ending involving a butterfly and a final image of boys marching with their background a graveyard, *All Quiet* is a bracing achievement, as blistering now as ever. It recognizes enemy soldiers as fellow pawns in a violence not of their making, goaded by nationalism into sacrificing much (sometimes all) and increasingly wondering why.

The Last Flight (1931) – Here's a genuine Lost Generation movie set mainly in 1919 Paris, a fragile gem from director William Dieterle, even though it's limited by a too-brief running time and insufficient character development. It works extremely well as both a mood piece and a time capsule, creating a haunting glow of disillusionment. (John Monk Saunders wrote the screenplay, based on his novel.) The focus is on broken veteran flyers who are referred to as "spent bullets," primarily Richard Barthelmess, David Manners, and Johnny Mack Brown. Each carries a noticeable post-war affliction: Barthelmess' burned hands, Manners' eye tic, and Brown's tendency toward crazy risk-taking. Unable to face going home to America, they remain rudderless. With no competition from Manners and Brown (two of the era's worst performers), the acting honors belong entirely to Helen Chandler (of recent *Dracula* fame, alongside Manners) as a rich, delicate kook. She's first seen in a bar holding a champagne glass filled with a set of false teeth—an alluringly strange introduction. She becomes pals with the boys, joining their lives of drink-filled carousing and becoming their childlike, eccentric mascot. She spouts marvelously nonsensical things, such as touting her ability to walk faster when wearing red shoes. In Lisbon, their circumstances worsen, which forces them out of their limbo. Even if much of the surrounding drama is weak, the film's aura of post-war pessimism lurks pervasively, while ultimately giving way to glimmers of hope. Too bad that Barthelmess, billed solo above the title, is such a stolid presence with no energy in his line readings. If he and the others could cast a spell as insinuating as Chandler's, then *The Last Flight* might have fully ascended. In a few short years, this entire ensemble would constitute its own lost generation, snatched from stardom and faded from the collective consciousness like so many of those who served.

The Man I Killed (1932) – Among those mournful looks at the war's impenetrable waste of human life, this uneven Ernst Lubitsch drama is actually most potent in visual terms (kudos to Victor Milner's cinematography), but deadly in its ineffective pacing. Phillips Holmes stars as a Frenchman who in 1919 is consumed with guilt regarding the German he killed in a foxhole. Traveling to Germany, he seeks forgiveness from the man's parents, Lionel Barrymore and Louise Carter, and fiancée Nancy Carroll. Though he befriends them and even falls in love with Carroll, he is unable to tell them the truth. There is healing and there is hope, but the plot never quite transcends its implausibility or its mawkishness. However, there are gorgeous Lubitsch touches throughout: a parade viewed from the space where an amputee's leg used to be, a row of gleaming swords jutting into a church aisle, a distant camera finding its way to Holmes' praying hands, and a lively montage of gossipy neighbors' scandalized reactions to Carroll and Holmes out walking together. With a title later changed to the vaguer *Broken Lullaby*, *The Man I Killed* was Lubitsch's final drama, hereafter committing himself to comedies such as *Ninotchka* (1939). Holmes gives one of his standard weakling performances, melodramatically flinging himself about. Though far from her best, Carroll is her warm, lovely self, and Barrymore, also reliably good, of course can't resist a little overdoing. Perhaps the film's most piercing moment comes when Barrymore describes victory as a case of old men celebrating the deaths of other men's sons. The movie might have increased its persuasiveness if, instead of everyone sounding American, Holmes had used a French accent, thus identifying him as the outsider, the former enemy. For all its flaws, *The Man I Killed*—the final teaming of Holmes and Carroll after romantic linkings in *The Devil's Holiday* (1930) and *Stolen Heaven* (1931)—still lingers as a thoughtfully troubled war-themed film from a war-sensitive peacetime.

Smilin' Through (1932) – Though based on a celebrated 1919 play first filmed as a 1922 silent, this deeply romantic drama clicked again. Its overt sentimentality, which includes a ghost, is offset by its genuinely tender and heart-aching components. It provided a showcase for three stars—Norma Shearer, Fredric March, Leslie Howard—with Shearer and March in dual roles, and Howard aging significantly. The main plot occurs in 1915 England with Shearer as Howard's adopted daughter, the orphaned niece of his great deceased love (also Shearer, but a blonde). The current Shearer loves March, an American from Cleveland who has enlisted in the war. Enraged by the Shearer-March romance, Howard flashes back, for Shearer's sake, to his impending wedding to her aunt (the other Shearer) and her gunshot murder by a rejected March (as his own father) whose bullet was meant for Howard. Got that? Shearer gets to romance the two leading men, one in each period, and she has a nice rapport with both of them. *Smilin' Through* certainly has the right tone for this era of WWI pictures, with its backstory of a young life cut short (her final line is "Isn't it a pity?"), as well as its sustained grieving. Howard's scenes with the ghostly Shearer—still a wedding-gowned vision of all that might have been—serve as comfort to anyone anticipating reunions with loved ones lost prematurely. The war is more directly addressed upon March's wounded return, after he's shot to pieces and walking on crutches. He shuns Shearer because—in grandly melodramatic, cruelly "unselfish" fashion—he doesn't want to burden her. Though this is one of MGM's Norma Shearer vehicles, its emotional arc is actually Howard's, charting his love-affirming release from clenching grudges. Directed by Sidney Franklin, who also directed the silent version, *Smilin' Through* is finally a soothing, softly lighted tearjerker. A 1941 Technicolor remake, starring Jeanette MacDonald, was part of the pre-WWII era's use of WWI to generate war-themed emotion. Though it was faithfully rendered, the material had by now pushed its luck one time too many, seeming as quaintly remote as a nineteenth-century ghost.

A Farewell to Arms (1932) – Beautifully refined by Frank Borzage (*7th Heaven*), this condensed adaptation of Ernest Hemingway's famed 1929 novel is stirringly effective, with Oscar-winning cinematography by Charles Lang and a surprisingly good team in Helen Hayes and Gary Cooper (whose heights are separated by about two feet). Primarily set in Italy, it's a love story between a British nurse (Hayes) and an American ambulance driver (Cooper), with the war a formidable hindrance to their happiness, even though it's this same war that brings them together. Though their love deserves to flourish, it's no match for a war with no patience for individual desires. When even so-called friends and allies contribute to keeping them apart, the whole apparatus seems heartlessly designed to keep love and happiness at bay for the duration. With this plum role, Cooper proved his acting credentials, giving a sensitive and emotionally bare performance. As for stage-star Hayes, she was never more vibrant onscreen (even though it's clear that "Coop" is the beauty of this duo). The stars bring out palpable tenderness in each other, conveying the emotional unreality of wartime: the sense of living speeded-up lives, grabbing what you can, and upending the rules. *A Farewell to Arms* can be a startlingly adult movie on the subject of desire. This is, after all, a pre-Code picture, meaning that much of its amatory intimacy wouldn't have made it into the film had it been produced just two years later. On the night they meet, there's a memorable post-coital scene with Cooper especially gentle in his response to Hayes' loss of virginity. She eventually heads to Switzerland to have their baby; Cooper deserts to find her. But who are they to challenge a world war? Unlike a warm chestnut such as *Smilin' Through* which employs the ingredients of melodrama, *A Farewell to Arms* intertwines love, war, and inexorable time with a more profound, all-encompassing ache. Unconcerned with details about the actual war, this film portrays it as a vague monster, an ever-hovering interference to Cooper and Hayes. Despite its sometimes rushed, truncated feeling, *A Farewell to Arms* presents war itself as the enemy above all others.

Cavalcade (1933) – Beating *Smilin' Through* and *A Farewell to Arms* for the Best Picture Oscar of 1932-33, *Cavalcade* is possibly the worst movie ever so honored, a laughably high-toned mediocrity. Based on Noel Coward's 1931 play—a celebration of Britain's stiff-upper-lip mentality—this Frank Lloyd-directed epic covers the time between two New Year's Eves, from 1899 to 1932. The hopelessly stagy results are superficial and stodgy, false and coy, filled with upper-crust condescension. Despite the inordinate expense, *Cavalcade* remains emotionally inert, working best as an unintended spoof. Basically, it's a big dead weight peopled by stick figures who aren't even sympathetic, an upstairs-downstairs collection of characters unified by their overwhelming Britishness, making the film an apparent orgasm for Anglophiles (including Academy members). The cast, mixing hams and no-talents, is led by Diana Wynyard who waffles between patronizing kindness and righteous indignation, her only two gears (both intended to inspire adoration). She and Clive Brook, her nonentity of a husband (a knighted military man), represent "upstairs," while married servants Una O'Connor and Herbert Mundin lead the "downstairs" crew. There's a self-consciously ironic scene aboard the Titanic (again, pure spoofery), followed by Frank Lawton (son of Wynyard and Brook) getting all excited by the prospect of WWI, in a cheerio-pip-pip sort of way. There's an endless, bafflingly repetitive WWI montage that achieves nothing, tirelessly rotating images of marching, explosions, and dying soldiers. The handling of the post-war era is somewhat better, with snippets, however fleeting, of blinded soldiers, gravesites, and talk of disarmament. Though *Cavalcade* is often downbeat, in a rife-with-importance manner, it sends mixed messages as it tries to be anti-war while almost choking on its blasts of rah-rah Britannia! *Cavalcade* does loosen its stiff-lipped countenance occasionally, as when two tuxedoed gay men are glimpsed in a 1920s club. One removes his bracelet and fastens it onto his mate's wrist. Blimey!

The White Sister (1933) – Helen Hayes, her confidence bolstered by Gary Cooper's ardor, now teams with Clark Gable! However, this remake of the 1923 Lillian Gish-Ronald Colman silent is no *Farewell to Arms* (though it is set in Italy, with both stars playing Italians). The huge budget of this overproduced movie reveals MGM's momentary belief in the stardom of Hayes, a recent Oscar winner for *The Sin of Madelon Claudet* (1931). The 1932 *Smilin' Through* was relevant because honest feeling seeped through its already old-fashioned plot, but *The White Sister* never overcomes its moth-eaten demeanor. Snappy Victor Fleming (*Red Dust*) is the wrong director for such soapy drivel, with even his reliably sure pacing gone astray. The plot is pretty much the same as what befalls Vivien Leigh in her version of *Waterloo Bridge* (1940), just substitute becoming a nun with becoming a prostitute (the two ladies' quite opposite reactions to the deaths of their soldier loves, both of whom are still alive, hence the dramas). Though Hayes clicked with Gary Cooper's puppy-dog beauty, she doesn't mesh with Gable's savvier glamour. It's hard to accept that Clark Gable (as an army lieutenant) would chase Helen Hayes (a prince's daughter) so relentlessly; she already seems a bit like a little old lady. During the war, pilot Gable is shot down and believed dead, not making it home until after Hayes has decided to become a streetwalker...I mean nun! Will she take her final vows before learning he's alive? If so, will he be able to convince her to renege? Can even a nun resist the King of Hollywood? Whichever way things resolve in Italy, *The White Sister* offers the promise, in *Smilin' Through* fashion, of an afterlife. This movie really isn't any worse than its silent original; it's just never credible enough to surpass its hoary nature, using WWI more as an exciting background than as a real and painful circumstance.

The Eagle and the Hawk (1933) – The plotting is prone to cliché but the sentiments are stingingly anti-war. Set mostly in France, it stars Fredric March as an American pilot and Cary Grant as a British gunner. March gives a strong, appropriately tortured performance wracked with grief and guilt: the more decorated he becomes, the more he boozes. He doesn't feel heroic and is tired of being congratulated for the deaths of young men while hating that his success has tagged him "a shining example." Grant, not yet as big a star as March and still unformed as a screen personality, seems miscast yet fares rather well. He's tough and hard, more butch than usual, and impossibly young and handsome. Carole Lombard shows up briefly (also bizarrely and pointlessly) for an eight-minute cameo billed as "The Beautiful Lady." Swathed in fur and satin, she meets March on his leave in London, telling him, "I want to be kind." (The stars were famously reteamed in 1937's *Nothing Sacred*.) Despite plenty of flying action and March's chill-inducing waking nightmare, director Stuart Walker's film isn't satisfactorily fleshed out. The screenplay is based on a story by John Monk Saunders, a key contributor to this era's WWI films; in addition to his work on *The Last Flight*, he also wrote the stories for *Wings* and *The Dawn Patrol*. For its over-the-top climax, involving suicide and falsified evidence, *The Eagle and the Hawk* mixes bleak anti-war feeling with movie hokum.

Heroes for Sale (1933) – Though only seventy-one minutes long, it's a wildly ambitious effort, taking on much too much, with each of its subjects worthy of an entire, *longer* picture. In the *I Am a Fugitive from a Chain Gang* tradition of examining veterans' post-war plight, *Heroes for Sale,* however impressive in its aims and passions, is frustratingly undercooked. Yet it's eminently watchable with issues still resonating today. Directed with heartfelt care by William A. Wellman (*Wings*), it manages to cover WWI combat, drug addiction, labor relations, and the Depression. Yikes! Unfortunately, the script is overly sadistic toward its main character Richard Barthelmess, who is *so* victimized. He's taken prisoner by the Germans, uncredited for his act of wartime bravery, put on morphine to manage his pain from a war wound, imprisoned for a riot he tried to stop, and treated like a bum after the crash. This woeful litany isn't helped by Barthelmess, a silent star clearly on his way out, who's physically and vocally lethargic; his motor is too slow to carry such a plot-revved movie. With him in the lead, the movie has no throbbing center. The most vital section involves his post-war morphine addiction, a war-related issue valiantly tackled, however briefly, with Barthelmess temporarily wrecking his life. Cured in rehab, he rises in the laundry business and marries the world's most beautiful laundress (an angelic Loretta Young). There's still so much more to come, sparked by the arrival of Robert Barrat as a German communist who becomes a rich right-wing capitalist! The new war is the Depression, a milieu of unemployment, soup kitchens, and Barthelmess riding the rails, all of which keeps *Heroes for Sale* a monumentally concerned and semi-hopeful movie from those socially committed Warner Brothers.

Pilgrimage (1933) – This John Ford movie opens in rural Arkansas, with old-time stage star Henrietta Crosman as a hard, selfish farmer trying to maintain control over son Norman Foster. He wants to enlist in WWI; she adamantly objects. But when he wants to marry sweet Marian Nixon, Crosman opts for the lesser of two evils and enlists him for service in the war. This first act, with its poetic compositions, is indeed striking (in a *Sunrise* kind of way), including the young lovers' hayloft tryst, which leads to Nixon's pregnancy. The all-American Foster will soon be dead in the trenches, yet Crosman wants no part of her grandson, even after the passing of ten years. As a Gold Star mother of the war, she is invited to make a French pilgrimage to her son's final resting place. There's a breathless moment when Ms. Nixon and her son bring Crosman a bouquet for Foster's grave: Nixon lifts it to Crosman at her train window and she silently accepts it, her black-gloved hand extended (and her face unseen). Ford's work grows more indulgent and less imaginative in France, as Crosman thaws, redeeming herself by befriending an American boy (Maurice Murphy) in Paris, someone like her son; she's soon playing fairy godmother to him and his girlfriend (Heather Angel). It's her second chance, intervening with the boy's mother (Hedda Hopper) in a rather overblown showdown, an all-too convenient absolving of the past. Crosman is a fine warhorse of an actress, an old-school technician, firmly weighted for the satisfying finale, an emotional catharsis promoting peace and love, which is an essential destination of all these WWI films of lamentation. Whether scalding or sappy, historical or made-up, the films' overriding message was to find a way to live together, a theme that could be transmitted for a few more years, until the Axis powers were emboldened and Pearl Harbor was attacked. Hollywood then found a more pressing message—to inspire the good fight—leaving anti-war sentiments back in the trenches of the war to end all wars.

The Whole Town's Talking: Neglected Comedy Gems of the Early Sound Era (1930-1935)

Coming off the silent comic peaks of the 1920s—including Buster Keaton in *Sherlock Jr.* (1924) and *The General* (1926), Charlie Chaplin in *The Gold Rush* (1925) and *The Circus* (1928), Harold Lloyd in *Safety Last!* (1923) and *The Kid Brother* (1927), Marion Davies in *The Patsy* (1928) and *Show People* (1928)—it would have been entirely logical for moviemakers and moviegoers to presume that talking pictures weren't going to be anything but a hindrance to the future of comedy on the screen. Wouldn't the glories of physical comedy be vanquished by performers suddenly more focused on being *heard*? Any such naysayers would soon be proven wrong. After the movies' awkward but mercifully brief technical transition to sound, the laugh makers took off in several wondrous directions, ultimately making the 1930s every bit as much a Golden Age of Comedy as the '20s.

Only Chaplin had the temerity to continue working silently, using sound but not dialogue in two films as great as anything he had ever done, *City Lights* (1931) and *Modern Times* (1936). Other funnymen, recently of the stage, scored brilliantly in the new era, mixing verbal ingenuity and flawlessly executed slapstick. The Marx Brothers brought their merry lunacy to pictures, including *Duck Soup* (1933), still a candidate for funniest movie ever made. W.C. Fields honed his beloved snide persona in a series of blissful vehicles such as *You're Telling Me!* (1934) and *It's a Gift* (1934). Then along came sexually preoccupied Mae West, a constant challenge to those in the "decency" racket. She sashayed her way to box-office gold with her innuendo-driven hoots *She Done Him Wrong* (1933) and *I'm No Angel* (1933).

Film versions of Broadway comedies were logical fodder for the talkies, and before long, they were being adapted so smoothly that they seemed born for the movies. The screenplays often surpassed the original scripts, as in *Dinner at Eight* (1933), *Stage Door* (1937), and *The Women* (1939). Other sophisticated fare was provided by all those chic comedies set in Europe, many of them directed by the inimitable Ernst Lubitsch, including *Ninotchka* (1939), his most famous picture of the decade.

The year 1934 marked a turning point for movie comedy and was coincidentally the year the Production Code began being enforced. This meant that a noticeable amount of sexual content was excised from the screen's romantic-comic pairings, most obviously with the arrival of the dreaded twin beds for married couples. It must have seemed another dark day for the genre's future, and yet it turned out not to be a bad thing at all. Filmmakers absorbed the new guidelines and simply found alternative ways to be funny. Three of the final pre-Code comedies, all from the first half of 1934, turned out to lead the way: Frank Capra's *It Happened One Night,* which became the gold standard for romantic comedy of the next eighty-plus (and counting) years; *Twentieth Century,* Howard Hawks' Broadway-based farce, noted for its breakneck pacing and outrageous abandon; and W.S. Van Dyke's *The Thin Man,* which freshly melded marital comedy and murder mystery and was soon imitated by countless wannabes—including its own sequels— but never equaled. This trio appears to have been three steps on the way to a brand-new sub-genre, the screwball comedy, a purely '30s concoction that often portrayed the Depression-era rich as an oblivious lot. It was here that you could find beautiful people behaving in knockabout fashion, with witty dialogue between pratfalls. Women frequently dominated screwball comedy, including fearless Carole Lombard, memorably playing typically dizzy (and lovable) heiresses. Lombard's *My Man Godfrey* (1936) is the quintessential example of all things screwball, soon to be followed by a pair of equally marvelous works, *The Awful Truth* (1937) and *Bringing up Baby* (1938), both lucky enough to have Cary Grant along for the ride.

The 1930s clearly offered an abundance of varied comic riches, a time as hospitable to Irene Dunne as it was to Groucho Marx. In such a creatively fertile period it was sometimes hard to get noticed, or stay noticed as the years went by, which explains why so many worthy '30s comedies drifted into obscurity. Allow me to shine a light on some less-than-household names in the realm of movie comedy, from the high-comic to the low-comic, specifically from the fledgling first half of the decade, before the solidification of romantic comedy and screwball comedy as screen staples.

The Whole Town's Talking (1935): Jean Arthur and Edward G. Robinson

Holiday (**1930**) – This pleasing adaptation of the 1928 stage hit was an early sign that the talkies were not only going to find their way technically but relax enough to provide breezy, charm-filled entertainment. This particular movie has been neglected because of George Cukor's celebrated 1938 remake starring Katharine Hepburn and Cary Grant, which is certainly the more polished work. The earlier film is still a delight, with Ann Harding (in Hepburn's role) a likable and animated presence, sometimes positively radiant, and clearly capable of being so much more buoyant and playful than her later string of soap operas would suggest. Directed by Edward H. Griffith, *Holiday* centers on a super-rich family. Mary Astor (Harding's sister) is set to marry Robert Ames, an adventurous nonconformist who wants to "retire young and work old." Uninterested in the money-mad rat race, he's evidently made for Harding, the family renegade. In 1938, a dull, humorless Doris Nolan played the engaged sister and you knew on sight that she could *never* end up with Cary Grant! However, Mary Astor is a real force: sexy, smart, beautiful, and slyly manipulative. She's cold and hard, too. The plot doesn't feel as predetermined in this version because Astor is too fine an actress to dismiss her character as just another rich bitch. On the other hand, Monroe Owsley, as the alcoholic brother (a role he created onstage), can't compete with Lew Ayres' richer, more varied "brother" characterization, the standout performance of Cukor's film. Both versions have their plusses and minuses, which means it's time for the 1930 picture to get some respect beyond its footnote status as the only film for which Harding received an Oscar nomination. For trivia trackers, it's also got an old actor named William Holden playing the father, and then there's Edward Everett Horton in the same comic-relief role he would play in the '38 version. The film's male leads, Ames and Owsley, aren't well-known because they died soon after—Ames in 1931, Owsley in 1937—both gone before the release of Cukor's remake.

Platinum Blonde (**1931**) – Here Frank Capra tries out many of his soon-to-be signature components while proving himself an already accomplished director of talking comedy. The plot is typical—ordinary reporter Robert Williams marries society girl Jean Harlow and they quickly clash—but the film glides on its diverting incidentals. Capra puts the emphasis on casual humor over big laughs, on making dialogue sound like natural conversation, and on the chemistry between his players. Despite the title tilting Harlow's way, Loretta Young is top-billed as the newspaper gal (known only as Gallagher) who pines quietly for Mr. Williams, her colleague and pal.

Wait, shouldn't Harlow and Young switch roles? It would seem so, yet both are enormously fresh and impossibly pretty. Clearly two superstars in the making, they are entirely relaxed and self-assured under Capra's guidance. As with most triangular comedies, you can guess where this one is headed, yet it's filled with surprises, like the lovely scene in which Williams and Harlow spontaneously sing their dialogue to each other (to a "Farmer in the Dell"-ish melody), turning a disagreement into frisky foreplay. The gifted Williams, a visual cross between Crosby and Mitchum, was dead before the year's end, but this easygoing, offhand comedy remains a tribute to his potential. (Harlow would soon be gone, too, in 1937.) *Platinum Blonde* offers the pleasures of spotting connections to Capra classics to come: the reporter-heiress romance and "ordinary people are resourceful, rich people are useless" theme of *It Happened One Night* (1934); the mentions of Williams' character as "Cinderella Man" and his scene with butler Halliwell Hobbes as their voices echo in the cavernous mansion, both of which returned in *Mr. Deeds Goes to Town* (1936); and Williams playing a Mr. Smith (without having to go to Washington). Even Ms. Young's character seems to be an outline for the Jean Arthur roles in *Mr. Deeds* and *Mr. Smith*. However, *Platinum Blonde* is more than something to be studied, with Capra (still billed with his middle initial R.) having had the confidence to focus on the intimacy and humanity that turns simple stories into deeply charming comedies.

Million Dollar Legs **(1932)** – It's the best anarchic farce *not* made by the Marx Brothers. Set against the real-life Los Angeles Olympics, this giddy, irreverent romp begins in Klopstokia, a bankrupt country whose president, W.C. Fields, is dealing with an evil cabinet led by Hugh Herbert. When American brush salesman Jack Oakie arrives, he falls instantly in love with Fields' daughter (Susan Fleming) and gets the brainstorm that a big win in LA could save the day for Klopstokia. It turns out that there's much natural athletic talent just going to waste, including Fields' crazy weightlifting prowess. As Oakie trains the team, villain Herbert hires femme fatale Lyda Roberti for sexual sabotage. She's Mata Machree, the woman no man can resist. Not a pretty girl, no, but man can she gyrate! Her number, "When I Get Hot," is a pre-Code sensation. My favorite idea here is Ben Turpin as a mysterious cross-eyed spy in a black hat and cape, so good at his job he even once appears *inside* a painting. Oakie gets to sing a love song to Ms. Fleming in genuine Klopstokian: "Woof Bloogle Gik." Directed by silent-era gag man extraordinaire Edward Cline and co-written by none other than Joseph L. Mankiewicz (in a far cry from his

All About Eve), *Million Dollar Legs* is a madly merry mix of lewdness and innocence, delivered in a joyous spoofy manner by a crackerjack ensemble of nutcases. The only flaw is that it doesn't end with a comic button from the scene-stealing Mr. Turpin.

Trouble in Paradise (1932) – What's this Ernst Lubitsch classic doing here? Isn't it already an acknowledged masterwork of 1930s comedy? Yes, but it's one of those classics that isn't really famous beyond devout classic-movie lovers. If there is a more gloriously sophisticated sex comedy—one so sparkling you can almost hear the tiny champagne bubbles popping—well, I haven't seen it. Lubitsch's work is so purely cinematic—seamless, fluid—so exquisitely crafted that the talking picture seems already perfected. It's about as un-static as a literate comedy can get. Not only gorgeous to look at, *Trouble in Paradise* boasts a witty, suggestive script and an expert cast. Elegant thieves Herbert Marshall and Miriam Hopkins meet in Venice, fall in love, and become a thieving duo. He's so good at his work he can pickpocket her garter! In Paris, they set their sights on Kay Francis, a wealthy widow and owner of a perfume business. Marshall becomes Francis' secretary and then hires Hopkins as his own secretary, with the film becoming a love triangle. Hopkins is light and appealing and Marshall is impeccably fine, but Francis is the revelation. Never has this limited actress seemed so bright and accomplished, so much more than merely the epitome of '30s glamour. *Trouble in Paradise* is a hypnotically sensual movie, and, thanks to Lubitsch's unerringly graceful interplay between words and images, a shimmering piece of fairy dust.

The King's Vacation (1933) – If he's remembered at all, Oscar winner George Arliss was Warner Brothers' pre-Paul Muni king of the biopics, usually billed "Mr." when playing everyone from Disraeli (his Oscar role) to Alexander Hamilton to Voltaire to Cardinal Richelieu. If I tell you that I'm about to recommend an Arliss comedy, it may sound like an oxymoron, like a Bogart musical or a Sonja Henie western. In his dramas, Arliss can seem like an outdated theatrical star with a bag-of-tricks acting style, but in comedy, in this film and *The Working Man* (1933), his warmth and shrewd wisdom suddenly make you understand why he was popular for so long. Here he's the titular king, a puppet figurehead in a mythical country run by crooked politicians. Originally fourth in line to the throne, he has "ruled" eighteen years. At the start of his reign, he was forced to give up his marriage to commoner Marjorie Gateson so he could have a proper arranged marriage to queen Florence

Arliss (the star's real-life wife). Liberal-minded, the king is in favor of the mounting revolution and happily abdicates, amicably parting ways with his queen. When he returns to Ms. Gateson and their grown daughter (Patricia Ellis) in France, he finds that he and his great love are no longer in sync. She's become a materialistic society lady, while he craves a simple, uncluttered life. What so irresistibly transpires is a burgeoning relationship between the two Arlisses, virtual strangers all those years as king and queen, now accidentally discovering each other and falling in love. It's a touching, disarming older-person romance with a splendid fairy-tale mounting and a script of honest feeling and emotional irony, plus Mr. Arliss' wily yet gentle acting. *The King's Vacation* is a real sleeper, a royally good piece of adult whimsy directed by Arliss favorite John G. Adolfi.

State Fair (**1933**) – This is the first and best of three film versions and also the most realistic of the trio. It's a pre-Code picture unafraid to show us a fair that's less than idyllic, a bit seedy, grubby, and in no way Disneyland, yet it's still a captivating movie. Delicately crafted by director Henry King, it stars box-office powerhouse Will Rogers as the farmer father, a perfect role for his laid-back charms. His wife, Louise Dresser, feels like a real farmwoman on an authentic (not storybook) farm. Their young-adult children are squeaky-voiced ingénue Janet Gaynor (whose yearning feels right, even if she does simper) and son Norman Foster, pre-Jimmy Stewart in his boyish manner. At the fair, Sally Eilers is the trapeze artist with whom Foster has a lot of sex, spending three nights at her place. She actually says to him, "I think I'll get into something more comfortable." Eilers is a glitzy heart-of-gold tramp, while Gaynor's love interest is newspaperman Lew Ayres, such a natural actor besides being handsome and sexy. It all feels like a genuine slice of life, folksy but never overly cheerful or prettified. The 1945 Rodgers and Hammerstein version is tuneful but suffocatingly wholesome and colorful beyond reason, all very efficient and impersonal. Though it's scrubbed clean—the trapeze artist is now a ladylike band singer—there's an inadvertent alcohol-fueled putting-to-bed scene between the son, Dick Haymes, and song plugger Frank McHugh, in which you'd swear that McHugh is about to perform oral sex on the shirtless, in-bed Haymes, with McHugh actually reaching for Haymes' belt buckle. The second remake, from 1962, retains Rodgers and Hammerstein but is updated, including the ferocious sexual energy of Ann-Margret (as the trapeze artist turned band singer turned stage performer). Despite her mod presence, the material feels old-fashioned and moralistic, not helped any by mom Alice Faye's song, "Never Say No to a Man." If you want to enjoy a purely human and refreshingly unsentimentalized piece of Americana, head back to 1933 and this Best Picture Oscar nominee.

Topaze (1933) – The major event here is John Barrymore's performance as a chemistry professor at a boys' school. In an impressive counterpoint to his fantastically hammy turn in the following year's *Twentieth Century*, Barrymore carries this winsome charmer with a sweet, mild-mannered demeanor. With a pointy beard, mustache, and glasses, Barrymore imbues this eccentric character role, Mr. Auguste Topaze, with enviable wit and a childlike appeal. He's a man who is all about honesty. Fired for not coddling the nitwit son of an old baron (Reginald Mason), he accepts the baron's job offer, not knowing it's for a corrupt scheme to pass off tap water as a curative tonic. Barrymore believes he's been hired as a chemist and proceeds to develop a tonic formula, never told that the drink ultimately produced is a sham. The baron's mistress, Coco, is a much-younger Myrna Loy who is being "kept" in a fabulous apartment. A year away from major stardom with her Nora Charles role in *The Thin Man*, lovely Loy is beautifully at ease. Based on a Marcel Pagnol story, with a clever screenplay by Ben Hecht, *Topaze* tingles with seemingly genuine Gallic charm. Directed by d'Abbadie d'Arrast (the best name in pictures), *Topaze* shifts when Barrymore learns the truth, devastated that dishonesty can be rewarded, which engenders his transition to cynicism. Barrymore's effervescent acting keeps the comedy lighthearted with more than able assistance from the modern low-key style of Ms. Loy.

Bombshell (1933) – By now the Jean Harlow persona was fully formed, thanks to the pre-Code sizzle and street-wisdom she brought to *Red-Headed Woman* (1932), *Red Dust* (1932), and *Dinner at Eight* (1933). Having some fun with Harlow's own stardom, *Bombshell* is a raucous and affectionate satire of Hollywood, with Harlow playing a very Harlow-like star complete with three large sheepdogs, her very own stalker, and not a moment to herself. It turned out to be one of her best vehicles, a portrait of the Golden Age dream factory as a three-ring circus. It mixes fact and fiction, with Harlow, as Lola Burns, called to do retakes on *Red Dust* and asking, "Where's Clark?" as she's about to redo the famous rain-barrel scene. Lola is a meal ticket for her extended family, including her perennially drunk, freeloading father (a very funny Frank Morgan). Harlow is a wonderful combination of sass and innocence, a wisecracking delight while stunning in her Adrian wardrobe. The central joke is that she craves great-lady publicity but can't get any. The only thing that the studio publicity man (Lee Tracy) wants to provide is sex and scandal, stressing Lola's bombshell appeal. (MGM is fictionalized here as Monarch Films Inc.) Tracy is in his all-out fast-talking scammer mode, and nobody did this sort of thing as unstoppably well. He and Harlow make a terrific team, highlighted by their endlessly entertaining screaming matches. Directed with enthusiastic zest by *Red Dust*'s Victor Fleming, *Bombshell* is a priceless Hollywood time capsule that also features Una Merkel as Harlow's secretary, Louise Beavers as her trusted maid, Pat O'Brien as her director/love interest, and Franchot Tone as a man she meets at a desert resort. When Tone sweet-talks her, a moony Harlow tells him, "Not even Norma Shearer or Helen Hayes in their nicest pictures were ever spoken to like that." Face it, Jean, aren't you much happier spewing one-liners back and forth with Lee Tracy in a movie as loud and likable as this one?

The Whole Town's Talking (1935) – Edward G. Robinson could be an astonishingly versatile actor, never more blatantly than in his dual role as coincidental lookalikes: a gentle-mannered nobody and Public Enemy Number One. What a pleasure to see Robinson as the complete opposite of his star-making gangster persona, while also giving the audience what it expected: another Robinson killer. He not only shares scenes with himself but also gets to play each character impersonating the other. Who can resist a great star kidding his own stardom *and* playing it straight in the same movie? Bad-guy Robinson is on the lam after a prison break; good-guy Robinson is an office clerk (and amateur writer). The plot kicks in when clerk Robinson is arrested, mistaken for the snarling hoodlum. The winning screenplay, by Robert Riskin and Jo Swerling, was directed by none other than John Ford, who did a neat job in what feels like Capra territory. The meek Robinson, who lives with a cat and a canary, pines for sassy co-worker Jean Arthur. She's good fun, too, on her way to settling into her own star personality, solidified (by Capra) in next year's *Mr. Deeds Goes to Town*. We know who the big hero is going to be here, but who would have guessed that Little Caesar himself could be one of the funnier guys around?

If You Could Only Cook (1935) – Here's another enchanting comic bauble with a warm Depression-era mix of rich and poor. This one stars Herbert Marshall as a New York millionaire, an auto magnate angry at his board of directors and unfortunately engaged to a fortune-hunting society snob (Frieda

Inescort). He wanders into the park and meets down-and-out Jean Arthur. Assuming he's unemployed too, she convinces him to go with her to apply for butler/cook jobs (intended for a married couple) at the estate of mobster Leo Carrillo. Arthur is actually a great cook and wows Carrillo at her audition when she holds garlic six inches above her sauce, rather than dropping it into the pan. The picture's droll high point has Marshall seeking instruction from his own butler (well-named Romaine Callender) on how to *be* a butler; it's a memorably civilized bit of role reversal. By one year, this movie predates *My Man Godfrey*, another film in which a rich man poses as a butler. There are some silly late-breaking complications and a too-abrupt finish, but *If You Could Only Cook*, directed by light-comedy pro William A. Seiter, is a beguiling winner. Arthur displays her scrappy radiance and vulnerability, and Marshall is his ever dapper, crisply humorous self, with Carrillo and Lionel Stander extremely funny as tough guys. Finally, who among us can resist this comedy's dual forces of great food and true love?

"Code" Breakers: Loose-Living Ladies of the Pre-Code Era (1931-1933)

The now-revered half-decade known as pre-Code Hollywood (1930-1934) came about, ironically, as part of the industry's response to assorted watchdogs who felt that the movies of the 1920s constituted a moral cesspool. Hedonism ran rampant, not only on the screen but in scandalous headlines about the stars themselves. The moguls, already dealing with various stripes of censorship within individual states, were fearful that the outcries of religious groups might lead to federal regulation. The Motion Picture Producers and Distributors of America (M.P.P.D.A.), a trade association, agreed in 1930 to a Production Code, a catalogue of all things *unfit* for the screen. Not only had the Roaring '20s brandished the reckless excess of sheiks and flappers, but talkies allowed for even freer expression, with characters inflecting their words as no title card ever could. The Code, the industry's voluntary guidebook, was promptly ignored, merely paying lip service to the so-called problem. How could movies clean themselves up while the Depression was worsening and when hard times were intersecting with Prohibition's culture of gangsters, bootleggers, and speakeasies? Movies thus continued their freewheeling ways, intertwining the reality of social unrest with the vicarious and escapist thrills of sex and violence, offering charismatic hoodlums, scantily clad chorines, plus drugs, unwed pregnancies, breadlines, prostitution, etc. Mobster characters made stars of Edward G. Robinson and James Cagney, and carnally inclined one-liners made blonde bombshells out of Jean Harlow and Mae West. Without such an environment, would Harlow or West—with their slinking toughness and smart-mouthed innuendos—have ever even become movie stars? More than anyone else, it was Ms. West who received the blame for pushing things too far, signaling the industry equivalent of a speakeasy raid.

Facing threats of boycotts from staunch religious organizations, Hollywood opted for actual enforcement of the 1930 Code, beginning July 1, 1934. All movies would thereafter require certificates of approval from a Production Code Administration within the M.P.P.D.A. Self-regulated censorship was, again, the preferable option, but this time it took. Scripts would have to meet Code standards, with cuts demanded if moral lines were crossed. Any questionable content would have to be resolved with onscreen punishment, the messages being that "crime doesn't pay" and pre-marital sex leads to misery. Hollywood's mission—most famously in the form of Andy

Hardy—was to set good examples for America's youth. You know the rest, the Code's chokehold on screen content for three decades, keeping movies on the straight and narrow. It's hard to complain too much about the results. Despite the strictures, or sometimes *because* of the creative (including subtextual) solutions produced by those boundaries, an undeterred Hollywood had no trouble making great movies. Here began the glory days of Fred and Ginger, Clark and Spencer, Mickey and Judy, Errol and Olivia, not to mention the birth of screwball comedy, the heyday of romantic comedy, and the reign of dramatic queen Bette Davis. The audience apparently absorbed the abrupt transition without complaint, perhaps not even noticing it, having been properly thrilled and delighted without interruption. Had those pre-Code days ever really happened? After all, Shirley Temple was the screen's number-one box-office attraction between 1935 and 1938, followed by Mickey Rooney from 1939 to 1941.

The Code's grip wouldn't begin to slip until it started being directly challenged, as when *The Moon Is Blue* (1953), with its harmlessly "indecent" dialogue, bravely defied Code disapproval and found popular success anyway, paving the way for an increasingly less Hollywoodized version of the world. As movie content continued to gain maturity—thanks to the influence of European cinema, as well as American writers such as Tennessee Williams and William Inge—the Code steadily crumbled, eventually replaced in 1968 by the ratings system. Screen permissiveness would soon travel far beyond anything that could have been imagined in the early '30s.

Made in that brief span between 1930 and mid-1934, pre-Code movies are often able to shock modern-day audiences because they don't seem to operate like "old movies," a term that conjures images of married couples in twin beds. Instead, these oldies are graced (or *dis*graced) with a sexual openness, an understanding that people want to have sex, actually might enjoy it, and don't necessarily want to wait for procreation-minded marriage to indulge. Plenty of such pre-Code gems vanished for decades, considered unsuitable for reissue (not without sufficient editing for Code approval). Some beloved pre-Code examples, such as *A Farewell to Arms* (1932) or *King Kong* (1933), were recut for re-release (and any subsequent television airings). In both cases, the footage has been restored, though not all similarly abused pre-Code films have been as lucky.

Since so much has been written about the pre-Code era and its startling pleasures, I choose to focus on one classification: provocative one-word titles. These constitute a menu of temptations on offer, brazen intimations of shameless behavior. Whether or not they live up to the promise of their titles is debatable, but they were certainly willing to slip into something more comfortable.

Ex-Lady (1933): Bette Davis and Gene Raymond

Illicit **(1931)** – Barbara Stanwyck, a child of divorce, has "modern" notions, believing that love cannot withstand the strains of romance's enemy: marriage. She and boyfriend James Rennie, both of the Park Avenue set, are sleeping together without heading for the altar. Though Stanwyck prefers to continue their unconventional arrangement, unconcerned about her reputation, she eventually acquiesces to Rennie's desire for wedlock. However, romantic rivals arrive in the form of slick Ricardo Cortez and bad-actress Natalie Moorhead. When all of Stanwyck's marriage fears are realized and their union dissolves, they return to their pre-marital state as "playmates." Can they pull it off? *Illicit* was Stanwyck's first film after becoming a star in *Ladies of Leisure* (1930), and she's expectedly likable, though ill-at-ease as an upper-cruster, lacking society diction and poise. Mr. Rennie is clearly headed for leading-man oblivion, but it's always a pleasure to see Joan Blondell (sixth-billed), here as Stanwyck's pal. The ladies are quite good together, even though Blondell is about as Park Avenue as Stanwyck. The film remains an eye-opener for its sexual nonchalance but never builds into a probing drama and ultimately loses most of its nerve. *Illicit* is racy twaddle, with static direction from Archie Mayo, never surpassing its tantalizing opening, with both stars in robes, soon sharing an omelet, only *then* revealed as being unwed. Later, you'll have to forgive a few lines between Stanwyck and Ms. Moorhead about how much each of them loves "Dick" (referring to Mr. Rennie's character name, I assure you).

***Forbidden* (1932)** – It's Stanwyck again, back with Frank Capra, the director who made her a star, though this is the weakest of their five pictures together, a typical back-street soap. Pairing her with a musty Adolphe Menjou, as her married lover, does not make for an exciting couple. Stanwyck begins as an old-maid librarian (with glasses) who uses her life savings for a cruise to Havana, getting herself glamorized enough to attract Menjou. The script anticipates *Now, Voyager* (1942) and *Summertime* (1955), and, later in the plot, Stanwyck's own *Stella Dallas* (1937). Menjou climbs from lawyer to D.A. to mayor to congressman to senator to governor, with Stanwyck out of the spotlight while giving birth to their daughter and then allowing the baby to be adopted by Menjou and his invalid wife (Dorothy Peterson). Stanwyck, fittingly, gives advice to the lovelorn in a newspaper column, while her editor (Ralph Bellamy) pines for her. Though Capra also penned the story, there's no distinctive Capra-esque presence anywhere on display; this isn't the kind of thing at which he excels. The plot reaches a melodramatic fever pitch, headed for a wages-of-sin ending of sacrifice and masochism. *Forbidden* is best when it shows some pre-Code personality, as when Bellamy, in pursuit of Stanwyck, tells her about the sexual abandon of hard-to-get women: "The longer they say 'no,' the harder they say 'yes!'" To which Stanwyck offers some fake outrage: "Please, Mr. Holland!"

***Shopworn* (1932)** – Stanwyck appears to have cornered the market on one-word pre-Code sensationalism, this time in the oft-told situation of an honest poor girl in love with (and loved by) a rich boy (Regis Toomey), a set-up somewhat similar to Stanwyck's upcoming *Stella Dallas*. After they spend a night together, his scheming, domineering mother (Clara Blandick, pre-Auntie Em) tricks them into splitting. She gets Stanwyck, who refuses to be bought off, sent to a reformatory for ninety days ("in violation of public morals") and takes Toomey to Europe, convincing each of the other's betrayal. Stanwyck has a miscarriage while imprisoned. From there, the film becomes maniacally plot-driven, including Stanwyck's rise to stardom in the theater, a twenty-second montage of theater programs and clapping audiences. She is never seen onstage, nor is any hint provided as to what her talent might be; it's all just a halfhearted ploy to bring some glamour into the movie. Six years will have passed before big-star Stanwyck and big-surgeon Toomey meet again. The emotionally hardened Stanwyck feels vindictive but soon softens, again headed for the sacrificial-masochistic route. It's an arduous melodramatic journey to get these two crazy kids together, with Stanwyck unsurprisingly more comfortable initially as the wisecracking diner waitress than as the grand and supposedly "notorious" actress she becomes. Her raw talent is obvious, but she's simply not yet the seasoned professional she'd soon be. Future character actor Toomey (a supporting player in later Stanwyck pictures *Union Pacific* and *Meet John* Doe) is in his brief phase as a leading man, not helped at all by the dizzying plot or the formulaic turns. *Shopworn* does have one of the pre-Code-iest of moments: young Stanwyck, trying to better herself by memorizing the dictionary, is up to "E" when Toomey reads aloud three words from her notepad, the third one being *ejaculate*.

Unashamed (**1932**) – While Stanwyck would surpass herself in the age of Code enforcement, other actresses had their brief career highs as pre-Code stars. Take comely and competent Helen Twelvetrees, who got herself into all manner of early '30s mischief. Here she's a wealthy, foolish girl who falls for fortune-hunter Monroe Owsley. Though she's close to her father (Robert Warwick) and her kid brother (Robert Young), she defies them by wanting to marry Owsley, believing it's *her*—not her three million—that he wants. The couple decides to spend a night together in a hotel, just so Twelvetrees can then *tell* her father, forcing him to give his consent! Of course, she could lie—say she did it when she hasn't—but, no, she goes through with it. Afterward, she asks her lover, "Do I seem a terrible sinner?" When the family confrontation arrives, Mr. Young, the angry brother, shoots Owsley dead. The film shifts to courtroom drama, with Young refusing "the unwritten law" defense, unwilling to sully his sister's reputation to save himself. On her way to selfless redemption, Twelvetrees engages in some tarty witness-stand playacting. Short on logic, long on overcomplication, *Unashamed* certainly doesn't blush.

Faithless (1932) – Tallulah Bankhead was among the stage stars who answered the talkies' call for actors with aesthetically pleasing voices, and yet her husky alto did *not* translate into movie stardom. (She wouldn't really succeed in films until she returned for *Lifeboat* [1944]). But in *Faithless*, the final film of her 1931-32 screen sojourn, she really gave it her all, imbuing lesser material with honesty and pathos, as well as some theatrical flair. The first part consists of a tediously identical series of financial tiffs between Bankhead, a still-rich girl in post-crash America, and Robert Montgomery, her working-man fiancé. She wants to live high; he wants her satisfied with his earnings. She finds out she's broke the same day he loses his advertising job, prompting her to break their engagement, thus instigating her downward spiral from professional houseguest to kept woman to hitting the skids. An accidental run-in with the also down-and-out Montgomery leads to their marrying, finding happy destitution. After he's injured in a labor-relations incident, Bankhead becomes a prostitute so she can pay for his medicine. Returning from her first night on the streets, she relates to the still-weak Montgomery with an acute mix of shame and tenderness. The most pre-Code element is his reaction to the revelation of just how she has saved his life. Instead of being furious and disgusted, he's moved by how much she loves him, her resorting even to *that*. Prostitution has come to the rescue, surprisingly *not* leading to murder, suicide, or illness. In fact, streetwalking is her redemption, her proof of unselfishness. For all the criticism of Bankhead's failed bid at 1930s film stardom, she definitely comes across here, descending plausibly from careless rich girl (amid gorgeous Art Deco trappings) to someone frightened, desperate, and degraded, eventually discovering her humanity and a deepening capacity to love. Montgomery, a smart, natural actor, assists his co-star in a joint mission to override a script prone to coincidence and rushed plotting. Though hoary (and "whorey"), *Faithless* gets points for its pre-Code absence of retribution for "sin."

Virtue (1932) – The first half is a pure delight, but it then devolves into third-rate melodrama. Such a shame, even though what lingers is the sharp, snappy Robert Riskin dialogue at the outset, enhanced by the charming chemistry between ex-hooker Carole Lombard and cabbie Pat O'Brien. Their tough, sassy courtship and subsequent marriage make for a sweetly appealing, funny-touching combination. As a newlywed, Lombard proves to be a perfect wife and homemaker. She had tried to keep her past a secret, but O'Brien learns the truth (from a cop) on their wedding night. Refreshingly, they still try to make a go of it, creating a happily wisecracking marriage, with O'Brien dreaming of having his own gas station. If the film had stayed on this path, as a grown-up comedy about a relationship with some challenging baggage, it might have remained fresh, zingy, and poignant. But melodrama swoops in, with outside characters mucking things up with scamming, accidental death, wrongful arrest, plus O'Brien mistakenly suspecting that Lombard is back to tricking. Again, time as a prostitute proves no detriment to a happy ending. Applaud director Edward Buzzell for his winning first half, then wag your finger at him for the rest. Of note is Ward Bond, as O'Brien's pal, mentioning Clark Gable (Lombard's future husband), and the fact that every significant female in this movie is a whore, an inconceivable notion just two years later. There are some choice one-liners tossed around, such as Lombard's to O'Brien regarding his face: "It's okay for you, you're behind it." And Mayo Methot as, yep, a likable tramp, is asked by Lombard if she's ever been married: "So many times I got rice marks all over me."

Flesh (1932) – The age-old plotting and characters are reshuffled with a change of genre and location. American Karen Morley is released from a German prison after she and lover Ricardo Cortez took a rap for some unseen crook. Morley is hard-bitten and sarcastic, broke and homeless, but German Wallace Beery, a wrestler and beer-garden waiter, falls unwaveringly in love with her. (Fresh from *Grand Hotel,* Beery kept his German accent; fresh from his Oscar win as a boxer in *The Champ,* he's back in the ring.) In his big-hearted-lug mode, Beery is primed for masochistic love, all set to be used and abused. Oh, Morley likes him, but she *loves* heel Cortez (who impregnated her before her prison stay and then ditches her upon his own release). She marries Beery, allowing him to believe that her baby boy is *his* and that Cortez is her brother. As Beery rises in the wrestling world, the movie shifts to America, with ever-unctuous Cortez managing him while again dangling Morley, even getting her to convince Beery to go crooked. With a story by Edmund Goulding (who directed *Grand Hotel*), dialogue by Moss Hart, and direction from John Ford, you expect there to be more to *Flesh* than there is. It's lively but it isn't memorable or convincing, feeling like collected bits of familiar plots from *They Knew What They Wanted* to *Fanny*. Cortez is a one-note sleaze, and Morley such a limited actress and presence, but at least Beery is sweet and innocent (if not much else) in a genuine way, occasionally offering a vivid, spontaneous emotion. The "flesh" is his but the title also acknowledges Morley's struggling need for the rotten Cortez. (At one point, he tells her, "You won't starve," not caring a whit if she must resort to hooking.) Funny how a false happy ending can seem subversive, by virtue of no moralizing punishment doled out (as it would be automatically by the Code). Morley's trajectory is overwrought, but she is another pre-Code fallen woman who fights for redemption and survives to achieve it.

Ex-Lady (1933) – Based on the same source material as *Illicit* (a story by Edith Fitzgerald and Robert Riskin), this second Warner Brothers version tones down the high-society aspect in favor of a more career-minded angle. Bette Davis, during her startlingly blonde period, is a successful commercial artist, an illustrator of books and magazine covers, as devoted to her career as she is to Gene Raymond, her boyfriend and lover (and every bit as blonde as she is!). Though they are emotionally connected and sexually compatible, Davis wants nothing to do with marriage, valuing her independence: "I want to be a person on my own." After Raymond finally convinces her to marry him, she joins his ad agency as art manager and junior partner. Professionally, she's more highly esteemed than he is, leading to resentment, as well as his susceptibility to having a mild dalliance. As in *Illicit,* the duo splits to return to their pre-marital bliss of occasional sex and companionship, with Davis saying, "Let's be separate people, and not try to be *one*." Of course, feelings, including jealousies, interfere. Directed more persuasively (by Robert Florey) than *Illicit,* and ultimately seeming less compromised, *Ex-Lady* acknowledges that there are no easy answers when it comes to relationships. The Davis-Raymond reunion feels like ever-imperfect reality for two people whose love finally outweighs everything else. The film succeeds as pre-Code provocation, notable, too, for its absence of any talk about Davis abandoning her thriving career and artistic gratification. Wearing some showstopping Orry-Kelly creations, she is certainly chic and glamorized while remaining clear-eyed; her acting is confident, concentrated, and electric (without any fireworks). She also has a pleasing rapport with the affable Raymond; his relaxed warmth seems to agree with her. *Ex-Lady* reaches a wordless pre-Code peak at a Havana nightclub, as the married pair is aroused by the rhythmic undulations of a half-naked female dancer. They grow frisky enough to exit, moving to a bench on the grounds, soon horizontally out of sight. Unrevivable once the Code was enforced, *Ex-Lady* was resurrected for *What Ever Happened to*

Baby Jane? (1962), by then sufficiently enough forgotten to be used briefly as onscreen proof that "Jane" was a no-talent.

Penthouse (1933) – No connection to the adult magazine, the title evokes glamorous splendor, not just monetarily but sensually, a place where dreams come true, where elegant decadence resides. The film itself is a murder mystery, a precursor to *The Thin Man*, complete with the 1934 classic's director (W.S. Van Dyke), writers (Frances Goodrich and Albert Hackett), and leading lady (Myrna Loy). It has the *Thin Man*-ish light tone, and its lead role—a society lawyer with a taste for sensational criminal cases—would have easily fit William Powell, including the character's soft spot for likably disreputable company. As played by a post-*42nd Street* Warner Baxter, he is properly easygoing and dapper. Sure, there's a murder and a frame-up, but it's so incidental, secondary to the Baxter-Loy relationship. She's a party girl, a high-class whore with a knack for suggestive dialogue. When she goes home with him, expecting to have sex, he'd rather talk about the murder. Regarding any clues she may have to offer, she tells him, "Cheer up, maybe I talk in my sleep." (When he exits, she's dumbfounded and checks her mirror reflection for any obvious loss of appeal.) She certainly has a breezy wit, and she does help with the case, making this truly seem like her audition for Nora Charles, though a flirtier and certainly more forward "Nora." As a murder mystery, *Penthouse* is pretty crummy, and utterly forgettable, but it makes for quite entertaining churned-out fare, the kind that coasts on film-star sparkle. It ends with a proposal, without concern over anyone's virginity. I do wonder if Baxter's early line to Loy is as dirty as I think: "I've got some eggs at my place that are just longing to be scrambled by you."

Female (1933) – A key product of pre-Code sexuality, despite its climactic cave-in, *Female* dares to engage in full-scale role reversal, not only by having Ruth Chatterton as president of a car company, but because of her advances upon a stable of attractive male employees, leading to invitations for "evening conferences." Publicly, Chatterton is a strong leader, tough and respected and accomplished, even feared, while privately she's interested in sex rather than marriage, wanting no emotional involvements. As a sex-flipping satire, *Female* is a gem, with men turning needy and insecure while Chatterton remains detached and unsentimental. Men are playthings: "A woman in love is a pathetic spectacle." Yet there's nothing trashy about Chatterton; she's a great lady with plummy speech. *Female* was co-written by a woman, Kathryn Scola, along with Gene Markey, the team who had recently written the scandalous *Baby Face* (in which Barbara Stanwyck literally sleeps her way to the top). Watch Chatterton set a trap for strapping employee Johnny Mack Brown: she beds him, then she's done with him. Another fellow becomes so emotionally attached that she's forced to transfer him. Why can't men separate sex from *feelings*? As part of her man-trapping lair, Chatterton has a Busby Berkeley pool (the one from *Footlight Parade*) and an organ planted in a wall (complete with organist). Unfortunately, you know where this is going, with her meeting her match in real-man George Brent (her true-life husband at the time), a new hard-to-get engineer. At only sixty minutes, *Female* is much too short, but Chatterton, a precursor to Bette Davis in flash and self-possession, brings a magnetic charge to this gender bender, until the big fat cop-out in which she chooses domesticity, putting Brent in charge of the company so she can play wife and mother (planning on nine kids). In typical pre-Code fashion, her promiscuous past does not preclude conventional happiness, but it's nonetheless dispiriting to see her sideline her audacious adventures of career building and sexual exploration, instead seeking conformity and peace. With Brent set to assume her position, it has the look of a man taking his "rightful place," a place the Code would do its best to make sure he occupied for at least the next thirty years, and with as little feminine interference as possible.

Hollywood's "Crash" Course: More Than Just Escapism (1931-1934)

It seems ironic at such an exciting and promising, however scary, time in Hollywood—the overhauling transition to sound—that the country was about to plunge into the Great Depression, instantly replacing all those onscreen college boys and jazz babies with hoods and shopgirls. The talkie "boom" made steady headway throughout 1929, only to be met with an even bigger boom, the stock-market crash in October. How would Hollywood's newfound potential—its state-of-the-art advancements, its moment of forward-looking expansion—serve a country whose immediate future suddenly looked so bleak? The movies simply acknowledged the new normal and adjusted accordingly. The result—American studio filmmaking of the 1930s—has been called the Golden Age of Hollywood, an era primarily associated with Depression escapism. After all, this era delivered the loopy antics of the Marx Brothers, the ever-fantastic thrills of Universal's horror series, the kaleidoscopic wonders of Busby Berkeley's imagination, the fleet-footed sensuality of Astaire and Rogers, the nonchalant sleuthing of Powell and Loy, and the spawning of a Depression-inspired sub-genre: the screwball comedy.

But there was a flip side to all those delights, a grimy alternative to feel-good distractions. The best remembered movies within this darker realm of Hollywood's early-'30s output are from the gangster genre, particularly its legendary Holy Trinity: Edward G. Robinson in Mervyn LeRoy's *Little Caesar* (1931), James Cagney in William A. Wellman's *The Public Enemy* (1931), and Paul Muni in Howard Hawks' *Scarface* (1932). These brutal classics continue to represent Hollywood's Depression-era toughness and rather startling ugliness, despite the pleasures of larger-than-life personalities at their centers. This was, don't forget, the raw pre-Code era, which, while addressing the new Depression, was also covering the dying days of Prohibition with its bootleggers, speakeasies, and police raids.

As king of the crime pictures, Warner Brothers established a reputation for grit and guts (which carried beyond the pre-Code era), employing those qualities even where it wasn't expected, making what might be called reality-based escapism. Look at *42nd Street* (1933), a musical that would never have soared minus its flavorful Depression context, with a host of chorines seeking employment (perhaps just steps from working the pavement) and a big-deal director (Warner Baxter) wiped out by the crash, desperate for a hit. Applying a Cinderella climax, in which one lucky nobody (Ruby Keeler) becomes an overnight sensation, *42nd Street* delivered a fantasy rooted in the truth of its day. Over at Columbia, another kind of Depression movie found its quintessential expression. *Man's Castle* (1933), starring Spencer Tracy and an impossibly lovely Loretta Young, is a poor person's love story, all about finding heaven amid hell. Despite some unfortunate late-breaking melodrama, director Frank Borzage offered a graceful, visually intoxicating, and poignantly acted romance set in Hooverville squalor. Like *42nd Street,* its moments of rapture are set against a background of recognizable authenticity.

Possibly the greatest American pre-Code Depression-based film is Frank Capra's multi-Oscar-winning *It Happened One Night* (1934), also from Columbia. Though a romantic comedy, it's entirely informed by Depression America, partly in its rich-girl/regular-guy romance, but mostly in the way it uses the country's present situation as its unmistakable backdrop, the canvas on which this road movie plays out (with details such as hobos on a passing train, or a hungry mother and son encountered on a bus). Claudette Colbert is the runaway heiress, a prisoner of privilege, helpless and useless but with a touch of recklessness, and Clark Gable is the reporter on her trail, representing all the working mugs in the audience. Part of the movie's infectious appeal derives from the value it puts on ordinary folks, with Colbert learning from Gable rather than the other way around. She's the one who doesn't know how to do anything, while he seems able to do everything ("I ought to write a book"), until the irresistible switcheroo of the hitchhiking scene. Before then, though, it is he who knows how to do things *properly,* such as dunking a donut or simply undressing. Anything *worth* knowing! With its air of sustained spontaneity and those two brilliant, light-comic turns, *It Happened One Night* is both ageless and a perfect marker of a very definite moment.

Hollywood's Depression-era grappling with contemporary times seeped into all types of movies, beyond the visceral flash of the gangster genre, the life-changing possibilities within backstage musicals, or the love-conquers-all assurances of romantic fare. What they all share is the quest for survival, whether immediate or long-term, without any way of knowing where it was all headed (or how much worse things could get). These movies displayed the industry's willingness to confront and reflect dark days.

Employees' Entrance (1933): Loretta Young and Warren William

Stolen Heaven (1931) - Though consistently melodramatic and straining plausibility, it's got a good hook, triggering an absorbing concoction of realism and what-if fantasy. Streetwalker Nancy Carroll and robber Phillips Holmes, virtual strangers, leave NYC for Palm Beach, armed with the twenty grand he just stole. Their plan is to spend all the money on fancy clothes and at a posh hotel and then kill themselves. They complicate their unsentimental deal when they fall in love. The adorable Carroll is so warm and sweet, while Holmes is not quite her equal in star quality. Though both stars are now forgotten, this was a reteaming after their big success in *The Devil's Holiday* (1930), for which Carroll received her one and only Oscar nomination. Also on hand is Louis Calhern as an unctuous rich guy lusting after Carroll. Crime may not pay, but it does serves as a springboard to true love, leading to newfound hope in pessimistic times. Directed and adapted by Broadway legend George Abbott,

Paramount's *Stolen Heaven* offers sin, adventure, and material excess—all very sympathetic to the desires and daydreams of those in the audience.

American Madness (1932) – Ever since the crash, any movie about a bank was automatically fraught with drama and suspense, including this impressive early Frank Capra effort for Columbia. As a bank president battling his board of directors, and then facing a robbery-induced panic, Walter Huston is his usually excellent self. But can his bank be saved? You can't help but be reminded of the similarities to Capra's *It's a Wonderful Life* (1946), with Huston a George Bailey type (having faith in people, making loans on instinct), right up to the sentimental ending, with the "little people" averting a disaster. Despite its crisp flair for dialogue, Robert Riskin's screenplay indulges a melodramatic side. The plot is motored by employee Gavin Gordon's assistance in the robbery (because of gambling debts), plus his flirtation with Huston's neglected but faithful wife, Kay Johnson. On the plus side is Pat O'Brien as the chief teller; he matches Huston's naturalism, appropriately, considering their almost father-son bond. As for Capra's visual skills, he makes dazzling use of the bank vault, so gleaming and exotic-looking, almost a palpable character, especially in the stunningly photographed heist sequence.

Employees' Entrance (1933) – It's set in a department store, yet it has the life-and-death urgency of a combat movie. A real doozy, call it a juiced melodrama—hectic and dirty and fun. Warren William stars as the store's volatile, ruthless, and unfeeling general manager who's so good at his job that he can get away with bullying his board of directors. He's so maniacally all-business that the character verges on the comical. Loretta Young is the unemployed beauty who succumbs to his advances, resulting in a job as a store model (looking swell in her Orry-Kelly fashions). She finds workplace love with Wallace Ford, Mr. William's protégé (and then assistant), and keeps secret her former dalliance with the boss. A woman-hating womanizer, William is single and anti-marriage, so Ford keeps quiet his marriage to Young. It's rather shocking when Young, now a married woman, sleeps with William a second time, after getting drunk at a party (following an argument with Ford). She must be a little hot for William, though Young's performance, fine as it is, doesn't dare suggest that possibility. The movie becomes a souped-up triangle, with Young and William fighting for Ford's soul, which includes gunfire and the taking of poison! Furiously paced, and sometimes veering toward the ridiculous, *Employees' Entrance* is a prime Warner Brothers quickie (at just seventy-five minutes), snappily directed by Roy Del Ruth. It wouldn't be as much fun as it is if Mr. William seemed more human.

Gabriel over the White House (1933) – Now for something truly weird (and unexpected from MGM), a fascinating curiosity of Depression filmmaking that opens with Walter Huston's inauguration as US President. He's someone with no interest in helping people or in keeping campaign promises; he's all about his (unnamed) party, otherwise apathetic and detached. He's a bachelor who makes his mistress (Karen Morley) his "confidential secretary." Following a car-accident coma, Huston wakes a new man, ready to do good, becoming a firm, straight-talking leader devoted to helping the unemployed and the hungry. He even stops having sex with Morley (who finds love with Franchot Tone, Huston's actual secretary). Is Huston possessed by the angel Gabriel? The only special effects involved in his transformation consist of fluttering curtains and lighting changes, a rather mild activation of this craziest what-if among all Depression movies. Huston's leadership soon takes a dark turn, morphing into dictatorship because it seems to him the only way to effect positive change. Cut the red tape! He has several racketeers executed, adjourns his useless Congress, and fires his Cabinet. Amid calls for his impeachment, he's still the only one in power who wants to help the needy. He goes after the Europeans who owe us money, creates jobs, and ends the arms race, decrying the money wasted on war. In his warning about the *next* war, he cites its "inconceivably devastating explosions." (Even the Japanese sign his "covenant.") Directed by Gregory La Cava, *Gabriel* is mesmerizingly offbeat and bizarrely centered on a bleeding-heart dictator; it's a unique mix of patriotism and radicalism, idealism and cynicism, growing increasingly talky (and heavy on the speech-making) and more ideologically unhinged. Huston is ideal casting, an actor of such gravitas; his intelligence grounds things considerably. The film's profound yearning for big solutions and true leaders is equaled by its lack of faith in our government. Based on an uncredited novel, Carey Wilson's screenplay, in its assumed passion concerning national woes, resorts to shocking tactics, in the grip of a possibly angel-controlled tyrant-hero. Amid the movie's confusing mixed signals, Morley and Tone continue to look upon Huston adoringly, as some kind of savior.

Gold Diggers of 1933 – Following what *42nd Street* started, this Busby Berkeley extravaganza from Warner Brothers famously opens with Ginger Rogers, in her glittery costume of coins, delivering the news that "We're in the Money," a hopeful yet decidedly ironic ditty for 1933. The title characters maintain their enormous likability because they include three expert wisecrackers: Joan Blondell, Aline MacMahon, and Ms. Rogers. As the lovebirds, Dick Powell, a secretly wealthy songwriter, and reliably lousy Ruby Keeler, a standard bearer of optimism, provide the wide-eyed counterpoint to all that fast-flying sass. This time it's Powell, rather than Keeler, who goes on for an ailing performer. Yes, it's a backstage musical, with all the woes of having to raise money to put on a show and all those chorus girls wondering how they'll make ends meet between gigs. (Producer Ned Sparks mentions the Astaires with Rogers in the room, *before* her first picture with Fred.) Warren William plays Powell's disapproving older brother, accompanied by family lawyer Guy Kibbee, which leads to all sorts of mistaken-identity complications manipulated by Blondell and MacMahon. The movie ceases to be a musical for too long a stretch, but director Mervyn LeRoy is mostly a whiz at keeping energized this type of slam-bang frivolity. As for Berkeley, the film climaxes with two of his finest hallucinations: "In the Shadows," the electric-lit violin number with all those swirling gals in tiered bell-like gowns; and "Remember My Forgotten Man," the most blatant Depression-oriented musical number of the period, with Blondell talk-singing about discarded WWI veterans now on breadlines, featuring stylized recreations of both the war and the present, bringing downbeat contemporary subject matter right onto the musical stage. *Gold Diggers* also peddled sumptuous black and white, lilting Harry Warren-Al Dubin tunes, and risqué humor. Nowhere else but at Warner Brothers could you be simultaneously reminded of the Depression and so deliriously distracted.

The Mayor of Hell (1933) – Here's another example of Warner Brothers' ability to serve grunge with a smile, combining despairing content with an overlay of highly charged uplift. Sort of a pre-Code *Boys Town*, *The Mayor of Hell* takes a problem-picture topic (reform schools) and then solves all its problems. (Reform-school pictures are essentially prison movies for kids.) As outrageous and over the top as this movie gets, it's also immensely entertaining and satisfying, mostly due to the star power of James Cagney who's used to full advantage in what is really a supporting role. Focused on one of the great heartaches of the Depression—its impact on the future of America's youth—the setting is a nightmarish institution run by the evil Dudley Digges...that is until Cagney takes charge. He's just a racketeer using his new cushy post as a front, but he becomes dedicated to saving these boys who remind him of himself. He's further committed because of the school's lovely progressive nurse (lispy Madge Evans). There's a real melting-pot of boys, plenty of them stereotypically presented, and yet their sheer diversity is refreshing. Cagney and Evans instigate a "self-government republic" for the boys, with their own court, police, store, etc. It amounts to a simplistic fairy tale, but it's quite pleasing to watch Cagney find a purpose and become the boys' champion. For a climax, there's a riot, followed by an abrupt resolution, but Cagney's remarkable electricity holds it all together. Using the studio's patented formula, *The Mayor of Hell* offers an illusion of stark reality, a platform from which to spin an outlandishly movie-ish yarn.

Three Cornered Moon (1933) – And what of the once-rich poor? This charming, relaxed pre-screwball comedy from Paramount, based on a play by Gertrude Tonkonogy, centers on a wealthy and rather useless Brooklyn family, who learn that they are made of stronger stuff after losing everything (thanks to widowed matriarch Mary Boland's bad investments). Her children are Claudette Colbert, who finds work in a shoe factory; William Bakewell, an actor who gets one line ("Yes") in a play; Wallace Ford, a law clerk, who, in the film's emotional climax, passes the bar; and Tom Brown, a college student who becomes a lifeguard. Hardie Albright is Colbert's beau, a helpless-artist type (an aspiring novelist), and Richard Arlen is a doctor who loves her, as well as being the tenant sharing the family's mansion. The movie has little sympathy for Albright, a failed artist portrayed as a lazy user. He lets everyone down when he refuses a job offer, though you could say he's unfairly treated as the plot's scapegoat. Things get pretty grim when the family actually goes hungry, and there's even some overwrought hysteria, but *Three Cornered Moon* is primarily playful, funny, and honest. Director Elliott Nugent elicits solid performances from his ensemble. The standout is Boland, a dizzy delight in one of the earliest depictions of the screwy matron of '30s comedy. The message here is the opposite of *It Happened One Night;* the rich prove to be quite capable, stepping up in hard times and fending just as well as poor folks.

Turn Back the Clock (1933) – This is another novel post-crash fantasy from MGM, but much lighter fare than *Gabriel over the White House.* Lee Tracy begins as a forty-four-year-old cigar-shop owner, a modestly fixed WWI veteran who's married to Mae Clarke and about to have a mid-life crisis. Should he have instead married rich girl Peggy Shannon and become the guaranteed success her businessman father would have made of him? Hit by a car and on an operating table, Tracy dreams of going back in time and making different choices. There's a lovely scene of him waking *into* the dream, discovering his long-dead mother (Clara Blandick) frying breakfast in her kitchen. It's just another morning for her but a profoundly moving reunion for him. (Blandick, later Auntie Em, shares a brief scene with Charley Grapewin, later Uncle Henry, six years before *The Wizard of Oz*.) Inside the dream, Tracy marries the rich girl (unhappily) and rises professionally to a bank presidency. No surprise: the dream teaches him to appreciate his real life. The moral is pat, that money doesn't bring happiness. In fact, it's often a curse! Despite such an elaborate ruse to make a banal point, the movie manages to stay fresh and alert, graced with Tracy's charismatic panache. Add winning direction from Edgar Selwyn (who co-wrote with Ben Hecht) and *Turn Back the Clock* is a real sleeper (forgive the pun). Its most bracing scene comes when the dreaming Tracy, in his role as wealthy citizen, addresses WWI troops about to go overseas. Rather than deliver the expected patriotic blather, he speaks honestly (from his actual doughboy experience), not only of mud and barbed wire but about a veteran's difficulty in finding a job...if he's lucky enough to return at all.

Wild Boys of the Road (1933) – Probably the roughest of Depression movies focused on youngsters, it has a documentary-like visual authenticity, especially in its scenes on trains and at rail stations (across many states). Extremely well-crafted by William A. Wellman for Warner Brothers, it's essentially an Andy Hardy picture that goes horribly wrong. Frankie Darro (the main boy from *The Mayor of Hell*) and Edwin Phillips are middle-class teens whose families are feeling the hard-times crunch. To help out, the boys quit school and run away to look for work, hopping a freight train. In no way delinquents, they are wonderful kids (perhaps too much so), but nothing goes their way. Dorothy Coonan (soon to be Mrs. Wellman) is a girl (dressed as a boy) with whom they form a solid trio. There's some overcooked melodrama (involving Coonan's shady aunt Minna Gombell), but also some wrenchingly powerful moments: railroad "dicks" brawling with homeless youths; revenge on a brakeman who rapes a girl; and, in the film's unforgettable centerpiece, a train running over a crawling boy's leg, leading to an amputation. As affecting as this movie undoubtedly is, it would be stronger with an appropriately harsh ending, instead of the too-easy, too-upbeat wind-up it was given. Yet how many who've seen this movie even remember that it has a cop-out ending? What stays with viewers are those agonizing episodes, the worsening struggle of young people trying to right an upended world. *Wild Boys of the Road* probably scared many worried teens into toughing things out at home, perhaps saving their lives.

He Was Her Man (1934) – Like *Stolen Heaven,* it's a love story between bruised losers, a Warner Brothers movie marked by Depression-tinged weariness. A no-options Joan Blondell agrees to marry Victor Jory, a thick-accented Portuguese fisherman, before falling for ex-con James Cagney, making this drama feel like an uncredited version of *They Knew What They Wanted.* The mustachioed Cagney is Flicker, a hood who turned stool pigeon on the two mugs who hung a rap on him; hitmen are now after him. Not at all the expected mug-and-moll shoot-'em-up, *He Was Her Man* is a bittersweet tale of second chances, compromises, and sacrifice. It's graced with two natural performances from Cagney and Blondell (in their seventh of seven films together), with an especially low-key turn from a no-fireworks Cagney. After a chance meeting, a hideout-seeking Cagney accompanies flat-broke Blondell—likely an ex-hooker, with the requisite heart-of-gold tenderness—on her way to Jory (who knows all about her "past" and still wants her as a wife). The main action is set on the coast, south of San Francisco, where director Lloyd Bacon establishes a tangy fishing-village ambiance. When unplanned love blooms between the stars—Blondell still knows nothing about his dangerous situation—it complicates her plans with Jory (who is so lively and kind and pretty hard to take). The plot is Cagney's redemption, the basis for this touchingly restrained tale of true love among this generation's battered masses. Cagney and Blondell are best remembered together in the musical *Footlight Parade* (1933), which was also directed by Bacon, but their teamwork topped itself here, even though this film went unnoticed. Perhaps that's not too surprising for a work so hauntingly infused with sadness, a quality that many films of this era tried to whitewash in favor of optimistic endings. Among the last of pre-Code films, and steeped in unresolved yearning, *He Was Her Man* is unusual and delicate, yet I've never read a nice thing about it. In *Gold Diggers of 1933,* Blondell had asked moviegoers to remember her forgotten man; what about this forgotten movie?

Mandatory Makeovers: Re-Accessorizing for the Production Code (1934-1938)

The major male stars of the early 1930s didn't have to make much of an adjustment when the Production Code began enforcement in mid-1934. Though the violence in gangster pictures was certainly toned down, Edward G. Robinson and James Cagney continued to be tough guys and continued to resolve issues with gunfire. Audiences loved Cagney just as much in *Angels with Dirty Faces* (1938) as they had in *The Public Enemy* (1931), easily absorbing the sentimentality added to the formula. Gary Cooper, back in his French Foreign Legion uniform, didn't womanize in *Beau Geste* (1939) the way he had in *Morocco* (1930), but moviegoers still found him transportingly romantic and adventurous. When Clark Gable capped the decade opposite Vivien Leigh in *Gone With the Wind* (1939), wasn't he every bit as sizzling as he had been with Jean Harlow in the pre-Code *Red Dust* (1932)?

Female stars bore nearly all of the burden of reinvention in a Code-dictated era. Gone from production rosters were the more explicit plots about hookers (*Rain, Virtue*), or those concerning schemers sleeping their way to the top (*Red-Headed Woman, Baby Face*). Unwed pregnancy was still a viable subject, if used for tearjerking purposes—with punitive suffering a must—as in *A Woman Rebels* (1936) and *The Old Maid* (1939). Yes, penance was key, meaning that if a prostitute did manage to appear—Marjorie Rambeau in *Primrose Path*, Vivien Leigh in *Waterloo Bridge*, both in 1940—there was no chance of the happy ending once possible for pre-Code women. For many early-'30s actresses, for whom these types of characters were their daily bread—Dorothy Mackaill, Helen Twelvetrees, Nancy Carroll, Sally Eilers, Ann Dvorak, Mae Clarke, among them—the Code swiftly quashed their stardom. Admittedly, most of them were in decline by 1934, having starred in too many similar films, perhaps already played out. Without Code-era reboots, they drifted into supporting roles, B pictures, or retirement. Plenty of male stars followed suit—John Boles, Gene Raymond, Ricardo Cortez, Warren William, even talented Chester Morris—but mostly because they were outshone by superior newcomers, not because their types of roles dried up.

By mid-1934, what melodramatic torment had not been endured by Ann Harding, Kay Francis, or Constance Bennett? If they, or any of the aforementioned ladies, tried continuing in their usual fare it was to be without the pre-Code spice that had enlivened their vehicles to begin with! Of course, age was another factor, always a hurdle in stars' transitions. Ruth Chatterton was now past forty, and though Ms. Bennett would have a big success with *Topper* (1937), she, too, was approaching a mature-lady grandeur that signified narrowing opportunities. Beyond the problems of changing content, advancing age, or a fickle audience, some of these ladies were perhaps too representative of an early post-crash atmosphere, just as some silent stars were too identifiably of their era and couldn't *belong* to the talkies. Mae West made more movies, but the Code did its best to interfere with her no-angel ways. Poor Fay Wray, forever fixed in the palm of *King Kong* (1933), was soon relegated to cheap programmers. As for the Busby Berkeley gals, Ruby Keeler was far too emblematic of Depression-centric escapism to last much longer, while Joan Blondell saw her splintering one-liners sandpapered. By the mid-'30s, it just wasn't their world anymore.

Norma Shearer held onto her status as MGM's First Lady, adding three more Oscar nominations in the Code era, even if it was mightily apparent that her days were numbered; she retired in 1942. Greta Garbo reached an artistic pinnacle with two Code-era triumphs, *Camille* (1937) and *Ninotchka* (1939), then bolted after flopping in *Two-Faced Woman* (1941). Both Joan Crawford and Katharine Hepburn suffered major setbacks in the early years of the Code's enforcement, each labeled box-office poison in 1938. Their sensational comebacks would have to wait until the next decade: Hepburn in *The Philadelphia Story* (1940), Crawford in *Mildred Pierce* (1945). Meanwhile, Barbara Stanwyck, working at a furious clip, made her transition without noticeable effort or perceptibly altering her persona, all the while playing a variety of parts. The multi-hankie *Stella Dallas* (1937) gave her an Oscar-nominated boost as the 1940s—her peak decade—approached.

While pre-Code actresses were scrambling, stagnating, or recalibrating, they also had to contend with a crop of females whose stardom was just blossoming in the mid-'30s, not only new arrivals like Olivia de Havilland and Rosalind Russell, but others, toiling for years, who were bursting into their full-blown stardoms, including Bette Davis, Ginger Rogers, and Jean Arthur. The most fascinating '30s ladies are the ones who had been defined by the pre-Code era yet were able to alter that identification and stay relevant, often flourishing as never before. An interesting trend was the new prominence of female-driven comedies: a late '30s heyday of romantic comedy and screwball comedy, both of which recharged a number of female stars, indelibly rebranding them. One thing was certain: there was going to be a lot of "ladylike" behavior from this batch of leading ladies, these mothers of reinvention.

The Gilded Lily (1935): Fred MacMurray and Claudette Colbert

The Thin Man **(1934)** – Though technically a pre-Code movie—released just one month before the Code's enforcement—*The Thin Man* appears to capture Myrna Loy wisely anticipating her Code-era transition, introducing a new Loy perfectly primed for the rest of her career. As an up-and-comer of the late '20s and early '30s, she somehow got herself typecast as an "exotic," playing characters with such names as Azuri, Yasmani, Nubi, and Carmita. Her peak of embarrassment is as Fah Lo See, Boris Karloff's daughter in *The Mask of Fu Manchu* (1932), wearing long press-on fingernails and being aroused by watching a hot guy get whipped. Much more promising was her intelligent allure as one of the pre-Code era's slinkiest, more provocative females in films such as *Love Me Tonight* (1932), *The Animal Kingdom* (1932), and *When Ladies Meet* (1933). After appearing with William Powell in *Manhattan Melodrama* (1934), they were reteamed for *The Thin Man*, which established a legendary Loy persona: "The Perfect Wife." Her Nora Charles is wealthy, beautiful, and nonchalantly stylish, but she's "perfect" because of her shrewd wit and playful bantering skills. Loy and Powell turned conversation into foreplay, their verbal volleying denoting a subtly sexy marriage of equals. Alert to each other's every comic twinkle, these masters of understatement generously shared their offhand merriment with moviegoers. Whether ordering "five more martinis" so she can catch up to Powell, or announcing, at the dinner-party climax, that this is "the best dinner I ever listened to," Loy was on her way to becoming one of the later '30s most bankable stars. It must be said that the murder mysteries within the six-picture *Thin Man* series are forgettable, growing weaker with each successive film, hard even to endure in the scenes in which neither star appears. Though this first picture has a pre-Code disrespect for Christmas (with Powell shooting balloons off their tree), it already has the couple in twin beds. (Nick Jr. doesn't come along until the third film.) Loy would be voted "Queen" in the same 1937 national poll that made Gable "King," extending her reign with marvelous dramatic work in *Test Pilot* (1938) and *The Rains Came* (1939). She was a down-to-earth screen goddess, casting a spell of deceptively casual enchantment, so approachably likable and warmly unassuming. Is it any wonder America adored her?

The Gilded Lily (1935) – The 1934 transition to a Code-ruled Hollywood coincided with Claudette Colbert's breakout into superstardom, courtesy of a trio of mega-hits that year: the pre-Code romantic comedy *It Happened One Night*, followed by two Code-approved dramas, the soap *Imitation of Life* and the epic *Cleopatra*. Talk about versatility! Of the three, it was Colbert's Oscar-winning work in Frank Capra's magical *It Happened One Night* that set the tone for the bulk of her long-running stardom. Though she never topped it (after all, it *is* perfect), she came close twice, with *Midnight* (1939) and *The Palm Beach Story* (1942). The pre-Code flourishes of Capra's film—the Depression-era physical details, Clark Gable's how-a-man-undresses lesson, the sexy haystack scene—were unlikely in the Code era, but this classic's sturdy rom-com foundation was highly influential, with Colbert herself headlining many inferior wannabes, bolstering them with her charm offensives and high-sheened self-assurance. *The Gilded Lily* is perhaps the best of all second-tier

Colbert comedies. The setting is still Depression-based, with stenographer Colbert having to choose between newspaperman Fred MacMurray (her best pal) and Ray Milland (whom she later learns is an English lord). A break-up with Milland makes her a tabloid celebrity, "The 'No' Girl," which leads to her nightclub act even though she hasn't any talent (an anticipation of "reality" stars). The film's one great sequence is Colbert's opening night. By virtue of coming clean about her lack of performing skills, she is a sensation, captivating the gawkers with her irresistible self-deprecation. Whether blanking on her lyrics or spinning uncontrollably onto a patron's lap, Colbert is a sheer delight, believably enrapturing the club's audience while offering a lesson in high-comic style and elegant bewitchery. The Code rears itself when Milland proposes a week-long getaway, sans wedding ring, sending Colbert into MacMurray's waiting arms. Both novice leading men show that they have the goods, but Colbert is deservedly solo above the title, gilding an average lily into pure gold.

Wife vs. Secretary **(1936)** – How in the world was Jean Harlow going to survive the Code? Her sense of uninhibited fun, tied to a brazen sexuality and loose-flying wisecracks, had made her a major star in 1932 with *Red-Headed Woman* (as a gold digger) and *Red Dust* (as a prostitute). What's a smart-mouthed, unrepentant sex goddess to do? After the 1933 highs of *Dinner at Eight* and *Bombshell*, Harlow made a disastrous initial transition to the Code era with *The Girl from Missouri* (1934), a defanged *Red-Headed Woman*— she's a gold-digging *virgin*, protecting her virtue! Things didn't improve with two melodramatic stinkers, *Reckless* (1935) and *Riff-Raff* (1935), nor even *China Seas* (1935), a popular but watered-down *Red Dust* (again with Clark Gable). *Wife vs. Secretary* is no great shakes, far below the caliber of its superstar trio—Harlow, Gable, and Myrna Loy—but it effectively formatted Harlow into a Code-era soap, casting her somewhat surprisingly as a super-efficient secretary. Gable is her boss, a wealthy magazine-publishing magnate, and she's his indispensable 24-7 right hand. It's refreshing to see her as a smart young woman, still likable yet believably brainy. Loy, meanwhile, is Gable's cool, pampered wife; they are happily married, also childless. Just an ordinary girl, Harlow won't quit her exciting job to please fiancé James Stewart, unable to admit (even to herself) how attached she is to Gable. In this situation, the old Harlow would have been a homewrecking seductress, a coarse climber, but here she's on the level. She's nicely relaxed, too, which often wasn't the case when this actress broached melodrama. Whether or not anything happens to change the friendly all-business relationship between Harlow and Gable, their erotic chemistry is undeniable. Unfortunately, *Wife vs. Secretary* is overly contrived and insufficiently bright, with too much business nonsense complicating the plot. Naturally, there's a climactic Harlow-Loy confrontation, but the movie's main value is as proof that there *was* a place for Harlow in this new era, further verified by a later 1936 picture, *Libeled Lady* (also with Loy), which confirmed Harlow's laugh-getting ability in a screwball-comedy arena. Alas, she was fatally ill the next year, gone at twenty-six, leaving us to wonder how she might have fared as the 1940s neared, when young Lana Turner was emerging as Gable's next blonde partner at MGM.

My Man Godfrey (1936) – Carole Lombard was one of those early '30s leading ladies who seemed destined to vanish, showing glimmers of promise but never really clicking in a distinctive way. Thank goodness for *Twentieth Century* (1934), among the first of truly screwball comedies, released two months before Code enforcement. Lombard, not especially known for hilarity, connected as never before. As a lingerie model molded into a glamorous superstar by producer-director John Barrymore, she perhaps showed more gumption than skill, more enthusiasm than inspiration, but what an infectious playfulness! She proved herself a game co-star, truly keeping up with the sensationally outrageous Barrymore, as though releasing her comic gusto from its genie bottle. *My Man Godfrey* is the film in which Lombard's screwball precision caught up to its promise, making her the poster girl for the genre's scatterbrained heiresses. Alongside a flawless William Powell (her former real-life husband), she is a sparkling mix of fearless abandon and childlike vulnerability (and brattiness). You can feel her influence on Lucille Ball, another drop-dead beauty able to access the kid (and the clown) inside her. Lombard giddily portrays a dimwitted rich girl sweetly infatuated with Godfrey (Powell), the new butler, the "forgotten man" she finds on a scavenger hunt (though he's also a man of mystery). Her soaking-wet scene, shouting "Godfrey Loves Me!" is deliriously inventive in its all-out freedom and glee. She's an adorable whack job bouncing around the room, the perfect counterweight to Powell's impeccable refinement. He's sane, as is Lombard's harried father (Eugene Pallette), but the screwballs, led by Lombard's mother (divinely dizzy Alice Brady), are certainly pleasure-forging life forces. Directed by Gregory La Cava with a freewheeling zest, *Godfrey* is a touching, big-hearted comedy, a Depression fairy tale that mixes hard times and frivolity. In her only Oscar-nominated performance, Lombard unleashed her special glow, enhanced by her fresh and impossibly fast line readings, becoming one of the prime comediennes in an age of staggeringly gifted competition. With the Code, she reached the top, in dramatic pictures as well, until her plane-crash death at thirty-three in 1942.

***The Garden of Allah* (1936)** – Marlene Dietrich was in trouble. Her seven-film association with director Josef von Sternberg, which produced the hits *Morocco* (1930) and *Shanghai Express* (1932), was no longer seducing crowds. *The Scarlet Empress* (1934) and *The Devil Is a Woman* (1935) were both box-office duds. Had her increasing exoticism finally enervated audiences? By 1938, she was box-office poison, only to be resurrected in 1939 when she ventured where no one expected—into the western *Destry Rides Again*. Back in 1936, finished with von Sternberg, she returned to some of the *Morocco* elements that had made her a US star. She reteamed with Gary Cooper in *Desire*, a highly underrated sophisticated comedy, and then made *The Garden of Allah*, which plays like a Code-modified *Morocco*-influenced romance. Directed by Richard Boleslawski with a seamlessly heady flow of images, *Allah* might be called lusciously deluxe kitsch. It's one of the earliest three-strip Technicolor movies, remaining among the more rapturous color experiences of all time, breathtaking in its palette. (What *Morocco* did for black and white, *Allah* does for color.) Though Dietrich is again in North Africa, again ready to give all for love, again in a plot of mesmerizing hokum, she herself is far from her pre-Code *Morocco* character—no longer a world-weary woman with a past. Instead, she's convent-raised and devoutly religious. Rich and lonely, too, she's searching for *something* (Gary Cooper?), giving the desert a try. Meanwhile, Trappist monk Charles Boyer has run away. When he meets Dietrich, he keeps his past a secret. They fall in love and marry, a dreamy couple with a smoldering chemistry. Based on a 1904 novel, the *Allah* story is unsurprisingly old-fashioned, filled with clichés and dragging a heavy religiosity. It works as an excursion into glamour and color, both of which infuse the emotions and heighten the palpability of the soap opera. (If the plot is moldy, the treatment is state of the art; if Dietrich is still encased in exotica, well, Technicolor gave her a fresh coat of paint.) Her endless array of fashions is stunning, especially when billowing in assorted winds. The desert is presented as a dreamscape, a paradise, and, most importantly, as the idyllic honeymoon. *Allah* cost too much to turn a profit, keeping Dietrich's career in a shaky position. She would have to find a more grounded and seemingly realistic screen persona, particularly if she intended to carry a fan base into the next decade. She succeeded, bawdily seeing "what the boys in the back room will have" in *Destry*, as well as making three films with John Wayne, proving that this sensually rarefied creature could come out from behind the veils of her mystique.

Tarzan Escapes (1936) – Here's a unique case, an actress playing the same character six times between 1932 and 1942, beginning in the pre-Code era and finishing at the start of WWII. Maureen O'Sullivan's Jane in MGM's *Tarzan* series, opposite Johnny Weissmuller, may be the single most fascinating figure in the transition from pre-Code to Code. The opener, *Tarzan the Ape Man* (1932), ostensibly an adventure movie, is, in reality, a "woman's picture"—a fantasy of forbidden love in which the central character is not Tarzan but Jane. When the spirited O'Sullivan arrives in Africa to see her ivory-hunting father (C. Aubrey Smith), her initial encounters with Weissmuller trigger a sexual odyssey. She gives herself over to animal instincts, a proper English rose succumbing to passion and very quickly choosing to remain, to live in sin! *Tarzan and His Mate* (1934), the other pre-Code picture in the sextet, continues the hokey erotica, with O'Sullivan still the plot's center (while surrounded by jungle-action antics). Both stars are uninhibitedly sexy, not to mention practically naked for most of the movie, including Jane's notorious skinny-dipping sequence (with an O'Sullivan body double). These first two movies are essentially about a young woman unlocking her wild nature, thrilled by her primal state. When the Code moves in, there's an unsurprising shift, with Jane more of a domesticator, bringing Middle America to the jungle. Like a missionary, she'll do some taming of Tarzan. In *Tarzan Escapes*, the duo still isn't married and is still quite amorous, yet all is not the same. When her cousins arrive from London, Jane shows off her domestic haven, the treehouse "townhouse" Tarzan built (which includes running water) with the kitchen she designed, plus an elephant-operated elevator, all of it seeming very *Flintstones*. As for hunting and gathering dinner, she tells Tarzan to "do the marketing." The most noticeable difference is O'Sullivan's costume which exposes far less skin than previously, while Weissmuller's is still skimpy and high-riding. (Did Code enforcers not realize that men could be objects of lust, too?) Throughout this nutty and absurd B-level adventure series, O'Sullivan maintained Jane's appeal, even while trickily transitioning from horny rebel to Loretta Young.

Love Is News (1937) – Speaking of Ms. Young, if you were as beautiful and innocent-looking as she was during the pre-Code era, you were bound to be harassed by men, just as she was in *Employees' Entrance* or *She Had to Say Yes,* both from 1933. She also epitomized the poignant Depression waif in *Man's Castle* (1933). The Code era would find her in spectacles like *The Call of the Wild* (1935), *The Crusades* (1935), and *Ramona* (1936), yet she didn't really find a sustaining niche until she cozied up to light comedy, the genre that would bring her an Oscar for *The Farmer's Daughter* (1947), followed by *The Bishop's Wife* (1947) and *Come to the Stable* (1949). At Fox in the 1930s, Young began a five-picture union with handsome newcomer Tyrone Power, starting with *Ladies in Love* (1936) but really igniting with *Love Is News,* a typical newspaper rom-com, fusing elements from *It Happened One Night* (1934), *Libeled Lady* (1936), and *Theodora Goes Wild* (1936). Power is too boyish to pull off a Gable-like reporter, and Don Ameche is at his worst as Power's frazzled boss. After some annoying interplay between the men, heiress Young enters with a blast of charm and star dust. The plot has her turning the tables on Power, the newsman who has been hounding her in print. She makes him a tabloid sensation by lying that he's her fiancé. It's a cute hook, before things get too frenetic with "hijinks." Young brings buoyancy to a routine effort, signifying her comfort within the genre. She may not be of Colbert's comic caliber, but she surely is a star, so chic and shimmery, furred and spangled, carrying herself with a breezy aplomb, far away from her Depression working girls and tenement dwellers. *Love Is News* was topped by the next Young-Power rom-com, *Café Metropole* (1937), the best of their quintet. Power would repeat his *Love Is News* role when the comedy was remade as *That Wonderful Urge* (1948) with Gene Tierney as the female lead (while Young, that same year, was busy accepting her Oscar).

Maytime (1937) – Jeanette MacDonald, the movies' first major female musical star, made her name in a series of sexy, effervescent musical comedies, often alongside Maurice Chevalier—the kind that might get her into a bathtub or at least a slip—including *The Love Parade* (1929) and the peerless *Love Me Tonight* (1932). After those champagne-popping Paramount musicals, MacDonald, now at MGM, made *The Merry Widow* (1934), again with Chevalier, a gem released with Code approval yet somehow retaining a risqué pre-Code spirit. MacDonald then broke with her early-'30s persona by starring with Nelson Eddy in the delightful *Naughty Marietta* (1935), rendering them the king and queen of screen operetta for eight movies, until

1942, an octet decidedly different from her "naughty" pre-1935 musicals. *Rose-Marie* (1936) was the team's silliest and campiest, but audiences loved it, and MacDonald next scored opposite Clark Gable in the disaster blockbuster *San Francisco* (1936), in which she's especially wholesome. *Maytime,* the best of her dramatic musicals with Eddy (*Marietta* is the best of their comic ones), is a flawed but splendid production, marred by a moralizing framing story, while musically it's an eclectically screwy mix, from "Carry Me Back to Old Virginny" to "Santa Lucia" to the opera *Les Huguenots.* The plot is a forerunner to *Love Me or Leave Me* (1955), with MacDonald as the songbird protégée of John Barrymore, mentored by him without any hanky-panky (though he loves and desires her). As the toast of Paris, she owes him everything and happily accepts his marriage bid, knowing nothing of true love, until, of course, she meets the struggling Eddy, a fellow American; their charming comic interaction denotes *real* love. At the May Day fair, the film reaches its musical climax with their duet ("Will You Remember?"), expressing a day of love to last a lifetime. *Maytime* is hyper-romantic, with MacDonald, soon saddened by her passionless marriage, reawakened by a New York reunion with Eddy (though, of course, she behaves herself). The drama benefits from Barrymore's restraint (not his usual mode by 1937); perhaps he's embarrassed by being in an operetta? He's both scary and sympathetic, and he raises MacDonald's limited acting skills. While still displaying her affection for him, she also conveys the tiring toll of it. It's nicely observed work, making this a love triangle of some heft (though Eddy is often on the sidelines). Extravagantly costumed by Adrian, MacDonald overflows with the finery of frills, bows, cloaks, flowers, and drapes: no more running around in a slip for her! By WWII, she and Eddy already seemed like nostalgia, yet that doesn't negate the fact that MacDonald's Eddy-fication had made her one of the late '30s biggest female box-office attractions.

The Awful Truth **(1937)** – Irene Dunne, like Carole Lombard, was a star transformed by a knack for comedy. Dunne achieved notice in the melo-driven worlds of *Cimarron* (1931) and *Back Street* (1932), reaching a pre-Code high with *Ann Vickers* (1933), in which she becomes an unwed mother *twice,* by two different men. The Code era brought her a big soap hit, *Magnificent Obsession* (1935), and her stardom was further expanded by her singing ability, featured in *Roberta* (1935) and *Show Boat* (1936). Yet I still wonder if her career, however versatile, might not have gone the same histrionically fizzling route as Ann Harding's had Dunne not found comedy, becoming more beloved in this vein than any other. *Theodora Goes Wild* (1936) was the transitional film, garnering her an Oscar nomination for her scrumptious two-tiered work as a proper girl who secretly writes a racy bestseller and, after unmasking herself, becomes a woman devouring a high-style high life. *The Awful Truth* is the great Dunne comedy, a screwball classic for the ages. She and Cary Grant divorce and then spend the rest of the movie plotting to wreck each other's new romances; it's obvious that the awful truth is their unshakable love. They simply need some fun-filled recharging: all that chemistry-fueled gamesmanship, the foreplay of sabotage, and the awareness of being so evenly matched. It's divorce as the ultimate aphrodisiac, a stunt to get the blood racing. (What new mate could ever compete with the partnership they already have?) Leo McCarey's Oscar-winning direction is an inspired mix of sophistication and slapstick, a series of superbly conceived comic set pieces effortlessly strung together. Dunne and Grant are beautiful sparring partners, experts at comic cunning, and never forgetting the subtext of love and sexual compatibility. As you savor Grant in his career-defining role, becoming his iconic comic self, both dapper and befuddled, Dunne is even more impressive, a faultless wielder of comic grace notes. There's an ingenious moment at her vocal recital when she deftly integrates a hiccup of a laugh into a song, her spontaneously tickled response to Grant's falling off his chair. Later, her gloriously low-down "Lola," Grant's embarrassingly tacky "sister," humiliates him while also bowling him over with her trashy ingenuity. *The Awful Truth* is a textbook example of how Code-era movies could still simmer with grown-up sex appeal, especially when assisted by an actress so accomplished in the art of the subtle, knowing wink.

Trade Winds **(1938)** – What if I told you that one actress made a successful transition to the Code era simply by dying her hair? It's true. Blonde Joan Bennett had been a lovely ingénue in pictures such as *Bulldog Drummond* and *Disraeli,* both from 1929, and, most famously, as Amy in *Little Women* (1933). Occasionally, she got to show some pre-Code sass, as in *Me and My Gal* (1932) with Spencer Tracy, but to many she was still the pretty kid sister of Constance Bennett (a major early '30s star). Despite a fine dramatic performance in *Private Worlds* (1935), the younger Bennett seemed destined to fade, to be overtaken by the next group of young and attractive blondes. Then came *Trade Winds,* which gave her an in-film makeover, a key part of the plot. It happens about ten minutes into the movie, when Bennett, avenging her sister's suicide, shoots a millionaire cad (Sidney Blackmer) and goes on the run from San Francisco to Honolulu (where she transforms into a brunette). With darkened hair, Bennett instantly goes from girl to woman, shedding her ingénue tag once and for all, and suddenly looks as if she had been pretending to be a blonde all along and was now, obviously, her authentic self. She found a look that would sustain her career for the next three decades, first as a queen of costume pictures (*The Man in the Iron Mask, The Son of Monte Cristo*), then as a noted film-noir femme fatale (*The Woman in the Window, Scarlet Street*), on to model of domesticity (*Father of the Bride, There's Always Tomorrow*), and, finally, as a television horror matron in *Dark Shadows*. *Trade Winds* is no more than entertaining nonsense, a comic-melodramatic adventure rather hectic and drawn-out in its series of locales and double-crosses, along with a ludicrous try at a *Thin Man*-ish climax. On Bennett's trail is ex-cop private investigator Fredric March, his secretary Ann Sothern, and dumb police detective (and comic relief) Ralph Bellamy. It'll be love at first sight for Bennett and March on the boat to Singapore. March's easygoing performance, as a womanizer struck by true love, is the main asset of this film directed by Tay Garnett, who also wrote the story (which includes a romanticism that occasionally evokes his far superior *One Way Passage* [1932]). Never a great actress, Bennett is merely competent here. While the other nine female stars in this chapter were refining their comedic skills and/or ladylike behavior, Joan Bennett proved how a bottle of hair dye could be as powerful a tool for career extension as a stack of good scripts.

Motion Picture Arts and Sciences: The Pasteurization of the Biopic (1936-1946)

The talking biopic got off to a lofty start with Warner Brothers' *Disraeli* (1929), featuring a "prestigious" (and eventually Oscar-winning) title-role performance from Mr. George Arliss, repeating his acclaimed stage role, which he had already filmed once before in a 1921 silent. Technically, the word "biopic" is too grand for *Disraeli*, focused as it is on one episode in the British Prime Minister's life. The film was a significant sound-era success for the good-for-you type of historical filmmaking. It now looks awfully stagy and old-fashioned with its creaky intrigue involving the Suez Canal and Russian espionage, but it's likable, too, tempering history with humor. Arliss shows off his carefully honed stage technique, supremely confident at radiating sly amusement, something audiences enjoyed sharing. *Disraeli* led to his becoming the king of biopics, starring, at Warners, in *Alexander Hamilton* (1931) and *Voltaire* (1933), and for United Artists in *The House of Rothschild* (1934) and *Cardinal Richelieu* (1935). He is essentially the same in all of them, shrewdly wielding his singular brand of overacted underplaying (or is it restrained hamminess?). Fairly similar and undistinguished, the films deal mostly with power, no matter their eras, locations, or cosmetic variations. *Rothschild,* a Best Picture Oscar nominee, was a cut above, but the Arliss biopics served as high-minded vehicles for an esteemed actor, secondarily functioning as shorthand history lessons.

Arliss' biographical output was soon surpassed, notably by Great Britain's *The Private Life of Henry VIII* (1933), with its agelessly ingenious Oscar-winning performance from Charles Laughton. Not to be outdone on the royalty front, MGM presented Rouben Mamoulian's visually luxurious *Queen Christina* (1933), starring a devastating Greta Garbo, who easily sways our attention away from the film's stock palace intrigue and hypnotically embraces romance with John Gilbert. Does Cecil B. DeMille's strikingly designed *Cleopatra* (1934), with its slinky Claudette Colbert, qualify as a biopic? Hardly, thanks to its comic-book theatrics and delirious appetite for camp, despite Colbert's tongue-in-cheek wit. If monarchy biopics stressed opulent production values over history, the most ostentatious of them all was W.S. Van Dyke's *Marie Antoinette* (1938); MGM hurled money at it. Too bad it's only so-so as a drama, with Norma Shearer her erratic self, occasionally affecting but mostly effortful. Her overworked costume designer, Adrian, reigns as the film's most triumphant contributor. Photographed in Technicolor, Michael Curtiz's *The*

Private Lives of Elizabeth and Essex (1939) is more a picture-book of chapters in Elizabeth I's life, rather than an all-out biopic, yet the fullness and intimacy of Bette Davis' characterization, in all its varied emotional compartments, makes it feel more definitive than it deserves.

If legendary bandits were more your thing, there was *Viva Villa!* (1934) with Wallace Beery as Pancho Villa in a script tailored to his luggish screen personality, and *Jesse James* (1939) starring a mustachioed Tyrone Power, butching up his pretty-boy persona. These films stressed action-adventure over biography, classifying them primarily as rip-snortin' entertainments. The flip side was nothing short of presidential, including dueling Abraham Lincoln portraits: John Ford's *Young Mr. Lincoln* (1939) and John Cromwell's *Abe Lincoln in Illinois* (1940). Ford's film, a small miracle of rustic beauty and unforced lyricism, is blessed with Henry Fonda's heart-stopping simplicity, while Cromwell's dully dutiful movie, lacking the Ford-Fonda resonance and poetry, features an impressively subdued, Oscar-nominated Raymond Massey repeating his stage triumph. The biggest, most ambitious of presidential biopics was Henry King's colorful yet disappointingly flaccid *Wilson* (1944), which mires itself in didactic, long-winded speechifying for its wartime audience. Alexander Knox's valiant Woodrow Wilson is stymied by the movie's wax-museum conception, leaving him stranded on his pedestal.

It's easy to appreciate the commercial value in biopics about war heroes, world leaders, famed outlaws, or any other real-life figures who inspire romantic curiosity and potentially offer vicarious sensation. What about a breed of biopic devoted to the decidedly uncommercial, those showcasing subjects who toiled outside of spotlights, often in the quietest of circumstances? How do you make "thrilling" the lives of scientists, inventors, doctors, and writers? How do you dramatize the act of *thinking*? Golden Age filmmakers managed to take some very important people—whose lives didn't exactly burst with sex and violence—and fashion their biopics not only into absorbing drama but box-office success. All types of biopics are subject to degrees of fictionalization—sometimes in the name of storytelling clarity (as in the use of composite characters)—but the so-called thinker-biopics were necessarily crafted to highlight and embellish their more relatable elements, such as courtship, marriage, and professional adversity. This could seem a compromise, certainly, but it was also a valuable skill that allowed movies to present brilliant minds by serving them with a spoonful of sugar, thus helping the medicine go down. You might describe this sub-genre as homework movies, more likely to be set in a laboratory than at court or on a battlefield and more attuned to the internal than the external. Such biopics aimed to engage moviegoers emotionally enough to have them stick around for any lessons to be learned.

There are no great films from this era of thinker-biopics, but they constitute an honorable bunch, with the most revered actors deemed qualified to play the most revered achievers, hence a landscape populated by Paul Muni, Edward G. Robinson, and Spencer Tracy. It was logical to have a glamorous movie star play the more "physical" real-life heroes, such as Gary Cooper, who was ideally suited to the soldierly duties of *Sergeant York* (1941) and the ballgame athletics of *The Pride of the Yankees* (1942), but when it came to microscopes and fountain pens, it was every bit as logical to see the unglamorous Paul Muni hunched over in deep thought. It was Muni, having been handed the Warner Brothers biopic baton from George Arliss, who got this particular brand of textbook biopic off and running.

Madame Curie (1943): Greer Garson and Walter Pidgeon

The Story of Louis Pasteur (1936) – It's impossible to imagine today's Hollywood putting a major star in a biopic about the chemist who fought anthrax. Not only did Warner Brothers cast Paul Muni in such a vehicle, but they managed to craft it into box-office gold, sparking the trend of turning science class into entertainment. Though Muni had already given his greatest screen performance in *I Am a Fugitive from a Chain Gang* (1932), he was about to enter his most identifiable career phase as biopic master, putting an impassioned stamp on the genre. *Louis Pasteur*'s story and screenplay Oscars were undeserved, but the writing denotes some kind of creative triumph, the setting of a standard for how to enliven heavy subject matter with well-placed dollops of melodrama, sentiment, and uplift, however simplistic and conventional. Director William Dieterle offers a speed-through of events, beginning in 1860 France with Muni developing vaccines for anthrax and hydrophobia in just eighty-six minutes. There's nothing probing here, in keeping with the film's Cliff Notes nature, but you also can't help but learn a little something. It certainly is satisfying to watch Muni fighting arrogance and ignorance in the medical community: those who don't believe in microbes, or the boiling of instruments, or even that doctors should scrub their hands. Muni's Pasteur brought him his only Oscar, a reward for the kind of righteously committed performance considered good for the soul. Hiding behind beard, mustache, and spectacles, Muni resides in the role's outer aspects, a strong presence matched to a showy part. His impact is enhanced by the fact that he's surrounded by stick figures, such as Josephine Hutchinson as his ever-supportive, cheerfully bland wife, and, in a romantic subplot, Anita Louise, as Muni's daughter, and Donald Woods, a young doctor. Finally, there's Fritz Leiber, another doctor, the film's powerfully skeptical villain (a genre necessity). It's easy to dismiss *Louis Pasteur,* but it's hard not to be slightly awed by any movie able to turn a sheep experiment into an emotional climax. For better or worse, *Louis Pasteur* turned two vaccines into a night at the movies.

The Life of Emile Zola (1937) – The *Pasteur* team—Warner Brothers, director Dieterle, star Muni—was back for more, topping their previous success, all the way to a Best Picture Oscar. (I can't believe that anyone still thinks *Emile Zola* is the film of its year, rather than *Camille* or *The Awful Truth*.) Instead of strictly following the *Pasteur* technique, *Emile Zola* put its focus on one particularly dramatic episode from its subject's life. Rather briskly, the film covers Zola's rise from struggling bohemian in 1862 Paris to best-selling provocateur, writing about harsh social conditions, thus stoking controversy. After some typical and-then-I-wrote plotting, the script compellingly shifts to the ruin of army captain Alfred Dreyfus (Joseph Schildkraut), wrongly convicted of being a traitor who gave secrets to the Germans. He's railroaded to Devil's Island. Zola's belief in Dreyfus' innocence leads to action, moving from his pen to the courtroom; he leaves behind wealthy complacency to confront an unjust military. Prestigious for its dramatization of the infuriatingly disturbing Dreyfus affair, *Emile Zola* suffers from choppy storytelling, colorless direction, and a second-rate supporting cast. Yet it still works, riling you as intended. In true Pasteur fashion, Muni seizes his role with an over animated gusto, again hiding behind beard, mustache, and glasses. His acting suggests a meticulously worked-out stage turn, the kind that might be best appreciated if you could only move your seat a few rows back. He does score in a nearly five-minute unbroken take to the jury, the climax of his libel trial, in which his staccato growl and ever-jutting chin are utilized to peak effect. An Oscar-winning Schildkraut, in his pivotal but small role, is quite moving in his transition from proudly dignified to nearly broken, aging from black-haired to all-white while clinging to hope. The film only hints at anti-Semitism (the word "Jew" is seen on paper, in relation to Dreyfus, but never uttered). How interesting to see a movie so openly suspicious of an ally's military (its refusal to admit wrongdoing *no matter what*), a subject inconceivable once WWII arrived. Superior to *Pasteur, Emile Zola* was nonetheless shaped by it, including its flavorless slot of the perfect "Mrs." (Gloria Holden) and its breathless Dieterle pacing. It's one of the biopics that announces, right at the top, its reliance on fictionalized elements.

The Story of Alexander Graham Bell (1939) – It was Fox's turn to try the Muni approach, delivering a purely formulaic biopic that pleased audiences by emphasizing romance over lab work. Don Ameche, famously cast in the title role, is paired with Fox princess Loretta Young in what might be described as lavishly pretty hokum. It begins in 1873 Boston, with Ameche as a teacher of the deaf who dreams about his idea for a telephone. He's a real pain, a bundle of rumpled earnestness, full of overeager intensity and an insufferable sincerity; it's a performance brimming with "eureka" moments. Far removed from Muni's customary gravity, Ameche is hard to take seriously. Ms. Young is the deaf daughter of wealthy Charles Coburn and Spring Byington, and her real-life sisters play her three siblings. She's so damned wise and inspiring, properly glowing in the eventual "Mrs." slot. As Bell's pal-assistant Watson,

Henry Fonda is unconscionably wasted in a comic-relief sidekick role. (Fonda and Young, in their only film together, share several group scenes but have no direct contact.) Serviceably directed by Irving Cummings, here's another biopic with a courtroom climax—a patent fight with Western Union. The case-winning proof is found, rather shamelessly, on the back of an Ameche love letter to Young (who saves the day by insisting it be read aloud). As Ameche pontificates in court, babbling on about "genius," you'll get one of several urges to hang up on him. Fox had cracked the science-biopic format so much so that satisfied audiences actually took to calling telephones "Ameches" for a while.

Dr. Ehrlich's Magic Bullet (1940) – Giving Paul Muni a rest, Warner Brothers cast Edward G. Robinson in the title role, a change of pace for an actor primarily associated with his star-making gangster roles. Helmed by biopic specialist William Dieterle, *Dr. Ehrlich* is as disease-related as *Louis Pasteur,* making it a perfect companion piece. Elevating the proceedings beyond the studio's established efficiency is a very fine and gentle Robinson performance, simpler and more contained than what Muni would have done. Robinson, however, does have the Muni "look"—mustache, beard, and glasses—no surprise since he's playing another great man from the 1800s. True, the character, so relentlessly good, isn't afforded much variety, but Robinson conveys shadings through his ingratiating honesty. Add Ruth Gordon as this year's model of the thanklessly perfect wife. It's a good film, with an Oscar-nominated script (co-written by John Huston), a 1940 movie about a German Jew who treated syphilis. Set in Germany in the late-nineteenth and early-twentieth centuries, the plot follows Robinson from hospital dermatology to his breakthrough in staining microbes onto slides, then on to his tuberculosis rest cure in Egypt and his fight against diphtheria with fellow doctor Otto Kruger. (The film's stirring centerpiece is their curing forty children in an epidemic.) Then, after a lull, wealthy Maria Ouspenskaya funds Robinson's syphilis work (and it's worth millions just to hear the old dowager say "syphilis"). There are plenty of scoffers, naturally, even after he wins the Nobel Prize. Like *Emile Zola, Dr. Ehrlich* climaxes with a libel case. The too-easy villain is Sig Ruman, representing all bad Germans; he's anti-Semitic and racist, speaking of "pure German blood," allowing Robinson at the end to offer some thinly coded anti-Nazi remarks about "diseases of the soul."

Young Tom Edison (**1940**) – Thomas Alva Edison became MGM's boy-man wonder, with his life conceived as a two-picture deal. The first installment, set near Detroit, unfolds before and during the Civil War. Directed by Norman Taurog and starring Mickey Rooney, it plays like a nineteenth-century Andy Hardy movie, with all the sentimental hearth-and-home trimmings, including Rooney's love of apple pie, his grace-saying churchgoing family, and their sing-alongs around a piano. Mr. and Mrs. Hardy (oops, I mean Edison) are George Bancroft and Fay Bainter, with Rooney as their teen genius-in-the-making. He's featured in primarily comic-tinged episodes (until two climaxes of souped-up melodrama). Incessantly inventing, Tom is misunderstood by the town and causes unintended mischief with his experiments, even getting expelled from school. As he self-educates, he starts his own vending business and prints war updates. The point is clear: Edison is, essentially, a typically resourceful and inquisitive all-American boy. He saves his mother's life by lighting her nighttime operation with an on-the-spot invention involving a mirror and multiple lamps and then rescues his two siblings, all in the same twenty-four hours! The second of these climaxes is ludicrous in a Rin Tin Tin sort of way: the bridge is out and a train is heading straight for it, until Tom deploys Morse Code via a train whistle! He wins the respect of his father; they bond by punching out another father and son. Though there's more "drama" than in the Hardy pictures, Rooney isn't noticeably different, and why should he be when this biopic is plugged more into the Hardy formula than the Muni mold? With Tom on his path to greatness, the movie ends with Spencer Tracy looking at an Edison portrait, a teaser for the imminent sequel released just three months later.

Edison, the Man (**1940**) – Mr. Tracy had recently won an Oscar for playing real-life Father Flanagan in MGM's *Boys Town* (1938), and he had just starred, on loan to Fox, as the first title character in *Stanley and Livingstone* (1939). (Not exactly biopics, but in the ballpark.) With Tracy as MGM's serious-actor answer to Muni and Robinson, it was high time that he carried a full-on biopic, the kind stressing brains over brawn. Unfortunately, Tracy dominates this *Edison* sequel more as a star than an actor, which is in keeping with Rooney's opening act. Tracy makes no attempt to disappear (in the Muni-Robinson tradition), and there's never any inkling of a specific Edison characterization. He's given a drearily humble modesty, inventing *for mankind's sake*, not his own glory, God forbid! Capably directed by Clarence Brown, it's all so well-intentioned and unexciting, an acceptably "nice" movie in which even the villain (Gene Lockhart) isn't too hateful. It never quite shakes off its Andy Hardy lift-off. (Don't worry, he still loves apple pie!) Edison is sustained by his goal of achieving electric light. The rest is the usual pendulum swings between success and failure, between money and no money, with all of Tracy's eventual employees adoringly devoted to him, the kind who remain even when he can no longer pay them. Rita Johnson, in the minor role of love-interest-turned-wife, gets to show more personality than most biopic spouses, beginning with their meet-cute in the rain, followed by their Morse Code-assisted courtship (tapping on a shared pipe, from separate floors, which includes Tracy's proposal). Of course, the scientific community denounces his attempts at electric light, all of which leads to his 1882 lighting of NYC. The worst scene comes last, with the elderly Edison being honored: Tracy, naturally, makes a speech, some questionable blather about "balance," regarding fears that science can turn destructive. It's Production Code nonsense, suddenly invoking God, as if believers would be offended by the film's awe toward Edison's discoveries. Was MGM fearful of looking more grateful to humanity than to God? Tracy even refers to "The Great Designer." His words put a real damper on the film's impact, an unconvincing almost-apology for everything that has come before it. Didn't Edison, a pioneer in the creation of cinema itself, deserve better than such cowardly hedging?

A Dispatch from Reuter's (1940) – Back at Warner Brothers, here's the second Edward G. Robinson-William Dieterle biopic of its year, again using the *Pasteur* formula, which by now probably seemed more predictable than clever in its handling of challenging material. All the inevitable components are here: a man of integrity, an ideal wife, firm opposition, neatly arranged crises, and the simplification of complex issues. As our hero is fought at every turn, the drama is standard but effective, grounded by Robinson's natural smarts. The sentimentality, positioned to make the plot more audience-friendly, includes a marriage proposal and its acceptance both achieved via pigeon post. Though inferior to *Dr. Ehrlich, Reuter's* is fast and compact, surely quite sensible goals when making a movie about a man devoted initially to his carrier pigeons, then to the telegraphing of news. With remarkable grace and economy, Robinson continued in his gentle Ehrlich mode, with Reuter another irreproachably wonderful guy, which, again, doesn't allow for much nuance. Though he often faces ruin, his struggles are always surmountable. The movie travels from 1833 to 1865, all across Europe and then to Lincoln's assassination. Edna Best, so warm and unruffled, is the next contestant in the woman-behind-the-man sweepstakes. Smoothly directed by Dieterle, and lathered by a pretty but overzealous Max Steiner score, *A Dispatch from Reuter's* is about making the world a smaller place; it's also a must for any pigeon lovers out there.

Madame Curie (1943) – With her great-lady status and air of class and distinction, Greer Garson had the eminent heft of Paul Muni; her persona easily lent itself to biopics. She had a major personal (and Oscar-nominated) success as real-life Edna Gladney in *Blossoms in the Dust* (1941), a colorful, soapy movie in which she fought the stigma of illegitimacy, the first of her eight teamings with Walter Pidgeon. After their biggest hit, *Mrs. Miniver* (1942), they played Marie and Pierre Curie in a female-oriented twist on what Warner Brothers had established with Muni. MGM seemed able to finesse a "woman's picture" out of any subject, even the discovery of radium. Set in France, *Madame Curie* never appears to mind that it can't make its science accessible, or interesting, focused as it is on being a period love story of the 1890s (and into the new century). However romanticized and elementary, this movie, like most of the smarty-pants biopics, is admirable for existing at all. Garson is a Polish girl studying math and physics at the Sorbonne, graduating at the top of her class. As befitting the subject of a worshipful biopic, she is Little Miss Wonderful, soft-spoken and well-mannered, sustaining a fairly angelic demeanor and never suggesting the consuming drive required for all she'll achieve. (She's allowed *one* outburst of frustration.) Much is made of her beauty, which was never an issue in a Muni or Robinson biopic, rendering Garson more believable as a movie queen than a scientific pioneer. A bearded Pidgeon, at first a shy science professor, is typically secondary to Garson, though he has enough meaty scenes for both of them to have received Oscar nominations. It's refreshing to see a marriage of equal partners (even though she's the real brains of the operation), which gives the film an unusually feminist imprint for its time. In their shed of a laboratory, the Curies spend four years separating radium from pitch blend. Ah, the wonder of studio-system filmmaking, able to turn such scientific drudgery into commercial romance, resulting in a mixed blessing of skillfulness and kitsch. Supported by a top-tier MGM mounting, the stars' "chemistry" is unfazed by Mervyn LeRoy's dullish direction. Garson's biopic success was spoofed by Judy Garland in the "Madame Crematon" sequence in *Ziegfeld Follies* (1946), in which an illustrious star announces her next project, a biopic about the inventor of the safety pin.

Devotion (1946) – Filmed in 1943 but released in 1946, it was one of a number of Warner Brothers movies stockpiled for the post-war audience. Like *Emile Zola,* it's a biopic about a writer, actually several writers: the Brontë sisters. There's no Devil's Island or any libel trial to enliven things, so, like *Madame Curie,* it goes the woman's-picture route, making a soap opera of their lives, including the siblings' angst surrounding their hopeless brother Branwell (Arthur Kennedy). Olivia de Havilland is Charlotte, Ida Lupino is Emily, and Nancy Coleman is Anne (a non-role), with much of their "devotion" focused on their beloved brother and his alcoholism. Thanks to Kennedy's vapid, uninteresting (and unsympathetic) performance, he isn't worthy of anybody's attention. It's Lupino, with her keen intelligence and a radiant soulfulness, who makes Emily the only character who comes alive. De Havilland does improve as the movie proceeds, once she's done with her girlish overacting, but it surely is hard to believe that she and Lupino could both fall for curate Paul Henreid, a rather grim romantic prize. Included are the publications of Emily's *Wuthering Heights* and Charlotte's *Jane Eyre* (which means de Havilland "writes" a role to be played onscreen by her real-life sister Joan Fontaine), but those classic novels take a backseat to the melodrama and the production values. *Devotion* seems to want to be *Pride and Prejudice* on the moors, desperate to keep things prettified. Directed by Curtis Bernhardt, it's a meandering and mostly uninvolving movie, working only in fits and starts (or whenever Lupino is around). What of those disappointing moors? They're strictly of the soundstage variety.

Sister Kenny (1946) – It's obediently respectful and drably serious, despite the potentially fertile content of a woman battling the old boys' club. Co-writer Dudley Nichols is lethargic as a director, delivering a repetitive drag of a movie. Rosalind Russell has the title role, opting for career over marriage, rejecting a military captain (Dean Jagger) so she can devote her life, in an inspiringly feminist manner, to infantile paralysis (polio). The love story feels dramatically imposed to foster our emotional investment, with Jagger no more than a device. It's the children who truly need her. The medical profession, however, wants her to disappear, seeking no part of the "Kenny treatment" simply because its language employs non-scientific terms. Elizabeth Kenny becomes "Sister Kenny" in WWI as an army nurse, on her way to opening various clinics throughout the movie. Though it's mostly set in Australia, it's free of anyone with an Aussie accent. There is a Scottish brogue from Alexander Knox in his service role as a doctor, a pal and ally of Russell's.

(Knox also co-wrote the screenplay.) Admittedly a tad grand, Russell does give a solid, thoughtful (and Oscar-nominated) performance. The part doesn't really play to her strengths—such selflessness does not become her. She's not helped by having to age into a crusty old lady. (Mr. Nichols also directed Russell the following year in the atrocious *Mourning Becomes Electra*.) It ends in the US during WWII, with the Americans giving Kenny her due. Like most of the biopics addressed here, the Kenny story concludes with a lecture, in her case delivered to orthopedic surgeons. *Sister Kenny* tries to jerk tears for its childless children's advocate, which is certainly a forgivable manipulation. In trying to realize important true-life stories for the screen, the makers of the thinker-biopics believed it was necessary to finish them off by wringing an emotional response from moviegoers. What better way to keep them thinking about what they had just learned?

Wuthering Lows: 1939, Hollywood's Worst Year?

Of course, I'm not serious. I am perfectly willing to acknowledge 1939 as the artistic peak of Hollywood's Golden Age, an honor it has held unofficially for decades. However, even a hallowed year produces its share of bombs, and 1939 was no different. It's just convenient to forget the lemons when the overall lemonade turned out to be the tastiest batch ever. Before I look at some of the worst movies of Hollywood's best year, what was it about 1939 that made it possible for the industry to hit such an unrivaled high? It was a serendipitous moment when all the elements came together, when the machinery of the picture business seemed to have worked out every kink.

The transition to talkies, somewhat shaky at the decade's start, was by 1939 a faint memory, with movies fully regaining their silent-era visual fluidity. Gone were those challenging days when camera operators stuck close to talking actors huddled near microphones, with everyone seemingly terrified of making a move. Another industry question mark of the early '30s was the ongoing experimentation with color, with full-spectrum three-strip Technicolor eventually making a well-received feature-film debut in *Becky Sharp* (1935). By 1939 the breathtakingly beautiful hues of Technicolor were already at an unsurpassable level of splendor. What a difference a decade makes with regard to sound and color.

The factory approach to moviemaking, known as the studio system, was at its well-oiled peak in 1939, having proven itself an enormously efficient and effective way to make quality films, primarily within the confines of soundstages and backlots. Though a number of stars are on record as feeling "owned" by their bosses, with some like Olivia de Havilland famously fighting them in court, it was the stars themselves who were the most indelible components of the studio system, the personalities responsible for Hollywood's Golden Age. While most of the silent era's idols had faded from public consciousness, the talkies created a more enduring breed of movie star, and by 1939 many of them had become the icons of their age, the prototypes for most of the stars who followed. For some, notably Bette Davis and Cary Grant, it took nearly the whole decade to get to the very top, but the stars of the 1930s continue to be the legends of classic film.

Finally, the movies of 1939 were made before World War II changed everything. Soon the European market would be cut off, and much of

American films' content would be focused on the conflict, with morale-boosting becoming "job one," perhaps leading to a less diverse output of movies than what had been produced way back in 1939. With the worst of the Depression over and Pearl Harbor yet to come, plus all cylinders working at maximum potential, 1939 had no excuse *not* to create its staggering list of all-time classics.

For laughs, 1939 was a comic bonanza, especially for sparkling females: Ginger Rogers, at her wisecracking working-girl best, starred in Garson Kanin's unpretentiously delightful *Bachelor Mother,* one of her happiest vehicles; Claudette Colbert, a peerless sophisticated comedienne, created effortless enchantment as a Cinderella stand-in in Mitchell Leisen's wondrous *Midnight;* Greta Garbo, stepping out of her comfort zone, was a Soviet "envoy extraordinary" and quite extraordinary herself, mastering a deadpan delivery for director Ernst Lubitsch's divine *Ninotchka;* and the astonishing all-female ensemble of George Cukor's *The Women*, featuring career-best performances from Joan Crawford and Rosalind Russell. If *The Women* is sexist and stereotypical, it's also a thrilling celebration of female comic talent.

If adventure movies were your thing, 1939 offered two beloved three-guy epics for youngsters of all ages: George Stevens' *Gunga Din,* a winningly friendship-driven, action-packed comic rouser (despite its racist streak), in which Victor McLaglen, Douglas Fairbanks, Jr., and a mugging Cary Grant are British army sergeants in India; and the more romanticized *Beau Geste,* from director William A. Wellman, with Gary Cooper, Ray Milland, and Robert Preston joining the French Foreign Legion, steeping themselves in lofty notions of valor and brotherhood. If a good old American-set action picture was more your speed, there was James Cagney in Raoul Walsh's *The Roaring Twenties,* a hokey but compulsively watchable gangster picture. Howard Hawks' *Only Angels Have Wings,* a South American flying picture (once underrated, now overrated), stars Cary Grant and Jean Arthur, both miscast in roles ideal for Clark Gable and Ann Sothern; it's a classic, alright, but its corny, macho sentimentality is an acquired taste.

It was also a prime year to get out your handkerchiefs. Carole Lombard, in her most luminous dramatic performance, is the center of John Cromwell's *In Name Only,* a juicily satisfying love triangle with Cary Grant and Kay Francis. The irresistibly charming Irene Dunne and Charles Boyer mixed laughs and tears in Leo McCarey's *Love Affair,* which is superior to *An Affair to Remember* (1957), its more famous remake. The soap queen of the year was Bette Davis, ruling the screen with such vitality and dramatic clarity, first in

Dark Victory, so moving as the playgirl with a fatal disease, then as *The Old Maid,* an unwed mother protecting her secret through the decades, another superbly controlled and penetrating portrait. Both films were directed by Edmund Goulding.

Davis gave a third great 1939 performance as Queen Elizabeth I in Michael Curtiz's *The Private Lives of Elizabeth and Essex* (opposite dashing Errol Flynn), a colorful pageant elevated by Davis' patented mix of cunning and vulnerability. History buffs could also revel in John Ford's laconically lovely and affecting *Young Mr. Lincoln,* with its magnificent Oscar-worthy central performance from Henry Fonda, who is utterly believable as an ordinary man capable of extraordinary things.

John Ford also gave birth to the modern western in 1939 with *Stagecoach,* to which every subsequent western owes something, though it's rarely been equaled thanks to Ford's overwhelming empathy for his characters. It also made a star of a young fellow named John Wayne. For more lighthearted western fare, there's director George Marshall's abundantly appealing *Destry Rides Again,* in which James Stewart and Marlene Dietrich make an unexpectedly wonderful team.

Literary fans could immerse themselves in William Wyler's limited but enveloping version of Emily Brontë's *Wuthering Heights,* enhanced by a hypnotically romantic Laurence Olivier (though he's out-acted by the sublime Geraldine Fitzgerald). John Steinbeck's *Of Mice and Men,* a more recent classic, received a powerful and poetic screen treatment, artfully directed by Lewis Milestone and featuring a shattering performance by Lon Chaney, Jr., as the lumbering, childlike Lennie. Based on James Hilton's novel, Sam Wood's heartwarming *Goodbye, Mr. Chips* is primarily a showcase for Robert Donat's Oscar-winning tour de force, but it also introduced a radiant Greer Garson to American movies.

And, finally, the two biggest of them all, both directed by Victor Fleming: *The Wizard of Oz,* not just a great movie musical or a prime showcase for the ageless artistry and simplicity of Judy Garland, but also the screen's apex of family entertainment; and *Gone With the Wind,* the supreme example of the Hollywood mega-production, a triumph of impeccable craftsmanship, made emotionally unforgettable by the red-hot chemistry and endlessly intriguing complexities of Vivien Leigh and Clark Gable.

Of all 1939's classics, the one I like least is Frank Capra's simplistic, preachy, and altogether shameless *Mr. Smith Goes to Washington* with James Stewart and Jean Arthur (who, more than Stewart, is the film's chief asset). It's just a coincidence that the inestimable Stewart stars in three of my ten losers of 1939, a fate that just as coincidentally befalls Lew Ayres.

Idiot's Delight (1939): Clark Gable and Norma Shearer

Idiot's Delight – As MGM's First Lady, Norma Shearer was at the top of the list for every prestigious Broadway property the studio brought to the screen, which explains why moviegoers saw her in *Private Lives* (1931), *Strange Interlude* (1932), *Smilin' Through* (1932), *The Barretts of Wimpole Street* (1934), even *Romeo and Juliet* (1936). Her performances were extremely uneven but mostly respectable until she acquired Lynn Fontanne's stage role in Robert E. Sherwood's Pulitzer Prize-winning *Idiot's Delight*, opposite Clark Gable (whose next film would be *Gone With the Wind*). This screen version, directed by an unusually clueless Clarence Brown, is a heavy-handed mess, failing as a commentary on the impending war, but also a flop as a romantic comedy. Set mainly in an Alpine hotel, the characters include a pacifist, a munitions maker, plus a scientist and a captain (both Germans). Gable is a low-rung song-and-dance man, and Shearer is a blonde with a heavy Russian accent (who may or may not be the redheaded acrobat who spent a night with him back in Omaha, years ago). As a fringe showbiz type, Gable is dandy, an especially game delight performing "Puttin' on the Ritz," accessorized with a straw hat, cane, and six chorines. It's Shearer, in a positively gruesome performance, who's embarrassing. She appears to be robotically mimicking someone, presumably Fontanne, but she has no wit nor high-comic flair to call her own. Irene Dunne or Claudette Colbert might have been splendid, while Shearer is only tediously effortful. Poor Burgess Meredith has the worst role as the ranting, righteous pacifist. *Idiot's Delight* aims for high-minded prestige-picture status, but it's ultimately just a pretentious disaster. They filmed two endings, both of them available, both of them terrible. Gable, mostly coasting on his reliable charms, emerges from the wreckage unscathed.

Made for Each Other – This highly regarded newlywed drama made the *New York Times'* ten-best list, despite being a relentlessly irritating and whiny movie about a supposedly average couple. Carole Lombard and James Stewart have a certain glow, but even they can't keep this one afloat. After meeting one weekend and marrying immediately, their life together is one dreary disappointment after another, not just a canceled honeymoon or a flop dinner party but bigger issues such as Stewart's shaky career as a lawyer. He's passed over for a promotion and forced to take a pay cut. Lucile Watson, as Stewart's formidable passive-aggressive mother, moves in with them, leading to an eventual Lombard-Watson showdown. The couple's debts pile up, yet they always have a servant. The director, John Cromwell, did far better work with Lombard later in the year with *In Name Only*, but here he's unable to uncover any interesting insights amid the overriding banality of these characters and their situations. *Made for Each Other* is simply an unpleasant waste of time. Worst of all is its whopper climax of high melodrama when their baby boy gets pneumonia. Will the life-saving serum, being flown across the country and through a blizzard, arrive in time? The grindingly manufactured suspense, including a parachuting pilot, constitutes desperate audience manipulation. The lovely, natural Lombard is too good for her role, while Stewart is charming until mired in tiresome self-pity. Even in their better moments, Lombard and

Stewart are not a good match-up; she seems too womanly for his boyishness. Producer David O. Selznick would redeem himself later in 1939 when Lombard's husband, Clark Gable, joined him for *GWTW*.

Tail Spin – Essentially, it's *Stage Door* (1937) for lady flyers, here known as "speed queens." Alice Faye has the Ginger Rogers role with the tough outer shell, but she seems more like an unappetizing cross between Jean Harlow and Shirley Temple, hard-boiled yet infantile. Faye's gift to the screen was her purring contralto singing voice, so why, after achieving success in musicals, is she in *this*? She sings once, and you're startlingly reminded, "Oh, that's why she's a star!" When she's not being the female Crosby, she's just another mediocre actress. Things improve with the arrival of Constance Bennett in Katharine Hepburn's *Stage Door* role as the socialite, now with flying ambitions instead of theatrical aspirations. Faye and Bennett soon dislike each other; both of them love handsome Navy pilot Kane Richmond. Bennett is her likable self, even though she's playing the girl no one likes. She and Faye have a pitiful brawl in the ladies' room, two slaps apiece; it's funny because it's so stilted. *Tail Spin* is a predictable yawn of clichés, a "B" picture with "A" leads. Continuing its borrowings from *Stage Door*, Nancy Kelly has the Andrea Leeds role, the noble suicide. Filling out the female flying ensemble are Jane Wyman, as animated "Alabama," and Joan Davis as Faye's comic-relief pal. As another flyer, Edward Norris plays one of those movie characters clearly marked for death from the moment he appears. Fifth-billed Charles Farrell, a huge star a decade ago, has only a minor role as a mechanic. The big climactic race is the "Powder Puff," an occasion for more selfless nobility. Though it's the gals who are racing, you'll always be way ahead of them regarding what comes next.

The Ice Follies of 1939 – Joan Crawford should be wearing her "box-office poison" sash throughout this one, clearly the lowest point of her MGM tenure. In the late '30s, Sonja Henie's ice-skating musicals were making a fortune for Fox. It's no surprise that MGM would want to make its own ice-pop of a musical, but why would they attempt that without an actual skating star? Who needs to see Crawford or James Stewart hit the ice? The dimwitted plot has Stewart dreaming of staging ice shows while wife Crawford can't help becoming a big movie star. She simply barges into studio head Lewis Stone's office and emerges with a contract. Stewart leaves her because of his wounded pride, but he quickly becomes the Ziegfeld of the ice world. Though this movie is spectacularly unsuccessful, the acquiring of success *within* the movie is ludicrously easy. The stars reunite for *A Song for Cinderella,* a film-within-the-film, designed to combine both their talents. For the lavish finale, this black-and-white movie turns to color, with extras who clearly raided the *Marie Antoinette* (1938) costume racks, and a redheaded Crawford making her three-strip Technicolor debut. (She's also seen with blonde and black hair in this picture.) Lew Ayres is utterly wasted as Stewart's old skating partner. It's such a demeaning waste of the star trio, with Crawford forced to be insufferably nice throughout (and seeming quite phony in the process). While she's being sickeningly kind, Stewart is a real jerk. There are tiresome scenes of him resenting her success and having to make dinner himself! Stewart didn't match well with Carole Lombard, and he and Crawford fare no better; no matter how soft she tries to be, she's too hard for juvenile Jimmy. With skating sequences both tacky and boring, *The Ice Follies of 1939* is a complete travesty and a must-see curiosity.

Broadway Serenade – Temporarily splitting up a popular team—so that the two stars could be showcased in separate vehicles—is supposed to double your profits. That's not what happened when Jeanette MacDonald went without Nelson Eddy for this depressingly routine showbiz musical. Why was she paired with non-singing Lew Ayres? He's certainly a better actor than Eddy, but what is she supposed to do with him? They play a struggling married vaudeville team, but, before you can say *Ice Follies of 1939,* she's whisked away to vocal superstardom, leaving him an emasculated pianist-composer working in dives, unsurprisingly leading to their divorce. Hey, don't worry, he's working on his rhapsody, toiling away in a garret. It's hilarious hokum when the gracious MacDonald sings for fans in a five-and-dime store, not knowing that the store's song-plugging pianist, the lowly Ayres, is her unseen accompanist. When his rhapsody finally sells, he feels worthy of her, comparably successful, but it's too late: she's engaged to Ian Hunter. (Why would Jeanette contemplate retirement for dull Ian?) But she consents to star in Ayres' rhapsody, staged by Busby Berkeley! She's a blonde through most of the number, a real kitschfest with masked singers, dancers, and musicians, even including unfortunate "hep" passages in the arrangement. Like Crawford in *Ice Follies,* MacDonald is always so damned sweet and wonderful, while Ayres would have been better served in one of his churned-out *Dr. Kildare* pictures. The brightest spot is Virginia Grey as a gold-digging showgirl always eager to shed some clothing, and it's also nice to see professional "sissy" Franklin Pangborn in a non-stereotypical role as a conductor-arranger. *Broadway*

Serenade is at least a half-hour too long, yet it manages to squander Frank Morgan as MacDonald's producer. I'd like more Morgan, not to mention some Nelson Eddy.

It's a Wonderful World – It's one of those painful screwball miscalculations, a disservice to all involved. Aiming for the *Thin Man* effect, it mixes comedy with a B-variety murder plot, but instead of arousing infectious fun, it's a pushed, frantic effort. Claudette Colbert and James Stewart, both miscast, have rarely, if ever, been so unappealing. For wit and breezy sophistication, no one could touch Colbert, which is why it's so frustrating to listen to her incessant wailing and whimpering, an almost constant hysteria. She plays a famous, dizzy poet. As for Stewart, he overacts the role of the tough, cynical private detective, often coming off as merely unpleasant and misogynistic. He's out to prove a framed client's innocence but is soon a wanted man himself. Colbert falls for him and becomes a pest he can't shake. The comic situations, including an encounter with a Boy Scout troop, are mostly overreaching ploys for laughs. With rote direction from *The Thin Man*'s W.S. Van Dyke and a disappointing script by Ben Hecht, *It's a Wonderful World* quickly becomes exhausting. There's no pleasure in watching great stars strain themselves and abandon their good judgment. You can kill the sour taste of it by watching Colbert in *Midnight* and Stewart in *Destry Rides Again,* restoring them to their 1939 comic glory.

When Tomorrow Comes – Here's the *other* Irene Dunne-Charles Boyer love story of 1939, hot on the heels of the far superior *Love Affair*. What a confounding narrative. It moves from romantic comedy to labor-relations drama to more serious romance to hurricane disaster movie to soapy love triangle. It can't make up its mind. Dunne is a waitress, aspiring singer, and union activist, while Boyer is merely a famous pianist. It turns out that he is married to Barbara O'Neil (soon to be Scarlett O'Hara's mother), a woman who's been mentally unstable since the death of her baby, a circumstance that allows Boyer to retain audience sympathy. In fact, he's so good and kind he's barely a character, which is equally true of Dunne and her role. Will O'Neil finally kill herself or go insane to allow for a happy ending? The stars blithely carry the movie, which is crowded with incident but doesn't add up to much. The hurricane sequence, short on special effects, won the film its Sound Recording Oscar, beating *Gone With the Wind*, which seems a bit excessive. The most interesting thing about this movie is the teaming of Boyer and O'Neil, a warm-up for the following year's infinitely better *All This, and Heaven Too,* in which they are again married, she's again unbalanced, and he's again honorable while falling in love with someone else (Bette Davis). *When Tomorrow Comes* was made by John M. Stahl who directed Dunne in two of her most memorable soap hits, *Back Street* (1932) and *Magnificent Obsession* (1935). This outing, based on a James M. Cain story and later remade as *Interlude* (1957) with June Allyson and Rossano Brazzi, is one of those big star vehicles that no one remembers.

The Return of Doctor X – Aside from *Black Legion* (1937) and *Dead End* (1937), there were few good screen opportunities for Humphrey Bogart between his name-making turn in *The Petrified Forest* (1936) and his graduation to stardom in 1941 with *High Sierra* and *The Maltese Falcon.* In 1939, not only did he suffer the indignity of being cast as an Irish-brogued horse trainer in *Dark Victory,* but he fell far lower, perhaps to his lowest career ebb, when he played the title role in this frightful "B" horror movie. *The Return of Doctor X* is a *Frankenstein* variation, with a well-intentioned mad scientist (John Litel) bringing the dead back to life, and also trying to invent synthetic blood, all in the heart of NYC! You'll suspect that Litel is sinister: why else would he have a goatee? Bogart is Litel's assistant, almost his Igor, and supposedly a medical genius. First seen petting a white rabbit, the glasses-wearing Bogart is gentle yet odd with a deathly pallor and a Bride-of-Frankenstein streak in his hair. Someone is killing people who have a special blood type; the victims are then drained of their blood. It's a *Dracula* rip-off too! Wayne Morris, a reporter, and Dennis Morgan, a doctor, are the bland good guys, and the unglamorous climax takes place in a New Jersey swamp. Bogart makes a decent, honorable try at creating a character, but it's still humiliating to see him here, two years from Sam Spade, so shockingly misused. He's not even in the first twenty-three minutes of a 63-minute movie.

Remember? – It's a very long eighty-three minutes, as Robert Taylor, Greer Garson, and poor Lew Ayres try to make something of this hopeless, head-scratching amnesia comedy which is neither funny nor charming. Co-written and directed by Norman Z. McLeod (who made the 1934 W.C. Fields masterwork *It's a Gift*), *Remember?* isn't even good-spirited. Ayres is betrayed by his fiancée (Garson) and his best pal (Taylor) when they fall in love and marry, which immediately leaves a mean-streaked bad taste from which this so-called comedy never recovers. Then comes the dismal conflict of Taylor's busy advertising agency interfering with his marriage, with divorce looming. You'll just have to accept my word that an amnesia powder (sprinkled by Ayres into martinis) erases the last six months for Taylor and Garson and restarts them conveniently on the day they met. This means they get to betray Ayres *again,* even more quickly this time around. Though the amnesia plot would seem to be the main thrust of the action, it doesn't occur until an hour into the movie. As Garson's mother, Billie Burke, doing one of her flighty socialites, is the only funny element, and the movie needs a lot more of her. With Laura Hope Crews (*GWTW*'s Aunt Pittypat) as Burke's sister, there's a priceless yet untapped opportunity for some ditzy teamwork, yet time *is* made for lame slapstick between Taylor and Garson on a fox hunt. Built on an unlikable premise, *Remember?* travels steadily downhill. You don't need amnesia to forget all about it.

Balalaika – Nelson fared no better without Jeanette, adrift here in his own kitschy vehicle. Ilona Massey is no Jeanette substitute, lacking any chemistry with Nelson. She's the anti-Jeanette, a cool blonde, hard and remote, even somewhat vampiric. (Massey and Eddy were previously together in 1937's *Rosalie,* with Eleanor Powell the female lead.) Eddy keeps trying to be playful with Massey, but she won't (can't?) play along. Not to be confused with *Ninotchka, Balalaika* is an absurdly ambitious musical which begins in 1914 Russia and includes an opera-house assassination attempt and the snowy trenches of WWI. At its heart, it's just a foolish operetta. Eddy is a prince and an army captain, but he mostly identifies as a singing Cossack. Massey, from a family of revolutionaries, sings at the Café Balalaika. Though on opposite sides politically, they fall in love. In support of the stars, Frank Morgan, C. Aubrey Smith, and Charlie Ruggles all have their moments, just not enough of them. There's an oddly eclectic musical program, including "Silent Night" (in German) and selections from *Carmen,* but nothing makes a real impression. Directed by Reinhold Schünzel—who had recently delivered the blow known as *Ice Follies of 1939*—*Balalaika* improves near its end, after the Revolution when our White Russians relocate to Paris and open a nightclub, with Eddy as their entertainer. If only the movie had started here, free to be light, amusing, and allowing all the character actors to shine. At the finale, Massey is decked out in one of Jeanette MacDonald's lavish costumes from *Maytime.* As if Eddy needed reminding about what's missing here.

Ruff Times: The 1940s Costume Picture (1940-1948)

Nowadays, Hollywood repeatedly sparks and inspires moviegoers' imaginations by leaping into the future, immersing itself in the constantly expanding potential of special effects, creating worlds (and universes) made possible by fast-changing technological advances. Taking off with the 1968 double whammy of *Planet of the Apes* and *2001: A Space Odyssey,* Hollywood escapism became increasingly led by action/fantasy and science fiction films. Prior to that, during the Golden Age of Hollywood, the "future" had been the realm of cheap black-and-white serials such as *Flash Gordon* (1936-40) and *Buck Rogers* (1939). Later, in the 1950s, science fiction exploded onto movie screens, yet, aside from a rarity like *Forbidden Planet* (1956), even the best of these, such as *Invasion of the Body Snatchers* (1956), were low-budget affairs. Flying saucers, robots, and aliens were not the stuff of "A" pictures and hardly the place to find stars and directors of stature. (Another good exception: Patricia Neal in Robert Wise's 1951 *The Day the Earth Stood Still.*) By 1977, with *Star Wars* and *Close Encounters of the Third Kind,* it all seemed permanently flipped around, with Hollywood seeming to spend the bulk of its financial resources on action/fantasy/sci-fi blockbusters, aiming forward into the unknown.

During the classic-movie era, the studios stoked the daydreams of moviegoers of all ages by delving *backward,* constructing a past of opulent beauty and lavish spectacle, far removed from everyday twentieth-century America. They presented idealized versions of bygone days in all their presumed grandeur, gallantry, and glamour. The catch-all term for this kind of enterprise is "the costume picture," which is a more frivolous term for "period piece." The difference is that period pieces don't have to be pretty, while costume pictures are generally an eyeful. A costume picture also has to have some size. There have to be *many* people looking pretty in their fancy duds. After all, costume pictures are nearly always "A" pictures. If not, how could they look good enough to attain such a classification?

Why did yesterday's audiences find such wonder in history, while today's ticket buyers are far more enraptured by the concept of tomorrow? Why such a radical shift? The most obvious reason is the way perceptions of history have changed over time. Old Hollywood peddled a limited and cleaned-up view of the past, and the mass audience didn't seem to mind the historical inaccuracies or the narrow perspectives. When watching *Gunga Din* (1939), we're never meant to ask, "What exactly are the British *doing* in India?" In *Beau Geste* (1939), no one ever explains why the French Foreign Legion is fighting Arabs on Arab turf. As history came to be taught and discussed with more ambiguity and sensitivity, and as moviegoers grew more willing to accept complex and possibly ugly realities, much of the past lost its innocence as movie fare, specifically as fodder for costume pictures (which can't really accommodate gray areas, anti-heroes, or revisionism). By the late 1960s, many of the screen's "historical" conventions were crumbling, in both the writing and in the physical details. The medieval world of *The Lion in Winter* (1968), with its grimy-looking castle, was certainly not the picture-book paradise that 1930s Warner Brothers would have made of it. *The Wild Bunch* (1969) dared to depict the inherent violence of westerns with the blood we'd been spared for decades, while *Little Big Man* (1970) portrayed an American historical figure (Custer) as a possible maniac. If history could no longer be sufficiently whitewashed and romanticized, and if mud, sweat, and chamber pots were now sullying screens, then maybe escapism had to look forward (despite occasional revisits from enduring characters such as those musketeers). After all, there's complete freedom in the future; you don't have to get anything *right*.

Costume pictures had acquired a new momentum in the mid-1930s, once the transition to sound was secure, with movies having regained the confidence to stretch out. When I say "costume picture," I don't mean prestigious literary adaptations, such as *Little Women* (1933) or *A Tale of Two Cities* (1935), and I don't mean historical biopics, such as *Queen Christina* (1933) or *Marie Antoinette* (1938). Nor would I include high-toned theatrical works, such as *The Barretts of Wimpole Street* (1934) or *Romeo and Juliet* (1936). Technically, these are all most definitely costume pictures, but a quintessential example of the genre would have to be something less edifying, less Oscar caliber, the kind of movie that just wants to entertain, which doesn't mean that it's automatically inferior to the aforementioned titles, just that its intentions are different. (Some might call *Gone With the Wind* the costume picture to end all costume pictures, but I'd say that *GWTW*'s complicated lead characters give it too much dramatic heft to warrant such a classification.) The typical costume pictures of the mid-'30s (*Anthony Adverse, The Gorgeous Hussy*) to the mid-'50s (*Désirée, Diane*) were supreme exercises in Hollywood craft, as much about art direction and background scores as anything else. Fashioned from historical tidbits and storybook melodrama, the genre devoted itself to romantic ardor, valorous thrills, and period splendor. Two consummate examples from the late '30s set a high standard for the next decade's costume-picture bounty.

The Prisoner of Zenda (1937), directed by John Cromwell, is the definitive version of an oft-filmed property, a majestic entertainment, as lively as it is piercingly romantic, with superb black-and-white camerawork from James Wong Howe, regal nineteenth-century sets and costumes, a great Alfred Newman score, and an irresistibly outlandish plot. Its sublime cast is led by a soulful and elegantly heroic Ronald Colman in the dual role of a new Ruritanian king and his British distant-cousin lookalike. Proving that every great costume picture needs at least one charming, slyly immoral, and self-amused rascal, *Zenda* has sexy, dastardly playful Douglas Fairbanks, Jr. Add heavenly Madeleine Carroll as royal love interest to both Colmans, plus a thrilling climactic swordfight and an affecting theme of duty versus personal happiness, and *The Prisoner of Zenda* delivers on every count on the costume-picture checklist.

After rocketing to stardom in the dramatically thin but stirring swashbuckler *Captain Blood* (1935), Errol Flynn reached his costume peak in *The Adventures of Robin Hood* (1938), probably the finest adventure film made during Hollywood's Golden Age. Directed by Michael Curtiz and William Keighley, it's an ageless, flawlessly sustained, and rapturously colorful entertainment, with Flynn a matinee idol, action star, and light comedian all rolled into one. He and Olivia de Havilland are among the screen's more entrancing couples, so tenderly intimate. *Robin Hood* boasts *two* iconic villains: Basil Rathbone *and* Claude Rains! Stressing loyalty and goodness while flaunting high-spirited comedy from its merry band of players, *Robin Hood* is a ravishing stunner, visually and aurally and emotionally.

In the 1940s, the costume-picture genre featured Mr. Flynn, Maureen O'Hara, Tyrone Power, Virginia Mayo, and other beautiful stars doing beautiful things in beautiful clothes. There continued to be costume pictures of the literary persuasion (such as *Pride and Prejudice*), and those that were theater-based (such as *The Little Foxes*), but let's keep the focus on the more escapist, fantasy-inducing entries. Even though Errol Flynn spent most of the '40s in war movies and westerns, he's still the star I think of first when contemplating costume pictures, so it is he who bookends this chapter.

The Sea Hawk (1940): Errol Flynn

The Sea Hawk (1940) – A knockout of studio-system craftsmanship, this is an exquisitely detailed swashbuckler from Warner Brothers, luxuriating in its black-and-white (and sepia) richness in much the same way that *Robin Hood* is vivified by its Technicolor. Reuniting Errol Flynn with *Robin Hood* director Michael Curtiz, *The Sea Hawk* doesn't have the emotional pull or the memorable characters of the former picture, though it does have another magnificent score from Erich Wolfgang Korngold. One might describe this movie as a melding of *Robin Hood* and another Curtiz-Flynn picture, *The Private Lives of Elizabeth and Essex* (1939), complete with its own Elizabeth (Flora Robson, assuming Bette Davis' throne). Flynn is the sea hawk, kind of a pirate or Robin Hood but also loyal to his queen. Though the film begins in 1585, it plays as an unmistakable metaphor for 1940 Germany, with the Spanish and their Armada as stand-ins for the Nazis, and Robson ending the movie with a propaganda speech aimed at "today." Despite some action footage lifted from the 1924 silent version, this *Sea Hawk* follows the Errol Flynn formula, allowing the star to be his charming, lightly humorous self, no matter the century, no matter the danger. The finest sequence comes early, a sea battle with Flynn and his men overtaking a Spanish ship, a beautifully edited, extremely exciting set piece of guns and swords. Some *Robin Hood* favorites return: Claude Rains is the Spanish ambassador; Una O'Connor a British servant; and Alan Hale, of course, is Flynn's sidekick. However, Brenda Marshall (as Rains' half-British niece) is a pallid Olivia de Havilland substitute, and Henry Daniell, as the main villain (a Brit in league with the Spanish), isn't quite Basil Rathbone. Mr. Rains, with a mustache, a goatee, and dark slicked hair, offers the most nuanced acting, while Robson is a crafty, likable Elizabeth (in a more limited role than Bette Davis' star-sized part). The movie lags in its Panamanian middle, but it gets big points for its galley-slave revolt and a climactic swordfight between Flynn and Daniell, a shadowy marvel of costume-picture art.

The Mark of Zorro **(1940)** – Tyrone Power, the decade's *other* great swashbuckler, became a star in *Lloyd's of London* (1936), an ornate but conventional costume picture. By 1940, he was a superstar, thanks to hits such as *In Old Chicago* (1937) and *Jesse James* (1939). As Zorro, he's a complete delight, and with his thin mustache, he looks sensational. When in the role of the masked superhero, sometimes all but his eyes are covered; at other times he wears only an eye mask. Like Michael Curtiz, director Rouben Mamoulian was another gifted filmmaker with a special zest for the pacing of action, plus a zeal for romance. With its lustrous black-and-white cinematography, handsome 20th Century-Fox production values, and a rousing Alfred Newman score, *The Mark of Zorro* is an ideal costume picture, gracefully balancing love and heroics. It begins in Madrid, with Power summoned home to California because his father (Montagu Love) has been ousted from office by a pair of usurping villains, a stupid puppet (J. Edward Bromberg) and his foxy second-in-command (Basil Rathbone, here to do for Power what he did for Flynn in *Robin Hood*). Also on hand is *Robin Hood*'s Friar Tuck (Eugene Pallette), still clergy but now "padre." It's extremely satisfying to watch Power, a cultured, privileged young man, find his true purpose. He assumes the role of fop, the better to go unsuspected as Zorro (the same surefire device in other famed properties such as *The Scarlet Pimpernel* and *The Desert Song*), leading to the wonderfully frustrating suspense of how long it will take before the truth is revealed. His love of magic tricks is a nice touch, a complement to his deft sleight-of-hand regarding his identity. Power heightens the stakes by making such a captivating sissy, such an amusingly bored snob. (When Rathbone stabs an orange, the effete Power states, "You seem to regard that poor fruit as an enemy.") As beautiful Lolita, Linda Darnell is a teenager of unspoiled radiance, the other half of the movie's lushly romantic duo. Power and Rathbone, both playing great swordsmen, have an outstanding screen duel, delivering the kind of climax demanded and earned by such a top-grade costumed adventure.

Son of Fury (1942) – Tyrone Power took his adventure skills from land to sea for more good old-fashioned fun in another gorgeous black-and-white production. It may be skin-deep in true costume-picture fashion, but it's also a compelling tale of revenge. Power begins as Roddy McDowall, a male Cinderella, the stable boy to his wealthy, villainous uncle (George Sanders). Because his nephew is believed to be illegitimate, Sanders has stolen the boy's title. When Power assumes the role, he's in love with his cousin (Frances Farmer), Sanders' daughter, a lovely but distant creature who's a bit lockjawed with breeding (and looking a lot like Jessica Lange, who played Farmer in 1982's *Frances*). Seeking his fortune, Power stows away to the Indies and becomes a sailor. In the worst scenes, he finds island paradise, which is conceived in coy, simplistic, and rather goofy terms, with native Gene Tierney (as Power's hula-dancing fantasy girl) doing her best Dorothy Lamour. She's sweet, but, honestly, it's an impossible role. Wealthy from all the pearls he's collected, Power returns to England ready to claim what's rightfully his. Directed by *Prisoner of Zenda*'s John Cromwell, *Son of Fury* features a prime supporting cast: John Carradine (Power's pal), Harry Davenport (touching as Power's grandfather), and, best of all, Elsa Lanchester in a cameo as a tarty barmaid who helps Power get out of England. All she wants in return is for him to walk with her, so that her rival will see her with a gentleman. In a seven-minute role as our hero's gentle savior, Lanchester is unforgettably, poignantly aglow. Sanders, however, gives a lazy too-familiar performance devoid of surprises. Hokey as this movie can be, it's elevated by the dashing good looks and impassioned nature of its star. Subtitled *The Story of Benjamin Blake*, *Son of Fury* was remade with Cornel Wilde as *Treasure of the Golden Condor* (1952), a color production but a far less sweeping version, lacking the original's wholehearted conviction.

Arabian Nights (1942) – The Technicolor images in Universal Pictures' series of six Maria Montez/Jon Hall adventures are truly something to see, like Disney cartoons come to life. Ecstatically colorful, sometimes hideously so, these movies (including the 1944 camp classic *Cobra Woman*) are B pictures adorned beyond expectations. The gaudy swirls help keep their dimwitted nonsense enjoyable. Here Ms. Montez, overly beaded and far too accessorized, is a dancing girl determined to be a queen, and Mr. Hall is the muscled Caliph whose brother (Leif Erikson) has snatched his throne. Sabu, as an acrobat, rescues the wounded Hall and protects his secret identity. Montez can't help falling in love with Hall, even though she thinks he's a commoner. As for her "acting," Montez is her usual dead-weight self, offering pricelessly numbed line readings. She's conveniently veiled for her big number, so her dancing double can take over. While easy to pick on, *Arabian Nights* is appealingly unpretentious and a magically pretty production (when it isn't too garish). Its action includes a climactic swordfight between the brothers, while the comic relief from the likes of Billy Gilbert and Shemp Howard is strictly kids' stuff. The Oscars noticed the A-factor in such B fare, nominating its color cinematography, color art direction, score, and sound. Perhaps best with the sound *off*, *Arabian Nights* remains a veritable eye-popper.

The Princess and the Pirate (1944) – One of Bob Hope's best and funniest vehicles, it was produced by Sam Goldwyn rather than Paramount (Hope's home studio). With fast, clever dialogue, here's a pirate movie filled with anachronisms, referencing the "road to Morocco," "Sinatra," "Gypsy Rose Lee," even providing "ye Goldwynne Girls," snippets of "Thanks for the Memory," and a cameo by Bing Crosby. Hope is "Sylvester the Great," a quick-change vaudevillian with an actorly ego, who is, of course, a coward. Virginia Mayo is the beautiful blonde princess on the run from an arranged marriage, headed to Jamaica to be with her commoner love. In her first major role, Mayo stakes claim to the genre, one of the prettiest things to happen to costume pictures for the next decade (including 1951's *Captain Horatio Hornblower*). Our stars meet aboard ship, captured by pirate Victor McLaglen ("The Hook"), leading Hope to assume the role of gypsy woman, rather hilariously. Topping his drag episode, Hope eventually impersonates McLaglen, a situation that reaches farcical heights when both men are giving orders aboard ship. Another big laugh-getter is the astoundingly versatile Walter Brennan as McLaglen's tattooer. Looking like *Snow White*'s Dopey, and with a cackling laugh, Brennan is kind of brilliant in his broad comic role. It's hard to believe it's the same actor who would soon play scary Old Man Clanton in *My Darling Clementine* (1946). More typically cast is Walter Slezak as a villainous governor in cahoots with McLaglen. (Funny that Hope, billed solo above the title, plays neither title role.) Despite its peak-form comedian and air of sustained zaniness, *The Princess and the Pirate* still qualifies as a genuine costume picture and not just a spoof, as transporting in its honest storybook wonder (enhanced by a lovely David Rose score) as it is in generating chuckles, all so ably modulated by director David Butler.

Kitty (1945) – For a more female-driven costume picture, here's a late eighteenth-century variation on *Pygmalion,* an enchanting, highly enjoyable "high" comedy. If the plot feels slight, well, the film is elevated by its overwhelming beauty: the awe-inspiring Karinska-executed costumes, the spectacular sets (especially those grand staircases), and the overall good taste in Mitchell Leisen's unceasingly attentive direction. Beginning in a London slum (Houndsditch) in 1783, *Kitty* charts the steep rise of a Cockney guttersnipe (Paulette Goddard, in the title role). After Gainsborough (Cecil Kellaway) paints her as "The Anonymous Lady," she's taken in by an upper-class but destitute fellow (Ray Milland) and his drunken aunt (Constance Collier), a pair who mold her sufficiently to land a rich husband. (So, Goddard is Eliza Doolittle, Milland is Henry Higgins, and Collier is Colonel Pickering.) Marriage leads to wealthy widowhood with Goddard eventually becoming duchess to an old duke (Reginald Owen, over the top, as usual). Beneath all the glorious frippery, Goddard is merely a gold digger and Milland her pimp, but she loves only him. A staggering number of things happen to Kitty in just two years, but will the man she loves ever see her as more than a guttersnipe? However, you probably won't want her to end up with this unlikable, undeserving fellow. (How much of that is due to Milland's polished yet unappealing performance?) Goddard's primary gift was her down-to-earth likability, rather than her comedic skills (which were so-so), though she's more than serviceable here. She has a "move your bloomin' arse"-type moment when she breaks her beads while dancing with the Prince of Wales at a ball, delightfully reverting to her former self: "Love a duck, me beads!" Ms. Collier is as deeply grand as she was in *Stage Door* (1937), exactly what you want, a larger-than-life addition to the fanciful proceedings. Despite its script's limitations, *Kitty* is a costume picture to devour, with Daniel L. Fapp's stunning black-and-white camerawork highlighting every inch of its Paramount-produced pomp.

Forever Amber (**1947**) – Based on Kathleen Winsor's bestseller, this was Fox's answer to *Gone With the Wind*. True, it's set in the Restoration England of the 1660s rather than the American South of the 1860s, and it features the Great Fire of London instead of the burning of Atlanta, but it was still hoping to be a comparable historical fiction epic. Though *Forever Amber* surely delivers color and opulence, it can't compete with *GWTW* on dramatic terms because it's purely romance-novel fare, a racy (if hardly steamy) costume picture that's all plot, plot, plot (including plague and unwed motherhood). Amber (Linda Darnell) chases Bruce (Cornel Wilde) for the entire movie, like Scarlett O'Hara chasing Ashley Wilkes. She is a country-raised orphan who follows her beloved to London and sleeps her way to the court of Charles II (George Sanders), eventually becoming the king's mistress. Along the way, Amber is swindled, goes to prison, becomes a thief, then an actress, and then a countess. Raven-haired Darnell became amber-blonde for this plum opportunity, and the film was a big box-office hit, but she never *owns* the movie the way Vivien Leigh owns *GWTW*. The always underrated Darnell does well enough, but despite fulfilling the role's sex appeal, ambition, charm, and British accent, she doesn't have the resources to fill in what isn't there, to make a plot-driven piece *feel* character-driven. Mr. Wilde acquits himself competently in what is essentially a man-candy role. More impressive is Sanders, so dryly witty, and often amusingly trailed by his half-dozen small dogs. Then there's Jessica Tandy, months away from creating the role of Blanche DuBois on Broadway, in a thankless supporting role, meeting Darnell in prison and later becoming her maid. *Amber's* unexpected director is Otto Preminger, who seems stymied by it all, unengaged enough to allow his design teams to dominate. The result is resplendent trash, a diverting bauble, given some true class by David Raksin's outstanding multi-themed score (which would be a classic if the film were better-regarded). Amber will have to pay for her sins in true Production Code fashion, but, as with Scarlett, you know you don't really have to worry about her.

Captain from Castile (**1947**) – After serving in WWII, Tyrone Power resumed his popularity in a lofty literary adaptation, *The Razor's Edge* (1946), but it was a dismissible effort compared to his next venture, the daringly downbeat and unfairly neglected *Nightmare Alley* (1947), which, though *un*popular, contains his best acting. Power's third post-war release, *Captain from Castile,* was safer fare, occupying familiar costume-picture territory. Visually ambitious, it is a Technicolor epic focused more on the Fox studio's impeccable craft and production values than it is on any drama or history, making it hard not to succumb to its boldly vivid palette of blacks, reds, and golds. As a spectacle, the movie seems to combine Power's two costume pictures of 1942, hijacking plot elements of *Son of Fury* and the color splendors of *The Black Swan,* not to mention returning Power to his Latino persona from *Zorro,* all of which carried the charismatic Power to another king-sized hit. It opens in 1518 Spain, as nobleman Power makes enemies with hateful John Sutton (a bigwig of the Spanish Inquisition). Sutton arrests Power and his family, leading to some nifty swordplay followed by an elaborate escape (mostly on horseback). Redheaded (and miscast) Lee J. Cobb is Power's trusted pal, and Jean Peters, making an appealing debut in the Linda Darnell slot, is the spirited servant who worships Power. The plot shifts when Power, Cobb, and Peters go to the Indies and join up with Cesar Romero's gold-driven Cortez (who promotes Power to "captain"). Despite Romero's significant presence, panache, and touch of madness, he isn't allowed much depth and the picture loses tension and momentum in the New World. Power's romance with Peters is one of the things slowing the movie down, including their klutzy "sexy" dance. The visuals continually trump the meandering story, with director Henry King always finding something good to look at. Things pick up when nasty Sutton comes to Mexico, ready to make trouble, leading to a ludicrous climax involving a stabbing. Though *Captain from Castile* is intriguingly critical of Spain and Cortez, it ends majestically with Romero and company on their way to further battles, victories, and glory. The movie wants to have it all ways, as vaguely as possible.

The Three Musketeers (1948) – Naturally, MGM was no slouch in the costume-picture department, reaping huge box-office returns for this color-saturated rendering of the Dumas classic. It does feel aimed at kids, and it lacks storytelling clarity, sometimes even good sense, but boy, it surely delivers playfulness, treachery, and an expensive budget. Director George Sidney, of *Anchors Aweigh* (1945) and *The Harvey Girls* (1946), gave it some MGM-musical movement and energy, notably in the exhilarating dueling sequences. Costume designer Walter Plunkett (*GWTW*) provided a sumptuous Hollywood take on the height of 1625 fashions, with Lana Turner his devastating mannequin. She's the villain, Lady de Winter, whose luscious blondeness is strikingly offset by the black mole on her face. At the center of the plot is a mustachioed Gene Kelly as d'Artagnan, indulging his Douglas Fairbanks fantasies and clearly having the time of his life. He's assisted by the titular trio of Van Heflin, Robert Coote, and Gig Young. As for the royalty, Frank Morgan (in his dithery mode) and Angela Lansbury are the King and Queen of France (with June Allyson a Lansbury maid). Kelly and Allyson fall in love hilariously fast, while Lansbury loves John Sutton, Prime Minister of England. Rounding out the all-star cast are Keenan Wynn as Kelly's comic-relief servant and Vincent Price as the evil Richelieu (who even strokes a cat while being villainous, just like James Bond's Blofeld). This romp can hardly be called an actor's movie, with not nearly enough of Morgan or Lansbury, and Allyson seems so out of place. Yet Heflin stands out, endowing the film with emotional layers and some dramatic weight, particularly in his storyline with Ms. Turner. Mostly, however, *The Three Musketeers* thrives on the melodrama of murder and suspense, the "fun" of heroism, and MGM's extravagant use of over-the-rainbow colors.

Adventures of Don Juan (1948) – Eight years after *The Sea Hawk,* Errol Flynn hadn't lost any of his swashbuckling oomph, with *Don Juan* his intoxicating, totally satisfying, and rather underappreciated return to form. Though nowhere near the equal of *Robin Hood,* it tidily refashions the Flynn formula for the early seventeenth-century. He still looks fit and handsome (though not for long), and he's better than ever with a sword. Viveca Lindfors, a smart and strong beauty, is the black-haired Spanish queen (from Austria) married to a weak, stupid king (Romney Brent). Doing justice to the Basil Rathbone role is Robert Douglas; he's the war-mongering black-clad duke manipulating the king. Some of the old gang is back, with Alan Hale happily where he belongs as Flynn's sidekick, and Una O'Connor in one scene as a servant. It may be a bit hard to believe Flynn as a Spaniard, but he's entirely plausible as both a fencing instructor and a great lover. He and Lindfors develop one of those aching loves, the kind that can never be. After all the lusty females fling themselves at him, Flynn is tamed by this true love, his first, and its impossibility gives the film a welcome emotional resonance. Like its star, *Don Juan* is primarily light and lively, boosted by breathtaking color photography and deservedly Oscar-winning costumes. How about that magnificent staircase at court? It's the fitting site of one of the best of all climactic swordfights. Well-paced by director Vincent Sherman, and exalted by yet another splendid Max Steiner score, *Don Juan* is a quintessential example of a type of costume picture at the beginning of its decline, the kind ostensibly set in places like England, Spain, and the New World, but more truly set in wondrous fairylands with names like Fox and Paramount.

Yankee Doodle Daffy: World War II, The Comic-Book Edition (1942-1945)

There's no question that Hollywood treated its responsibilities regarding World War II with utmost seriousness. Movies quickly became the widest-reaching and most stirring source of morale boosting and community spirit anywhere available. Beginning in the late thirties, with films such as *Confessions of a Nazi Spy* (1939) and *Espionage Agent* (1939), soon to be followed by *The Mortal Storm* (1940) and *Foreign Correspondent* (1940), Hollywood tried to explain what was happening in Europe, providing warnings about the Nazi threat and steadily building support for the Allies, well before the attack on Pearl Harbor. Once the US entered the fight, the war became the movies' central subject, splintering into several distinct sub-genres: those focusing on either the military, the home front, European resistance, and, to a lesser degree but none too surprisingly, Hollywood's own contribution to victory with pictures like *Hollywood Canteen* (1944). The industry went all the way, promoting unity and vigilance, as well as good old all-American know-how. In many of the WWII movies, someone invariably finds time to make a long speech about the war, supposedly aimed at a character or characters in the movie but actually intended for the audience. You might hear something about valor, patriotism, and resilience, or about never forgetting December 7th, or the inevitability of our enemies' defeat. (Joan Fontaine has a dilly of a monologue, all about England, in *This Above All* [1942], with background music surging for emphasis.) Among the more adult WWII movies were the fictionalized accounts of famous battles, including *Wake Island* (1942), *Bataan* (1943), and *Guadalcanal Diary* (1943). There were even a few nuanced and probing looks at the war, notably Andre de Toth's *None Shall Escape* (1944) and Fred Zinnemann's *The Seventh Cross* (1944), movies that were meant to stay with you, offering something to think about and talk about beyond optimism, basic training, and pin-up girls.

Though the industry accepted its wartime mission as essential, the movies themselves didn't always treat the subject with the gravity expected, even when tackling the assumedly sobering subjects of combat or underground uprisings. The oddest kind of World War II movie, among all those made *during* the war, is what I'll call the comic-book movie, the kind of picture that treated the war itself as escapism—more fun than any western, more transporting than any costume picture—movies ironically designed to take your mind *off* current events, or at least to filter those events for more comfortable digestion. The idea of combining the war's logical components—realities of battle, sacrifice, and fear—with dollops of derring-do, fantasy, and all manner of film clichés is a deeply bizarre notion. It was certainly a way to coddle audiences and shield them from anything too harsh, and it was also a way to be reasonably topical without asking anybody to think too hard, all in the name of rousing commercial entertainment. Some people must have been appalled by the so-called "comic-book movies," while others probably found relief in absorbing the war as a thrilling adventure, a chance to revel in boundless US and Allied ingenuity and courage. The Germans and the Japanese suddenly became the all-time best movie villains, the kind who smile and snarl at the same time, and the immediate recipients of the era's golden age of ethnic epithets.

Put aside, if you can, the war's bloodiest battles, the millions of lives lost, the unimaginable horrors, and enter a world in which the dizziest, most outlandish movies being made were not the frothy Betty Grable musicals, or those slapsticky Abbott and Costello comedies, but the action-adventure concoctions depicting the war as a page-turning potboiler, a glamorous intrigue, or a nail-biting whodunit. Rarely, there were clever and inventive comic-book war movies, such as Billy Wilder's *Five Graves to Cairo* (1943) and Alfred Hitchcock's *Lifeboat* (1944), but most of these movies survive as fascinating head-scratchers. They cumulatively form a priceless time capsule of that brief moment when Hollywood combined some basic elements—narrative naïveté, a strict avoidance of subtlety, and an unflappable surety—to create often compulsively watchable, shamelessly single-minded war movies without gray areas to muck things up. Of course, nearly all these films have dated badly, positively disposable since the day the war ended, yet most haven't lost their energy or their urgency. Whether their innocence seems real or calculatedly engineered, well, you be the judge. The war's comic-book movies will either make you want to wave the flag or roll your eyes, but they're almost certain to provoke an insatiable craving for popcorn.

Son of Lassie (1945): Peter Lawford and Laddie

Nazi Agent (**1942**) – Just prior to being immortalized as the quintessential Nazi villain, Major Strasser in *Casablanca* (1942), the great German actor Conrad Veidt got a rare leading role in Hollywood as good-and-evil German twins in what is decidedly a B picture. If all you know about twins is what you learned at the movies, you know that one of them is *always* evil, and that, before long, one of them will pretend to be the other. Set in America, *Nazi Agent* presents Otto, the good twin, a seller of rare books and stamps, and Hugo, the bad twin, a baron who, you guessed it, occupies the title role. Otto is bearded and wears glasses, while Hugo has slicked-back hair and sports a monocle. It's rather easy to identify who's good and who's evil. Hugo wants to use Otto's store as a front for his spy ring and blackmails the anti-Nazi Otto into accepting his terms because Otto entered the US illegally. In a tussle, the good Conrad Veidt shoots dead the bad Conrad Veidt, assumes his identity and is suddenly a double agent working for himself. He even manages to save the Panama Canal! He also gets a moment typical in this kind of movie, a longing gaze at the Statue of Liberty. The young director, Jules Dassin, displays more than a few nice visual touches, but *Nazi Agent* is just about entirely the Conrad Veidt show. His prodigious talent elevates what is, to put it mildly, a hopelessly implausible yarn. Veidt excels in both roles and is particularly fine when Otto is impersonating Hugo. This can't quite compare with Veidt's greatest performance, in the title role of the silent masterwork *The Man Who Laughs* (1928), but he was an actor who, no matter the circumstances or the budget, seemed always to give his all.

Invisible Agent (1942) – Here's a top candidate for the looniest of all the comic-book movies of the era. Are you ready? The Allies and the Nazis both want to acquire the services of the Invisible Man because, let's face it, he's the ultimate superspy. Jon Hall plays the grandson of the character created by Claude Rains in *The Invisible Man* (1933), and, don't worry, not only does he have the secret formula but he's volunteering for the Allies. As for the villains, we have Nazi Cedric Hardwicke and Japanese Peter Lorre (formerly the screen's Mr. Moto, when it was okay to *like* the Japanese). As a love interest for Hall, there's Ilona Massey, a German spying for the Allies, though her English is such a mess you have to wonder if her help is worth much. I just keep thinking about how cold Mr. Hall must be during all that supposedly naked invisibility. It would be nice to report that *Invisible Agent* is absurdist fun, but it's just plain silly. True, it intends to be fairly comic, but it's also not funny. Was it really that much of a comfort to know that the Invisible Man was on our side?

Desperate Journey (1942) – Here's the mother lode of the war's comic-book movies, a proudly preposterous series of cliffhangers strung together. Love it or hate it, you can't say you didn't get your money's worth. Essentially a combat picture, it's rather oddly comic and no one in it seems to take the war very seriously. Errol Flynn and company manage to best every single Nazi who crosses their path. He's an Australian RAF pilot on one of those planes in which the crew is a cross section of Allied nationalities, including Ronald Reagan as, duh, the American. When their plane crash-lands inside Germany, the survivors (our two stars and three others) have the best time anyone has ever had while being hunted down by Nazis. Flynn speaks German, which allows for many of the quintet's deceptions, while he and Reagan continually try to outdo each other in the rakish-charm department. The main Nazi is

Raymond Massey—recently Abe Lincoln, no less—with a most unconvincing accent. (Paging Conrad Veidt!) The fellas manage to blow up a chemical plant, steal a plane, and kill dozens of Nazis. Flynn refers to their antics as "all the fun." Directed by Raoul Walsh, *Desperate Journey* is what is known as a slam-bang entertainment, a nonsensical pleasure in which there's finally nothing to do but succumb to its make-believe vision of warfare. The message is that winning this war is going to be a snap, as long as we've got good-looking heroes with a talent for mischief, disguise, and one-liners. The famous final line says it all, with Flynn pumped for his next adventure: "Now for Australia and a crack at those Japs." Actually, it was Southeast Asia, when Flynn and Walsh reteamed for *Objective, Burma!* from early 1945. About as far from *Desperate Journey* as any war-era combat picture could be, *Objective, Burma!* (though fictional) is a physically and emotionally grueling experience, shaming the earlier film's immaturity.

***First Comes Courage* (1943)** – In Nazi-occupied Norway, glamour queen Merle Oberon is loathed by her community because she's the lover of elegant Nazi major Carl Esmond. In fact, Oberon is a spy for the Allies, selflessly incurring local hatred for the good of the cause. She's so darned brave, so sickeningly noble, all the while chic and beautiful in her *war*-drobe. Brian Aherne is a breezy British commando wounded by the Nazis and being hidden by Oberon in her basement. Former lovers, their romance is rekindled, yet Oberon still accepts Esmond's marriage proposal, determined to keep on spying. What a gal! Esmond learns she's a spy but marries her anyway. It's all plot, no nuance, and no attempt at seriousness. Oberon merely gets nobler and nobler, without any trace of depth to clutter her mind, offering attitudes and poses as her preferred means of expression. Too bad that Greta Garbo had retired before they made all those war movies set in Scandinavia. Such vehicles would have provided a convenient extension of Garbo's movie career, a logical transition to a new, if temporary, persona. *First Comes Courage*'s claim to fame is as the final film of trailblazing female director Dorothy Arzner.

***Assignment in Brittany* (1943)** – This time it isn't twins, just lookalikes. Jean-Pierre Aumont (billed without the "Jean") plays the dual role of two Frenchmen, one working for the British, the other a collaborator. Quite expectedly, good Jean-Pierre assumes the identity of bad Jean-Pierre on a mission to locate a Nazi submarine base on the French coast. (Bad Jean-Pierre has only one scene, in a hospital bed.) If you can accept the improbable set-up, the movie is enjoyable for a while, until its series of unrestrained climaxes. Director Jack Conway keeps things moving, and Aumont is reasonably charismatic (though it's clear that MGM does not have a new Charles Boyer on its hands). The good girl is pretty, sensitive Susan Peters (unfortunately costumed as a milkmaid) and the bad girl is Signe Hasso (a collaborator and a beret-wearing tart), while this season's elegant Nazi is George Coulouris. Then there's great old Margaret Wycherly, best remembered as Jimmy Cagney's "Ma" in *White Heat* (1949), as the mother of bad Jean-Pierre. In perhaps the film's freshest idea, Wycherly figures out that good Jean-Pierre is an impostor but decides she likes him better than her actual son. *Assignment in Brittany* lays on the martyrdom, the explosions, torture, and a firing squad. You won't believe a minute of it, but it's hard to dislike a movie that contains the following code words: "Cold Mutton and Goat Cheese."

Above Suspicion (1943) – It begins at Oxford in 1939 with the wedding of two Americans, professor (and Rhodes Scholar) Fred MacMurray and Joan Crawford (in her final MGM film for a decade). They agree to spy for the British on their Continental honeymoon. What could be more fun than that? They go from Paris to a Nazi-infested Central Europe, eventually winding up in Italy. There's some nonsense about a secret weapon (a magnetized underwater mine), but this strangely music-filled picture is mostly about Fred and Joan doing their best Nick and Nora Charles as they blithely make their way into Germany, occasionally singing, all the while following lame, impossible clues. They disguise themselves in Tyrolian get-ups, then as an elderly couple, and Fred eventually dons a Nazi uniform for the big escape. Taking a break from all her arch playfulness, Joan manages to get herself tortured. (Don't worry, she can take it!) With a bad accent, Basil Rathbone is the main Nazi, while ever-reliable Conrad Veidt (in his final film) is a welcome addition as a mysterious Austrian count/tour guide. Richard Thorpe's direction is thankfully fast-moving, yet nothing about *Above Suspicion* feels new, especially its direct steal from *The Man Who Knew Too Much* (1934): a concert-hall assassination timed to a musical peak. In the final analysis, who needs Niagara Falls when you can have an adrenaline rush of a honeymoon like this? Treating WWII primarily as a frolic, *Above Suspicion* is among the coyest of the comic-book movies.

Adventure in Iraq (1943) – Though its title evokes more recent times, it's actually a look backwards, a WWII reworking of that old chestnut *The Green*

Goddess, a George Arliss screen vehicle of both 1923 and 1930. (He also played it on Broadway in 1921.) In Arliss' place, Paul Cavanagh is a British-accented European-educated Iraqi sheik unhappy that his country is being controlled by the British Army, which is why he's a Nazi sympathizer. After their small plane makes a forced landing, a vaguely drawn trio—two men (British John Loder and American pilot Warren Douglas) and one woman (American Ruth Ford who is divorcing Loder and smitten with Douglas)—is given a lavish reception by Cavanagh. He then informs them that they will be executed, an act of revenge for the three Iraqi Nazi spies about to be killed elsewhere. This C picture mentions that Iraq is desirable to outsiders for its oil, and there are also disparaging remarks about Iraqis as "barbarians," "fanatics," and "devil worshippers." After a wireless message gets to the Americans in Cairo, the film climaxes with the bombing of Iraq. It's a clunky melding of an old-fashioned play, some contemporary international intrigue, plus a dash of *Arabian Nights,* but its accidental connection to future history does make it something of a minor jaw-dropper.

A Guy Named Joe (1943) – Screwy as this one is, it's not exactly fair to call it a comic-book movie because it's so heavy-handed and pretentious, taking itself too seriously to be enjoyed as foolish escapism. A gruff Spencer Tracy plays a great, reckless pilot who bravely bombs a Nazi carrier before crashing to his death. He goes to flying heaven—which looks very *Here Comes Mr. Jordan* (1941)—where he meets his new boss, Lionel Barrymore. Even in the after-life, Barrymore is his windbag self. Tracy is sent back to Earth as an angel, a "coach" to other flyers. Unseen and unheard, he uses some form of osmosis to get his supernatural suggestions across. (Where was Tracy's own angel when he needed one?) He gets assigned to young Van Johnson who is soon doing whatever Tracy tells him (despite not being able to hear him). Johnson becomes romantically involved with lady-pilot Irene Dunne, Tracy's former love, even though she seems like Johnson's mother. Unfortunately, Tracy and Dunne, two great stars in their only appearance together, stop having direct contact once he's dead, denying the rest of the movie its initial pleasures of acting sparks between them (even though the plot doesn't really start until Tracy's death). The bulk of this film is blathering gobbledygook and cloying whimsy, with an overall maudlin air. Victor Fleming's direction is much too leisurely, miring the movie in its patriotic smugness. Newcomer Esther Williams brightens things as a canteen girl who dances with Johnson, but, with only one scene, she can't help much. *A Guy Named Joe* is the kind of movie that can accommodate both the bombing of a Japanese ammunition dump *and* a heavenly chorus. Steven Spielberg apparently thought far more of it than I do, remaking and updating it as *Always* (1989) with Richard Dreyfuss and Holly Hunter, and with Audrey Hepburn as…Lionel Barrymore.

Passport to Destiny **(1944)** – The premise is so giddily appealing that you'll keep rooting for this movie, until it becomes too ridiculous to sustain your good will. Though it's merely a 63-minute B picture, it's still a rare leading role for the wondrous, delightfully eccentric Elsa Lanchester. She's a London charwoman, the widow of an army man: Charles Laughton (Lanchester's real-life husband), seen here only as a portrait with a most unpleasant expression. When she's a miraculous survivor of a bombing raid, Lanchester credits her husband's lucky piece (a magic eye), suddenly feeling invincible enough to head to Berlin expressly to kill Hitler. Bucket in hand, and cheerfully dotty as ever, she scrubs her way through France and into Germany. She gets nowhere by looking Hitler up in the phonebook but soon gets a job in a Nazi office building, pretending to be deaf and mute because she can't speak German. Though she does find her way into Hitler's office, it's disappointing when the film's suspense peters out. *Passport to Destiny* is never really as amusing as you want it to be, nor is it as much of a showcase for Lanchester as she deserves. However, she does parachute out of a plane, and that's not nothing.

Son of Lassie **(1945)** – Amid all these black-and-white movies comes this Technicolor cross between a war movie and an animal picture, a sequel to *Lassie Come Home* (1943). In just two years, Roddy McDowall has matured into Peter Lawford, with Donald Crisp back as the father. The son of Lassie is Laddie, and this movie might easily be retitled *The Nazis Are Mean to Laddie*. (Lassie herself has a supporting role.) This is practically a remake of the first picture, with Laddie now the collie on an exhausting journey home, with the significant added complication of WWII. Laddie is devoted to Lawford in an obsessive, almost crazed way, following the young flyer to his post (forty miles from home), then stowing away on his plane. He's practically a stalker. Most of the action takes place in Norway, after Lawford and Laddie are forced to make a parachute landing, with the Nazis chasing them for the remainder of the picture. The irony is how much danger Laddie unintentionally puts in Lawford's way, more than once leading the Nazis right to him. One Nazi shoots Laddie, wounding his paw. (If you didn't already hate Nazis, this would constitute the last straw.) The man-dog duo is separated for a long stretch, with Laddie cared for by some kids, including Helen Koford (later known as Terry Moore). Nils Asther, as a courageous Norwegian, is of questionable help to Lawford when he gives him a bright red sweater for his escape through the snow. Once reunited, Laddie and Lawford jump off a bridge together, go down the rapids, even over a waterfall. With its rapturously pretty natural scenery, storybook colors, and its canine hero, *Son of Lassie,* released in April of 1945, was perhaps Hollywood's final word on its treatment of the war as sweeping, transporting unreality. As victory approached, who better than a beloved collie to provide the war with its escapist comic-book capper?

Making House Calls: Hollywood and the Home Front (1943-1945)

While stars such as Errol Flynn, John Wayne, and Lassie were fighting the war on screens across the nation, the film industry did not overlook the issues being faced by those in the audience. It was one thing to see movies about far-off battles and war-ravaged territories, but quite another to experience movies depicting the world right outside the local movie theater. Home-front pictures were about American citizenry's role during wartime, about contributing to the war effort and holding the country together until the soldiers' return. Whether instructional or inspirational, soothing or cautionary, these movies took their function seriously. The big jump-starter among home-front movies was set not in the US but in England. Released in June of 1942, MGM's *Mrs. Miniver* follows a supposedly average (yet remarkably brave and capable) middle-class British family (with a maid and a cook) who confronts damaging air raids, personal tragedy, and even a downed Nazi flyer on their premises. Its point was to encourage Americans to behave accordingly if the war ever arrived in their neighborhoods. Carefully constructed to push all the right buttons, *Mrs. Miniver* had the perfect messenger, Greer Garson, so wonderfully (and impossibly) warm, wise, and charming in the title role (for which she won an Oscar). Though it often defies plausibility, and is certainly not subtle (with its climactic call to arms by a vicar and a staunch chorus of "Onward, Christian Soldiers"), *Mrs. Miniver* proved shrewdly effective, filled with memorable war-strifed scenes. The public flocked, the Academy named it Best Picture, and, though overrated, it remains a key marker of its moment. Who didn't want to be like the Minivers, sharing their pedestal of grace and fortitude?

There were other European-set home-front dramas that portrayed varying degrees of courage and capitulation, hoping to set proper (and improper) codes of behavior for a hypothetical Nazi occupation of the US. *The Moon Is Down* (1943), about a Norwegian village, and *This Land Is Mine* (1943), which unfolds in an unnamed European country, shared the message of many similarly plotted movies: fight back and never give up, whatever the sacrifice. Even a coward, like Charles Laughton's meek teacher in *This Land Is Mine,* could find redemption and become a hero. *The White Cliffs of Dover* (1944), MGM's attempt to top its own *Mrs. Miniver,* features an American heroine (Irene Dunne) who marries a British baronet and remains in England. Trapped in this stodgy soap, Dunne faces two world wars, loses loved ones twice, and all the while proves that the British didn't have a monopoly on Miniver-like nobility.

Most subjects covered in American-set home-front films could be spun positively or negatively, including the emigration of war-torn children. *On the Sunny Side* (1942), a pre-*Miniver* picture set in Ohio, concerns Roddy McDowall who is sent over from England for the war's duration and lives with friends of his parents. His experiences primarily celebrate the values of an all-American boyhood, from hot dogs to black eyes, with Roddy adapting rippingly. At the other extreme is the overwrought *Tomorrow, the World!* (1944), from the hit play, in which Skippy Homeier, a German orphan staying with relatives, turns out to be a Nazi youth (and junior saboteur) eager to unleash his ideology on apple-pie America.

The housing shortage in Washington, D.C., was played strictly for laughs. The best example of this sub-genre is George Stevens' *The More the Merrier* (1943), with its glorious comic trio of unexpected roommates: Jean Arthur, Joel McCrea, and Charles Coburn. Unfortunately, *The Doughgirls* (1944), based on a Broadway success, was given the abrasively strident Warner Brothers treatment, a fate that marred quite a few stage comedies during the '40s. (Remember *The Man Who Came to Dinner* and *Arsenic and Old Lace*?) A farce set mostly in a crammed hotel bridal suite, *The Doughgirls* has the bonus of Eve Arden, cast against type, as a Soviet sergeant (kind of an upbeat Ninotchka). Another play gone wrong was the underwhelming comedy *Over 21* (1945), in which novelist Irene Dunne follows husband Alexander Knox to officer-candidate school, living in a bungalow court with other wives. Even more cramped was *In the Meantime, Darling* (1944), set in a house near a military base, with women sharing rooms with their soldier husbands (who are waiting to be shipped out). Promoting unselfishness, it was a lesson movie aimed at young women, with Jeanne Crain as a spoiled rich girl newly married to a lieutenant (Frank Latimore); she does some growing up.

Writer-director Preston Sturges made two great 1944 home-front comedies, both slapstick screwball classics starring Eddie Bracken: *The Miracle of Morgan's Creek,* a provocative farce with Bracken cast as a nerd who can't pass a war physical, and Betty Hutton as a pregnant girl who can't remember which private she married; and *Hail the Conquering Hero,* with Bracken discharged from the marines because of chronic hay fever, yet unable to stop his out-of-control heroic homecoming. In such self-consciously morale-boosting times, Sturges managed an astonishing artistic objectivity and freedom. Without any disrespect, he delivered good-hearted satiric fun at the home front's expense, and, unlike most war-era movies, his comic double bill is agelessly good, with relevance beyond the war years. For a desperately unfunny wartime screwball comedy, try *Government Girl* (1943), with the all-time worst Olivia de Havilland performance (as a secretary at the war construction board who falls for boss Sonny Tufts).

Serious-minded romance was another favorite topic of home-front movies. *I'll Be Seeing You* (1944) is a nice little drama, a love story between Ginger Rogers and soldier Joseph Cotten, each harboring a painful secret. Though the writing is a bit problematic, the two stars' subdued turns make the movie work. *The Clock,* among the better remembered of WWII-era romances, was released in May of 1945, with the war nearly over. During a two-day leave in Manhattan, soldier Robert Walker falls in love with Judy Garland and marries her. Despite the stars' considerable charm, sensitivity, and chemistry, *The Clock* is an overrated Vincente Minnelli film, though it's quite exceptional in several scenes near its end. *The Impatient Years* (1944), a disappointment with Jean Arthur and Lee Bowman, is a comic version of a *Clock*-ish set-up: the pair married after knowing each other four days, then forced apart for eighteen months because of Bowman's active duty, winding up in divorce court, and then ordered to rekindle whatever it was they first felt. Amid so many rash wartime unions, it was a viable comic idea, but it fizzled.

As for wartime musicals, a quintessential example is the very popular *Two Girls and a Sailor* (1944), basically a stuffed-to-bursting variety show with June Allyson, Gloria DeHaven, and Van Johnson. The gals play a nightclub sister act who patriotically solicit servicemen on the street to come to their house for a private canteen. Dozens of uniformed strangers join them for... pop, sandwiches, and music! The boys had to have been expecting a brothel, so why do they stick around? Well, they have the best time ever! (I would love to see just one of them leave in abject horror.) Squeaky-clean beyond compare, *Two Girls and a Sailor* is home-front uplift at its most innocent and undemanding.

In its role as chronicler and influencer of the contemporary scene, Hollywood attempted to examine many facets of the home-front experience: the optimism and the grief, the pride and the guilt, the camaraderie and the opportunism, etc. With no assurances of the war's outcome (something we now take for granted when watching these movies), Hollywood hoped to reflect what was happening in America, while essentially making things look pretty flattering in the reflection.

Tender Comrade (1943): Ginger Rogers

The Human Comedy (1943) – With an Oscar-winning story by William Saroyan, this handsome MGM production, often touchingly observed, is forced in its lyricism, overimpressed with itself, and excessive in its speechifying (an occupational hazard of home-front pictures). Set in a small California town and enriched by atmospheric locations, *The Human Comedy* is about what we're fighting for, presenting American values on an ambitiously broad canvas. Leading an ensemble cast, Mickey Rooney is a high-schooler working part-time as a telegraph messenger, alongside an alcoholic telegrapher (a poignant Frank Morgan, in one of his best dramatic parts). Fay Bainter, who had recently been smartly understated in *The War Against Mrs. Hadley* (1942)—as a selfish matron who finds the war a nuisance (but not for long)—is the mother of Rooney, as well as Van Johnson (a soldier), Donna Reed, and little Jack Jenkins (later known as "Butch"). Because the script is extremely episodic, the movie is wildly uneven, sometimes suggesting a grandly mounted Andy Hardy picture, specifically in its school/teenager scenes (among the film's weakest). Rooney, however, is excellent—maturing believably, becoming man of the house—especially in his beautiful reading of a letter from his overseas brother. Another of the best episodes has three lonely soldiers—Robert Mitchum, Don DeFore, and Barry Nelson—accompany Ms. Reed and her pal, Dorothy Morris, to the movies. It's a sweet, unforced ships-in-the-night sequence. A standout player is Marsha Hunt, a breath of fresh air with a high-comic sparkle, as a flighty socialite with unsuspected depths. The low points include a highly improbable scene in which an entire trainful of soldiers join vocal forces for a rousing rendition of a hymn. There's an element of fantasy, too, with Ray Collins, who also narrates, as the ghost of Rooney's dead father, though no one can see him. (Collins was a dead narrator in 1944's *The Seventh Cross*, too.) He'll be joined by another ghost before long, with grief (and moving forward) very much on the movie's mind. Among the film's five Oscar nominations were those for picture, director (Clarence Brown), and lead actor (Rooney). When Brown's direction is at its simplest, *The Human Comedy* is a beauty. However, subtlety was rarely the goal of home-front films, which tended to be steeped in idealized overkill.

Good Luck, Mr. Yates (1943) – The plight of military-rejected young men (who yearned to serve) was played for laughs in Preston Sturges' wartime comedies, but here's a film that used the premise for a B-variety feel-good drama. Bland Jess Barker (soon to be Susan Hayward's real-life husband) is a teacher at a military academy who's unhappy with his educational deferment and even more unhappy when his perforated ear drum bars him from enlisting. Too embarrassed to return home after a big send-off, he moves away, takes a room in a boardinghouse, and assists in the war effort by working in a shipyard. So far, so good, until the script becomes mired in sentimentality and action-oriented melodrama, ditching its potential as an honest portrait of a young man's painful (and guilt-inducing) exclusion from serving. Barker lives *and* works with, among others, welder Claire Trevor and her dad Edgar Buchanan. (Top-billed Trevor has a thankless love-interest role.) Meanwhile, specialist Albert Bassermann is trying to repair Barker's ear. Poor Scotty Beckett has the worst role, the student who idolizes Barker and goes AWOL to unravel the mystery of what became of him, which unfortunately steers the movie into kids' picture terrain. A troublemaking co-worker (Tom Neal) mistakenly suspects Barker of being a Nazi, which leads to our protagonist's act of heroism and a promotion, all to get to the movie's point—civilian men like Barker are necessary to the fight, with vitally important jobs to do. His ear may be hopeless but not his usefulness to victory.

Watch on the Rhine (1943) – Based on Lillian Hellman's 1941 stage success, this once-prestigious drama isn't very good, despite its accolade from New York's film critics as the year's best film. Indelicately crafted, it's preachy and pretentious, and Ms. Hellman, unwarrantedly proud of her achievement, is credited not only for her play but for "additional scenes and dialogue." Its four Oscar nominations, for picture, lead actor (Paul Lukas), screenplay (Dashiell Hammett), and supporting actress (Lucile Watson), resulted in a win for Lukas (beating Humphrey Bogart in *Casablanca*), who, like Ms. Watson, was from the Broadway company, as was the director, Herman Shumlin (who proved to be no William Wyler with a camera). It's a half hour before Lukas, wife Bette Davis, and their three children arrive (from Europe in 1940) at the D.C. mansion of Davis' hearty widowed mother (Ms. Watson). Lukas, ill and exhausted, is a German anti-fascist activist who has, for the sake of his work, been moving the family across Europe. (Davis hasn't been back in America for seventeen years.) The kids are insufferably perfect and excruciatingly phony (with the two boys especially mechanical, like reverse Nazi youths). The least offensive is Janis Wilson, who's reteamed with Davis from *Now, Voyager* (in which she played Paul Henreid's daughter). Back in another Hellman play (after *The Little Foxes*), Davis works overemphatically hard at playing a woman too good to be true. Lukas is faultless, not at all stagy, and entirely convincing. It's a role prone to self-admiring martyrdom, but Lukas keeps things simple—he's a crusader born of necessity rather than ego. The plot has far too much melodramatic intrigue within Ms. Watson's home, with the amazing coincidence that another of her houseguests is George Coulouris (also from the Broadway cast), a Nazi-sympathizing Romanian count soon spying on Lukas. The play has been *too* opened up, with scenes at places like the Washington Monument and the German embassy, all tension-diffusing mistakes. The home-front focus is on Ms. Watson and her realization of a world outside her privileged cocoon. Moved by her daughter's sacrifices, she has her eyes opened: "We've been shaken out of the magnolias." *Watch on the Rhine* hoped to shake viewers out of their respective magnolias, rather strenuously, and occasionally goes over the top (assisted by one of Max Steiner's worst, most intrusive scores). Despite the expert restraint of Lukas and Watson, and the dry, cool bitterness of Mr. Coulouris, it's hard to be stirred by a movie that so clumsily and heavy-handedly assumes its own greatness.

Tender Comrade (1943) – A complete misfire, it concentrates on four women, all married to overseas soldiers and all working at an aircraft plant in LA. To save money, they rent a house together and run it with a "share and share alike" philosophy, a detail later used as a "red" flag in screenwriter Dalton Trumbo's shameful blacklisting. It's hard to accept that such a rotten movie could inflict any harm beyond its own tedious ineptitude. The quartet consists of everywoman Ginger Rogers, bad girl Ruth Hussey, saintly Patricia Collinge, and innocent Kim Hunter. They hire a housekeeper (Mady Christians), a Nazi-hating German married to a US soldier. The unhappily married Hussey is "bad" because she wants to go out on dates. Worse, she's anti-rationing. News of her husband's death—broadcast on the radio right after Rogers tells her off—transforms her. When he then turns up alive, she's a cleansed, newly devoted spouse. Despite all of that, Hussey gives the best performance. Her character's flaws give the movie its only recognizable humanity, its only edges. The rest are goody-goody mouthpieces in what must be the talkiest, most overwritten of home-front movies. Anything you want to know about the evils of hoarding? Sit back and get an earful. Never has the wonderfully spontaneous Rogers been so artificial and shallow, never have her instincts been so *wrong*, especially in three abominable flashbacks covering her relationship with Robert Ryan. (The more she overacts, the more he wisely underplays, burying her.) Her incorporation of stupid baby-talk, a coy attempt to get laughs, is beyond strained and entirely out of tune with the established mood. She also gets no help from Trumbo's tonally confused writing and Edward Dmytryk's shapeless direction. The gravest miscalculation is the finale: a long and completely implausible monologue by Rogers to her newborn, as falsely calculated as everything else here. The film's popularity confirmed that women craved contemporary stories, hoping to measure their wartime experiences against those of others, perhaps not even noticing that they deserved far better than the turgid pieties, misplaced laughs, and smug condescension of the inauthentic *Tender Comrade*.

Since You Went Away **(1944)** – Produced by David O. Selznick, it's no accident that it's the *Gone With the Wind* of the home front. Did it *need* to be scaled as an epic with an overture, intermission, and entr'acte? Never mind *GWTW*, here was Selznick also outdoing *Mrs. Miniver,* stating at its start that this was a story of "the unconquerable fortress: the American home." He wrote it himself, and though it's three hours long, utterly simplistic, and so obvious in its manipulations, it surely is a memorable soap. Photographed by Stanley Cortez *and* Lee Garmes, it's also a gorgeous black-and-white movie, notably at its big dance inside a hangar and, later, during a day in the country shared by Jennifer Jones and soldier Robert Walker, plus their lovely train-platform farewell. Claudette Colbert is ideally cast as a symbol of forty-ish American womanhood, Mrs. Miniver-like in her abundant warmth, charm, smarts, and the fact that there's really *nothing* average about her: she's a great-lady star. Married to a man enlisted in the fight, Colbert is home with her daughters: seventeen-year-old Jones and younger Shirley Temple (who, even as a teen, pouts all her lines). Jones, actually in her mid-twenties, plays younger by simpering, but her acting improves once she meets Walker. (In real life, they were separating so that she could eventually marry Selznick!) On hand for some amusing dissonance, crusty Monty Woolley becomes the family's lodger, an old military man and Mr. Walker's grandfather. The Woolley-Walker family conflict is an emotion-jerking plot device, but it's Walker, so appealingly insecure, who gives the film's most engaging performance. In addition to Woolley, further discord is provided by Agnes Moorehead and her carefully timed appearances as the person you're meant to hate, the local bitch, gossip, and snob, a blight on the home front and its good works. And she's divorced! Meanwhile, Colbert's husband is reported missing in action, adding some suspense. Conceived to inspire all wives and mothers, Colbert makes the transition from helpless to strong, useless to useful by becoming a welder in a shipyard. If all this weren't enough, there's Nazimova as a refugee who can (and *does*) recite the Statue of Liberty's words. The film received nine Oscar nominations, including those for Best Picture and cast members Colbert, Woolley, and Jones, but won only for Max Steiner's emotionally sweeping score. Though this movie was impeccably over-engineered by Selznick, director John Cromwell achieved delicate intimacies throughout, especially in the romance between Jones and Walker. Or the moment when Colbert is missing her husband and leaps into *his* twin bed and sobs.

Marriage Is a Private Affair (1944) – During his brief stint in the MGM writing department, Tennessee Williams supposedly spent some time assigned to this Lana Turner vehicle. Though there's no outright trace of Williams' presence, the film does seem to want to say something provocative about female desire, within the confines of Code-era women's pictures. The end result is whiny and drawn-out, with lazy overseeing from director Robert Z. Leonard, but in its favor is Turner. At twenty-three, she looks more dazzlingly beautiful than ever, with long blonde tresses; she's a particular knockout in a black-and-white striped gown and black opera gloves. Her presence is playful, easygoing, and humorous; she's not yet the rigid, tightly pulled Lana Turner of the '50s and beyond. Set among the rich, *Marriage* is about love in wartime, covering that popular topic of marrying a soldier you barely know. Turner marries flyer John Hodiak after knowing him just two weeks, but his orders keep him at home, working on range finders. She becomes a housewife (with a maid) and gives birth to a baby boy. Because she's the daughter of jaded, much-married Natalie Schafer, the film wonders if Turner will become her mother. Can she—so childish, selfish, and without any real problems—remain good and faithful? After being married a year, she needs to feel desirable, to be wanted by a certain major (James Craig). She even lies about having been to see *Mrs. Miniver* when she was actually at his place. The material is fraught with juicy possibilities, but the movie maintains an unchallengingly trite perspective, pumped with constant infusions of MGM glamour (such as a hat that looks like a very thin, very large crème-filled cookie). For the benefit of Turner (and all the wives in the audience), there's another cautionary character: the married Frances Gifford. She's having an affair with Hugh Marlowe, both of them good friends of Turner and Hodiak, as is Gifford's husband (Herbert Rudley). *Marriage* is built on the premise that Lana Turner's beauty gives her a free pass to flirt with misbehaving. After all, she's nobody's girl next door.

The Very Thought of You (1944) – One of the nicer of wartime romances, it's an absorbing drama whose requisite preachiness is overridden by the warmth within the love story. Young Eleanor Parker makes a real star impression; she's a beautiful newcomer who can act, an ingénue with sexuality. Primarily set in Pasadena, the film has Parker and her likable pal Faye Emerson working in a parachute factory. The guys are Dennis Morgan, an army demolition expert, and Dane Clark, Morgan's comic-relief sidekick who's conveniently on hand for Ms. Emerson. Parker, formerly a soda jerk, had a crush on Morgan when she used to serve him nightly (though he never noticed her). They meet officially on a bus, embark on a whirlwind romance, and (of course) marry a few days later. This time the cautionary female is Andrea King, as Parker's sister, married to sailor William Prince but cheating on him. King has several awful scenes, representing all married gals behaving badly during the war, which includes giving poor advice to Parker (who represents all the wonderful young women out there). Mr. Morgan, an actor I usually find entirely unappealing, has never seemed as attractive as he does here (though Dane Clark is reliably irritating). This is a consoling drama, with most everything resolving happily, abundantly so. Directed and co-written by Delmer Daves, it carries an authentic regular-people American flavor, earning both its romantic urgency and its generous uplift.

Sunday Dinner for a Soldier (1944) – You have to get through nearly an hour of overly cute tedium for the pleasing pay-off of its final third. Set on a houseboat secured on a Florida beach, it stars Anne Baxter as a capable and spirited young woman keeping her family together after the death of her parents in a car accident. She's raising her three younger siblings while looking after their lovably irresponsible grandfather (Charles Winninger). Baxter has a dull, rich suitor (Robert Bailey) able to turn her family's fortunes around, but she just doesn't love the guy. The family volunteers to host a soldier for dinner, but, due to complications not worth going into, no one is coming— even though they're all ready for him! Then Sgt. John Hodiak accidentally wanders by, as if he fell from the sky. (He's on a bomber crew.) What's nice about what transpires, amid fried chicken and roasted marshmallows, is that it's a two-way dream come true. Yes, the family delights in their soldier, but he's every bit as enamored with them, a ready-made happy family (something he's never had). Director Lloyd Bacon, who struggles with the poky first hour, savors the sentiment and joy of the climax, especially as Baxter and Hodiak come together. It's clear that they're right for each other because he, unlike her wealthy suitor, appreciates her pleasure in a nearby ruin of an unfinished hotel. He joins her fantasy of a make-believe palace of music and glamour;

they effortlessly improvise a fancy night out. (Baxter and Hodiak later married, together from 1946 to 1953.) As family-oriented home-front fare, *Sunday Dinner* qualifies as a light dessert.

A Medal for Benny (1945) – John Steinbeck is co-credited with the story, set among paisanos in California, similar in spirit to his *Tortilla Flat*. A good movie with a good message, it's one of those pictures in which the title character is only talked about. Unfortunately, it requires viewer endurance for its weak first half and schematic second half, paving the groundwork for a strong final fifteen minutes. As Benny's girlfriend Lolita, Dorothy Lamour looks pretty and is likably second-rate, complete with accent, while Oscar-nominated J. Carrol Naish is the whole show as Benny's illiterate, simple-minded father, a passive put-upon fellow. It's a typical Naish "accent" role, but a better one than usual; he's smart enough to know that restraint will serve his impact best. Benny hasn't been seen since a judge exiled him from the community for one year (over a brawl). The movie shifts with the news that Benny died a war hero—not even his father knew he had become a soldier. Benny singlehandedly killed a hundred Japanese in the Philippines and is set to receive the Congressional Medal of Honor. The movie halfheartedly aims for Sturges-like satire when the town leaders get excited about all this leading to a local economic boom. However, no one is happy with Naish's poverty; it doesn't fit with the mythologizing of Benny, which includes making Lolita (who has moved on to someone else) his great love. Naish eventually refuses to attend the ceremony, but will the movie really dare to keep him at home? *A Medal for Benny* refreshingly honors the diversity of the US and its heroes (and the people who raised them). It reminds us that heroes come from everywhere, so don't try to pretend they don't! Despite meandering direction from Irving Pichel, the film addresses the ways in which the stateside population absorbs the war's realities, mixing cynicism and sentimentality on the way to its worthy destination.

Allotment Wives (1945) – In 1944, *Youth Runs Wild* depicted juvenile delinquency unleashed by the war, with unsupervised teens running amok while their parents worked long hours at defense plants. Despite the intriguing premise, it's a terrible movie. *Allotment Wives* is another B picture with the gutsy sensationalism to place a dingy spotlight on no-good home-front behavior. Set between V-E and V-J Days, and released after the war's end, it's just about the last word on home-front movies, a camp hoot! In her second-to-last film, Kay Francis is a glamorous beauty-salon owner and the operator of a soldier's canteen, but it's all a front. A product of the slums and reform school, she's secretly heading a syndicate that scams the government's Office of Dependency, a provider of benefits to wives and kids of soldiers. She recruits girls nationwide to become bigamists, collecting lots of Uncle Sam's dough; she's like a madam building a prostitution empire. Ms. Francis co-produced the movie, which is sort of a poor man's *Mildred Pierce* (which was released a few weeks prior). Like Mildred, here's a successful businesswoman with a troublesome teenage daughter (who finally has to be slapped). Bossing men around, Francis overdoes the toughness. She's also prone to acting up a storm, which only heightens the shoddiness of her performance. This is cheap exploitation moviemaking, fun junk from poverty-stricken Monogram Pictures, not to be taken seriously despite its nasty set-up. The war was over and things would soon be returning to normal, right? There was no longer any need for inspirational bolstering from Greer Garson and Claudette Colbert, or all that mouthy fortitude from Bette Davis and Ginger Rogers, or any reason to fear Kay Francis. The home front had survived healthily, and Hollywood had worked tirelessly to do its part, to be there whenever audiences needed guidance, reassurance, or plain old comfort.

Lights Out: The Nocturnal Emergence of Film Noir (1945-1949)

Maybe you're one of those classic-film lovers who can't seem to get enough of this genre. That's okay, because there are so many examples of film noir that no one is likely ever to have seen them all. It was one of those genres, like horror movies, for which a big budget was not essential, meaning that you didn't have to be MGM or Paramount to excel at film noir. You could do just as well, if not better, at RKO or Columbia. Not enough money for first-rate sets? Just stick to black and white, cut your light sources to a minimum, and start creating something mysterious and steeped in shadows. If film noir seems like a genre ahead of its time, it's probably because of its cynical, knowing depictions of sex, criminality, and violence, which offer a more tarnished (and therefore modern) sensibility than most movies made during the enforcement of the Production Code. While the censors focused on the studios' more prominent efforts, the often lower-rung noir pictures could get away with more suggestive and unusually downbeat content.

How to define film noir? Said to have been coined by a French critic in 1946 in response to a distinctive darkness in American movies, the term "film noir" took decades to take hold and was eventually regarded universally as a wholly American amalgam of tawdry pulp fiction, detective-driven whodunits, post-war panic and uncertainty, and the visual influence of European film artists. Without meaning to, Hollywood had organically conceived a new genre. Classification as film noir can be arguable because movies can have noir elements or sequences without feeling like *pure* noir. One fan's film noir is another fan's plain-old crime picture or wicked melodrama. Is *White Heat* (1949) a terrific update of a 1930s-style James Cagney gangster picture or is it film noir? I'd say it's the former, but maybe you disagree and can offer a convincing defense. When tagging any movie as film noir, I go by a basic, admittedly *in*defensible principle: I know it when I see it. Film noir resides in the underbelly of society, dealing directly with the things being plotted while most of the rest of us are sound asleep. It's often the arena in which malleable mugs are manipulated by seductive dames, or where a group of thugs plan the perfect (yet doomed) crime/heist. You get the idea.

Stranger on the Third Floor (1940) has all the markings of being the first recognizable example of film noir, including such characteristic components as a stylized dream sequence, the use of voiceovers and flashbacks, and a story comprised of guilt, fear, and paranoia. The director, Boris Ingster, was a Latvian who worked with Sergei Eisenstein, and the cinematographer was Italian-born Nicholas Musuraca, the man who later lensed *Out of the Past* (1947), perhaps the quintessential film noir. With its striking, consistent flashes of visual invention, *Stranger on the Third Floor* heralded the arrival of film noir, even though no one seemed to notice. So much more than a "B" killer-on-the-loose picture, it's the genre's granddaddy, a *major* minor work, complete with Peter Lorre.

Based on Dashiell Hammett's novel, *The Maltese Falcon* (1941) is the screen's supreme private-eye picture, and yet, like *White Heat,* it has never felt "noir" to me, more like the best 1930s-style detective movie ever made and less like a harbinger of what was to come. Other novelists provided mid-decade Hollywood with sources that helped to establish film noir. Screen adaptations of James M. Cain books included *Double Indemnity* (1944) and *The Postman Always Rings Twice* (1946), similarly (and somewhat outlandishly) plotted yarns in which a man and woman plot to murder the woman's husband. (The moral may be "beware of blondes," or at least blonde wigs.) Though *Postman* bogs down in much too much plot and too many twists, *Double Indemnity* is noir's first classic. Directed by Central European-born Billy Wilder, *Double Indemnity* is set in pre-war Los Angeles, the city that quickly became film noir's most iconic playground, perhaps because of the potent built-in contrast that could be made with LA's dream-factory reputation. *Indemnity* makes tangy, textured use of the location, also offering stylish black-and-white visuals, cool-eyed treachery, and sharp quotable dialogue tossed off by Barbara Stanwyck and Fred MacMurray, all of which set a noir standard.

Novelist Raymond Chandler co-wrote the *Indemnity* screenplay, while two of his own books were made into noir classics themselves, both featuring his private eye Philip Marlowe, played by Dick Powell in Edward Dmytryk's *Murder, My Sweet* (1944) and by Humphrey Bogart in Howard Hawks' *The Big Sleep* (1946). Both are set in LA, naturally, with the famously incoherent plot of *The Big Sleep* carried by Bogart's wry likability, while *Murder, My Sweet,* with the equally good and sardonically funny Powell, is most memorable for its surreal drug-embellished nightmare. Despite tart dialogue, neither film is noted for emotional intricacies lurking within their plots. The same can be said for *The Killers* (1946), an expansion of an Ernest Hemingway short story. As directed by German-born Robert Siodmak, it was the most visually arresting noir thus far, making stars of Burt Lancaster and Ava Gardner in the process.

French-born Jacques Tourneur, a directing graduate of Val Lewton-produced horror movies such as *Cat People* (1942), made the noir leap brilliantly with *Out of the Past* (1947), in which the genre's key elements fell iconically into place, perfectly distilled. Consider its stunning high-contrast and insinuatingly mobile black and white, or the juxtaposition of pulpy twists and a plaintive post-war mood. Add a femme fatale, embodied by beautiful, smoldering Jane Greer (icy yet vicious), and an ideal anti-hero, an ex-private detective courtesy of Robert Mitchum, so smart, sexy, and tough (also sensitive and vulnerable). It's got the flashbacks and voiceovers, the zesty dialogue, and the California locales, but it's the tale's fatalistic inevitability and its encroaching sense of doom which provide the enduring ache, the pessimism that stings. Film noir, as never before, had uncovered a well of feeling, a humanity amid the gloom.

A late-'40s offshoot of film noir is the docudrama noir, a sub-genre that often combined noir's visual flamboyance with so-called realism to create rah-rah procedurals focused on US law-enforcement and government institutions, including the FBI (*The House on 92nd Street* – 1945, *The Street with No Name* - 1948), the Treasury Department (*T-Men* - 1947), the justice system (*Boomerang!* – 1947, *Call Northside 777* - 1948), NYC's homicide squad (*The Naked City* – 1948), and immigration (*Border Incident* – 1949). Most of these movies are somewhat square and over-glorifying, but the best of them, *Border Incident,* manages to make its official points and still be a sensational example of film noir, both in its darkened splendor and its violent agent-infiltration plot.

Among the lowest-budget film-noir examples, there's *Detour* (1945) from director Edgar G. Ulmer, another Central European. Though a no-budget quickie, *Detour* has textbook noir content and some inventive shots, plus a femme fatale (Ann Savage) without a single attractive feature. Formerly overlooked, *Detour* has come to be overrated. Joseph H. Lewis' *Gun Crazy* (1949), a riveting Bonnie and Clyde update, also went under the radar in its day. Ingeniously shot, it portrays crime as the most exciting aphrodisiac, with Peggy Cummins its shocking, deadly female, perhaps the genre's craziest.

Taking into account all these movies' unsavory behavior and snappy wit, their slinking ladies and trench-coated hunks, the shafts of light and accompanying shadows, and, most of all, all that cigarette smoke, there are still dozens of other black-and-white sleepers from the genre's vast output. The ten here are flawed but certainly worthwhile. So, light up, pour a shot, and try not to be such a chump.

Fallen Angel (1945): Dana Andrews and Linda Darnell

Fallen Angel (1945) – The success of *Laura* (1944), a splendid murder mystery (but too glamorous and genuinely romantic to classify as noir), led to this reunion of its director Otto Preminger, star Dana Andrews, cinematographer Joseph LaShelle, composer David Raksin, and costume designer Bonnie Cashin. Though not up to *Laura*'s high standard, *Fallen Angel* luxuriates in its moody, prowling camerawork and pleasurably pulpy set-up. Andrews, stranded and broke in central California, falls for slutty, sarcastic waitress Linda Darnell; they share a steamy rapport. As a way to finance his plans with Darnell, he pursues sweet, rich Alice Faye. After playing *Laura*'s tough but tender police detective, Andrews now excels as a hustler, a studly charmer with aggressive instincts. (Upon entering a seedy hotel room, Andrews says, "What a dump," four years before Bette Davis made the line *hers*.) He marries Faye, but he's also the prime suspect when Darnell is murdered. You'll be sorry when the luscious darkness of Darnell makes its final exit, especially because Faye (out of her musical-comedy sandbox) is lifeless in her non-singing goody-goody role. She may be top-billed, but it's Andrews and Darnell who shine, both film-noir models of smarts and simmering sensuality.

Cornered (1945) – Like Preminger and Andrews moving quickly from *Laura* to *Fallen Angel*, director Edward Dmytryk and his star Dick Powell followed the success of *Murder, My Sweet* with *Cornered,* an international noir—opening in London but primarily set in Buenos Aires—directly inspired by post-war insecurity. Like *Fallen Angel,* it cannot rate with its duo's previous film, though it's nonetheless a worthy follow-up. Powell is a shell-shocked former POW, a Canadian flight lieutenant, now seeking revenge on the Vichy war criminal responsible for the firing-squad execution of his wife, a member of the French Resistance. That's quite a hook, and the sleek visuals add luster, even though the film can be talky and confusing. Powell, about as far removed from his Busby Berkeley musicals as can be imagined, never smiles, by now having successfully completed his transition to hardened dramatic star. It's fascinating to watch this ex-juvenile actor playing so close to the edge, on the verge of breaking down. His new worn-out (yet obsessed) persona takes center stage, illuminating some of the enduring emotional ravages of WWII's survivors. Even sunny, chirping Dick Powell wasn't immune.

Desperate (1947) – With low-budget winners like this one, director Anthony Mann soon emerged as a key director of '40s noir, exhibiting a masterful control, and in this instance, even co-writing the story. *Desperate* deals explicitly with the perils of post-war anxiety and adjustment. Celebrating four months of wedded bliss, ex-G.I. Steve Brodie (a trucker with his own truck) and pretty blonde Audrey Long (who has just learned she's pregnant) are clearly on their way to achieving the American Dream. This is what we fought for, right? After Brodie unknowingly accepts a job linked to a warehouse heist led by Raymond Burr, the film turns into a nightmare with our perfect couple sabotaged by outside forces, perfect fodder for film-noir paranoia. In the film's most dazzling sequence, Brodie is beaten by Burr's thugs in their blackened hideout as an overhead light dangles from the ceiling, soon swirling about the room like a pendulum, plunging figures into alternating light and darkness, all of it superbly wrought by cinematographer George E. Diskant. (This is noir, folks!) With its young couple on the run, the film's driving force becomes Brodie's determination to protect his family and their future, whatever it takes. *Desperate* finally restores optimistic belief in our system, but not before immersing audiences in a series of high-stress situations, including a dilly of a showdown between Brodie and Burr: a pursuit traveling four floors of a walk-up apartment building. Brodie and Ms. Long are properly ordinary and nice-looking, while the nasty Burr dominates, notably in his obsessive attachment to his cop-killer brother. The plot is a fairly basic extended chase, but the tone is one of definite post-war discord.

They Won't Believe Me (1947) – Joining Dick Powell, Robert Young was another actor who shook up his light-comic image by "going noir." In Young's case it was with a kind of role usually reserved for females, a seductive yet unfeeling louse who uses and manipulates lovers for selfish, greedy ends. Dana Andrews had done this sort of thing in *Fallen Angel*, but what made it more startling this time around is that Young juggles three women: Rita Johnson, the woman he married for her money; Jane Greer, the magazine writer with whom he toys then dumps; and Susan Hayward, a gold digger. Young is debatable casting, not especially sexy or charismatic, yet maybe it's his very ordinariness and nice-guy professionalism which add that extra chill to his scheming. There's an appropriately troubling contrast between the women, all of whom really love him, and Young who is incapable of matching their emotions. Ms. Johnson, in the best role, is the standout and deeply touching as a woman who loves too much, unable to walk away even though she knows how little he's worth and how unloved she is. *They Won't Believe Me* has neat, clever plotting, but there's also room for the flashier flourishes of a fatal car accident, an off-screen leap off a cliff, and a memorable "shockeroo" ending. Irving Pichel's direction isn't always up to the script's crafty potential, but the movie effectively conveys the emotional divides between a heel and his women.

Raw Deal (1948) – In the year since *Desperate,* Anthony Mann has moved up in the world, directing three established actors—Dennis O'Keefe, Claire Trevor, Marsha Hunt—in this piece of beautifully Mann-handled pulp art. Photographed by John Alton, a Mann favorite, with especially stunning close-ups, *Raw Deal* is relentlessly, voluptuously visual. Set in San Francisco and the Northwest, it follows escaped prisoner O'Keefe (a noir regular), on the lam with moll Trevor and hostage Hunt. O'Keefe had taken the rap for crime boss Raymond Burr (back as another Mann villain), and now he wants the fifty grand Burr promised him. Burr, of course, would rather see him dead. The man-hunt plot is typical fare, but it's elevated by an interesting love triangle, to which most of the crime content takes a backseat. Trevor adores O'Keefe, but she knows deep down that he doesn't love her and never will. Though mighty hard-boiled, she's also insecure, threatened by good-girl Hunt (from the law office that defended O'Keefe). It's surprisingly affecting when Trevor, too smart for her own good, is the first to notice that O'Keefe and Hunt are falling in love before even they realize it. There's an expectedly pleasing contrast between trashy Trevor and ladylike Hunt, while O'Keefe is merely adequate, not innately hard enough for his macho role. In the film's bid for extreme noir brutality, Burr throws a flaming bucket of brandy on his girlfriend after she accidentally spills a drink on him. There's also a thrilling brawl between O'Keefe and two guys in a room filled with taxidermy (silent observers to the blistering action). *Raw Deal* is still Claire Trevor's movie. She provides its bruised heart and soul, which includes her plaintively self-aware narration. Incidentally, Trevor plays Pat Cameron, not Pat Regan (as it says in the final credits).

Cry of the City (1948) – With noir master Robert Siodmak (*The Killers*) at the helm, this feels like a noir-ish Italian-American riff on *Angels with Dirty Faces* (1938), as two neighborhood kids take opposing paths in adulthood, in this case as a homicide police lieutenant (Victor Mature) and a cop killer (Richard Conte). You might say that they are good and bad sides of the same coin. *Cry of the City* is a New York noir in which Siodmak and his cinematographer Lloyd Ahern make fine use of NYC locations and create a visual feast of rich, tingling images. Mature is just fine, but Conte (the Italian John Garfield) steals the show. Slick, charming, and scary, he has only one "good" quality—his love for girlfriend Debra Paget. If the drama feels uneven, the visuals never disappoint. The film's set piece is Conte's prison escape, with Siodmak meticulously sustaining the tension with dread-inducing details, as Conte, disguised as a visitor, carefully walks his way out of the joint. Baddie Hope Emerson has a great entrance, walking toward us from far back, an impossibly deep shot with the one-by-one additions of four light sources as she moves closer. The Italian-American ambiance feels fresh and convincing, and Mature, recently from the Italian-American world of *Kiss of Death* (1947), is Javert-like in his resolve to capture Conte. Again evoking '30s movies, their climactic showdown takes place outside a church. (For trivia lovers, this film features characters named Tony Rome, Mamma Roma, and Madame Rose.) As for Siodmak, *Cry of the City* is an overlooked feather in his noir cap, bookended by his two film-noir peaks, *The Killers* and *Criss Cross* (1949), with the latter the best of the trio, a flawless melding of the visual razzle-dazzle and the complex emotional undercurrents that constitute film noir at its finest.

Impact (1949) – Though convoluted and plot-heavy and with some hokey, silly touches, *Impact* is nonetheless an enjoyable grabber. Brian Donlevy is a big San Francisco executive who adores wife Helen Walker. After she was so devastatingly evil in *Nightmare Alley* (1947), it's no surprise that here Walker is a spoiled, calculating, and adulterous horror. In a page right out of James M. Cain, she and her lover (Tony Barrett) plot to kill Donlevy, but he survives being hit with a lug wrench and pushed into a ditch. It's Barrett who dies, in an explosive crash in Donlevy's car, with everyone assuming it's Donlevy who's dead. Depressed by it all, he ends up in Idaho and becomes a car mechanic at Ella Raines' gas station. The movie calms down while the tension builds over when he will finally confront Walker (who manages to raise her evil quotient). In the meantime, Raines is a pretty, sweet war widow and a convenient new love interest. When Donlevy goes on trial for Barrett's murder, Raines joins police lieutenant Charles Coburn (unlikely casting) to prove his innocence with help from no less than Anna May Wong (as Walker's maid). With its San Francisco locations, solid Donlevy performance, and decent direction from Arthur Lubin, *Impact* is a pleasurably overcomplicated noir. If there's any resonance to be found in its reliably churning plot, it comes from Raines' character. She represents all the war widows who, forced to change courses, were quietly creating new, uncharted lives for themselves.

Thieves' Highway (1949) – Playing a Greek-American, here's Richard Conte in his good-guy mode. Despite slackening pacing and plausibility, this is a particularly tough noir, intensely atmospheric in its gritty locations (mostly San Francisco). Conte is an ex-GI and ship mechanic who returns home to Fresno to find that his father lost his legs in a trucking accident, a set-up rigged by crooked Lee J. Cobb, a fruit and produce boss in Frisco. This is revenge noir, with Conte heading to Cobb, supposedly to sell him a truckful of apples. Nothing is easy in this movie, not even for a hardened GI, filled as it is with bad luck, reprehensible behavior, and harsh thrashings. Conte is extremely likable when he's strong and no-nonsense, but much less so when he disappoints us by behaving foolishly. The trucker scenes anticipate the great *Wages of Fear* (1953) in their visceral danger and grimy realism, including one terrifying sequence that ends in a fiery crash. Unfortunately, there's some bad casting: Cobb, our villain, overacts his way into absolute phoniness, laughing too loudly every chance he gets, and finally not believable enough to be legitimately scary; and Jack Oakie, a comic-relief trucker, is simply in the wrong movie and is too much his usual goofy self. As the Italian heart-of-gold tramp hired by Cobb to distract Conte, Valentina Cortese is no beauty but she's a nice mix of slinky and soulful. It's a good twist to have Barbara Lawrence, Conte's greedy fiancée, be a bad "good girl," and Cortese be a good "bad girl." There's a too-easy violent climax at a roadside cafe, certainly too easy for a movie in which everything has seemed such a struggle. Director Jules Dassin, soon to be blacklisted, offers tangible Californian ambiance and flavor, but he's less secure with the story and his actors. Despite needing more character depth, *Thieves' Highway* remains a good and unusual socially conscious noir. Its fatalism may be compromised, but that doesn't entirely negate the stark and disturbing world it brings teeming to life.

Red Light (1949) – Roy Del Ruth, best known for musicals, directed this offbeat, bizarrely original mix of noir and religiosity. The outstanding cinematography of Bert Glennon (*Stagecoach*) vivifies the drama, though the movie needs a more compelling actor than George Raft to carry it. Unfortunately, lovely Virginia Mayo is not a "bad girl" here, around merely to try to halt Raft's mad vengeance. It falls to portly Raymond Burr, by now an essential noir villain, to bring to the proceedings the necessary jolts. He went to prison for embezzling from Raft's San Francisco trucking company, and now he's seeking revenge by arranging the murder of Raft's beloved (and newly home) army-chaplain brother Arthur Franz. The riddle of Franz's dying words convinces Raft that the key to unmasking his killer lies within a missing hotel-room Bible. It's rather fascinating to watch this confused narrative attempt to balance its dirty murderous doings with its thick "inspiring" elements. However flawed, *Red Light* is certainly *not* run-of-the-mill. There's a knockout centerpiece, both a visual stunner and a throbbing nail-biter: Burr's hushed nighttime pursuit of Raft employee Gene Lockhart on the company grounds, creeping to a cruel crescendo. The rooftop climax in the rain is another showy eye-catcher, with its Raft-Burr confrontation on a blinking neon sign. Despite those strains of "Ave Maria," the film delivers the "noir" satisfaction to which its audience is entitled. It turns out that even God can have his fill of Raymond Burr.

Tension (1949) – The main event here is Audrey Totter, a premier femme fatale of film noir, an actress able to inhabit ever lower reaches of immorality and soullessness. Though it has its share of the genre's occupational hazard of lapses in believability (plus a sluggish pace from director John Berry), *Tension* is pretty good noir, elevated considerably by Totter's delicious rottenness. Dissatisfied with her war-veteran husband (Richard Basehart) and his low income as a drugstore manager, she's become a cheating wife, available to any man willing to spend money on her. (She comes with her very own promiscuous-sounding soundtrack, musically underscoring her every stinking move.) Cool-temperatured Basehart is the masochist who remains obsessed with her and is soon plotting a murder because of her. He creates a second identity in which his "disguise" consists only of wearing contact lenses rather than his usual glasses. (I wouldn't describe his plan as well-thought-out.) *Tension* is one of those movies in which someone can't go through with a murder, yet the intended victim turns up dead anyway. Thanks to nice girl Cyd Charisse, Basehart develops a less masochistic view of love, but, don't worry, Totter continues to be where the action is. Set in Southern California (of course), *Tension* is one of the last film-noir examples explicitly to address the post-war situation. The ugly marriage at its center is the result of Basehart being unable to fulfill the promise implied by how good he looked in his uniform. *Tension* confronts the corroding aftermath of post-war optimism—when prosperity didn't magically appear for wartime couples joined by little more than infatuation or lust—but it's not its social theme that holds the attention. When a guy approaches Totter at the drugstore counter, and is about to make an unwanted advance, she stops him dead with one word— "Drift." She almost makes you want to be a masochist, just so you can hang out with her.

Screwy Hooey: The Random Harvest Effect (1945-1950)

Sometimes one movie can spawn an industry of wannabes. *Rebecca* (1940) led to all those films about men of mystery and in-the-dark heroines residing in intimidating mansions, including *Rage in Heaven* (1941), *Dragonwyck* (1946), *Undercurrent* (1946), *Cry Wolf* (1947), and *Secret Beyond the Door...* (1948). *Meet Me in St. Louis* (1944) triggered a spate of period family musicals, such as *Centennial Summer* (1946), *Summer Holiday* (1948), and *On Moonlight Bay* (1951). *Samson and Delilah* (1949) was responsible for the Bible boom of the 1950s and '60s. Regarding Hollywood's mid-century propensity for looney-tunes melodrama, the culprit of inspiration was *Random Harvest*. Based on a James Hilton novel and released by MGM in December of 1942, *Random Harvest* was directed by Mervyn LeRoy and stars Greer Garson and Ronald Colman. It proved to be an essential piece of escapism for the home-front audience, a grandly mounted, dreamily photographed black-and-white movie arranged on storybook-England sets. The story's transporting appeal can mostly be explained by the fact that it has only the slightest resemblance to what might be termed reality. Yes, there has always been a taste for the addictive pull of outlandish movie melodrama—consider *Magnificent Obsession,* with popular versions from both 1935 and 1954, bookending the era being considered here. *Random Harvest,* however, upped the ante on outrageous plotting. An absurd amnesia-related love story—a situation that happens decidedly more frequently in movies than real life—*Random Harvest* is wacky enough to teeter along the edges of outright comedy. Let's just call it a screwball melodrama. Amnesiac Colman is mentally tangled between his former great love and his current wife of convenience, both played by Garson. The kicker is that she is not playing a dual role. Unbeknownst to memory-rattled Colman, she's the same person!

Colman's amnesia goes back to his service in WWI and 1917 asylum incarceration. When he emerges in 1918, he's immediately befriended by music-hall performer Garson who, too good to be true, quits her job to look after him. (He may have no memory, but she's got the screw loose.) They fall in love and marry, maintaining a polite platonic-feeling distance. (And who's paying for their darling cottage in Devon?) Colman is affably subdued, a shell of a man, and clearly no prize, yet Garson and, later, young Susan Peters, love him completely. (Plus, past 50, he's looking a tad mature.) Now here's where it gets daft. Hit by a taxi, Colman regains his memory but forgets the last three years (his life with Garson). Restored to his aristocratic position, he senses that something is missing. Garson, now his secretary, waits *patiently* for him to remember that she is his great love, dropping subtle hints. It's hard when the man you love is in love with someone else...*you!* When Colman enters politics, he proposes their marriage of convenience (legally she has become a widow). We wait for him—blasé about one Garson because he's hung up on another (whom he can't recall)—to sort it all out. She remains charming, beautiful, and radiantly warm, yet never a plausible character, just an exquisitely suffering movie queen. That, too, is part of the appeal, the satisfaction of watching wise, unperspiring Garson, so stalwartly undeterred in her hopes. After all, none of what happens could *ever* happen, keeping the drama, however inane, compulsively engaging. You don't believe a minute of it, but you can succumb with relish, just like wartime audiences did. (Talk about putting a world war out of your head!) The success of *Random Harvest* encouraged a cluster of movies aiming to emulate its narrative nuttiness (though never quite equaling it), piling on the twists and coincidences (as well as more amnesia), all involving circumstances unlikely to befall anyone. If audiences accepted Garson pining to be as loved as another woman— herself!—were there really any limits on how far screenwriters might dare to go?

Also from 1942 was the soapy sensation *Now, Voyager,* that irresistibly sympathetic portrait of an emotionally abused ugly-duckling daughter (Bette Davis) who, under the care of a psychiatrist (Claude Rains), becomes a swan with self-esteem. In addition to being one of Davis' finest hours, *Now, Voyager* solidified psychiatry as a major plot point of '40s melodrama, meaning that a number of movies had overtly psychological aspects to their over-the-top dramatic curves, including *Bewitched* (1945), *The Secret Heart* (1946), and *The Guilt of Janet Ames* (1947). Such films were meetings of lowbrow and highbrow, tying old-fashioned theatrics to newfangled psychology, the former a necessity to draw you in, the latter at-the-ready to explain everything.

Whether mental health was included or not, the *Random Harvest* effect provided the comfort of seeing problems—far more complicated than your own—tidily resolved. Here was an era in which most any plot, no matter how improbable, could be made consumingly enticing by charismatic stars, enveloping production values, and lubricating scores. What about *Mildred Pierce* and *Leave Her to Heaven,* two stylishly florid 1945 melodramas? Their respective themes—masochistic maternal martyrdom and psychotically possessive love—are too rational, too credible, for the all-out *Random Harvest* effect. The following films aren't about anything except plot turns. Cast aside the mundane to enter a world so eventful, so filled with secrets and deceptions, that your only recourse is surrender. Know that in the end, you'll be grateful your life is as comparatively boring as it is.

Love Letters (1945): Jennifer Jones and Joseph Cotten

Love Letters (1945) – Baldly inspired by *Random Harvest*, it's another amnesiac love story, and, like *Random*, the darn thing is both absorbing and appealing. Director William Dieterle crafted a fluid, attractive movie, enhanced by pretty Victor Young music, Lee Garmes' creamy black-and-white photography, and good dialogue from Ayn Rand (yes, *that* Ayn Rand). Joseph Cotten is a British soldier in Italy who plays Cyrano for a pal (Robert Sully), writing love letters to the guy's girl (Jennifer Jones) back in England. Like many a Cotten film, *Love Letters* is grounded by his gentle intelligence; there's nothing melodramatic about *him*. The focus eventually shifts to the now-amnesiac Jones and her quest to reclaim her memory. Jones' Oscar-nominated performance isn't in Cotten's league; she *is* melodramatic and also mechanical (though she does have a lustrous beauty). After her soldier love returned and married her, she became unhappy, disenchanted with her so-called letter-writing lover. Her memory loss has to do with his murder, for which she spent a year in prison (for manslaughter), though, of course, she's innocent. The film directly evokes *Random Harvest* when Jones marries Cotten, fearing he will never love her because he still loves someone else, not knowing that *she* is the other woman, the pen pal she doesn't remember being. (Before he meets her, Cotten refers to Jones as his "pin-up girl of the spirit.") The great Gladys Cooper, reteamed with Jones after *The Song of Bernadette* (1943), is Jones' adoptive guardian, giving one of her patented displays of formidable acting power and austere concentration. *Love Letters* instigates a free-for-all clash of British and American accents, with "British" Cotten so overwhelmingly American. (Jones gets off easily; she's playing a Canadian.) With its inviting country houses, heightened romanticizing, and contemporary *Cyran*-izing, *Love Letters* hits all the right buttons, steering clear of any reality check. Cotten, Jones, and Dieterle reunited for the sublime *Portrait of Jennie* (1948) whose fantasy plot feels truer and more emotionally resonant than anything in the supposedly earthbound *Love Letters*.

Spellbound (1945) – The most famous mix of psychiatry and unhinged plotting is this Ben Hecht-scripted Alfred Hitchcock hit, one of the director's weaker efforts. Utterly laughable in its simplistic psychobabble, *Spellbound* is straight-faced nonsense, a foolish romantic mystery tied to the cure-all of analysis. Ingrid Bergman is the wholesome, virginal, glasses-wearing psychoanalyst at a Vermont institution. Married to her work, she's told by a colleague that, romantically speaking, she's "like embracing a textbook." Will she ever be a *real* woman? The new boss (Gregory Peck), try though he might, can't conceal the fact that he's a crazy impostor and, yep, an amnesia victim. The stars fall in love instantly, and when Peck bolts to NYC and Bergman follows, she hopes to treat him on the run. Because Peck is just a good-looking cipher, she also has to do all the acting. He ought to be vulnerable and sexy and—due to the possibility that he's also a murderer—scary! Where's the alluring menace? Instead, he's all poses, all actorly uncertainty. Peck is a leading man in search of a performance, stranded by a script that keeps him in just a few stifling gears, his woodenness occasionally disrupted by a mad expression. The character can't bear lines, such as fork marks on a tablecloth or the design on a bedspread, but, don't worry, Bergman will explain everything perfectly, including Peck's Salvador Dali-designed dream. There's no end to her reckless, noble bravery, all that capable efficiency and resourcefulness, plus the doctorly gobbledygook she spouts so assuredly. Famed for its hyper-surging (and Oscar-winning) Miklós Rózsa score, *Spellbound* is never boring. It's high-minded twaddle, with glamorous stars, occasional visual treats from its director, and a speed course in brilliant analysis that must be worth at least three credits.

Tomorrow Is Forever (1946) – In keeping with the *Random*-inspired mix of the emotionally compelling and the dramatically confounding, this soap also follows the former film with a well-spent budget, which allowed for a Max Steiner score and Jean Louis fashions. Like *Random*, it begins with WWI's finish, with Claudette Colbert receiving a telegram that her husband, Orson Welles, died "over there." (We see them together in one flashback, at the time of his enlistment.) But Welles is alive, so badly wounded (including a disfigured face) that he chooses to keep his identity secret and remain "dead" in Europe. Married only a year, he left Colbert pregnant. Though Welles remains her great love, she marries wealthy chemical-company owner George Brent, who treats her son like his own. Set primarily in Baltimore, the plot jumps to 1939, with Richard Long the grown son, followed by a second son. When Welles returns, it's with a blonde-braided moppet (Natalie Wood, speaking German and giving a lovely, accomplished performance) whose parents were killed by the Nazis. Welles limps, uses a cane, and now has an Austrian accent, but, though bearded and gray, he still looks like himself. Brent has—are you ready?—coincidentally hired Welles as his specialist chemist, with neither man knowing that they are both married to *the same woman*. And Long doesn't know that Brent isn't his real father. Will Colbert recognize this Viennese scientist as her husband? If so, how long will it take? How insane that he's accidentally back in her life, another great love recast in the role of stranger (like Greer Garson before him). Welles really lays it on—makeup, accent, beard, limp, etc.—but Colbert gives a strong, persuasive performance, one of her best. With its return of a dead spouse, *Tomorrow Is Forever* is like a solemn reworking of *My Favorite Wife* (1940), but this time the "resurrected" hopes to remain a ghost.

A Stolen Life (1946) – It's a juicy opportunity for Bette Davis, playing well-fixed good-and-evil twins, but it's all plot over character, which is what makes it so mindlessly watchable. Davis puts on quite a show: properly reserved and pitiable as sensitive-artist Kate and glossy and brittle as no-good Pat. (It doesn't start feeling campy until Pat's delayed entrance.) The effect is that of watching *both* Bette Davis personae of the '40s meeting head-on: the victim (*Now, Voyager*) and the monster (*In This Our Life*). Or like seeing Davis play both roles—hers and Mary Astor's—in *The Great Lie* (1941). Glenn Ford is the boyish, dopey fellow, a New England lighthouse inspector wanted by both sisters. Though he and Kate are soulmates, he opts—no surprise—for the more sexual Pat, the Kate with "frosting." A convenient storm at sea has both Bettes (and no life jackets) in a sailboat, and bad Pat is knocked into the sea. All that good Kate is able to hold on to is Pat's wedding ring. With the ring now on Kate's finger, she is assumed to be Pat, wife of the man she loves! While trying to imitate her dead sister, she learns that the marriage is on the verge of divorce, and so she tries to win him back. (Because he no longer wants any part of slutty Pat, the movie can skirt the issue of Kate potentially jumping into bed with a man who isn't her husband.) Like Ronald Colman, Ford is now "married" to the person he truly loves but doesn't know it! Its crackpot plotting seems to exist in its own far-off universe, yet it's all smoothly served by director Curtis Bernhardt and set to a lushly incessant Max Steiner score. (Like *Random Harvest*, *A Stolen Life* received a classic spoof on Carol Burnett's television variety series, and, in both cases, little altering was needed to make the material screamingly funny.) As a none-too-bright object of desire, Ford, walking on eggshells as an actor, is an uninspiring lump, overwhelmed by one Davis, never mind two! (The stars reteamed, but were no longer romantically paired, for Frank Capra's dismal 1961 *Pocketful of Miracles*.) Despite Davis' dual-role flashiness, neither role has much depth, requiring her star power more than her artistry. The trick photography of the two Bettes works very well, part of an overall first-class mounting (at the tail end of Davis' reign as the queen of Warner Brothers). You can dismiss this movie as gimmickry, but when Davis made another twins melodrama, *Dead Ringer* (1964), it suddenly made the idiotic fun of *A Stolen Life* look like a probing exploration of sibling rivalry.

The Locket (1946) – Like the WWII movie *Passage to Marseille* (1944), *The Locket* is remembered, if at all, for its wild flashback structure, literally a flashback within a flashback within a flashback. Don't be alarmed, it's got plenty of fashionable (and hopeless) psychology to interpret everything. Following the *Random Harvest* playbook, *The Locket* intertwines emotional cliffhangers with ridiculous storytelling. Unfortunately, its star, Laraine Day, is a lackluster actress, never enthralling enough to be the central figure in such a deranged plot. Three men have come under her spell. She's about to marry Gene Raymond when psychiatrist Brian Aherne arrives to warn him about her (in the first flashback). Within Aherne's account, painter Robert Mitchum (miscast) arrives to warn Aherne about her (in the second flashback). After Day steals a bracelet, she recounts a childhood memory to Mitchum (in the third flashback), the locket episode that traumatized her, leading to later incidents involving theft, suicide, and murder. With a whammy of a final twist and some deft visual flourishes from director John Brahm, *The Locket* is intriguing yet unfulfilled, marred by uneven acting, analytical anemia, and its convoluted structure. Yet it is held together by the sheer chutzpah of its sensationalized doings.

Night Song (1947) – More than any other example, *Night Song* comes closest to achieving a *Random Harvest* state of unfathomable lunacy, duplicating its two-person love triangle. Dana Andrews is torn between Merle Oberon and Merle Oberon, not knowing she's the same woman. Just replace amnesia with blindness, and off we go! Andrews is a blind pianist-composer, a WWII veteran who lost his sight after the war, due to an accident caused by a drunk driver, leaving him angry and bitter. As a San Francisco socialite, Oberon, out slumming in a dive, becomes haunted by his music. Pretending to be blind, she befriends him and inspires him to finish his concerto. She arranges a composition contest, which he wins fair and square; his prize is the $5,000 needed for his vision-restoring operation. There's a lovely moment when he offers her his winnings to correct her own sight; she tells him she's beyond help. After his successful operation in NYC, Andrews balks at returning home. But what about that blind girl? Oberon hightails it east as herself, meeting him as the wealthy—furred, jeweled, and Orry-Kellyed—Oberon (photographed in all her black-and-white glory by then-husband Lucien Ballard). Speaking of his blind friend back home, he tells her, "Her voice was like yours." Yeah, exactly like it! Gently manipulating him—the way Greer Garson nudged the confused Ronald Colman—Oberon hopes he'll choose her blind counterpart, the *right* choice. Can he resist the fabulously devastating, liquid-eyed Oberon? We're complicit in her hope that he'll reject her, for *her*. Considering what he's up against, Andrews gives an especially restrained performance, and he's also quite credible in both his blindness and piano playing. Oberon fares less well acting-wise while still being ideal, offering hypnotic romanticism and a star's aura, both of which add more to *Night Song* than any great acting could. It shares its kitschy "serious" music background with other high-toned melodramas, such as *Deception* and *Humoresque,* both of 1946, offering a veneer of class, though, deep down, it's just enjoyably shameless hokum. Earnestly directed by John Cromwell, *Night Song* may also inspire you to finish that concerto buried in your piano bench.

Embraceable You **(1948)** – Here's an especially maudlin entry, which is probably why you haven't heard of it. The plot feels like something that might have worked as a late '30s vehicle for John Garfield and Priscilla Lane, but it actually stars Dane Clark and Geraldine Brooks, who seem like third choices and lack the personality to put it over. Clark, a getaway-car driver for a NYC gangster, rams into Brooks in a hit-and-run. Wracked with guilt, he visits her in the hospital, though he doesn't make a confession. It turns out that she has an inoperable aneurism and nowhere to go. Cop Wallace Ford, guessing Clark's guilt, forces him to care for Brooks, which includes a swell furnished apartment. She doesn't know she's dying but Clark *does*. There's an unintentionally funny scene when Brooks, a dancer, collapses during a tap audition (laughable because you see it coming a mile away). Naturally, a love story unfolds, even though Clark is like a sexless Garfield, generating few sparks with his co-star. Will Brooks figure out her fate, and that it was all Clark's doing? Can love conquer all? How many couples have a how-we-met story to match theirs? Though evoking *One Way Passage* (1932) with its law-troubled man and fatally ill woman and *Magnificent Obsession* (1935) with its female not knowing that *he* is the cause of her health crisis, *Embraceable You* is too morbid to be rivetingly make-believe.

The Forbidden Street **(1949)** – An odd duck that melds Victorian melodrama, Grand Guignol, backstage content, dual-role romance, and sex comedy, *The*

Forbidden Street shifts tones so often and so perplexingly that you can't get a handle on its intent. Director Jean Negulesco, often vitally good at creating unified worlds, can't achieve one here, despite the evocative design and moody black and white of a slummy English mews. Maureen O'Hara plays a rich girl of Victorian England, willfully marrying bearded Dana Andrews, a poor alcoholic painter. She moves into his mews address, soon feeling miserable and unloved. He conveniently dies in an accidental fall, but another Dana Andrews (clean-shaven) appears. I always hate it when an actor plays dual roles with the same voice, but that doesn't happen here. Andrews' first character is dubbed (by someone veddy British); the second character has Andrews' own (but British-accented) voice. The dubbing is unsettling but sensible, though both characters, however intriguing, are vaguely constructed devices. You might expect a mystery over whether or not it *is* the same guy, but the movie instead has the new Andrews starting a puppet theater. What? More expectedly, he and O'Hara fall in love. The best section involves a witch-like rag lady (a terrific and scarily believable Sybil Thorndike) out to blackmail O'Hara, but too much of *The Forbidden Street* borders on parody, strangely unbalanced between the overwrought and the lightweight, mired in coincidences and implausibilities. Where's the secure, however demented, narrative anchor and drive of a *Random Harvest* or a *Night Song*? Ms. O'Hara simply doesn't exhibit the presence or the variety to maneuver this misguided vehicle over its roughest passages.

The Secret Fury (1950) – Claudette Colbert is a concert pianist, making this another piece of preposterous trash with classy pretensions, even though it's at its best when luxuriating in film noir. Directed by Mel Ferrer, it begins when Colbert, about to wed architect Robert Ryan, is stunned when their ceremony is halted by allegations that she's already married. All kinds of people are soon recalling her marriage to a man she's never met, with no one seeming to believe Colbert's fierce denials. Is she crazy, or being driven crazy? With a title referring to insanity, *The Secret Fury* delivers two surprises unrelated to the plot: a bizarrely numb cameo from José Ferrer (as a musician) and a hotel-maid role for a pre-*I Love Lucy* Vivian Vance. Eventually on trial for murder, Colbert is prosecuted by Paul Kelly, the man she jilted for Ryan! On the witness stand, she howlingly overacts and who can blame her, what with the amount of unendurable distress flung her way? She gets a stint in a mental institution, but why, oh why, does no one ever consider who might have a motive in persecuting her? Once the victimized Colbert is locked away, *The Secret*

Fury ironically peaks, covering Ryan's action-packed noir-like investigation, which actually includes waterboarding. The movie adds up to a whole lot less than it might have, after all the hysteria is unsatisfactorily explained, but it surely provides a contagiously good ride. The similarly plotted (though quite differently motivated) British period thriller *So Long at the Fair*, also of 1950, is monumentally superior, but its emotional suspense operates on the same pleasurable principle of maddeningly elaborate machinations.

No Man of Her Own (1950) – You knew Barbara Stanwyck had to show up in this chapter. If nothing else, *No Man of Her Own* is consistent—ludicrous all the way. The whopper of a plot has Stanwyck flashing back to when she was pregnant in NYC and begging lover Lyle Bettger not to abandon her. Instead, he gives her a train ticket to San Francisco. On board she meets a nice married couple: Richard Denning and the also-pregnant Phyllis Thaxter. In the washroom Stanwyck tries on Thaxter's wedding ring and—BOOM—train wreck! Stanwyck wakes in a hospital having given birth to a boy, assumed by all to be Thaxter, still wearing the ring (*A Stolen Life* all over again). With Thaxter and Denning dead and with his family never having seen Thaxter, Stanwyck plays along for her baby's sake. She is welcomed by Denning's wealthy Illinois family, including bland John Lund as Denning's older brother. The family soon adores her and Lund falls in love with her, but, naturally, Bettger arrives, wanting a piece of Stanwyck's good fortune. Past forty and seemingly aware that she's too old for her role, Stanwyck appears to be on automatic pilot, while Bettger, not satisfied with playing a mere louse, is pure evil. The plotting grows more inconceivable, if possible, including the dumping of a body. This is a disappointing reteaming for Stanwyck and Mitchell Leisen, the man who directed her arguably greatest performance in *Remember the Night* (1940). Coincidentally, the two movies share a battered Stanwyck unexpectedly embraced by a loving family, but *No Man of Her Own* has none of the earlier film's enriching textures or intimate delicacy. It takes some head-scratching finagling to get to the happy ending, but that's why fans inhale the screwball melodramas, for their defiant vanquishing of the boundaries of logic. After toppling basic good sense and furnishing vicarious thrills and oversized emotions, only then do these movies restore us to a world in which a love triangle actually requires three people.

Pink Elephant in the Room: The Astonishing Stardom of Clifton Webb (1946-1954)

How does an actor make his talking screen debut at age 55, become a full-fledged movie star four years later, and, two years after that, the seventh biggest box-office attraction in America? It would be an impressive achievement for anyone, but it's downright incredible that the man in question was the formidably queer Clifton Webb. Adding to the amazement is the fact that this happened between 1944 and 1950, a most conservative time in the industry—not only while the Production Code ruled unconditionally but as the Red Scare was gaining traction, with all types of progressives headed for blacklisting. Yet this was the moment when a rather stereotypically gay man reached the heights of commercial success. Looking back on Webb's incontrovertibly prissy persona, one can't help but be reminded of what an innocent time, regarding sexuality, the mid-century was. Besides, no one really wondered (or cared) what middle-aged actors did in their bedrooms, and since there was no such thing as being "out," America was comfortably able to accept Webb as a "confirmed bachelor." But how did he get moviegoers to embrace him so wholeheartedly? Well, by sneering at them. The key to his popularity was his enviable way with a putdown, leveling people with his withering wit and giving audiences the vicarious thrill of wielding an indomitable verbal power. Webb's defiantly superior airs and rarefied manners suggested no interest in baser human instincts (of any orientation), rendering him among the nonsexual, those *beyond* sex, leaving fans to admire his real-life (and lifelong) devotion to his ever-present mother. That must be why he never married and had kids, *right*? (When Webb's mother died in 1960, Noel Coward is said to have quipped, "It must be terrible to be orphaned at 70.") By being too old for matinee-idol status, Webb never had to worry about potentially career-toppling exposure. He was free from the kind of anxiety that probably led to many sleepless nights for other gay actors, such as Ramon Novarro, Rock Hudson, and Tab Hunter. Juvenile Ross Alexander, whose homosexuality led to his suicide at 29 in 1937, had starred in *Here Comes Carter* (1936), ironically about a radio personality who dredges up the *real* dirt on Hollywood stars. With no public interest in his private life, Clifton Webb could be venerated as the epitome of amusing acerbity, and like Liberace, hide in plain sight.

Blithe bitchiness was Webb's specialty, but hadn't Claude Rains and George Sanders already projected a similarly waspish quality? Yes, but they played a wider range of characters than Webb, who became more of a personality star, someone who wouldn't veer *too* far from what you expected of him, which in his case meant a somewhat queeny performance. (Unlike gay Charles Laughton, Webb was no man of a thousand faces.) Yes, there were other gay-seeming characters throughout the Production Code era, including those fussbudget sissies played so extravagantly well by Franklin Pangborn, or all those bone-dry elitists etched by Henry Daniell, or the occasional bow-tie-wearing secretary such as Dan Tobin in *Woman of the Year* (1942) or a girl's best friend like David Wayne in *Adam's Rib* (1949). Webb upped the ante, parlaying his haughty grandeur into above-the-title stardom, well beyond the status of a prized supporting player.

Improbably, there was a gay peer of Webb's: Monty Woolley. One year Webb's senior, he became a film star not too long before Webb's sound debut in *Laura* (1944). In 1942 Woolley headlined *The Man Who Came to Dinner,* repeating his 1939 stage triumph, followed by *The Pied Piper* for which he received a Best Actor Oscar nomination. Audiences adored Woolley for the same snippy and persnickety ways soon to be capitalized upon by Webb, though Woolley tended to be more curmudgeonly than Webb (who drifted more toward flamboyance). Woolley would soon be relegated to supporting roles, just as Webb was rising to all-out stardom. Both men were American—Webb from Indianapolis, Woolley from NYC—yet many filmgoers probably mistook them for British because of their impeccable speech and breeding. Today, gay eyebrows arch when Woolley, as an old military man in *Since You Went Away* (1944), says, "I have handled men for 35 years." In *Night and Day* (1946), in which he plays himself opposite Cary Grant (as Woolley's also-gay pal Cole Porter), he calls Grant out on acting "like a guy who shouldn't have gotten married in the first place." After he sends flowers to Grant (laid up in a hospital), Woolley tells him, "One can only send them to a man when he's flat on his back."

Clifton Webb was born in 1889 as Webb Parmalee Hollenbeck (a perfect name for a Webb screen character). He made his Broadway debut in 1913, on his way to becoming a star of musicals, revues, and comedies—a real song-and-dance man. Though he made a handful of silent films, he mostly prospered on New York stages, in Jerome Kern's *Sunny* (1925) with Marilyn Miller, Rodgers and Hart's *She's My Baby* (1928) with Beatrice Lillie and Irene Dunne, and the Gershwins' *Treasure Girl* (1928) with Gertrude Lawrence, in which he introduced "I've Got a Crush on You." Among his comedies was *Meet the Wife* (1923) with a young Humphrey Bogart. Webb had a major success in Irving Berlin's revue *As Thousands Cheer* (1933), with Ms. Miller and Ethel Waters, and, in 1941, reached his theatrical peak when he starred in the original Broadway production of Noel Coward's *Blithe Spirit*. Who in his right mind could have predicted that Clifton Webb, past fifty, was about to become a major movie star?

Webb would make twenty films between 1944 and 1962, all of them for Twentieth Century-Fox. Otto Preminger's *Laura,* a gloriously moody and glamorous murder mystery, introduced him as Waldo Lydecker, a columnist who writes "with a goose quill dipped in venom." Waldo established Webb's star-making persona, effete and snotty, yet so appealing for his devilish humor, his ever-entertaining aplomb with an insult. Luckily, the sophisticated ambiance and witty dialogue matched his skills. Is Waldo gay? Yes, in his desire to love Laura (Gene Tierney) not in a literal sense but as a possession, like the other beautiful, priceless objects he has acquired. He molds her into a woman worthy of his refinement and makes her his supreme accessory. Webb takes definite notice of detective Dana Andrews, a hunky inferior, referring to him as "muscular and handsome in a cheap sort of way," a man who brings the possibility of actual sex into Laura's life. Waldo is a complex, mesmerizing fellow, and Webb is superb, acting with intricate artistry and nuance, garnering a Best Supporting Actor Oscar nomination. His next film, *The Dark Corner* (1946), cast him as a Waldo wannabe in a film-noir setting. It isn't bad, but it's no *Laura,* with Webb a gallery owner/art collector in another plot in which a female portrait is significant. Though he's married this time, Webb again seems to be a gay man obsessed with beautiful things.

The big years of Webb's career, 1946-1954, arrived after *Laura* had made him a name, continuing through a series of enormous box-office hits, helped along by a character who would prove to be more associated with Webb than even Waldo, a guy asexually named Lynn, also known as Mr. Belvedere.

The Razor's Edge (1946): Clifton Webb and Gene Tierney

The Razor's Edge (1946) – "If I live to be a hundred, I shall never understand how any young man could come to Paris without evening clothes." That says it all about Webb's character, Elliott Templeton, a high-society snob, probably the most effeminate character he ever played ("I have a flair"). Elliott is a wealthy, useless man, with no wife nor any love life. He's pals with Somerset Maugham (Herbert Marshall) who also happens to be the gay author of the novel on which this film is based, here taking part as a dry observer. This popular Best Picture Oscar nominee was a comeback for Tyrone Power, who had been off the screen three years for his service in WWII. It's a tony literary adaptation that plays as high-minded drivel. Power is a WWI veteran who leaves Chicago society to embark on a remote quest for enlightenment, which includes blue-collar jobs, Parisian bohemia, and a trip to India, all of which lead to his glazed beneficence. Stymied by the role's hollow spirituality, Power languishes in a boring higher-plane trance. This is a long, lavish affair, primarily set in France, with handsome 1919 and '20s period flavor. Its box-office appeal was derived from its soapier aspects, especially Gene Tierney as its lovely over-the-top bitch, a rich brat who marries John Payne while yearning for Power. Webb is imperiously prissy as Tierney's uncle (a reunion for them after *Laura*), and his performance would be just another Waldo variation if not for his deathbed climax, in which he's emotionally bare, reeling from a stinging social snub. Highlighting the man's pitifully trivial nature, Webb locates the insecurity beneath the façade, the awareness of how soon he'll be forgotten, his armor replaced by touching vulnerability. Webb was Oscar-nominated, but the film belongs to an Oscar-winning Anne Baxter for her deeply felt performance as a sweet ingénue destroyed by tragedy, a showy, alcoholic downward-spiral that's vividly alive and achingly fragile. *The Razor's Edge* has a high gay quotient, not just because of Webb and Maugham but also Edmund Goulding, its director. It is downright clairvoyant when Mr. Marshall (as Maugham) tells Webb that he's "sitting pretty."

Sitting Pretty (1948) – This was Webb's first screen comedy and first onscreen leading role, and it brought him his third (and final) Oscar nomination (for only his fourth Fox film). It was his sole nomination as Best Actor, even though he's third-billed and doesn't enter until twenty-five minutes into the 84-minute movie. But it's his show all the way. Essentially, the premise transplants Waldo Lydecker into a suburban sitcom, a good (if one-joke) set-up, allowing for plenty of Webb's traffic-stopping glares and snide one-liners. Shiny, optimistic post-war America is no match for the high standards of Webb's Mr. Belvedere. In answer to an ad, he becomes resident babysitter to the three sons of Maureen O'Hara and Robert Young. (The movie is so completely Webb's that, if you've seen it, I'll bet I had to remind you who plays the top-billed parents.) Belvedere has *been* everything and can *do* everything ("I am a genius"). He's a bow-tie-wearing, yoga-loving vegetarian and, oh yeah, he hates kids. In a stereotypically female job, he's a Mr. Mary Poppins, transforming the entire household overnight. Webb became a resounding star at one particular moment, his famous reaction to being pelted with cereal by the high-chaired baby: he dumps the bowl on the kid's head. Though you probably recall the moment, it actually happens off-screen; what's *seen* is the crying boy wearing the bowl. (Belvedere might have looked too mean if actually caught in the act.) The sons love him almost immediately, even though there isn't any reason why. How interesting that there's another feminized male in the neighborhood, an iris-breeding mama's boy and gossip (Richard Haydn), but Belvedere loathes him, in no way seeing him (or anyone else) as a possible kindred spirit. Competently directed by Walter Lang, *Sitting Pretty* is conventional and pleasantly uninspired, elevated considerably by Webb's unflagging precision and caustic delivery. Though there's more going on with Belvedere than is first revealed, Webb isn't really challenged, merely doing his thing, ever so expertly.

Cheaper by the Dozen (1950) – In a real twist, Webb played the father of twelve in this wildly popular family comedy in which none other than perfect-wife Myrna Loy was his spouse. An example of wholesome period Americana (set in 1921, primarily in Montclair, NJ), *Cheaper by the Dozen* is plotless and episodic, as well as being pat, square, and overly sure of its charms. Webb plays an industrial engineer (an efficiency expert) and a militaristic patriarch. He has a large personality, pushy and opinionated, as usual, but with a key difference: he's a real softie at heart, an affectionate husband, a committed father, and no longer a Lydecker, more a watered-down Belvedere. While allowing for some of his typically grand airs, the movie sentimentalized his appeal, and it worked. The public's acceptance of husband-father Webb expanded his casting possibilities, unexpectedly adding "family man" to his range. I don't especially enjoy watching him engage in domestic huffing and puffing, nor uncharacteristically pushing for laughs. Loy, maybe in response, underplays to the point of being strangely muted, seeming all tired out, perhaps because she's given so little to do, even though she's playing a psychologist. Poor Jeanne Crain: at twenty-five she's cast as a sixteen-year-old, *after* playing in *A Letter to Three Wives* and *Pinky,* both major adult hits of 1949. While trying to convince us of her youth, she's threatened by Webb with exile to a convent whenever she shows interest in makeup or boys. You'll perk up for Mildred Natwick (from Webb's Broadway stint in *Blithe Spirit*) and her one scene as a member of Planned Parenthood who speaks about birth control. (She is shocked to learn that Loy has twelve kids.) As "cute" family goo goes, the movie (directed by *Sitting Pretty*'s Walter Lang) isn't too bad, and, if nothing else, proved that audiences would believe Webb had slept with a woman twelve times. After pulling at your heartstrings, there's a fresh feminist ending, all leading to 1952's *Belles on Their Toes.*

For Heaven's Sake (1950) – Teaming a top-billed Webb with Fox's other later-life star, Edmund Gwenn (an Oscar winner for 1947's *Miracle on 34th Street*), resulted in this fairly awful (and unofficial) pairing of Belvedere and Santa, courtesy of *Miracle* writer-director George Seaton. This cloying whimsy features the duo as angels, but the emphasis is on treacle rather than laughs. It's a '50s pro-procreation fantasy that labels childless married couples as unfulfilled and selfish. Robert Cummings is a Broadway director-producer, and Joan Bennett is his star-wife, both too career-driven to become parents. Here's where it gets creepy: Gigi Perreau plays the couple's unborn child, desperately waiting for them to wise up, fornicate, and bring her into the world. (Why is she currently a nine-year-old?) To intervene properly, Webb becomes mortal and poses as a Texan "angel" interested in backing the couple's new play. Modeling himself specifically on Gary Cooper in *The Westerner* (1940), Webb is more game than hilarious, while wonderful Joan Blondell is wasted in the degrading role of a playwright out to seduce him! An utterly misguided venture, it's far beneath Seaton's usual skill level; he had recently made the marvelous *Apartment for Peggy* (1948), also with Gwenn. The one and only bright spot here is Jack La Rue as a gangster-playing movie actor who thinks he's *really* a tough guy. It is noteworthy that Ms. Bennett plays (eventually) a pregnant woman in the same year she was Elizabeth Taylor's mother in *Father of the Bride*. Bob Cummings makes a casual mention of one of their previous stage productions, *Footsteps on the Ceiling,* a made-up title also featured in *All About Eve* (from earlier in 1950). Aside from these tidbits of trivia, this sorry slop is worth enduring for one moment: after descending a staircase in painful cowboy boots, Webb announces, "These high heels are killing me."

Mr. Belvedere Rings the Bell (1951) – After the boffo success of *Sitting Pretty,* Webb was next seen in *Mr. Belvedere Goes to College* (1949), a limp follow-up, with everyone's favorite snarky babysitter going through four years of college in one year (and becoming valedictorian). The sequel foolishly mired itself in a romantic subplot between Shirley Temple and Tom Drake, but Webb still got to make crepes and give waltz lessons. The movie's "high heels" moment comes when he's jailed and makes his one phone call…to pal J. Edgar Hoover! Far superior was the third and final installment, based on a 1948 non-Belvedere play, *The Silver Whistle,* altered to accommodate him. Webb is crisply civilized as ever, and the film, directed by Henry Koster (*The Bishop's Wife*), is a modest treat. It's the rare movie about old people, with Belvedere crashing an old folks' home and reviving the spirits of some lonely, forgotten seniors. At 62, Webb is playing a 46-year-old man passing himself off as a spry 77. (It's easier to believe him as 77 than 46.) The home is church-sponsored but has fallen on hard times, with Hugh Marlowe the reverend in charge and Joanne Dru his smitten nurse. You expect their subplot to be irritatingly coy but, refreshingly, it isn't. Belvedere is on a personal investigation of old age, ditching his lecture tour in the process. (He is, oh yes, a best-selling author.) Webb refuses to let the film become nauseating; it remains winning, likable, even poignant. When contrivances arrive, well, you're already hooked by then. Treating the aged with dignity and sympathy, this movie is *Cocoon* without aliens. In his three years of playing fairy godfather, Belvedere graduated from little kids to college students to the elderly.

Dreamboat (1952) – In *Elopement* (1951), a minor Henry Koster comedy, Webb plays the industrial-designer father of an overachieving Anne Francis. Its final line, uttered by Webb in response to Francis' marriage to William Lundigan, is, "And, as for children, well, her favorite movie is *Cheaper by the Dozen.*" You know you're a huge star when you can make a joke like that and it's assumed *everyone* will get it. A year later, Webb played Francis' father again, in the far superior *Dreamboat,* a bright little comedy teaming Webb with Ginger Rogers. He plays a college professor, Thornton Sayre, a widower with a dark secret: he *was* "Bruce Blair," a Douglas Fairbanks-like silent-screen star. Current television showings of his films, hosted by his former co-star (Rogers), embarrass and anger him, prompting his trip to NYC to stop the station's airings. The generous clips of the two stars in their fake silents are nicely detailed and highly enjoyable (the same year that *Singin' in the Rain* was having similar fun). Webb is a delight in one of his best roles, and Rogers is awfully good, too, though given far less to do. Written and directed by Claude Binyon, *Dreamboat* gently satirizes television, as well as affectionately lampooning silent-film clichés. Ms. Francis is paired with Jeffrey Hunter; they're attractive in a predictable subplot. However, as the unmarried president of the college, Elsa Lanchester makes the most of her supporting role, dropping a proper exterior to reveal her crush on "Bruce Blair," *throwing* herself at Webb three times! He resists, of course, but it's such a joy to watch Lanchester lose her dignity in pursuit of her idol, hijacking yet another movie. It ends with a preview screening of *Sitting Pretty,* seen here as Bruce Blair's comeback vehicle. Once a star, always a star.

Titanic (1953) – The success of Lynn Belvedere and *Cheaper by the Dozen* meant that Webb was a comedy force, and projects like *Laura* and *The Razor's Edge* might never come his way again. One might have expected him to play

Addison DeWitt, the Oscar-winning George Sanders role in Fox's *All About Eve* (1950), but perhaps he was, by then, too big a box-office name to accept supporting roles. He did undertake a change of pace, starring in the John Philip Sousa biopic *Stars and Stripes Forever* (1952), and it was another popular success, but *Titanic* was his most serious endeavor thus far into the '50s. Call it *Grand Hotel* with an iceberg; it's banal and soapy yet undeniably effective and good-looking. It surmounts its shallower aspects because of director Jean Negulesco's sure pacing and an admirably convincing climax. Aboard ship is dapper captain Brian Aherne; married socialites Barbara Stanwyck and top-billed Webb, their teen daughter Audrey Dalton, and younger son Harper Carter; filthy-rich (and underused) Thelma Ritter, a fictionalized Molly Brown; and Richard Basehart, an alcoholic defrocked priest. Stanwyck isn't at her best; she's frozen-faced, with occasional outbursts of emotion, trying to escape an unhappy marriage. Webb, meanwhile, is customarily priggish, with his nose in the air. Ms. Dalton is snooty like her father until she warms to a dreamy tennis-playing Purdue boy (Robert Wagner), making them the Leo and Kate of this version. Stanwyck admits to Webb that their son isn't *his*, the result of a one-night stand! This means Webb wants nothing more to do with the boy who, of course, adores him. When Webb says, "I am not a man of character," it is an obvious set-up for his emotional redemption. The iceberg doesn't arrive for sixty-seven minutes, and even then, it doesn't really steal focus from Webb. Well before his moving climax with the boy, Webb owns this movie. Though more dramatically efficient than the overrated 1997 blockbuster, this *Titanic* received an excessively kind reward, an Oscar for story and screenplay.

Mister Scoutmaster (1953) – They might as well have called it *Mr. Belvedere Gets a Merit Badge*. As a television personality who needs to reach a younger demographic, Webb decides to find out what kids like and becomes a scoutmaster. He's in a childless marriage with Frances Dee, but, honestly, can an adoption be far behind? It's typically pandering, '50s-sitcom domesticity, and before you can say *Sitting Pretty*, Webb is dumping a dish of melted ice cream on a bratty scout's head. Unlike the more adult *Dreamboat*, we're back in one of Webb's tepid and mushy "family" comedies. When he goes "camping," it's not the kind you may be hoping for. (But here he is breaking the ban on gay scout members, leaping decades!) As usual, the scouts come to love Webb though we can't guess why. He thaws, expectedly, but the inferior material spotlights the fact that this formula has been too many times to the well. Reuniting with Webb after *For Heaven's Sake,* Edmund Gwenn, as a reverend, is squandered. Gwenn quotes John Donne's words—"...for whom the bell tolls; it tolls for thee"—which is bizarre because Webb's character name is Robert Jordan, the same as Gary Cooper's in *For Whom the Bell Tolls* (1943). Webb was reportedly offered the plum role of Jeffrey Cordova in MGM's *The Band Wagon* (1953), another supporting role out of line with his star standing. Despite Jack Buchanan's fey brilliance in that part, Webb might have been equally fabulous had he gotten his gloves on it.

Three Coins in the Fountain (1954) - A massive box-office hit and a ludicrous Best Picture Oscar nominee (in a year that overlooked *Rear Window*), *Three Coins* was buoyed by its Oscar-winning title tune (sung by Frank Sinatra). As a glossy, colorful CinemaScope travelogue (of Rome and Venice), tied to daytime-serial plot threads, it's all so coy, virtuous, and dated in its frightful marriage-mindedness. Following his *How to Marry a Millionaire* (1953), Jean Negulesco made this other three-girl buddy picture, mingling the romantic escapades of American secretaries working in Rome, with Jean Peters falling for virile co-worker Rossano Brazzi, and Maggie McNamara setting a trap for wealthy prince Louis Jourdan. As for Dorothy McGuire, she's pining for Webb, an American novelist, having been his indispensable secretary for fifteen years, silently and masochistically in love with him when she could be chasing cute Italian boys. Such a self-pitying drag, how can we feel sorry for her? Webb is a 60-ish, urbane bachelor, undoubtedly a gay man, a gent with dyed reddish hair, including a mustache and goatee. He has a substantial ego, and this mediocre movie could use much more of his sting. When McGuire finally threatens to return home, Webb realizes he'll be unable to function without her. He proposes, speaking of "companionship," "respect," and "no surprises" (as in "no sex"), telling her she's the only woman to whom he would make such a "rash offer." He also claims, at his age, to be beyond passion. Webb's acting is elegantly understated, offering a delicacy nowhere else present. He is, as usual, top-billed, but *Three Coins* is slick schlock, a thin and whiny crowd pleaser that even his classy-old-queen performance could carry only so far. Webb and McGuire reteamed for *The Remarkable Mr. Pennypacker* (1959), a poor attempt at mixing *Cheaper by the Dozen* with sophisticated adult comedy, with Webb a bigamist in, no kidding, the sausage business. He's a free thinker with two families (unknown to each other), totaling seventeen children! Wouldn't it make more sense to discover that it was a man he had stashed away?

Woman's World (1954) – Again, it's Negulesco, three central ladies, and Webb top-billed, this time for a female-centric comic slant on *Executive Suite* (from earlier that year). Fashionable and skin-deep, it's mildly entertaining, though drearily tied to '50s conformity, with a mixed message celebrating both homespun values and consumerism. Compensating for the script's shortcomings are the all-star cast and a CinemaScope travelogue of NYC. As owner of a car company, Webb is seeking a replacement for his deceased general manager, inviting three of his district managers (and their wives) to New York to compete for the job: Cornel Wilde and June Allyson (Kansas City, three kids), Fred MacMurray and Lauren Bacall (Philadelphia, two kids), and Van Heflin and Arlene Dahl (Dallas, no kids). The three candidates are good, dull fellows, played accordingly, while Webb is in eunuch mode, unmarried, naturally. His wall of nine photos of glamour girls, meant to imply his history as a womanizer, instead just makes him look like a diva-worshipping gay boy. The movie asks us to find Allyson lovable for her unpolished Middle-American "authenticity," also giving her points for disliking Manhattan. She's so condescendingly "down to earth" that you want to swat her. Bacall comes off well because she's likably low-key, while Dahl, the film's voluptuous goddess, is set up as "bad" because she's childless, ambitious, and sexual. She, of course, *loves* New York! What can she be thinking when she makes a play for Webb? She kisses him, and after she leaves, he wipes his mouth. Hey, she could still show up on his wall of "beards." Webb made a fourth and final Negulesco film, *Boy on a Dolphin* (1957), which introduced Sophia Loren to US audiences. A junky, clunky B-movie adventure with great Greek locations, it cast Webb as a cultured collector of ancient treasures. Its most Webb-ish moment comes when he responds to a man proudly brandishing a switchblade: "I suggest you use that on your fingernails."

CODA: Webb, who died at 76 in 1966, also starred in *The Man Who Never Was* (1956), a solid thriller that cast him against type as a British officer in a real-life WWII caper. It was the butchest role he ever got which he handled quite plausibly, flashing wit without being too flashy. *Holiday for Lovers* (1959) was the last of his forced family comedies, this one pairing him with Jane Wyman as parents of two daughters. Within the film's bad-taste sense of fun, their South American adventure includes a family strip search at an airport. Leo McCarey's *Satan Never Sleeps* (1962) was Webb's final film, a superficial stinker based on a Pearl S. Buck novel, an off-key comedy-drama set at a mission in 1949 China, a two-priests movie in the tradition of McCarey's

Going My Way (1944), again following a young priest (William Holden) and an older one (Webb) at odds. A white-haired Webb fusses around, dryly bitchy, best in his more emotional scenes. Ironically, it was *Going My Way*'s old-priest Barry Fitzgerald who beat Webb when he was first Oscar-nominated for *Laura*. Though there never was an Oscar awarded to Clifton Webb, there were eighteen years of acclaim, popularity, a defining signature role, plus a lavender legacy like no other.

Heaven Can't Wait: The Post-War Appetite for Fantasy (1947-1949)

When most classic-film fans think of the immediate post-war era in American film, they probably think about the screen's new maturity, a product of the nation's recent experiences with loss and sacrifice (notwithstanding victory), as well as the acceptance of a reality which contained such unfathomable truths as the Holocaust and atomic bombs. Hollywood grew up in a way it hadn't since its pre-Code days, a time when it had dealt with the Depression, organized crime, Prohibition, and adult sexuality. The issues were different a decade later, but the impulse seemed similar, to move closer to reflecting the world as it was *right now*. This obviously included America's transition to peacetime, best exemplified by William Wyler's masterpiece *The Best Years of Our Lives* (1946), a moving time capsule in which three servicemen make unsteady but ultimately optimistic adjustments to civilian life. The era's new openness went beyond the specifics of the war's impact on our nation with movies delving into subjects previously shied away from or addressed less directly: alcoholism (*The Lost Weekend,* 1945), anti-Semitism (*Gentleman's Agreement,* 1947), rape (*Johnny Belinda,* 1948), mental illness (*The Snake Pit,* 1948), and racism (*Pinky,* 1949). Another development was the emergence of a new genre, film noir, which was a more stylized expression of post-war maturity, noted for its mood of disenchantment and its pessimism about victory's promising aftermath. Hollywood's new penchant for darker fare was also influenced by the stunning neo-realism coming out of war-ravaged Europe with movies such as Roberto Rossellini's *Open City* (1945) bringing a visceral rawness to narrative film. Amid the adult issues, the noir angle, and the Italian imports, there was also an accompanying rejection of it all, a spate of comic fantasies that luxuriated in soothing comforts, complete faith in the future, and welcome intervention from all manner of magical fix-its.

This sudden rush of fantasy films (most of them aimed at adults) provided blatantly alternative choices for those uninterested in downbeat, once-forbidden subjects. After all, not everyone was wishing that movies were closer to real life, and there will always be people who tell you that they don't want to see movies designed to make them *think*. The fantasies of the late '40s now look like a cuddly (but defiant) antidote to the movies' swerve toward a loss of innocence. They were all-out assurances that the movies were still the best place to escape one's worries and blot out the real world. Yes, there had always been fantasy films, just not so many big ones clustered together. Ironically, or perhaps logically, the trend of issue-oriented realism spawned the companion trend of consoling fairy tales, two honest (and popular) reactions to recent history.

There's no getting around the fact that fantasy, specifically when meant for adults, is about mortality, or, rather, the avoidance of it. In the wake of so many thousands not coming home from the war, here were movies proclaiming that there were other forces at work: angels or ghosts or whatever (and usually played by the most charismatic movie stars). Whether you were religious or not, there was something mysterious and wondrous happening at the movies with a hint that just maybe those lost loved ones were part of this happily-ever-after beyond reality.

There had been some notable fantasy films made during the US involvement in World War II, occasional visits to the genre that don't appear to signify any kind of trend. Comedies such as Ernst Lubitsch's *Heaven Can Wait* (1943), with its scenes set in Hell, and Rene Clair's *It Happened Tomorrow* (1944), in which a knowledge of the future proves to be dangerous, were period pieces removed from the war. (Mr. Clair also made the slight, self-explanatory 1942 *I Married a Witch*.) Other films melded fantasy into the war, including the bathetic *A Guy Named Joe* (1943), in which a dead flyer turns guardian angel, and *Between Two Worlds* (1944), a wartime update of the sentimental old chestnut *Outward Bound,* with a ship headed to the afterlife and its passengers judged by "examiner" Sydney Greenstreet! Two other war-themed fantasies starred Robert Young: *The Canterville Ghost* (1944), a "spirited" but flimsy comedy with ghost Charles Laughton roaming an English castle; and *The Enchanted Cottage* (1945), another update, an exceedingly romantic account of a house's "response" to the love between a sad, homely woman and a disfigured WWII flyer. Among the final fantasies of the war era were two musicals: *Where Do We Go from Here?* (1945), a misstep with some merit, in which Fred MacMurray takes a genie-induced odyssey through US history; and *Wonder Man* (1945), with *two* Danny Kayes, one of them the ghost of a nightclub headliner.

It would seem that in December of 1946 one picture decidedly kicked off the post-war fantasy spurt, a film beloved as few films are. However, *It's a Wonderful Life,* despite its Best Picture Oscar nomination, didn't do for post-war audiences what it has been doing to movie lovers at least since its rediscovery in the '70s. Perhaps the combination of Frank Capra and James Stewart was deemed *so* last decade, so *Mr. Smith,* denoting a pre-war datedness, even though the film itself is unexpectedly dark. It's that very darkness, the way it brings all-American Stewart to the brink of suicide, from which it derives its primal power. Capra's film represents a perfect mix of post-war panic (plunging a man from promise to despair) and fantasy (thanks to an angel's visit and the nightmare he presents). It's hard to believe that the film's theme—that each of us makes countless positive differences in the world— could ever *not* resonate. And yet *It's a Wonderful Life* famously didn't set box offices afire, and therefore can't take credit for instigating the post-war trend of fantasy-inspired entertainments. It was a few hits from 1947 that proved audiences' hunger for such distractions, through to the end of the decade.

Comedy seemed an important component of the post-war fantasies embraced by the public. A dramatic example, and a box-office disaster, is the romance *Portrait of Jennie* (1948), a finely honed, hypnotic work about a love outside time, with Joseph Cotten and Jennifer Jones trying to synchronize themselves despite fate's error. Another affecting dramatic fantasy is *The Boy with Green Hair* (1948), a flawed but extremely offbeat anti-war allegory aimed at kids. For the most part, this was an era of merrymaking fantasies, from obscurities such as *Heaven Only Knows* (1947), in which Robert Cummings is an angel out West, to box-office champs like the unenchanting *A Connecticut Yankee in King Arthur's Court* (1949), in which Bing Crosby time-travels from 1912 to 528. Here are ten more ways that post-war moviegoers warded off reality, just as a new threat—the Cold War—was becoming the latest worry.

One Touch of Venus (1948): Ava Gardner

Miracle on 34th Street (1947) – After making one of the era's worst fantasy films, the morbid treacle known as *Sentimental Journey* (1946), Maureen O'Hara and John Payne were reteamed for one of the best. Like *It's a Wonderful Life*, it earns its joyful destination by acknowledging and confronting skepticism and disillusionment. Macy's employee O'Hara, bruised by divorce, is anti-fantasy and does not want her daughter (second-grader Natalie Wood) to grow up with lies about true love and fairy-tale endings, raising her to be precociously realistic (and no fun at all). Payne is a lawyer who hopes to make O'Hara believe in love again and to help Wood enjoy childhood. Enter Kris Kringle (Edmund Gwenn, in his Oscar-winning performance) and his challenging mission to cure mother and daughter of their tarnished outlooks. The magic isn't just Santa but Gwenn himself; it's the perfect meeting of actor and role. Gentle yet strong, wise yet funny, his touch couldn't be lighter, his charm couldn't be greater. He develops an engaging bond with young Wood, who, incidentally, makes such a skillful transition from practical to playful that it's hard to believe she didn't get one of those special Oscars generously awarded to remarkable child performances in the 1940s. It is deeply satisfying and touching to watch O'Hara and Wood come out of their ruts, and to see O'Hara warm up to Payne. All of it is gracefully assisted by Gwenn, who gets the last word in the unforgettable capper. With its background of Christmas consumerism run amok, plus Gwenn's sanity on trial, the movie deftly keeps the real world in view, a land of cynics (in business, politics, the justice system), which, again, makes the triumphant whimsy all the more gratifying. Written and directed by George Seaton (who won an Oscar for his screenplay), *Miracle* was a Best Picture Oscar nominee. It also introduced the great Thelma Ritter, who, as a shopper perplexed by Macy's new Santa-inspired customers-ahead-of-profits policy, parlayed a scene-stealing three minutes into a major career. The film's big line is, "Faith is believing in things when common sense tells you not to," as good a mantra as any for this era's fortifying fantasies.

The Ghost and Mrs. Muir (1947) – Combining comedy and drama, it's primarily a captivating romantic fantasy about an impossible love between a beautiful widow and the ghost of a salty sea captain. Though the film is set at the dawn of the twentieth century, it's reasonable to assume that WWII's many bereaved females connected with its heroine, Mrs. Muir (Gene Tierney), in her striving for an independent new life, leaving London behind for supposed tranquility. At Gull Cottage, a seaside house atop a cliff, she must contend with the house's ghostly tenant (Rex Harrison). So much for tranquility!

He likes her spunk, and their verbal sparring is indeed enjoyable. It's a sexy set-up. After all, they share a bedroom, allowing Harrison sly suggestions of possibly improper uses of his ghostly state. Tierney's British accent is shaky, and her acting is uneven—sometimes bewitching, sometimes artificial— but Harrison is perfection. He's hearty, commanding, and stingingly funny, quite convincing in his coarse bluster and bellowing delivery. Dashing in his beard and mustache, he also provides the film with its warm undercurrents of deepening ardor. When smoothie George Sanders enters as a womanizing (but *alive*) love interest for Tierney, you'll mourn Harrison's absence and sorely miss him. Delicately directed by Joseph L. Mankiewicz, this is a lovely movie, a comedy that modulates into a bittersweet tale of a love that cannot be (a year ahead of *Portrait of Jennie*). Gorgeously mounted, it's exquisitely detailed in every department, including its truly haunting Bernard Herrmann score. Natalie Wood is Tierney's daughter, but her role, unlike her assignment in *Miracle on 34th Street*, is incidental. With its surefire hyper-romantic climax, *The Ghost and Mrs. Muir* refuses to allow death to get in the way of true love, an especially comforting message for post-war audiences still grieving.

Down to Earth (1947) – A sequel to the immensely popular *Here Comes Mr. Jordan* (1941), which abounded in clever afterlife shenanigans, *Down to Earth* adds Technicolor and is essentially one of Columbia's worship services to the beauty of Rita Hayworth. If judged solely on that score, it's the greatest movie ever made. It does for Rita in color what *Gilda* (1946) had just done for her in black and white, solidifying her as the screen's Love Goddess. It's a cute idea to cast her somewhat literally as Terpsichore, the Greek goddess of song and dance. She's not amused when she learns that Larry Parks' Broadway-bound musical, *Swinging the Muses,* is depicting her as a "man-chasing trollop." Offended by such vulgarity, she arranges an earthly visit, courtesy of Mr. Jordan (Roland Culver, formerly Claude Rains in 1941) who runs things up there in the clouds. Soon starring in the show, Hayworth intends to make it classy, but all she's really doing is making it boring, cutting all the jive! In this regard, the film predates *The Band Wagon* (1953), another musical in which a lighthearted show is nearly ruined by pretentiousness and saved only when it returns to its "pure entertainment" intentions. Though Edward Everett Horton (as a heavenly messenger), James Gleason (now a theatrical agent), and director Alexander Hall are all back from the first film, this is a silly and labored follow-up. Mr. Parks may be fresh from his triumph in *The Jolson Story* (1946), but he is utterly lacking in screen presence. What's a goddess to do when her love interest is a walking piece of white bread? There's plenty of nonsense about his life-threatening gambling debts, plus a few bad musical numbers, including an unfunny polygamy song (for Hayworth, Parks, and Marc Platt), and an elaborately ineffective playground sequence. Jack Cole's choreography includes a highbrow "Ancient Greek" number that bores the onscreen out-of-town audience, though I much prefer it to all the low-down "hep" stuff that replaces it. The best scene has Hayworth, in a green dress, vigorously dancing with two snappy chorus boys, flinging her red tresses exuberantly and showing what real movie-musical magic was in 1947. As for her acting, she's solid in the more dramatic moments but overanimated (straining to be witty) in her comic scenes. Naturally, Hayworth eventually craves to be human. (It's always a comfort to the humans in the audience when otherworldly creatures are jealous of us.) This kind of fantasy wants to clear all rational thoughts from your head, without seeking to replace them with any *other* thoughts, aside from the inarguable conclusion that Rita Hayworth is a goddess.

It Had to Be You (1947) – Here's fantasy as screwball comedy, though Ginger Rogers, one of the era's premier funny ladies, is unable to make it work. The script, by the talented team of Norman Panama and Melvin Frank, is overcomplicated despite getting points for being oddball and adventurous. The silliness finally outweighs any brightness, and its air of frantic foolishness becomes a chore to sustain. I never like Rogers when she's playing dim (as she does in *Tom, Dick and Harry* – 1941); she was usually at her best when playing the savviest person in the room. Here she uses her coy and pouty little-girl voice (not unlike the one she employed so brilliantly as a put-on in *The Major and the Minor* – 1942). Rogers plays a sculptor, a millionaire's daughter who has left three guys at the altar and is once again engaged. Cornel Wilde, an Indian in her dream, is there in her train compartment when she wakes. He's going to help her find the right guy. Wait a minute, this man from her subconscious can not only be seen by her but by everyone else. That's a plot point the film is unable to make plausible, even in the context of a zany fantasy. It's no help that Wilde is a gregarious pain. He also plays a fireman, someone Rogers knew as a child and is coincidentally a three-time runaway groom. She pursues the real Wilde relentlessly, yet they seem a terrible match, a daffy rich girl and a macho fireman. Worse, the stars have no chemistry. In the light-comedy arena, he's no Cary Grant, and as a frazzled heroine, she's no Jean Arthur. *It Had to Be You* is an honest attempt at an off-the-wall "finding Mr. Right" comedy, but it never gets over its illogical hump—having a subconscious manifestation visible to all as a three-dimensional human being. Even in the midst of a fantasy boom, there are still some things that moviegoers are unlikely to swallow.

The Bishop's Wife (1947) – Surprisingly, it was made by many of the people (producer Sam Goldwyn, co-writer Robert E. Sherwood, composer Hugo Friedhofer, photographer Gregg Toland, costume designer Irene Sharaff) who had just made *The Best Years of Our Lives* (1946), the reality-check opposite of this feel-good piece of angelic mischief. Who could resist the charming trio of Cary Grant, Loretta Young, and David Niven? Raising money for a new cathedral, bishop Niven is miserable. He misses his small parish church. In answer to Niven's prayer, angel Grant arrives, revealing his true identity but taking on the public role of Niven's new assistant. Young has the title role, and it is she, a mere mortal, who provides supernatural warmth and radiance. Yes, Grant is inexhaustibly appealing, but he's also a bit constrained by his angelic status, while Niven is to be commended for his ability to be so harried and moody without losing his likability. Brushing up against all the family-picture niceness is a naughty/harmless love triangle. It is somewhat risqué for an angel to be wooing a married woman, even if it's all in the name of making the bishop jealous enough to become a proper husband again. (And the movie ultimately makes it quite clear that Young would *not* succumb to Grant.) Gladys Cooper plays a Scrooge-like character ("Mrs. George Hamilton"), a rich, imperious, and selfish widow to whom Niven must kowtow. Like Scrooge, she has a climactic transformation, a shining moment for a great actress. There's also Elsa Lanchester, delightful as a servant with a crush on Grant, and a restrained Monty Woolley as an old scholar with no religion. (Only Niven and Woolley know that Grant is an angel.) Like Hayworth in *Down to Earth*, Grant seems to want to stay beyond his mission, another fantasy-film reminder of just how lucky we are down here. The movie's post-war messages involve tolerance and peace, but the real message is to sit back and let yourself be lifted by three transporting stars. Based on a Robert Nathan novel (as was *Portrait of Jennie*), *The Bishop's Wife* can claim impeccable production values, amusing effects, a lilting score, even two youngsters familiar from *It's a Wonderful Life*. Director Henry Koster mostly employs his light touch but misplaces it in the scenes with cabbie James Gleason, as well as in the performance by a boys' choir. *The Bishop's Wife* and *Miracle on 34th Street* lost the Best Picture Oscar to the sincere but painfully self-congratulatory *Gentleman's Agreement*. The new realism had beaten two of the era's best, most devout proponents of pure make-believe.

Abbott and Costello Meet Frankenstein (1948) – Universal-International combined two of the studio's franchises—monster movies and Abbott and Costello comedies—at a time when both needed a boost. After 1945, Universal's horror series was dead and buried having fallen pretty low with too many tired-out sequels. Meanwhile, Bud Abbott and Lou Costello, the nation's top box-office attraction of 1942, were no longer in the top ten by the war's end. Teaming the comic duo with resurrected monsters proved as enlivening as one of Dr. Frankenstein's electric jolts—comedy and horror have rarely blended so winningly. (Another Abbott and Costello post-war fantasy, *The Time of Their Lives* [1946], which cast Lou as a Revolutionary War ghost, is the team's *other* best film; both pictures were directed by Charles T. Barton.) Because Bela Lugosi is the head monster here, the title really should be *Abbott and Costello Meet Dracula*. Returning for the first time to his signature role, Lugosi proves himself a game comic actor and a good sport. Dracula's plan is to replace the Frankenstein Monster's fiendish brain with a simpler, more malleable one (enter Lou). It's hard not to smile each time Lugosi refers to Lou's "Wilbur" as "*Vilbur*." His light, self-amused work is a treat, without sacrificing any of his Transylvanian oomph, which includes taking a bite out of Lenore Aubert (a second-string Hedy Lamarr). She's the beautiful surgeon who romances Lou all the way to the operating table. As the Monster, Glenn Strange is no Boris Karloff—he's more like a piece of furniture. Lon Chaney, Jr., back for his fifth time as the Wolf Man, scores as Lou's *other* straight man. Chaney's solemn demeanor, exactly what it was in his other Wolf Man movies, gives the comedy a core of earnestness; he's the only one who believes that any of this is actually happening. Adding to the sustained laughs and scares, there's a "House of Horrors" sequence, a trick wall in a castle basement, and a climactic showdown between Lugosi and Chaney. There's even a cameo from the Invisible Man! The film's success launched a series of Abbott and Costello collisions with other horror legends, none anywhere near this one's enduring pleasures. With their popularity recharged, Bud and Lou were the number three box-office attraction of 1948.

Mr. Peabody and the Mermaid (1948) – With a title like that, you're expecting Esther Williams, but the mermaid role is decidedly secondary to William Powell's Mr. Peabody. This mild, leisurely paced fantasy skirts around a very real subject: Powell's mid-life crisis over turning fifty. He and pretty wife Irene Hervey, married fifteen years, also seem susceptible to outside flirtations, having lost some of the zip in their long-term relationship, a second *real* subject merely grazed. They are Bostonians wintering on a tiny Caribbean island and ensconced in a lavish beach house with a built-in pond/aquarium. (What exactly does Powell do for a living?) Struck by a girl's singing voice calling to him, he ventures out in his sailboat and catches a mermaid (Ann Blyth). Don't worry, he tastefully covers her bosom with a bathing-suit top. She can't walk or talk, but she laughs and cries, and she learns to understand English in a flash. Blyth's hair and makeup, despite all that water, are always flawless. Her role isn't much; she mostly gets to be wide-eyed. Powell teaches her to kiss and then it's all she wants to do, whenever she's not eating the fish in the pond or sinking her teeth into presumed rival Andrea King. Clearly, Blyth makes him feel young again. Another impossible love story, and never as funny as it ought to be, it's whimsy without wit. The polished Powell does his best to carry it, but in his way are Irving Pichel's bland direction, a muddle of a sea climax, and an unsatisfying tie-up. Coincidentally, Glynis Johns played a vivacious, chatty mermaid in the same year's *Miranda* in Britain.

One Touch of Venus **(1948)** – If Rita Hayworth could play a goddess in a musical, then why couldn't Ava Gardner? This property had been a 1943 Broadway hit with Mary Martin, but Gardner's casting considerably upped its goddess quotient (though her singing was dubbed). Universal-International's film version was modestly budgeted and shot in black and white; it's friendly and unpretentious but also second-rate. With its Kurt Weill-Ogden Nash score disrespected, the result is a halfhearted semi-musical with just three songs (though they're all marvelous). Robert Walker is the longtime department-store window trimmer who kisses the Venus statue and awakens her, unraveling his life while providing her with a grand adventure. Though efficient in his goofiness, Walker seems a bit worn to be behaving in such a boyishly stupid manner. Gardner's acting may seem tentative, but she's still seen to advantage with her soft sweetness and a sexuality both heated and giddily playful. She's also wonderfully costumed (by Orry-Kelly) and rapturously photographed (by Frank Planer). Dick Haymes (Walker's roommate), Olga San Juan (Walker's perky girlfriend), and Tom Conway (the department-store owner) round out the cast, but it's Eve Arden, as Conway's pining secretary, who steals each of her scenes, wisecracking her lines with enviable precision. Despite William A. Seiter's perfunctory direction, *One*

Touch of Venus is tuneful and pleasant, and, no surprise, things work out well romantically for everyone who comes in contact with the goddess of love. Whatever is lacking here, one thing is certain—Venus couldn't have taken a more convincing human form than Ava Gardner.

The Luck of the Irish (1948) – Hoping for another *Miracle on 34th Street,* Fox produced this leprechaun comedy with an Oscar-nominated Cecil Kellaway in the so-called Edmund Gwenn slot. It's no *Miracle,* but it's also not bad. Tyrone Power, fresh from the dramatic challenges of *The Razor's Edge* (1946) and the far superior (but unpopular) *Nightmare Alley* (1947), is snugly at home in a light-comic vein. Anne Baxter, coming off her well-deserved supporting Oscar for *Razor's Edge,* is fresh and winsome as his Irish-brogued leading lady. This was the third Power-Baxter collaboration; the first was the WWII action picture *Crash Dive* (1943). Kellaway delights, whether waddling, skipping, hopping, scurrying, or drinking! It's just that his leprechaun role is no Kris Kringle. The screenplay is too heavy-handed in its moralizing, with Irish-American Power having to choose between good and bad. "Good" is Ireland, Baxter (a maid), and his job as a newspaperman, while "bad" is New York City, working as a speechwriter for politician Lee J. Cobb, and marrying fiancée Jayne Meadows (Cobb's daughter). The deck seems stacked, the choices therefore tilted and simplistic. Kellaway, grateful that Power doesn't want to steal his pot of gold, becomes his devoted servant. He shows up in NYC to save Power from selling out (in both love and work). Baxter arrives in NYC, too, with everyone seeming to be vying for Power's soul as he moves closer to learning what is truly golden. *The Luck of the Irish* is a middling effort from director Henry Koster (*The Bishop's Wife*), but it's quite a handsome black-and-white movie. However, if ever anything cried out to be in color, it's a leprechaun movie!

It Happens Every Spring (1949) – Ray Milland, the epitome of the new realism with his Oscar-winning alcoholic performance in *The Lost Weekend* (1945), went over to the fantasy side in 1949: first going the Satanic route in *Alias Nick Beal,* then starring in this baseball comedy, a return to the lighter fare of his pre-*Lost Weekend* days. He's a university chemistry professor who accidentally discovers that his new formula repels baseballs from wood. He takes a leave of absence, changes his name, takes off his glasses, and is soon pitching (unbeatably) in the major league. In a colorless role, Jean Peters is his girlfriend, as well as his student and the daughter of the university president.

(It's simply matter of fact that a female college student would be scouting for a husband among the faculty.) Milland's team knows nothing of his past, and his past knows nothing of his present. He becomes pals with Paul Douglas, the team's catcher. (Douglas appeared in another baseball fantasy, 1951's gooey but tolerable *Angels in the Outfield*). *It Happens Every Spring* becomes a real head-scratcher, also morally questionable, particularly for its Production Code era. Milland is not only a liar but a cheater on a grand scale. Even in an innocuous, frivolous comedy, he doesn't deserve to be a winner. It is hard to root for him as he reaps money and acclaim. The basic premise and the special effects are amusing, but the movie has trouble sustaining the merriment, increasingly leaving a bad taste, all the way to the World Series. Since Milland's initial ball-playing motivation is to make enough money to marry Peters, is the movie a plea for better pay for teachers? Hardly. And why not just sell the formula? Under the workmanlike direction of Lloyd Bacon (*42nd Street*), this fantasy might be described as unintentionally subversive, not quite as delightful as it thinks, cheerily rewarding ill-gotten gain. With no one ever learning the secret to his success, Milland becomes a baseball legend, gets the girl, and even a school promotion. I'd applaud the Code-bashing daring and the lack of old-time moralizing if the movie were making pungent, satiric societal points, but it isn't. By 1949, had Hollywood temporarily run out of genuine ways to charm the heck out of escapist-loving filmgoers?

Sensitivity Training: Issues, Messages, and Controversial Terrain (1947-1950)

The distracting pleasures of fantasy notwithstanding, let's face so-called reality and immerse ourselves in the previously mentioned post-war penchant for mature subject matter, a delving into untapped areas. As if cued by victory, this new era of exploration officially began with the November 1945 release of Billy Wilder's *The Lost Weekend*. From Paramount, Wilder's film not only enthralled critics and audiences with its down-and-dirty foray into an alcoholic's mind but had the jolting effrontery to star light-comedian Ray Milland, instantly heightening the film's built-in shock value. *The Lost Weekend* no longer packs quite the same punch it once did, yet it's still pretty potent, elevated by the veracity of its Manhattan locations, moody black and white by cinematographer John Seitz and unforgettable set pieces (including Milland's stealing a woman's handbag, and his at-home hallucination of a mouse attacked by a bat). Thanks to Milland's complete availability as an actor, tinging his downward spiral with self-loathing, dark humor, and poetic delusion—all of it perfectly aligned with Wilder's smart, inventive direction—*The Lost Weekend* hit a nerve. Not everyone craved fantasy or escapism; some moviegoers were clearly ready for anything Hollywood might tackle.

The war's influence on this adult trend was explicit in those films about post-war adjustment, with RKO's *Till the End of Time* (1946) beating producer Samuel Goldwyn's *The Best Years of Our Lives* (1946) into theaters by four months. Both films follow three returning servicemen's transitions to civilian life, with *Till the End of Time* tracking Guy Madison, Robert Mitchum (with a silver plate in his head), and Bill Williams (who lost both legs). The result is only moderately successful—insufficiently persuasive, probing, or even affecting—and so the film was relegated to oblivion once *The Best Years of Our Lives* became the definitive account of its subject, with infantry sergeant Fredric March, Air Force captain Dana Andrews, and sailor Harold Russell making *their* adjustment in William Wyler's indelibly moving work. It now has a priceless time-capsule aura without having lost any of its stirring immediacy. March and Russell won Oscars, yet the film belongs to the un-nominated Andrews, its true center, who returns to his soda-jerk job and a faithless wife (Virginia Mayo). Whether in the poignancy of March's reunion with wife Myrna Loy, or real-life veteran Russell's aching depiction of creating a new normalcy after the loss of his hands, or Andrews, amid a sea of scrapped planes, feeling equally useless, *The Best Years of Our Lives* authentically conveys the resounding hopes and fears of its very particular moment.

Fox's *Gentleman's Agreement* addressed anti-Semitism, with Gregory Peck as a gentile who goes "undercover" as a Jew so he can write a magazine article about first-hand prejudice. Though earnestly well-intentioned, it proves to be overwritten, naive, and condescending. Courtesy of Moss Hart's smug screenplay, everybody talks in speeches, notably Peck as an especially righteous stiff. This movie wears its "lesson" mantle all-too proudly, with Elia Kazan exposing little of his directorial conviction. Self-consciously impressed with itself, *Gentleman's Agreement* confused worthiness with excellence, and many people were fooled. Like *The Lost Weekend* and *The Best Years of Our Lives,* it won the Best Picture Oscar. Here was more proof that Hollywood enjoyed patting itself on the back for its presumed courage, real or imagined.

Issue-oriented works could also be female-focused as was the case in two of 1948's most highly touted vehicles: an Oscar-winning Jane Wyman in Warner Brothers' *Johnny Belinda* and an Oscar-nominated Olivia de Havilland in Fox's *The Snake Pit.* Wyman's picture, nurtured by director Jean Negulesco, deals with a deaf and mute young woman taught sign language by a gentle doctor (Lew Ayres, formerly Dr. Kildare). This fragile story takes an upsetting turn when Wyman is raped and impregnated. It might sound like too much for one drama, handling both disability and sexual assault, but this Nova Scotia-set movie sustains itself through a strong sense of place, deepening family ties, and the wondrously unaffected and understated performances from the stars. If you can get through Wyman's signing of the Lord's Prayer (kneeling beside a deceased loved one) without your eyes moistening, well, you're made of sterner stuff than I am. Whereas *Johnny Belinda* holds up exceedingly well, the same cannot be said of Anatole Litvak's *The Snake Pit,* despite the thrilling vividness—those flashes of anger and terror—within de Havilland's emotional unraveling. The issue of mental illness is intensified by de Havilland's nightmarish institutionalization. It's absorbing, alright, but the writing now seems hopelessly dated, simplistic, and unsatisfying as it extols the magic of psychiatry.

Those three Best Picture winners and two female tours de force were, in addition to their acclaim and forward-moving impact, *all* box-office smashes—mostly, I'd say, because of their optimism. Despite their baring of warts and occasionally stark ugliness, each was filled with hope, usually in a too-easy, excessively reassuring manner designed to coax commercial appeal. (It's okay to put people through the ringer, just don't leave them depressed.) Add to the list Fox's *Pinky* (1949), in which Elia Kazan *does* display his cinematic gifts, providing this racism drama with a swampy, flavorful ambiance of Southern decay. Jeanne Crain plays a black nurse who's been passing for white (up north), and, though the point is that she *doesn't* look black, did Fox really have to cast the whitest actress on the lot? (Why not Linda Darnell or Anne Baxter? Borrow Jennifer Jones?) Even so, *Pinky* is surprisingly good and piercing. Crain has run from William Lundigan's marriage proposal—he doesn't know she's black—and back to her loving washerwoman grandmother (Ethel Waters). No more than sincere at best, Crain is outacted by crusty-wise dowager Ethel Barrymore, in what amounts to an extended deathbed role, and a bone-chilling Evelyn Varden as a loud-and-proud racist. Again, a message promoting hope; again, a hit.

One issue not confronted directly at this time was homosexuality, though two Warner Brothers films unmistakably veered rather close without actually qualifying as issue-oriented. Alfred Hitchcock's *Rope* (1948) tells a Leopold-and-Loeb story of an obviously (and matter-of-factly) gay and cohabitating couple (arch John Dall and overwrought Farley Granger) who engage in a thrill murder. However grisly, *Rope* is stagy and overheated, empty and pretentious. John Cromwell's *Caged* (1950), hardly a film about prison reform, is a female-centric melodrama about how sweet Eleanor Parker is systematically turned into a hardened inmate, a nice girl going *bad*. Much of *Caged* is unexpectedly solid and straightforward (not *too* campy), and it's even adult enough to acknowledge female sexual needs, including those of lesbians, with enough innuendo to go around (from both inmates and matron-from-hell Hope Emerson).

Up to now, I've made no mention of MGM, a studio that had trouble adapting to this post-war sea of change, cautiously maneuvering themselves. Their typical idea of a prestige picture was something like the lavish period epic *Green Dolphin Street* (1947). After a few years of fumbling attempts, they eventually found their way. This chapter looks at two kinds of the era's "issue" movies: worthy entries overshadowed by the aforementioned biggies and intriguing failures with their hearts in the right place.

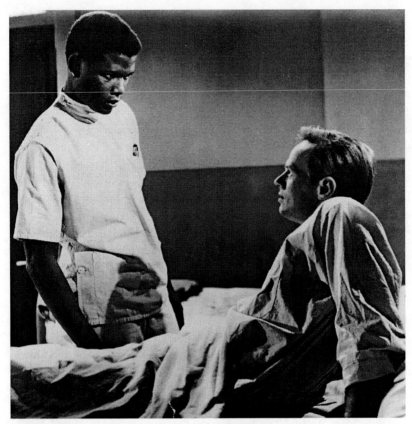

No Way Out (1950): Sidney Poitier and Richard Widmark

The Beginning or the End **(1947)** – What could be more serious than a movie about the new atomic age? Unfortunately, MGM hedged any potential impact by approaching the subject as skittishly as possible. Why else would they assign director Norman Taurog, Oscar winner for *Skippy* (1931) but most recently known for his Mickey Rooney and Judy Garland movies? Why give the lead role, a Columbia scientist, to drearily unappealing Tom Drake, the boy next door from *Meet Me in St. Louis* (1944)? It begins as a documentary with the burying of a time capsule—not to be disturbed until 2446—which includes a print of this movie. (Future moviegoers are not going to be pleased.) Maybe it was too soon to make a movie about our dropping of the bombs on Japan, but it certainly didn't have to be so square and awkward, featuring clunky dialogue about the pros and cons of using the bombs and of atomic energy itself. Though dealing with the recent past, the film is also inherently about

1947 because there's no going backward. Does this halfhearted, unconvincing movie really think it's grappling with the big new-world issues it dares to raise? It wants to be morally complex without earning it, falling back on self-congratulation and strenuous uplift. Despite a big-name ensemble, with Brian Donlevy and Robert Walker as army officers, almost no one qualifies as a real character, meaning that there's very little humanity on display in a film aiming to address our vulnerability as a species. Included is the race with Germany to acquire the bomb, but you'd literally have to be from another planet to find this suspenseful. Ludwig Stossel shows up as Einstein, leading a parade of historical cameos. (Look, there's boy-next-door Drake chatting with Einstein!) On view, from the air, is the Hiroshima bombing, but the hopeful ending invokes God, through the ghostly form of a character who died in a radiation accident, speaking now of our having "the secret of the power of the universe," then going further: "Atomic energy is the hand *He* has extended." Can't wait for the reviews in 2446.

***Smash-Up: The Story of a Woman* (1947)** – It's a female *Lost Weekend,* the alcoholism drama that put Oscar nominee Susan Hayward on the A list. Though not as memorably harrowing as Billy Wilder's groundbreaker, it's still worthwhile, much more than a mere copycat (with Dorothy Parker and Frank Cavett receiving an Oscar nomination for their "original story"). Hayward seizes her opportunity, showing not only guts but both softness and ferocity, not to mention beauty and glamour. She plays a talented vocalist who gives up her career for husband Lee Bowman's singing ambitions. He becomes a radio star, leaving her to feel increasingly useless, bored, and shut out. She may seem to have it all, both a penthouse in Manhattan and a country house, but not even a baby girl (who has a nanny) can make her feel necessary. She already had a weakness for liquor (to calm backstage jitters), but soon she can't stop, drinking to bolster her courage and confidence, to assuage her nerves and insignificance. What the movie offers is a feminist portrait of a gifted but subjugated woman, swirling in a crisis triggered by the sudden end of her promising career. Bowman hardly has the sufficient pop-star appeal, and he's rather dull overall, but his character is also woefully underwritten, too easily dismissible as an oblivious jerk. Marsha Hunt, though, scores as the "other woman," a sly operator, best when she's bitchy; she and Hayward engage in an all-out powder-room brawl. Eddie Albert, here as a nice-guy songwriter, would later appear with Hayward in her more famous alcoholic drama *I'll Cry Tomorrow* (1955). Made for Universal, *Smash-Up* is a noir-ish-looking musical drama no more than capably directed by Stuart Heisler, leaving it to Hayward to do all the burrowing beneath the surfaces, including several believably timed descents into drunkenness. Things will have to get worse—there's a kidnapping and a fire at the climax—before they can get better, eventually arriving at a hopeful ending. The most positive aspect of all is Susan Hayward's boozy breakthrough into big-league stardom.

The Unfaithful (1947) – It may not sound like an "issue" movie, not dealing with anything as "big" as life in the atomic age, or an alcoholic tailspin. A post-war home-front picture, *The Unfaithful* pulls down the covers on wartime female infidelity. Unlike no-good Virginia Mayo in *The Best Years of Our Lives,* how about a sympathetic portrait from a woman's point of view? And what if the result was an unofficial but blatant remake of *The Letter,* following its 1929 and 1940 film versions, repositioned among Southern California's high society? Still a juicy melodrama, surely, but tweaked with contemporary relevance. During the war, Ann Sheridan married Zachary Scott despite knowing him only two weeks. While he was serving overseas, she had an affair with a sculptor. She ended it, but the guy persisted. In the present day, the lover assaults her and she stabs him dead. (We barely get a look at the guy; his death, inside her house, is filmed from outside, glimpsed only in violent shadows.) The incriminating proof is no longer a letter; it's the sculptor's identifiable bust of Sheridan. (Should it therefore have been titled *The Bust*?) Handsomely mounted on vast, glamorous interiors, this is a stylish-looking woman's picture from director Vincent Sherman, yet it opts for character over plot, with its topic surmounting soap opera. Sheridan, who got few choice roles, is at her best: honest, intelligent, and emotionally true. Lew Ayres is a family friend and coincidentally a divorce lawyer; he's gentle and caring, warming up for *Johnny Belinda,* and sounds like an American Ronald Colman. Eve Arden, cast against type as Mr. Scott's bitchy high-living (and divorced) cousin, proves what an incisive dramatic actress she could be, slowly revealing unsuspected depths, beyond her smart-talking expertise. Her big scene arrives when she defends Sheridan (and all wartime wives) to a disillusioned Scott (who becomes more interesting as the movie proceeds). Viewers of *The Unfaithful* may be enticed by the sex and murder but are then rewarded with refreshingly meaty conversations and adult, intimate feelings. With the focus on marriage, how could the ending be anything but optimistic? Production Code-era movies couldn't condone divorce nor infidelity, which explains the movie's fine-line preaching, wanting Sheridan and Scott to stay together while careful not to sanction her actions! I wonder how many wives were terrified that wartime dalliances might come back to haunt them. Not to mention their busts.

Crossfire (1947) – Though it beat *Gentleman's Agreement* into theaters by nearly four months, *Crossfire* was overshadowed by Elia Kazan's film, which became *the* anti-Semitism drama and beat *Crossfire* in the Best Picture Oscar race. However, the sharp, visually striking *Crossfire* holds up better than *Gentleman's Agreement,* utilizing a film-noir technique that makes it feel less like a lecture than Kazan's film. Tautly directed by Edward Dmytryk on a seemingly low RKO budget, *Crossfire* was stunningly photographed by J. Roy Hunt, notably in its opening murder, seen on wall shadows produced by a lamp—one man beating another, no faces visible. Set in Washington, D.C., the film is based on writer-director Richard Brooks' novel *The Brick Foxhole* in which the murder victim was gay rather than Jewish, showing just what was acceptable (and not) in '40s groundbreakers. (The Milland character in *The Lost Weekend* novel is also gay, a closet case.) Brooks' book goes unnamed in the credits, cited only as a novel, as if too notorious even to mention. *Crossfire* famously stars three Roberts: Young, Mitchum, and Ryan. Sam Levene is the unmarried Jew beaten to death, just for being Jewish, by the bigoted Mr. Ryan. Ironically, Levene's scenes retain a gay vibe, with him approaching a cute "sensitive" soldier (George Cooper) alone at a bar, engaging him in conversation, patting him on the back. The scene suggests a pick-up attempt, though Levene has a female date, possibly a beard. (Cooper is then alone with Levene in Levene's hotel room.) Mr. Young is the police captain, unfortunately saddled with the protruding anti-hate sermons, which are clearly aimed more at the audience than anybody in the movie. In his only Oscar-nominated performance, Ryan is a scarily effective villain, but I prefer the work of the faultlessly natural Mitchum, strong yet warm, bringing some welcome sardonic humor to his role as a sergeant drawn into the case. *Crossfire* faces post-war confusion and insecurity, tying these anxieties to the scapegoating of minorities. Tough yet tender, this movie teems with the boiling-over tensions of nocturnal activities.

Possessed (1947) – Following her 1931 pre-Coder with Clark Gable, here is Joan Crawford's *other* movie titled *Possessed.* From her Warner Brothers heyday, this second *Possessed* is something of a hybrid, wanting to be part of the screen's new plunge into psychiatry while not veering too far from its star's Oscar-winning *Mildred Pierce* (1945) formula. *Possessed* has too much going for it to be dismissed as one of those ludicrous post-war psychological potboilers, such as *Spellbound* (1945), instead getting the jump on *The Snake Pit* by attempting to dissect a woman's mental disintegration. Of course, *Snake Pit* had the boldness of being set primarily within the walls of an institution, whereas *Possessed* resides in far more glamorized settings, also steeping itself in classical music. Besides, while Crawford gives an able Oscar-nominated performance, it can't compare with Olivia de Havilland's go-for-broke immersion into a broken psyche. Crawford is more of an emotional indicator, not exactly simmering with depth but perfectly in tune with her film's melodramatic comfort zone, including a *Mildred Pierce*-like mother-stepdaughter conflict over a man (Van Heflin). *Possessed* opens with a great sequence: a zonked Crawford wanders through LA, asking people for "David." She's hospitalized for her catatonic stupor, under the care of a doctor (Stanley Ridges, who gets to utter all the dull, dated psychobabble), all a set-up for the flashback of her story. Crawford, a nurse, was deliriously in love with Heflin, but he dumped her because she was too smothering, loving *too much*. (In *Leave Her to Heaven* [1945], Gene Tierney also loves obsessively, but she's deranged from the start; Crawford at least gets to play a psychologically structured descent.) Heflin is especially good, making "David" a real, regular heel, not a movie-ish swine, just ordinarily selfish and insensitive. Crawford marries wealthy widower Raymond Massey, and his grown daughter, Geraldine Brooks, starts dating older-guy Heflin, igniting Crawford's schizophrenic tendencies, fusing reality and fantasy, leading to a second great sequence, her hallucination involving a flight of stairs and a hairbrush. *Possessed* may seem schizophrenic itself, but its mix of mental instability and Hollywood trappings works well, with the dark shimmers and sensual jolts in Curtis Bernhardt's direction creating a pleasurably hypnotic excursion into love and madness.

Homecoming (1948) – Though it's the best of the four Clark Gable-Lana Turner movies, that isn't saying much. As MGM's notion of a *Best Years of Our Lives*-type story, *Homecoming* is far too obvious and simplified, with two-geared direction from Mervyn LeRoy, either glossy or stodgy. Playwright Paul Osborn's screenplay is a slow and repetitive variation on the old redemption plot from *The Citadel* (1938), with prosperous surgeon Gable, living a perfected life, empty with success. Childless, he and wife Anne Baxter have lived selfishly. Now, as a colonel, he returns home from the war having learned what it really means to care about people. Gable, the film's chief asset, brings his smarts, subtlety, and verve to the movie and makes it—and other post-war movies of his, such as *Adventure* (1945) and *The Hucksters* (1947)—seem better than deserved. The other kind of person—good and unselfish—is represented by John Hodiak as Gable's college pal (Gable and Hodiak are too far apart in age to play collegemates) and fellow doctor, someone who cares for the poor, and also by Ms. Turner, Gable's indispensable war nurse, a widow with a boy of six. Instead of delving into Gable's post-war change of outlook, and confronting the contemporary scene (and the movie's title), *Homecoming* is primarily (and disappointingly) a wartime flashback opting for the safety of the past (in France and Italy). It's a *MASH* atmosphere, with no fashions for Turner, just army and medical garb. She gives a confident performance, bonding with Gable, changing his life, and making him more compassionate. Unfortunately, the movie is never challenging enough, too secure in the surefire Gable-Turner chemistry. Their love is chaste for a while, eventually consummated in a bombed-out building as the war rages nearby. Neither Hodiak nor Baxter, married in real life, is well-served; he's a device, and she's mired in a soap. Though concerned with how the war may have improved and inspired people, *Homecoming* is a failed message picture, too comfortable with warming generalities. Like other "serious" MGM movies of the post-war—*Cass Timberlane* (1947), *B.F.'s Daughter* (1948), and *The Doctor and the Girl* (1949)—*Homecoming* seems misguided, wrongfully convinced that its approximation of reality comes close enough.

An Act of Murder (1948) – Here's an issue-oriented movie ahead of its time about the choice to end the life of a terminally ill person, long before anyone ever heard of Dr. Kevorkian. Released by Universal, this low-budget drama, set in Pennsylvania and attentively directed by Michael Gordon, is a grabber. Fredric March is a by-the-book judge and Florence Eldridge (March's real-life spouse) is his wife, with Geraldine Brooks their daughter, a first-year law student, and Edmond O'Brien, her boyfriend, a lawyer at odds with March. The stars have a wonderful twenty-year marriage, but Eldridge, suffering from spells, goes to see friend and neurologist Stanley Ridges. Nobody ever says brain tumor but that's what it is, inoperable and hopeless. Ridges and March decide not to tell her, but she learns the truth and keeps it to herself. Must she die an agonizing death? Will March do something about it? Will she? This all leads to a car crash in the rain and a courtroom climax (remember that March is a judge). Both leads excel, with Eldridge experiencing a memorably distressing moment in an amusement-park fun house. *An Act of Murder,* also known as *Live Today for Tomorrow,* introduces issues of legal innocence, moral guilt, intent, as well as the head versus the heart, and ultimately raises more questions than it can answer.

***Intruder in the Dust* (1949)** – One of the era's finest social-issue movies and from MGM no less! Directed by Clarence Brown, who had recently done such sensitive work in the family pictures *National Velvet* (1944) and *The Yearling* (1946), *Intruder* is a palpably atmospheric message picture that keeps its speech-making to a blessed minimum. Visually enveloping, with vital black-and-white location use of a Mississippi town, it places an ensemble cast in a pre-*To Kill a Mockingbird* plot. African-American Juano Hernandez, owner of ten acres and his own house, is jailed for the murder of a white man (shot in the back). Will he be killed by a white mob before he can be proven innocent? A white teenager (Claude Jarman, Jr. of *The Yearling*) knows the suspect a little and wants to help him, as does the boy's lawyer uncle (David Brian) and a brave old spinster (Elizabeth Patterson, *I Love Lucy*'s Mrs. Trumbull). Set in an unnamed state and based on a William Faulkner story, *Intruder* has a potent simplicity, building in quiet power and grace. Though young Jarman investigates the crime daringly, the most indelible scene arrives when Ms. Patterson, volunteering to stand guard at the jail while doing her mending in the entryway, bravely defies the mob. It's a crowning role for an old pro rarely given such a substantive opportunity; she's likable and admirable in an unfussy way. Also impressive is Hernandez, acting with unsentimental dignity and stubbornness (marvelous, as well, in the next year's *Stars in My Crown*). Kudos, too, to Will Geer as the open-minded sheriff, Porter Hall as the dead man's one-armed backwoodsy daddy, and Jarman himself, nicely unaffected. *Intruder in the Dust* is forceful yet smartly restrained and made with care, taste, and a small-town pacing. Still neglected, it's deserving of *Mockingbird*-sized attention.

***No Way Out* (1950)** – A different kind of racism drama, this one is centered on an African-American doctor (Sidney Poitier, in his film debut). Marred by melodramatic hysteria, it's nowhere near as good as *Intruder in the Dust* or *Pinky,* but it's a best-intentioned, honorable work, co-written and directed by Joseph L. Mankiewicz the same year as his *All About Eve.* Though outdated and oversimplified, it effectively alternates its focus between four main characters: Poitier, who makes a grounded and personable impression as the young physician facing racism at a hospital (including a white woman spitting in his face); Stephen McNally, as Poitier's boss and mentor, a forgettable good-guy role; top-billed Richard Widmark, a stick-up hood arrested and wounded alongside his hood brother; and Linda Darnell, a girl from the wrong side of the tracks (in Beaver Canal). When Widmark's brother dies while being treated by Poitier, Widmark accuses him of murder. An autopsy can prove Poitier was correct in his actions, but Widmark, a flaming racist, won't allow it. (He's quite free with the N-word.) *No Way Out* is tainted by Widmark's over-the-top acting which is phony, hammy, and, of course, smirking. Darnell gives a good hardboiled performance, making a plausible transition to good girl, including sympathy for Poitier. She plays the dead guy's ex-wife, no fan of Widmark's, and ultimately, hers is the best part, the character who changes the most. It's great to see young Ruby Dee (as Poitier's sister), Ossie Davis (as Dee's husband), and also Mildred Jo-Anne Smith as Poitier's wife, evidence of a big studio (Fox) giving quality screen time to gifted, underused African-American players. Yet it's Widmark, as the movie's out-of-control monster, who keeps demanding attention, especially in the fevered climax, while Poitier retains his dignified humanity. Despite its many flaws, *No Way Out* deserves notice for exposing unashamed (if overacted) racism, violently front and center.

Outrage **(1950)** – The directorial career of actress Ida Lupino is noted for its tackling of unusual content—polio in *Never Fear* (1949), bigamy (no surprise) in *The Bigamist* (1953)—but most pointedly in *Outrage,* in which the subject is rape. *Johnny Belinda* certainly dealt with this issue as sensitively as it had ever been thus far, but it was one of several things covered in the movie. *Outrage,* on the other hand, is entirely about a rape, the horrific incident itself but primarily its agonizing aftermath, and Lupino shows not just skill but honesty and mettle. She also co-wrote the script, which isn't at all heavy-handed, nor does it feel old-fashioned. Mala Powers is engaged to handsome Robert Clarke who just got a raise. After working overtime as a bookkeeper, and while walking home, she's chased and then assaulted. All she sees is the man's neck scar, not his face. Photographed by Archie Stout with remarkable depths and shadows, it's a terrifying sequence filled with a suspenseful dread. Powers can no longer face her fiancé, plus there's gossip and the stigma surrounding what happened to her. She runs away and is rescued by a minister (Tod Andrews) who helps her find lodgings and a bookkeeping job (on an orange ranch). Though it appears she's starting to heal, it's not that easy, her terror rising if she feels threatened. *Outrage* is a B movie ahead of its time, acknowledging post-traumatic stress disorder. It bogs down a bit in the minister's goodness, and nothing in it can equal the emotional anguish and filmmaking force of the rape sequence. Naturally, *Outrage* is ultimately hopeful, reliably so, continuing the trend of this era's issue-oriented fare. Present your subject as baldly as possible, but don't leave anyone feeling despondent, not if you want them to return for the next provocative drama.

Chilly Receptions: Welcome to the Cold War (1948-1956)

What a difference a victory makes. The United States and the Soviet Union, allies of World War II, had managed to overlook their governmental and philosophical differences to fight the good fight, but, ironically, they were *not* brought closer together by defeating a common enemy. America's next big fear was the spread of communism, which put the two nations at odds in an our-way-versus-your-way conflict, a situation with world-war potential. Instead, the result was the Cold War, an undeclared battle between ideologies that lasted over four decades, a mostly covert operation capable of eruption at any moment (as in Korea, 1950-53). And don't forget the era's new panic—fear of nuclear annihilation—perfect for keeping people up at night. It was essential to try to control the Cold War's temperature.

Yet, in the *very* recent past, the Hollywood of WWII had made the Soviets and their lifestyle a part of the screen's Allied propaganda machine. A small sub-genre of war-era films simply couldn't get enough of happy Russian peasants, so endlessly hardworking, so devoted to their families. They were— oh, my God!—just like *us,* only in different costumes and able to wield a plow, also valiantly capable at fighting a Nazi onslaught. The quintessential example of this admiring yet condescending simple-folk approach is *The North Star* (1943), directed by Lewis Milestone (*All Quiet on the Western Front*), written by Lillian Hellman, and starring Walter Huston. It makes the grotesque assumption that Russians rarely stop singing and dancing, tireless in their merrymaking (until forced to become guerrillas). With an esteemed ensemble including Dana Andrews, Ann Harding, and Erich von Stroheim, *The North Star* arrived with class and prestige, complete with an Aaron Copland score. Aside from an occasionally chilling episode, as when the Nazis use Russian children for blood transfusions (sometimes draining them to death), *The North Star* is embarrassing mush.

Song of Russia (1944) was more of the same, promoting U.S.-Soviet unity, again trotting out the happy-peasant formula. American Robert Taylor is a world-famous conductor on a pre-war Russian tour, and lovely Susan Peters is the villager with whom he falls in love (a talented pianist who can also ride a tractor, handle a machine gun, and make a Molotov cocktail). Again, the Nazis put an end to the pleasant monotony of country living, and, again, the native response is fire: in *The North Star,* the village burns itself down, leaving no resources for the Germans; in *Song of Russia,* they burn all their crops, depriving the enemy of food. The same basic thing happens in *In Our Time* (in Poland) and *Dragon Seed* (in China), both from 1944, emphatically convincing viewers that this was the best (and obviously also the worst) recourse when an Axis power invades. These movies usually end with a big climactic speech of uplift, whether by peasant Anne Baxter (in *The North Star*) or peasant John Hodiak (in *Song of Russia*). Hollywood's pro-Soviet fare, which also includes *Mission to Moscow* (1943) and *Counter-Attack* (1945), raised eyebrows the minute the war was over, with some Red-Scare proponents wondering why certain film professionals had been so sympathetic, prompting a witch hunt for those deemed *too* sympathetic.

The bullying "patriotism" of the House Un-American Activities Committee, and the shameful blacklisting of "suspicious" characters working in the movie industry, signified Hollywood's about-face regarding our old ally. With post-war America in the grip of anti-communist fervor, movies would no longer depict Russians as a brave, resilient people; they were now not to be trusted, lying in wait to overturn capitalism, meanwhile hoping to recruit the gullible. Basically, the movies retracted every nice thing they had said about the Russians during wartime.

Not all Cold War-themed movies revolved around the sneaky tactics of espionage. Take Robert Wise's *The Day the Earth Stood Still* (1951), one of the best of them all, fusing the science-fiction craze and Cold War content into a seamless fit. Here's a smart, restrained fantasy in which an elegant and superior alien (Michael Rennie) comes to Earth to warn us about weapons of mass destruction, particularly our potentially dangerous misuse of them: we will be destroyed if deemed a threat to Rennie's union of planets. The anti-nuke message is delivered with force, a direct rebuke to the U.S.-Soviet arms race. (Whereas most of this era's Cold War movies have a hawkish right-wing slant, *The Day the Earth Stood Still* is a liberal-leaning peace-promoter.) In a sly yet unmistakable metaphor for the corrosive force of communism, *Invasion of the Body Snatchers* (1956) has alien forces creating dehumanized versions of all of us, crushing individuality. With their tingling spins on the subject, these two sci-fi classics positively submerged themselves in Cold War panic.

The Cold War picture also found a snug home in B movies of a film-noir variety. Look at *The Whip Hand* (1951), in which a Wisconsin ghost town is actually a secret cell of commies, including an ex-Nazi scientist working on germ warfare, experimenting on humans! *Shack Out on 101* (1955) has diner-waitress Terry Moore an unlikely figure poised to save us all from communism, while Ruth Roman in 5 *Steps to Danger* (1957) tries to get guided-missile information to a German physicist who escaped the Soviets. Higher budgets didn't automatically ensure coherence or credibility. Leo McCarey's *My Son John* (1952) suggests that Robert Walker became a communist spy because he moved away from God and got too many school degrees, not that it offers any idea of what a commie spy actually *does*. Speaking of God, William A. Wellman's *The Next Voice You Hear...* (1950) is a turgid fantasy in which the Big Guy takes over the nightly airwaves for a week. This whiny misfire, made to allay modern-age fears (without directly mentioning communism or nuclear war), relies on bland platitudes: count your blessings; make your own miracles; and, most of all, *don't be afraid*.

The Cold War movie peaked with two masterpieces of the 1960s. John Frankenheimer's *The Manchurian Candidate* (1962) is a magnificent paranoiac thriller, a tale of brainwashing, assassination, political ruthlessness, and, unforgettably—thanks to Angela Lansbury—mommy issues. A harrowing black comedy, *The Manchurian Candidate* seems not to have aged a day. Neither has Stanley Kubrick's *Dr. Strangelove* (1964), the other '60s triumph, a doomsday satire and outrageous nuclear-war comedy with an expectedly hilarious performance from Peter Sellers (in three roles) and an *un*expectedly hilarious performance from George C. Scott (in only one role). Sidney Lumet's *Fail-Safe*, from later in 1964, is virtually a straight-faced, appropriately somber version of *Strangelove*'s plot, but it's also heavy-handed and pretentious, wearing its grimness proudly, and is ultimately far less potent than *Strangelove*. Set in 1964 but released in 1959, Stanley Kramer's *On the Beach* is a far better radioactive-apocalypse drama, with some excellent performances (especially Ava Gardner's) and a matter-of-fact tone that makes humanity's demise indeed plausible. A cold war might feel more insidious than a war you could actually put your finger on, and yet it was somebody's finger, pushing a button, that remained the scariest thought of all.

But let's get back to the beginning, when the Cold War arrived, when post-war reality revealed itself and a new post-Axis world order was established. With a broken Europe painfully reassembling, the U.S. and the Soviet Union were major players as never before.

Big Jim McLain (1952): John Wayne

***Berlin Express* (1948)** – Since Cold War movies were the natural offspring of World War II movies, there was logically some overlap between the two classifications, a period of transition. At first, Hollywood was reluctant to let go of the Nazis as their ideal villain, most famously in Alfred Hitchcock's extraordinary *Notorious* (1946) in which post-war Nazis regrouped in South America. A lesser-known example is *Berlin Express*, from film-noir specialist Jacques Tourneur (*Out of the Past*), a socially conscious film noir residing within a ravaged post-war Germany (the same location for that year's *The Search* and *A Foreign Affair*). Adroitly blending the grimy realism of such stark devastation with the artful artifice of a nightmarish, nocturnal black-and-white world—while tying worries about Germany's future to a cloak-and-dagger plot—*Berlin Express* might be described as docudrama noir flanked by international intrigue. (It also happens to be a nifty train thriller, at both its beginning and its climax.) The plot hinges on the kidnapping of a German doctor, head of a fact-finding commission whose focus is the reunification of Germany. He hopes that America, France, Great Britain, and the Soviet Union—each currently occupying a German sector—will stay on friendly terms. Heading to Berlin (from Paris), he is to present his findings to the Allies. (It isn't clear what he needs to tell them; just accept that it's "important.") However, Nazi-like Germans have formed an underground movement, intending to wreak unrest and kill the doctor. Characters aren't necessarily who they seem to be, which allows for some enjoyable twists. The doctor's French secretary (Merle Oberon, with a dreadful accent) leads the search for her missing boss, assisted by four Allied representatives: American Robert Ryan, Frenchman Charles Korvin, Englishman Robert Coote, and Russian Roman Toporow (surprisingly attractive and unsurprisingly severe). One of them is an assassin intending to murder the doctor. However farfetched and implausibly fast-paced (with clues falling too easily into the quintet's path), *Berlin Express* is skillful, satisfying, and prone to dazzling visuals from cinematographer Lucien Ballard: a shootout in an old brewery, a brawl in a water tank, and a climax sparked by a train-window's reflection. It ends at the Brandenburg Gate where there's an especially hopeful coming together of the American and the Russian, both so touchingly oblivious to the stalemate ahead.

The Iron Curtain (1948) – Set between 1943 and 1946, this William A. Wellman drama makes a literal transition from actual war to virtual war, but it's not about Americans. Set in Ottawa, it begins with Allied Canadians and Russians working together. The wartime setting suggests one of Hollywood's pro-Soviet appraisals, but because it's a post-war movie the Soviets are suddenly more akin to Nazis, those of Hollywood's sinister comic-book variety. Dana Andrews, a cipher clerk from the USSR, arrives in Canada to work at the Soviet embassy. Later, his pregnant wife, Gene Tierney, joins him. (Neither has a Russian accent, but they speak English with the stilted phrasing of those not entirely fluent in a second language.) Ottawa offers a fresh black-and-white location for wartime fare, yet the film grows increasingly drab and shallow. Andrews' character is rather a cipher himself, an obedient blank, resulting in a halfhearted and uncomfortable performance marred further by an insufficiently motivated transition from loyal Soviet to anti-Soviet hero, a ridiculously rapid case of having one's eyes opened. Tierney's role is a nothing, which is rather perplexing considering her great run of hits for

Fox between 1944 and 1947, including *Laura* (1944) with Mr. Andrews. The subtext is that both husband and wife are simply too nice to remain among those shifty communists. Consider their purity when puzzled by the sounds of a church choir wafting onto the street, having been denied such beauty in their atheist homeland. Halfway through the movie, the war ends, which allows for the more contemporary Soviet content: the spying over atomic-bomb information, and the plan to turn Canada into a communist country. What once would have been an overemphatic war-era movie about Russians working diligently alongside Canadians instead became an overemphatic movie about dirty commies showing their true colors.

The Red Danube **(1949)** – As in *The Iron Curtain,* the Soviets in question are another country's problem. The good guys are the British in 1946 Vienna, with a blustery Walter Pidgeon as a one-armed colonel assigned to repatriate *forcibly* any displaced Russian citizens to the Soviets, including sweet ballerina Janet Leigh (of German descent). Leigh takes refuge in a convent run by Mother Superior Ethel Barrymore (in her smugly grand mode). Then there's Angela Lansbury, sorely wasted as Pidgeon's right hand, pining for Peter Lawford (a Scottish major), as Lawford and Leigh fall in love (insipidly, generically). Meanwhile, Louis Calhern is reduced to a cartoon as the Russian colonel pursuing Leigh. *The Red Danube* was shot by Charles Rosher in a lushly gorgeous black and white marked by soft shadings and vibrant close-ups, looking almost like a Garbo movie. The roles and the plot aren't up to the merits of the subject, and George Sidney's direction skims along the surface of things. Lansbury is reteamed with Sidney after *The Harvey Girls* (1946) and, coincidentally, "Atchison, Topeka" is heard as underscoring in one of her scenes. Based on a novel, *The Red Danube* makes typical points about the Soviets being louses, again stressing their atheism. This thoughtful movie becomes leisurely and longish, slackening any tautness surrounding Leigh's hiding, leveling into a flattened-out earnestness. Coincidentally, Lansbury and Leigh later appeared in *The Manchurian Candidate* (1962), a daring, provocative counterpoint to *The Red Danube*'s hazy conviction.

I Married a Communist **(1949)** – Also known, rather boringly, as *The Woman on Pier 13;* it doesn't teach you one thing about communism. Merely Red-crazed pulp, it portrays commies in established movie terms as garden-variety gangsters who just want to impose havoc, specifically aiming to foil waterfront negotiations between good-guy owners and good-guy union members in

San Francisco. Wouldn't real communists be fighting hard on the side of the workers? Here they're just bad-guy instigators. Directed by Robert Stevenson (*Mary Poppins*), this is a film noir with a social message, a cautionary tale of home-grown terror that intends to ring the alarm about possibly evil dealings across the plain old USA. Robert Ryan is surprisingly uninteresting, even kind of a drag as a former party member—a once-disaffected kid who fell in with the wrong crowd—now unable to break free. He's a successful V.P. in the shipping business, newly married to an interior decorator (Laraine Day) and being hounded by a party leader (Thomas Gomez, another commie cartoon) and by his own ex-girlfriend (blonde bombshell Janis Carter). Ryan is strong-armed into doing their bidding, helping to sabotage labor talks. Ms. Carter, a communist femme fatale, toys with innocent John Agar (as Day's brother); then, in true noir fashion, she falls in love with the schnook. Savor the black-and-white glories of Nicholas Musuraca's camerawork, while trying to guess what in fact commies want! *I Married a Communist* looks like nothing more than usual-suspect baddies trying to harm a few nice movie stars.

Big Jim McLain (1952) – By now, with the blacklist in full swing and with Hollywood terrified of making the slightest move that might be labeled unpatriotic, some movies treated their anti-communist mission as being every bit as vital as the industry's morale-building of WWII. A film that dives into the deep end of right-wing propaganda, *Big Jim McLain* is a flagrant tribute to the House Un-American Activities Committee. (It is stated that we owe them a great debt.) Ex-marines John Wayne and James Arness are investigators for the Committee, sent to Hawaii to root out a cell of offenders. These secret Red agents are led by an elegantly heartless and unnecessarily British Alan Napier. He and others are up to no-good by causing dissension between employers and unions; their goal being a labor stoppage in island shipping. Nancy Olson, bland and unthreatening, is perfect for the pallid rom-com romance she shares with Wayne. But *Big Jim McLain* is black and white in every way with Wayne all swaggering righteousness and bravado (and nothing underneath). Directed by Edward Ludwig, its biggest crime is simply being a bad movie, a Red-baiting wet dream in which Wayne decks plenty of commies. He even expresses open contempt for the Fifth Amendment (because our enemies use it to go free). This isn't the screen-actor John Wayne of *Red River* (1948) or *She Wore a Yellow Ribbon* (1949); he's just a hulking windbag throwing his weight around.

Man on a Tightrope (1953) – Elia Kazan, in addition to being a great director of stage and screen, was famous for naming names to the committee in 1952. This anti-Soviet tract seems to be part of his self-defense, a further justification for what he did (in case anyone was skeptical). Fredric March stars as a circus manager (and clown) in 1952 Czechoslovakia. It's no surprise that March's tense, impassioned performance is the main event here. He's surrounded by a worthy plot and some keen suspense, plus the heartening theme of artists who want only to practice their art, with March forced to take a stand to *save* his art (which is, in Kazan's eyes, what he had done). March's plan is to lead the circus beyond the Iron Curtain, right into Bavaria. Unfortunately, the film isn't as good as it sounds, especially superficial when judged against March's sustained depth of character. Kazan's own work is solid but impersonal (as if his heart isn't *really* in it), and playwright Robert E. Sherwood's screenplay is too melodramatic to generate a contemporary urgency. Coming a year after *The Greatest Show on Earth,* a circus-themed Best Picture Oscar winner from Cecil B. DeMille (Hollywood's outspokenly right-wing director), *Man on a Tightrope* borrows *Greatest Show*'s Gloria Grahame who, ironically, did better work for broad-stroked DeMille than actor's director Kazan. As March's slutty second wife (an emasculating bitch), Grahame is cast to type yet pretty awful, so utterly phony. Terry Moore is also no prize as March's daughter, in love and lust with Cameron Mitchell (ridiculous-looking with big curly hair). Adolphe Menjou, another fierce Hollywood Red-hater, is amusingly cast as a commie big shot, and, naturally, there's a spy skulking inside the circus. Thanks to the veracity of its locations, the black-and-white grit, and Mr. Fredric March, *Man on a Tightrope* teeters far less than it might have.

Never Let Me Go (1953) – Gene Tierney is a Russian (again), another of her people's distressed ballerinas, in this improbable but entertaining movie conceived more as MGM gloss than political treatise (*Waterloo Bridge*-ish in its combination of war, romance, and toe shoes). It's set right after V-E Day as a love story between Tierney and US war correspondent Clark Gable. In Russia for four years, Gable speaks the language while Tierney, correcting her *Iron Curtain* performance, speaks English with an accent. The stars marry but the authorities won't permit her to leave the country with him. Tierney is too wonderful for words—sweet, lovely, and doll-like—also dimly limited, rather wind-up. As for Gable—still looking pretty good—he brings, as usual, some weight and smarts to a movie in need of both. And it's nice to see him stretching his acting muscles with British actors from outside the

MGM stable: Kenneth More, Richard Haydn, and Bernard Miles. The central plot involves Gable's rescue of Tierney by boat, with any stock villains no match for the King. Delmer Daves' direction keeps the action disappointingly lightweight and simplistic, so lose yourself in the stunningly lighted deep-focus photography of Robert Krasker (*The Third Man*). Despite the silliness of some awfully deft code deciphering, the suspense reaches its climax when Tierney, formerly number-four swan and now a prima ballerina, is suddenly set to star in *Swan Lake,* upsetting Gable's plan. As a chase ensues (thanks to an evil ballerina), the Cold War is served as pop entertainment with the Soviet Union simply the nasty enemy *du jour.*

Pickup on South Street (1953) – Though surely uneven, it's still one of the top Cold War movies of the '50s, feverishly pumped by Samuel Fuller's direction, further vivified by cinematographer Joe MacDonald's bracing close-ups. Set in a Manhattan in which the enemy is among us, *Pickup* is a jazzy, particularly brutal film noir starring Richard Widmark as a pickpocket (a "cannon"), an ex-con who, by stealing Jean Peters' wallet, inadvertently foils a communist plot involving a stolen chemical formula. Ms. Peters is a tramp, a real tomato, sadly accustomed to abuse from men, now innocently abetting ex-boyfriend Richard Kiley, a secret commie agent. Suddenly, both the Reds and the Feds are looking for Widmark. No matter, the film belongs to Thelma Ritter in an Oscar-nominated performance as Moe, a tired-out Bowery-dwelling stoolie with one aim: to have enough money for her burial plot and headstone. Ritter is extraordinary in a dramatic role, so touchingly exposed and believably broken-down; it's a plain, pure, and intuitive piece of movie acting. Widmark, however, gives a typically smirky and giggly performance. (When playing hoods, he always lacked the appeal and variety of a James Cagney.) Leading lady Peters is hardly great, but she certainly gives her all to a character part, working conscientiously in a role that Jan Sterling could have easily tossed off. The message is that even America's underbelly—represented by Widmark, Peters, and Ritter—is prone to patriotism. They may be lowlifes, but, hey, they're not commies! *Pickup* resonates as a tale of losers purified by fighting something beyond the confines of their grubby little worlds. Slimy Widmark is capable of heroism, while Kiley, the Red, is not only violent but cowardly. The unlikely Widmark-Peters romance puts a strain on what is, essentially, a sordid story: it's laughable to hear strains of "Again" every time they clinch. Although there's some late-breaking excitement involving a dumbwaiter, why did the climax have to be so rushed and unsatisfying? Cold War America's vague hyper-paranoia about commies is summed up earlier by Ritter: "I know one thing...I just don't like them."

Trial (1955) – A good courtroom drama with a Cold War slant, *Trial* is certainly compelling, yet typically hyperbolic. It begins in June 1947 with a girl murdered on a beach; the prime suspect is a teenage Mexican (Rafael Campos). Glenn Ford is a university law professor whose job is in peril because of his lack of courtroom experience, leading to his summer employment with lawyer Arthur Kennedy (who will defend Campos). Ford is on his way to more than he bargained for, soon to be shaken from his academic illusions. Playing an idealist, Ford gives one of his mannered "natural" performances, utilizing a forehead-furrowed earnestness and a boyishness past expiration. Add Dorothy McGuire as Kennedy's secretary, John Hodiak as the prosecutor, and Katy Jurado (in constant hysteria) as Campos' mother. Ford and the refined McGuire fall in love, sharing a rather adult screen relationship for 1955. There are hints that they are sleeping together, even living together. *Trial,* however solidly packaged by director Mark Robson, can also be overwrought, notably when the subject of communism is introduced. A disgusted Ford, such an innocent, will find himself at a rally of 20,000 commie sympathizers. What's most interesting about *Trial* is its balance. Yes, it offers blatant Red-stained villainy, but it also presents right-wing extremists such as two anti-Mexican bigots leading a segregationist mob. *Trial* dares to meld conservative anti-communist furor with liberal-minded sympathies toward minorities (including Juano Hernandez as a gentle African-American judge). It's something for everyone! Unfortunately, *Trial* recedes from any gray-area shadings, wrapping things up too swiftly and neatly. Its message is blunt: like the crooked folks in *Pickup on South Street,* and like good-guy Glenn Ford, we *all* need to wake up. And, believe it or not, we all have what it takes to thwart the enemy.

Toward the Unknown (1956) – A sub-genre of the Cold War covered military movies designed to flaunt American hardware, reassuring nervous citizens by showcasing our intimidating state-of-the-art arsenal. The intent couldn't be clearer: it's okay to sleep at night because, well, we're awesome! *Strategic Air Command* (1955) is no more than a commercial for the defense department, about our weaponry being the best tool in "keeping the peace," our main deterrent to oblivion. The USA "must be combat-ready 24 hours a day" in order "to prevent a war from ever starting." The movie fetishizes bombers, spewing streaks of pretty-colored smoke against sunny skies. (Also in this category of uniformed muscle-flexing is *The McConnell Story* [1955] and *Bombers B-52* [1957].) Dramatically anemic, these movies save all their energy and artistry for the beauty of metal in flight. Mervyn LeRoy's *Toward the Unknown* fits right in, reliably routine and predictable on land, but stimulated whenever aircraft rises against blue expanses. There are two other assets: the film's eye-catching primary-colored palette and William Holden, deploying his patented intelligence and unvarnished humanity. His backstory—as a POW of the Korean War—may be the script's only non-standard element. Brainwashed by the Reds, and a victim of prolonged solitary confinement, Holden broke and gave them information. He also tried to kill himself. *Toward the Unknown* is set at an Air Force base for test pilots, which is what Holden used to be and hopes to be again. Everyone, of course, is leery of him. Redemption is the obvious thrust of the plot, though, like everything else in this movie, including a dull love triangle (among Holden, Virginia Leith, and Lloyd Nolan), it takes a backseat to any military prowess soaring through the heavens. Like many a Cold War movie, *Toward the Unknown* hopes to leave you with the overwhelming comfort of knowing that, as an American, you are in good hands, and that it's safe to come in from the cold.

"Home" Movies: Domesticity in Post-War America (1948-1956)

Movies of the 1930s seem to be about two groups: rich people and poor people. After the interruption of World War II, Hollywood had a new subject, a middle class forging ahead in something called suburbia. It was part of the post-war boom, a new era's possibilities, an America invigorated by victory, all of which was reflected at the movies. *Mr. Blandings Builds His Dream House* (1948) is the quintessential comedy of post-war expansion, as one family braves the transition from a cramped NYC apartment to spreading out in CT. While many '30s comedies were escapist larks about well-off screwballs, post-war comedies aimed to show more relatable adventures, stoking laughs with reminders of the types of misadventures being shared across the nation. It was no longer an Art Deco world dressed in satin gowns and tuxedoes; instead, it was more ordinary, a place of mortgages, ice-cream trucks, and freshly mowed lawns. It was as if the movies had decided to start with "Happily Ever After" and see how couples were actually faring with their houses, jobs, and kids. As Mr. Blandings, Cary Grant, out of dinner clothes, is just your average harried husband/father, an Everyman. Amid the movie's many money-hemorrhaging laughs, there's something real stewing: Grant's emasculating insecurities regarding all that's expected of him as a provider to wife Myrna Loy and their two daughters. (Whereas adult comedies of the '30s were sparsely populated with children, post-war domestic comedies put kids front and center. The title *Family Honeymoon,* of 1948, says it all.) *Mr. Blandings* is a bright, if conventional, take on contemporary middle-class values, making good fun of the uphill battle to have it all. It's perfectly pitched to its intended audience of all those folks reaching for the American Dream.

In the same vein as *Mr. Blandings* was the even more popular and acclaimed *Father of the Bride* (1950), a savvy, enjoyable comedy in which Spencer Tracy is the put-upon father (a lawyer), with Joan Bennett his more even-keeled spouse. Instead of a money-pit house, Tracy faces an out-of-control wedding. It's another perfect family with Tracy warm and loving, Ms. Bennett doing her best Myrna Loy, and a radiant eighteen-year-old Elizabeth Taylor as America's perfect daughter (plus two far less significant sons). Like *Mr. Blandings,* *Father of the Bride* plays on the notion of universal experiences, yet, in both cases, the so-called middle class is clearly *upper* middle class, complete with maids. These films' laughs derive from the pressures (mostly financial) to keep everything from collapsing. Audiences smiled in recognition of such woes, but they could also feel encouraged by seeing everything work out.

However, it wasn't always fun and games. In addition to movies that celebrated and reinforced America's post-war values and conventions, there were also movies that questioned them, and they might be from any genre, even musicals, and just as easily focused on women as men. The subjects might be domestic struggles or dissatisfactions, including misguided dreams of attaining total bliss (as often promised at the movies!). In this family-sitcom era, epitomized by Ozzie and Harriet, it's especially interesting to acknowledge films which defied all that so-called "perfection." This includes those that broached feminism, though most of them softened and compromised their initial impulses before their status-quo fade-outs. In *I Can Get It for You Wholesale* (1951), Susan Hayward starts out as not only career-minded but uninterested in marriage. However, she must be taught a lesson, which includes winding up in Dan Dailey's arms. Screen females of this period often take one step forward and then maybe three back. In the never-dull *Crime of Passion* (1957), columnist Barbara Stanwyck, firmly anti-domesticity, implausibly marries police detective Sterling Hayden and is thrust into suburbia, soon focusing all her drive, ambition, and sexuality into furthering her husband's career. How long before she snaps? Not long, soon resorting to murder. Whether you were male or female, how could the pervasive cultural messages of consumerism and conformity as cure-alls, whether absorbed from movies, television, or advertising, *not* incite some discontentment and rejection?

The following ten movies are reactions to the contemporary landscape. While some embrace ordered domestic ideals, others subversively balk at such buttoned-up notions. Some of the films' characters are desperate to have all that's been promised while others are disillusioned by their supposed attainment of picket-fence dreams. The thing about flawless domesticity is that it doesn't exist, even if you thought you saw it in such banalities as *Father Was a Fullback* (1949) or *Mother Didn't Tell Me* (1950). Creating photoplays that depicted neatly mapped-out lives is perhaps a logical reaction to the ever-hovering anxieties of life in an atomic era. What better distraction than to try to control every detail of your own small world? But that doesn't mean you won't also feel suffocated. Despite their varied circumstances, here are characters grappling with the great expectations of family life in mid-century America.

Pitfall (1948): Dick Powell and Jane Wyatt

***Pitfall* (1948)** – Dick Powell seems to have it all: a good job at an LA insurance company, a perfect wife (Jane Wyatt), and a young son (Jimmy Hunt). But at breakfast he's sarcastic, feeling very much in a rut, triggering this cautionary film-noir tale. It's aimed at other husbands and fathers who might also be feeling trapped, as well as tempted to shake things up, despite not really having anything to complain about. Powell's company is investigating Lizabeth Scott, looking into her possibly ill-gotten assets from her boyfriend, an imprisoned embezzler (Byron Barr). Though Ms. Scott is clearly a path out of Powell's rut, their subsequent affair soon unsurprisingly threatens his whole life (even though the affair is brief and ends amicably). The effortlessly scary villain is (no surprise) Raymond Burr, a private detective obsessed with Scott, becoming her stalker. It's refreshing that Scott is no femme fatale here, just a nice girl, a model. Wyatt, later an iconic sitcom wife on *Father Knows Best,* is not only intelligent but has believably "married" interplay with Powell, who, though solid, sometimes underplays to the point of near-unconsciousness. *Pitfall* is another good movie from director Andre de Toth, the maker of *None Shall Escape* (1944), a singular WWII movie, and *Crime Wave* (1954), a terrific film noir. Abetted by its fine use of LA locations, *Pitfall* is built upon domestic boredom and an unglamorized reality. In risking his marriage and his home, Powell gets more than he bargained for, including being beaten to a pulp and firing a gun. Though the movie dares to suggest an is-that-all-there-is response to achieving the American Dream, its moral, finally, is to remind men to appreciate what they have and beware any reckless impulses. *Pitfall* gets major points for a happy ending that isn't rose-colored, free of any guarantees that life can completely return to what it had been. Here's an adult, probing film rooted in a character who feels stifled by the confines of everything he's been told will make him happy.

Strange Bargain **(1949)** – Another good noir-ish LA picture, it's a fast and brief (sixty-eight minutes) low-budget murder mystery directed by Will Price (Maureen O'Hara's then-husband). Though it's too easy to guess the ending, it's not bad at all. This portrait of suburbia is far from idealized, with a model American family doing everything correctly yet struggling to survive. They go to church and say grace at meals, but they're having trouble meeting their monthly nut. That can't be right! Gray-templed Jeffrey Lynn (in a better-than-usual performance) has worked twelve years as an assistant bookkeeper. Martha Scott is his wife, and they have a son and a daughter. Lynn's financially strapped boss (Richard Gaines) seeks Lynn's help in his suicide plan, paying Lynn ten thousand dollars to make it look like murder (so Gaines' family can collect the insurance money). Lynn tries to stop him but finds him dead, so he follows the plan as instructed. But did Gaines commit suicide or was he murdered? This movie was intriguingly revisited as the basis for a 1987 *Murder, She Wrote* episode with Lynn, Scott, and Harry Morgan (the police lieutenant) returning to their original roles for a plot-shifting riff on the screenplay—complete with clips from the film as flashbacks. *Strange Bargain* is an interesting portrait of flawed post-war circumstances, with domestic instability inviting high melodrama. Though seemingly doing everything expected of him, Lynn's character is unable to succeed in 1949 America.

The Reckless Moment **(1949)** – The great German-born director Max Ophüls (*The Earrings of Madame de…*) made this fascinating female-driven suspense film, a look at domestic life when a woman must fend for herself. Joan Bennett is a wife and mother called upon to handle a distressing family situation without any aid from her never-seen husband (on a business trip in Berlin). In her care are her kind but useless father-in-law (Henry O'Neill), her seventeen-year-old daughter (Geraldine Brooks) and her pubescent son (David Bair). Despite Bennett's attempts to stop them, Ms. Brooks and Shepperd Strudwick (a sleazy art dealer) are fooling around. When Strudwick appears at the family home (on Balboa Island, fifty miles from LA), there's a violent confrontation with Brooks, leading to his accidental death. Brooks begins the film like another Veda Pierce (Mildred's horrid teenager), but after Strudwick's death, she moves to the periphery (weeping mostly). Suddenly, Bennett is dumping the body, essentially doing anything and everything to protect her brood. (She's played both parents before, already tested when her husband was overseas during the war.) In a sly counterpoint, the film is set the week before Christmas, placing its matron in anything but a holiday mood. Then an Irish-accented blackmailer (James Mason) arrives, seeking five grand for Brooks' love letters to Strudwick. Mason is unusual for being kind and sympathetic to Bennett, defying plausibility by falling in love with her. (It surely is convenient to have an amorous blackmailer.) Bennett is ideal as a typical American mother (as she'd be, next year, in the far lighter *Father of the Bride*), though Mason seems ill-at-ease in a less well-drawn role. Alongside the Christmas irony, there's a rich subtextual detail concerning Bennett's son, often half-dressed and exposing skin, which never fails to irk his mother. The fact of his being in the midst of puberty—a second child soon to be sexual—is a reality Bennett isn't ready to accept. She's being forced to learn that she's unable to stop either of her children from growing up, a potent realization for mommy. *The Reckless Moment* is a stirring testament to mothers as the protectors of the home, capable of meeting any challenges flung their way, with those in Bennett's care shielded from most of what transpires. Despite too much melodramatic action at the climax (which includes Mason's evil partner), this is a vibrant melding of highly charged tension and honest domestic issues, elevated further by Ophüls' signature long takes and mesmerizing tracking shots, plus a brisk pace and a fresh locale.

Everything I Have Is Yours (1952) – There's every reason to expect that this MGM vehicle for the dancing duo of Marge and Gower Champion will be just another backstage musical. Yet it's actually about bigger things than the mechanics of creating hit shows. It opens with a triumphant Broadway debut for the married team, but Marge, after one performance, learns she's pregnant and leaves the show. Gower continues successfully with Monica Lewis as his new partner. The plot takes a decidedly feminist stance with Marge itching to return to dancing by the time her daughter is nine months old, not wanting to retire just because she's a mother. Why shouldn't she go back to the work she loves, the work at which she excels? Well, Gower is against it, hoping she'll stay ensconced in their CT home. He's a jerk for much of the movie, while, naturally, Ms. Lewis is a bitch who's hoping to steal him for herself. *Everything I Have Is Yours* shows a wife and mother seeking fulfillment outside the home, craving the artistic self-expression she once had. The couple eventually splits, and so Marge, undeterred, pursues her comeback without him. The movie had the potential to dig deeper; it seems like an outline for a more serious exploration of the central issue. Even so, it's an acceptable, even ambitious try, with the stars embracing their best-ever screen opportunity. Both of them do surprisingly well in the acting department, especially Marge (who always had more personality and presence than Gower, even if it was he who had the film-star looks). There are three major Marge-and-Gower dances—a tappy up-tempo, a sexy "Casbah" number, and a Fred-and-Ginger-ish dream ballet—which display the team's boundless versatility. By avoiding a sexist cop-out ending, *Everything I Have Is Yours* feels more progressive than many Golden Age films, those that eagerly hand their career women pink slips.

Easy to Love **(1953)** – Another MGM musical, but, while *Everything I Have Is Yours* feels forward-thinking, *Easy to Love* is cringingly dated. Esther Williams' character has everything: she's beautiful, smart, and talented. But she's fixated on getting a wedding ring from her boss, Van Johnson, head of Cypress Gardens in Florida. Williams is the water park's main attraction, doing four shows daily, plus secretarial work for Johnson, all for $75 a week. For eight years, she's been slaving away, all in the hope of being Mrs. Johnson (something that's never crossed his mind). Not only is he all business, but he's surly, selfish, and manipulative. Though it's all in the name of romantic comedy, it's excruciating to watch this incredibly capable woman accept all his degrading nonsense; for some unclear reason, she loves him. There are suitors—womanizing musical-comedy star Tony Martin and nearly always shirtless swimming hunk John Bromfield—and other, better professional offers ($300 a week for a NYC water follies), but, no, rather than break free, she craves her dysfunctional relationship with Johnson. (It's no fun watching her use the other two guys to try to make him jealous.) The bathing-suit numbers are a mixed bag, and though Busby Berkeley's water-skiing finale is impressive, it has nothing to do with Williams' strengths as a swimmer. Mr. Martin carries the musical load (singing some tepid new songs quite well), and the film also benefits from director Charles Walters' tasteful color sense and designer Helen Rose's lovely clothes. As usual, Williams is at home onscreen, while Johnson, obviously, is at his least appealing. Supposedly oblivious to her love all these years, he finally realizes, most unconvincingly, that he *does* love her, leaving no reason for viewers to feel anything but skeptical about this doomed happy ending. I hope that girls in the audience were questioning Williams' actions, ultimately disappointed in her "victory" of nabbing a creep. *Easy to Love* was intended as a frivolous amusement, but there's no avoiding the bad taste of its message to get a proposal at any cost! It's especially depressing after the feminist impulses of Williams' 1952 pictures, *Skirts Ahoy!* and *Million Dollar Mermaid,* films that might truly inspire girls and make them want to be like Esther Williams.

Executive Suite **(1954)** – The bane of onscreen 1950s domesticity was June Allyson. She seemed to be passing herself off as the perfect wife, the new Myrna Loy, but, in truth, she was a frightful and coyly guilt-inducing nightmare, not just here but in the same year's *Woman's World* and *The Glenn Miller Story.* (Was she popular with women because she clearly was no threat to anybody?) *Executive Suite* is a corporate drama, about the sudden death of the president of a Pennsylvania furniture company, leading to behind-closed-doors power plays regarding who's going to replace him. It's a good, absorbing black-and-white ensemble piece with an all-star cast, cleanly directed by Robert Wise, though essentially a soap opera, a drama without gray areas. It all comes down to good guy William Holden, the head of design and development, and bad guy Fredric March, the company controller. Holden represents high-quality aspirations and pride in your product; March is all about the bottom line and the stock holders. Holden is ambivalent about being a leader; March is grasping for power. It's art versus commerce, idealism versus cynicism, a fight for the soul of the company, a microcosm of the soul of America. Plus, oh no, March appears to be single. Certainly the forces of the American family can defeat a suspiciously unattached climber! Though Holden stands in for all husbands and fathers, as well as American exceptionalism, the shrewd, scheming March steals the movie. A once-beautiful leading man, March was by now a great character actor, artfully delineating a maneuvering (and hungry) shark. Holden's character is less magnetic thanks to all that virtuous baggage, plus his having to contend with wife Allyson. Though it makes sense that she's very interested in her husband's career, why does she come off as meddling and annoying? I think it's Allyson's smug tone, which includes her off-putting and pandering effort to court audience adoration. (Ms. Loy made us love her by just *being*, without a firm eye on how she was coming across.) As nurturers go, Allyson is awfully steely. Even when engaged with her little-league son, whom she pushes to be a better pitcher, she's more insistent than helpful. Allyson and Barbara Stanwyck (overacting as the suicidal daughter of the company founder) both have nearly immobile faces and scary voices, Allyson's rasp versus Stanwyck's bass-baritone. *Executive Suite* is a liberal-minded big-business movie, an anti-greed tract celebrating American vision and know-how. Its message: never underestimate the potential of the U.S. family, and, more importantly, you can achieve the American Dream without sacrificing your wholesomeness.

The Tender Trap (1955) – A CinemaScope adaptation of a recent Broadway comedy, it's by no means short and sweet, slackly directed by Charles Walters (*Easy to Love*), but, even worse, lacking any chemistry between Frank Sinatra and Debbie Reynolds. He's a theatrical agent and ladies' man; she's an actress. As Sinatra's boyhood pal, David Wayne, newly separated from his wife (and three kids) back in Indianapolis, arrives at Sinatra's NYC apartment, a pad with a revolving door of lovely ladies, everyone from Carolyn Jones, his dog walker, to Celeste Holm, a classy violinist. The main problem here is Reynolds' character. First of all, she's only in the theater until marriage comes along. Her cavalier attitude about showbiz makes her quickly unlikable, not to mention ungrateful, apparently oblivious to her good fortune at being employed in a show. She's an unpleasant device, a mechanized creation salivating to be a Stepford wife. She falls for Sinatra when she sees him sitting in a chair in a home-show furniture display. As the last piece of her preordained fantasy, she "casts" him in the role of would-be husband, all according to a stupid image in her head. It leads to an empty, perplexing relationship. Why is this swinger dating a virgin? Why is she chasing a known womanizer? Entertaining though it can be, *The Tender Trap* is deeply marred by being so drearily committed to a quest not only for domesticity but conformity. Sinatra must be tamed! Sure, he resists, but the movie (and Reynolds) know what's good for him. (How low had our comic heroines sunk since the joyously freewheeling days of Irene Dunne and Carole Lombard?) The expert Holm gives the best performance, raising the film with her sophisticated comic grace, though even she's saddled with an awful stereotype, the sad career girl, still unmarried at 33 and desperate! Mr. Wayne is also skillfully low-key, developing nice rapports with both Holm and Sinatra (who is in full ring-a-ding-ding mode). Reynolds is everything she's supposed to be, but, really, who wants to be around *that*? The best sequence is the first, Sinatra's hipster delivery of the title tune, sauntering toward a far-off camera, growing taller against a blue sky.

There's Always Tomorrow (1956) – One of the best and least-known of director Douglas Sirk's domestic melodramas of the 1950s, its title is an ironic comment on what proves to be a thematically resonant soap opera about Fred MacMurray's mid-life crisis. He's another American male who seems to have it all, running a successful toy company in California, married to Joan Bennett, father of three, able to afford cook/housekeeper Jane Darwell. Yet no one, especially Bennett, has any time for him. Like Dick Powell in *Pitfall*, he's a decent man in a rut, but this time the woes go deeper than mere boredom. Call it suffocation. Meanwhile, Bennett revels in the whirls of domestic life, and, in the process, always puts her kids first, thus neglecting her romantic life with her husband. An explicit metaphor for MacMurray is his robot toy, both of them moving automatically. Then old friend and former co-worker Barbara Stanwyck returns after twenty years, now a successful NYC dress designer, out west to open a new shop. Extremely glamorous and beautifully dressed, Stanwyck looks sensational. Currently divorced and lonely, she had originally left home because of her unsatisfied love for MacMurray. They start spending time together, rather chastely, reviving a past that appears to have been semi-romantic. There are some contrived coincidences to keep the plot going, but the movie rather daringly sets up a logical situation for adultery, all the while questioning MacMurray's supposedly enviable sitcom-like lifestyle. In a piercing scene, the disenchanted MacMurray can't even bring himself to enter his own house. And how about the startling private moment when he deliberately raises his newspaper to block a family photo from view? Refreshingly, there's no Stanwyck-Bennett confrontation, although two of the kids (the grown son and teen daughter) confront Stanwyck in a rather forced, unconvincing scene. Shot in almost noir-ish black and white, and competently acted, *There's Always Tomorrow* improves upon a 1934 version (same title) starring Frank Morgan. It's also the fourth and final teaming of Stanwyck and MacMurray, the first two of which are masterworks: *Remember the Night* (1940) and *Double Indemnity* (1944). No matter its ending, no matter its pitting another sad career girl against the American family fortress, and no matter how it pulls back from its most provocative notions, *There's Always Tomorrow* remains memorable for the stings of its central character's doubts and yearnings.

The Catered Affair (**1956**) – It's Paddy Chayefsky doing for the Irish what he did for Italians in *Marty* (1955). This modest, likable movie is about "little people," complete with Marty himself, Ernest Borgnine, now a Bronx cabbie. Well-made by director Richard Brooks, it's literally a poor man's *Father of the Bride*, about the planning of a wedding without an upper-middle-class bank account. As Borgnine's wife, Bette Davis is wildly miscast in a role created on television by Thelma Ritter, an actress born for this type of ordinary-person role. Ritter might've gotten an Oscar had she played it onscreen, whereas Davis, however committed, offers an effortful accent and an overly controlled performance. Unalterably fancy and mannered, she's never loose enough, unable to "throw away" a single line or gesture. (Great together in 1950's *All About Eve*, Davis and Ritter were hardly interchangeable.) Daughter Debbie Reynolds announces that she and schoolteacher Rod Taylor are getting married and don't want any fuss, but Davis hopes to give Reynolds something she'll always remember. Life isn't so great, the movie seems to say, so why not have one shining day to look back on? Of course, Davis wants to make up for her own pitiful wedding, which perhaps was a harbinger for her unhappy union. Why not a wedding breakfast with all the trimmings? In true *Father of the Bride* fashion, things get out of hand money-wise, with Davis increasingly needing and fighting for her catered affair. Based on Chayefsky's teleplay, Gore Vidal's screenplay balances its downbeat outlook with late-breaking uplift and pat assurances. This movie was a real breakthrough for Reynolds. She's marvelous, without a trace of her MGM-musical pizzazz, and with a touching stripped-bare honesty, plus a palpably sexy kissing scene with Taylor on his Murphy bed. Who could have expected that Debbie Reynolds would wipe the floor with Bette Davis? One actress simply resides inside her character; the other self-consciously maneuvers hers. Also in the cramped household are a son (Ray Stricklyn) and Davis' bachelor brother (Barry Fitzgerald). With one bathroom for five people, *The Catered Affair* evokes Depression-era tenement films, while also providing a welcome lower-class edition of the 1950s domestic drama.

Bigger than Life (**1956**) – If Dick Powell in *Pitfall* and Fred MacMurray in *There's Always Tomorrow* were suffering from the suburban blues, what to make of James Mason as a husband and father who becomes a scissors-wielding maniac? Though this film is ostensibly about prescription-drug addiction, it's *really* about the domestic nightmare of constant financial pressures. As with Jeffrey Lynn in *Strange Bargain,* things just aren't working for Mason, a schoolteacher forced to moonlight as a cab dispatcher (a secret he keeps from wife Barbara Rush and young son Christopher Olsen). Everything looks perfect at first, like a color episode of *Father Knows Best,* including Ms. Rush's immaculate chocolate cake (the surest symbol of a healthy America). In this world of bridge-playing and twin beds, why is Mason feeling sick, having pains, and collapsing? It turns out he has a rare inflammation of his arteries and only a year to live, but cortisone can keep him alive. The drug puts him on an energetic high, until the cure proves worse than the disease, leading to mood swings, to the point of psychosis! How can you not feel that Mason is simply allergic to his life, the choking conformity, the mounting bills, the entrapment? It's a nice touch to have his home decorated with posters of Italian cities, a suggestive visualization of escape fantasies. Mason is excellent, throwing himself into the role's mania, tears, and rage, eerily pushing his son toward the kind of perfectionism that may have led to his own unraveling. This is incisively detailed work, but the overall conception is too limited by the era's censorship, avoiding much of the ugliness we expect here, in terms of language, violence, and sex. And Mason, who also produced the movie, is too British for such an American story, too rarefied to be an Everyman. The film is laughably dated and naive with regard to drug use and doctors, but, with its psycho unleashed on suburbia, it remains a striking attempt at offbeat fare. Director Nicholas Ray provides the same kind of colorful vibrancy and fevered intensity (plus a thrilling use of CinemaScope) that he had recently brought to *Rebel Without a Cause* (1955). Ray visually darkens the palette as Mason's situation worsens, notably when his shadow looms. There's also an inspired image of Mason's face in a cracked bathroom mirror, jaggedly splitting him into both Jekyll and Hyde. If its transitions seem abrupt and theatrical, well, *Bigger than Life* is a heightened experience, turning the quest for the American Dream into a flat-out horror movie.

Dark Victory: WWII for Grown-Ups (1949-1962)

Once Allied victory was deemed inevitable, the movie industry began moving away from its staunch morale-building, away from comic-book renditions of the Axis powers. One might have expected war-themed movies to have grown more optimistic as victory approached, but actually the reverse happened. The major war movies of 1945, whether released before or after the war's end, are mostly sobering elegies. Imminent victory ironically, or perhaps sensibly, signaled that the time had come to take stock of the last four years, to feel the shared losses, to express gratitude toward those not coming home, thereby enabling the movies to look at the war in more realistic terms. With morale no longer a concern, Hollywood was able to let go of its war-effort functions and try to make sense of all that had transpired. Overall, movies matured considerably in the late 1940s, in no small measure because the nation had come through a world war and was now living in an atomic age.

Released between V-E and V-J Days, William A. Wellman's *Story of G.I. Joe,* from United Artists, is probably the finest war movie made during the war (and one of the all-time great WWII movies). Seen through the eyes of real-life war correspondent Ernie Pyle (Burgess Meredith), *G.I. Joe* is an uncompromising tribute to the grunt soldier, a plotless and episodic combat film about the constant filth, mud, and exhaustion—the overall grind—facing U.S. soldiers traipsing through Italy. Shot in a pseudo-documentary style, *G.I. Joe* also boasts the first outstanding Robert Mitchum performance. He's the commanding officer, a man of integrity and top-notch leadership skills but privately worn-out, burdened by self-inflicted guilt regarding those in his charge now dead. Mostly absent of clichés, propaganda, and politics, *G.I. Joe* permits viewers to absorb the war's casualties, especially in its tremendously moving ending, amplified further by Pyle's war-related death before the film's release.

In December, four months after V-J Day, John Ford's *They Were Expendable* arrived, another somber show of respect, doing for the navy what *G.I. Joe* did for the army (though not quite as successfully). Starring real-life navy hero Robert Montgomery and John Wayne, both cast as lieutenants in the South Pacific, this MGM production is generally regarded as a masterpiece, even though its leisurely storytelling has little momentum, and no one among its characters is well-defined or even interesting. It cannot be faulted for its physical authenticity, especially in the precise and admiring attention aimed at the war's initially undervalued PT boats. However emotionally affecting this movie is occasionally, most of its dramatic excitement comes from seeing those boats in action.

Also in December came the release of Lewis Milestone's *A Walk in the Sun,* another combat movie, a Fox film set in 1943 Salerno, dealing solely with an infantry unit's moment-to-moment mission. Like *G.I. Joe,* it addresses relentless discomfort, ongoing wounds and deaths, and mounting grief. With narration delivered by *G.I. Joe's* Burgess Meredith, the mood is contemplative and pensive. As for the "walk," it's a six-mile trek from their beach landing to a Nazi-held farmhouse, with Dana Andrews substituting for the cracked-up commander. Despite the you-are-there realism, there's too much self-conscious poeticism in the writing (and unwelcome assistance from an accompanying ballad on the soundtrack). The climax, an excellent battle sequence, is nearly ruined by the jarring inclusion of heroic American songs, suddenly distorting a war-is-hell movie into a patriotic rouser about U.S. might and belying most of what precedes it. It surely is interesting that Wellman, Ford, and Milestone, the directors of this trio of primarily sensitive and penetrating WWII movies, had all made renowned WWI films in the years after the armistice: Wellman's *Wings* (1927), Ford's *Four Sons* (1928), and Milestone's *All Quiet on the Western Front* (1930). Details change, but war's laments do not.

Premiering a week before V-J Day, Delmer Daves' *Pride of the Marines,* starring John Garfield, is based on a true story about a soldier blinded on Guadalcanal in 1942. Tracking Garfield's healing process, this Warner Brothers film is wildly uneven and sometimes heavy-handed, but it's nonetheless adult and effective and paved the way for Marlon Brando as a paraplegic veteran in *The Men* (1950) and Arthur Kennedy as another blinded soldier in *Bright Victory* (1951). As Garfield's character makes his painful transition home, his story was part of a logical shift for home-front movies. With the war's end, the traditional home-front dramas were supplanted by those involving returning servicemen's post-war assimilation, notably including *Till the End of Time* and the Oscar-winning Best Picture *The Best Years of Our Lives,* both from 1946, followed by, among others, *Living in a Big Way* (1947) and *Apartment for Peggy* (1948). As for further exploration of the actual war years, Hollywood took some time away from the subject, time for increased objectivity and reflection. Among the few major war movies of 1946 are *13 Rue Madeleine, O.S.S.,* and *Cloak and Dagger,* while 1947 delivered *The Beginning or the End* and just about nothing else, with none of these especially good. In 1948, Hollywood addressed the overseas post-war situation, dealing with lost children amid the rubble in Fred Zinnemann's *The Search,* and mixing Occupied Germany and romantic comedy (uneasily) in Billy Wilder's *A Foreign Affair.*

Three years after 1945's plaintive, last-word looks at the war itself, MGM ushered in a new era of WWII movie, assuming that the audience was ready to absorb and examine reality, fortified by the consoling knowledge of the war's outcome. Opening in December of 1948, and based on a hit Broadway play by William Wister Haines, Sam Wood's *Command Decision* boasted a big-name cast led by Clark Gable and Walter Pidgeon. Probably the talkiest war movie ever made (its obvious stage origins undisguised), *Command Decision* is an Air Force picture, set in 1943 London, about daylight precision bombing over Germany. How do you send men to likely death? Are the continual sacrifices worth it? Such complicated questions were unlikely to be confronted in wartime movies but proved to be fair game in a victorious peacetime. Also from MGM was *Battleground,* another admirable William Wellman WWII picture opening in November of 1949. Like *G.I. Joe* and *A Walk in the Sun,* it's a combat film; instead of Italy, the evocative setting is a snowy, foggy, and otherworldly France and Belgium of 1944 (the Battle of the Bulge). Though both tough and thoughtful, *Battleground* can also be a bit bland, with some lightweight actors such as Van Johnson (also in *Command Decision*) and George Murphy. Such a movie (a huge hit) can never mean today what it did back then, when so many in the audience had been directly touched by the war, making this burgeoning era of WWII movies part of a national closure.

The 1950s brought occasional returns to the comic-book antics of WWII action movies—*American Guerrilla in the Philippines* (1950), *Sealed Cargo* (1951)—and also saw the war used as the basis for comedy-mystery (*Stalag 17*), glossy soap (*Battle Cry*), and hokey melodrama (*The Sea Chase*). However, '50s Hollywood often strove to uncover aspects of the war not previously exposed. Combat movies offered bracingly fresh settings (the Underwater Demolition Teams of 1951's *The Frogmen,* or an Australian infantry unit fighting in Africa in 1953's *The Desert Rats*), while other movies taught history lessons: about Rommel in *The Desert Fox* (1951); the dropping of the atomic bomb in *Above and Beyond* (1953); and the elaborate "Operation Mincemeat" caper in *The Man Who Never Was* (1956). You could find an ingenious and velvety black-and-white spy picture (*5 Fingers* – 1952), a colorful wide-screen account of a brave missionary in China (*The Inn of the Sixth Happiness* – 1958), or Marlon Brando's fascinatingly multi-dimensional Nazi in an otherwise wanting drama (*The Young Lions* - 1958). WWII worked as fodder for intimate stories, such as *Heaven Knows, Mr. Allison,* or spectacular epics like *The Bridge on the River Kwai,* both of 1957. Finally, the devastating truths of the Holocaust would come to screens via *The Diary of Anne Frank* (1959) and *Judgment at Nuremburg* (1961).

But let's go back to December of 1949, as the new era was taking shape, when gray areas and ambiguities were welcomed into WWII movies (as they had been in WWI films in the '20s and '30s). With most WWII newsreels and war-era Hollywood pictures shot in black and white, movies continued to present WWII primarily as a black-and-white event, nicely matching any usable war footage, while *Fighter Squadron* (1948) and *Task Force* (1949), both lemons, exist merely as excuses to showcase *color* war footage. Nine of this chapter's ten films eschewed color for grays both visual and thematic.

Twelve O'Clock High (1949): Hugh Marlowe and Gregory Peck

Twelve O'Clock High (1949) – The psychological toll of command is a crucial war-film subject, famously tackled in the WWI flying yarn *The Dawn Patrol* (1930) but never handled better than in this Best Picture Oscar nominee. The set-up is the same as in *Command Decision*: in 1942 and '43 England, an American unit is engaged in daylight precision bombing raids over German industry. Without the former film's staginess, *Twelve O'Clock High* (based on a novel) is infinitely superior, while still being talkier than most war movies. The film presents opposing styles of leadership from two group commanders: Gary Merrill, beloved by the men and sensitive to their needs, yet unsuccessful in the job; and Gregory Peck, Merrill's replacement, hard-nosed and demanding, feared and disliked, but yielding better results and increasing the men's pride. Peck deliberately assumes an inflexible persona. "Consider yourselves already dead," he tells his men, his advice on how best to approach their mission. There's a telling scene of Peck having a cigarette outside his car, right before assuming command, taking his last free moments before inhabiting his "character," before having to keep his emotions in check and becoming the seemingly unfeeling fellow he needs to be. (He's like an actor in the wings, preparing for his entrance.) How long can anyone force himself *not* to get emotionally involved? *Twelve O'Clock High* portrays war as a mind game, separate from the agenda of defeating the Germans. These mental challenges are about sustaining your ability to do your job and getting others to do *their* best. If anything, this makes such men even more heroic, facing complex internal struggles, seeming far more human than heroic characters who operate like automated stick figures. Peck is unerringly intelligent and tensely committed, though I'd say his role has even more rumbling textures than his fine performance can accommodate. Tautly directed by Henry King (who next directed Peck in the 1950 western masterpiece *The Gunfighter*), *Twelve O'Clock High* is visually stark with most of its intensity of an interior variety. It's not the kind of film anyone would have wanted to see in 1943, but 1949 audiences accepted this intricate examination of the private, invisible warfare within fighting men.

Three Came Home (1950) – Based on a true story, it's one of many real-life WWII accounts that were coming to light in post-war America. Set primarily inside a female prisoner camp run by the Japanese in Borneo, it features one of Claudette Colbert's top dramatic performances, an impassioned handling of a grueling experience. It's the third film in director Jean Negulesco's unofficial trilogy of woebegone women following Ida Lupino in *Deep*

Valley (1947) and Jane Wyman in *Johnny Belinda* (1948). Atmospherically convincing and dramatically restrained, *Three Came Home* finds a center in a most unusual connection between Colbert and her colonel captor played by Sessue Hayakawa. An American, Colbert is married to Patric Knowles, a British colonial official; they are parents of a four-year-old boy. She's also the author of a book of which Hayakawa is a fan. (He's chillingly friendly when he asks her to sign a copy, not finding it at all awkward that she's also an "occupied" citizen.) Though there's none of the comic-book villainy depicted in many war-era films, the film doesn't stint on Japanese brutality, including a wrenching sequence, cruelly set across a watery ditch, in which the male captives bid farewell to the women and children. The title may give away the ending, but it's still an agonizing struggle, including beatings and starvation. (The elegant Colbert gleefully resorts to eating retrieved garbage.) The film's most harrowing scene is Colbert's nighttime assault by a camp guard while she's trying to collect laundry during a windstorm. She fights him off, but her formal accusation leads to her own torture. It's especially fascinating, for 1950, when, near the end, Hayakawa tells Colbert that his wife and three kids have been killed at Hiroshima. The movie suddenly displays the grief and humanity of the enemy, even allowing Hayakawa a sobbing emotional release. He has remained civil and respectful to Colbert, and his evenhanded mix of warmth and barbarity seems to say that war is war, so what can you do? (Hayakawa was in training for his 1957 running of another prisoners' camp in *The Bridge on the River Kwai*.) The surefire finale has all eyes trained on the top of a small hill, anticipating the surviving men's return, a deeply poignant finish to a strong, offbeat WWII movie. It ends in 1945 on September 11, a date as yet untainted, filled only with profound joy.

Force of Arms (1951) – I'd label it mostly routine, attempting to conjure *A Farewell to Arms*. Director Michael Curtiz brings it to life for a thrillingly good mid-section before its return to convention. William Holden, a man without family or any ties, is a sergeant promoted to lieutenant after showing sterling leadership in 1943 Italy. He romances Nancy Olson, a nice-girl schoolteacher turned WAC; they meet in a graveyard. The war is suddenly just a backdrop for their abrupt love story, but what will love do to this soldier's performance? Now with something to lose, Holden is no longer fearless. He turns cautious in battle, providing "safe" leadership, leading to his possible responsibility in the death of his pal (Frank Lovejoy) as well as others, even though no one blames him. Instead of fighting harder because of a future he's fighting *for*, he's ironically weakened by his newfound love, made self-conscious and self-protective by it, becoming a potential combat liability. Tantalizingly raised, this issue, as well as Holden's subsequent guilt and need for redemption, offers a potent war-movie subject that, unfortunately, gets too fleeting attention. The plot reverts to more familiar action, choosing improbable movie-ish turns over challenging and perhaps disturbing content. At least Holden, fresh from *Sunset Blvd.* (1950) and again opposite the adequate Ms. Olson, further displays his hard-bitten dark side which compensates for some of the film's romanticizing (fitted to a lush Max Steiner score).

Decision Before Dawn (1951) – A virtually forgotten Best Picture Oscar nominee (in a year that overlooked *The African Queen* and *Strangers on a Train*), here's a spy movie refreshingly devoid of glamour and exoticism. Based on true events of 1944, it concerns German POWs who agree to spy for the Allies. The extraordinary Oskar Werner—sad-eyed and sensitive, evoking a blond Montgomery Clift—is a German corporal, a medic. He volunteers to assist the Allies *because* he loves Germany and believes that the sooner she's crushed the sooner she can be healed. Despite American stars, Richard Basehart and Gary Merrill (in admittedly peripheral roles), Werner is the whole show, endowing the drama with its only fully dimensional characterization. What's so emotionally compelling is his friendless isolation, spying on his own people while considered a traitor by the Allies. (His painfully ironic code name is "Happy.") Unfortunately, his five-day mission isn't terribly interesting, suspenseful, or easy to follow. The best sequence has the undercover Werner unexpectedly assigned as a medic to an ailing Nazi colonel (O.E. Hasse), a one-on-one of perilous tension, the kind mostly lacking elsewhere. Overall, director Anatole Litvak is better at handling action and creating atmosphere than achieving storytelling clarity, though everything comes together in the final half hour, once Werner is on the run. With its gritty capturing of authentic locations (in France and Germany), the film has a tangible credibility, and its melancholy theme—a head-bowed acknowledgement of heretofore unappreciated sacrifice (unknown to all but a few)—hits its mark. *Decision Before Dawn* honors those who thanklessly served a cause without living to see the fruits of their courage. Its solemn gratitude is graced with that enriching, soulful Werner performance, so full of contradictory feelings.

The Man in the Gray Flannel Suit (1956) – In a way, it's *The Best Years of Our Lives* ten years later, a check-in on our servicemen's presumably completed adjustment to civilian life. But what lurks within? What has remained unspoken? The plot deals with sex, family, and money, but it yearns to be more than a facile tale of suburbia. Based on Sloan Wilson's 1955 bestseller, this Technicolor adaptation is a mixed bag: ruminative, relevant, and absorbing, but also soapy, overlong, and misshapen (with a clumsy structure of WWII flashbacks). Writer-director Nunnally Johnson should have parted with large chunks of his screenplay, yet he's clearly more comfortable with words than a camera. In the title role, Gregory Peck, husband to Jennifer Jones and father of three kids, commutes to NYC from Connecticut. His career looks very *Mad Men-ish* with his new job in public relations at a broadcasting firm owned by Fredric March (whose son died in the war). Worse than Peck's money woes is his private, lingering guilt over the men he killed in WWII, including the accidental grenade death of a pal. He was already married to Jones back then, but still engaged in a genuine love affair with Italian Marisa Pavan. His burden is his secret past, something perhaps shared by many veterans in the audience. (Peck eventually learns that he and Pavan produced a son.) There are unnecessary subplots given much too much time, wrongfully stealing focus from Peck and our interest in the impact of his past on his present. Ms. Jones is little help, a bit Lady Macbeth yet never quite emerging, remaining off-puttingly remote (even when overacting). Reunited from *Duel in the Sun* (1946), she and Peck scored this second box-office hit, with Peck ideally cast to represent a generation. Yet it's no surprise that Mr. March comes off best, giving another of his rivetingly accomplished middle-aged performances. (Inexplicably, March's wife isn't played by his ubiquitous real-life wife Florence Eldridge; instead, it's Ann Harding.) Despite its many flaws, including an over-the-top climax, *The Man in the Gray Flannel Suit* is an immediate grabber, generating enough good will to allow for ample forgiveness whenever it strays or stagnates.

Attack (1956) – Like *Command Decision* and *Stalag 17*, it's a WWII movie based on a play: Norman Brooks' *Fragile Fox* (1954). From a solid foundation—just the right balance between combat and dialogue—*Attack* feels ahead of its time, daring to suggest that not everybody in the U.S. military is good, brave, or competent. Character-driven in a *Twelve O'Clock High* manner, it examines the war being fought within a unit, amid clashing personalities in oppressive confines. Set in 1944 Europe, it's a Robert Aldrich movie (made eleven years before his testosterone-fueled fantasia *The Dirty Dozen*, which is about as far from the questioning *Attack* as any WWII movie could be).

Lee Marvin, a lieutenant colonel, and Eddie Albert, a captain, are from the same part of the South. Albert is also a coward, helped along militarily by his judge-father's influence but ever-burdened with daddy issues and the obvious psychological pain of being unable to prove himself a real man. *Attack* opens with inaction on Albert's part, resulting in the deaths of fourteen of his own men. Jack Palance, a lieutenant and a model soldier, is enraged by Albert's dangerous unworthiness, but Marvin won't place Albert elsewhere, hoping to take advantage of his connections after the war. At fifty, Albert is far too old for a role that would make infinitely more sense as a confused, immature youth. Marvin and Palance are more typically cast, the former slickly self-serving, the latter properly intense. All the way to its shocker of a climax, *Attack* has little to do with beating Hitler. It uses WWII to look at fighting men on the same side, a group of fallible human beings in extreme circumstances, saving and harming each other.

Verboten! (1959) – One of writer-director-producer Samuel Fuller's best films, not quite *fully* realized but singularly adventurous. Sure, it's lopsided, and it has a botched ending, plus the worst title tune of all time (sung by an uncredited Paul Anka), but Fuller gets points for taking chances, for being so crazily ambitious. Call it low-budget or just plain cheap, there's no denying Fuller's exceptional filmmaking, notably his superb opening combat sequence through a bombed-out German village. James Best is the handsome U.S. sergeant who falls in love with Susan Cummings, the local German girl who treats his gunshot wound (in the rear), hiding him until the Americans arrive. The war is on the wane, and Cummings hopes to prove to Best that not all Germans are Nazis. The bulk of the film takes place in the post-war era, which gives it a fresh sense of time and location, despite recurring clunkiness. At first, Cummings marries Best so she can use him, but then she really falls in love with him. He becomes a civilian in post-war Germany, landing a job in Cummings' village, a U.S. military-office position. Leaving behind the Best-Cummings relationship, *Verboten!* shifts attention to post-war Nazi activities, specifically a Hitler Youth group reorganized into a secret terrorist organization. Then, turning almost into an all-out documentary, the movie visits the Nuremburg trials, including footage of the atrocities, beating *Judgment at Nuremburg* to the screen by two years. There's interesting, unusual content throughout, from the war's dying days to German resistance to the Occupation, and Best remains a sweet, earnest center, but *Verboten!* is an editing mess, all the way to its bizarre dead-stop ending.

Hell to Eternity (**1960**) – Beginning in Depression-era Los Angeles, it's another true story, an imperfect movie worth your time. An orphaned Caucasian boy is embraced by the family of his Japanese pal. The boy becomes a member of the family, learns to speak Japanese, and grows up to be Jeffrey Hunter. Then comes the attack on Pearl Harbor, experienced here from a Japanese-American perspective, unlike that of any U.S. film preceding it. Anti-Japanese sentiment leads to the internment of Hunter's "parents," while his "brothers" go to war in Italy. This first section is original, eye-opening, and touching, and the film is never again quite this fine or flavorful, becoming more standard once Hunter is a marine. The tension evaporates, and the film bogs down in military humor and soldierly horniness. The action then travels to the war in Saipan, and Sessue Hayakawa (who else?) shows up as a Japanese general. Luckily, the movie recovers from its slump once Hunter starts rescuing starving Japanese civilians hiding in caves, connecting with them as people, eventually called the Pied Piper of Saipan. Hunter is appealingly affable, but his character has surprisingly little depth. We're also denied any emotional catharsis regarding his Japanese family. Directed by film-noir master Phil Karlson—who made the smashingly good *Kansas City Confidential* (1952)— *Hell to Eternity* can be a frustrating mix of the stirring and the forgettable, but the remarkable novelty of its subject sustains it through its lapses.

Bridge to the Sun (**1961**) – If *Hell to Eternity* seemed new and daring, then *Bridge to the Sun* further upped the ante on war stories moviegoers hadn't seen before. Another true story, another strong movie, but it should have been more moving, more rattling, and never quite lives up to the potential of the material. Directed by Étienne Périer, it centers on an interracial love story followed by a war-torn culture clash. Carroll Baker, a Tennessee gal visiting D.C. in 1935, meets James Shigeta, the secretary to the Japanese ambassador to the U.S. They date, fall in love, marry, move to Japan, and have a daughter. Baker is informal and demonstrative, not at all submissive, but she tries her best to adapt. The Pearl Harbor attack occurs while they're back in the U.S.; all enemy diplomats are instantly deported. Baker opts to return to Japan with Shigeta (who is against the war), and she's there until after the bombs are dropped. Baker and her child spend most of the war at a house in the country, with Shigeta on the run for his anti-war stance. Beginning with a bubbly Southern charm, Baker is rather good, even though she sometimes resorts to shrill overplaying. Like *Three Came Home*, here's another real-life American woman's incredible saga, inconceivably trapped between two worlds, unprepared for what awaited her.

Hell Is for Heroes (1962) – Lacking gloss, sentimentality, and gung-ho attitudes, this combat movie is as spare and no-nonsense as its lean budget. As in *G.I. Joe* or *Attack,* there are no concerns about politics or patriotism, just the goings-on within a fighting unit. Set in 1944 France and directed by Don Siegel (*Dirty Harry*), its set-up is streamlined: six U.S. soldiers are ordered to hold a ridge while outnumbered by nearby Germans. Steve McQueen is the nominal star but this is truly an ensemble cast, including James Coburn, and, as comic relief, both Bobby Darin and Bob Newhart. (Here are McQueen and Coburn between *The Magnificent Seven* and *The Great Escape*.) Scruffily unshaven, McQueen is expectedly cool and sexy, but he's not playing a likable fellow. Instead, he's unfriendly, distant, and terse, a loner who's nobody's buddy, nor a team player. A private, he's technically a bad soldier—a nuisance to his superiors, disagreeing and disobeying—yet he's the unit's toughest fighter, signifying that one has nothing to do with the other. He is actually the kind of guy who wins wars, perhaps unfit for anything else, but the movie wants to have it both ways. After all, our anti-hero is still a dazzling movie star doing brave, macho things in traditionally heroic movie terms, particularly in his super-human initiative at the climax. Yet the film's impact nonetheless feels anti-war, with director Siegel showing special interest in depicting combat death as ingloriously agonizing as possible. Like *Verboten!* here is a war movie that ends abruptly, in mid-battle, perhaps a comment on the seeming interminability of warfare, at least for those in the thick of it. *Hell Is for Heroes* impressively balances tension with its visceral blasts of violence, and, in McQueen, adds a formidably off-center good guy to the screen's post-war exploration of WWII. After being released from the topicality and morale-boosting obligations of the war era, and whether dealing with true-life experiences or more generalized war content, Hollywood has never lost its appetite for WWII. After spending 1942-45 helping the populace get through the war, the industry has been putting the war in perspective, never more committedly than in the years when WWII was still a fairly recent event, still a palpable part of so many lives in the audience.

Starlet Rising in the West: The Unsteady Climb of Marilyn Monroe (1950-1953)

I'd say that 1953 delivered more than its share of Hollywood milestones: *The Robe* introduced CinemaScope, and the public resoundingly approved; *House of Wax* gave 3-D a fleeting moment of widespread popularity; the Academy Awards got their first-ever television broadcast; Frank Sinatra made his sensational comeback in *From Here to Eternity*; and major stardom was achieved by a female headed for icon status. Make that *two* female icons: Audrey Hepburn, who, having gained experience in European movies and on Broadway, seemed to come out of nowhere for Oscar-winning stardom in *Roman Holiday*, and Marilyn Monroe, who, different from Hepburn as can be imagined, had been toiling in plain sight, observed by early-'50s moviegoers as she worked her way to the pay-off of her three 1953 releases. First, in January, she was Joseph Cotten's rotten, cheating wife in *Niagara*, and then, in July, she was a musical-comedy gold digger, alongside Jane Russell, in *Gentlemen Prefer Blondes*, and finally, in November, she joined Betty Grable and Lauren Bacall for more comic gold-digging in *How to Marry a Millionaire*. Suddenly, Marilyn Monroe was the new queen of Twentieth Century-Fox, having had the baton passed to her by none other than Grable herself.

The Monroe persona, secured by her Lorelei in *Gentlemen Prefer Blondes* and Pola in *How to Marry a Millionaire*, put a unique spin on "the dumb blonde," a broad classification that had recently reached blissful heights via Judy Holliday in *Born Yesterday* (1950) and Jean Hagen in *Singin' in the Rain* (1952), both of whom were coarser and more street-smart than Monroe's more innocent variations. Though naive about most everything else, Lorelei and Pola do know how to make the most of their physical assets. In these modest, intensely likable vehicles, Monroe made a cuddly bombshell, a sweet-natured glamour queen, but, mostly, she was an original and wondrous comedienne. Who can forget Lorelei's giddy materialistic glow ("I just love finding new places to wear diamonds"), or Pola's vain refusal to wear glasses, hilariously tripping or walking into walls? Who but Monroe could be so adorably blank?

She ranked as the top box-office female in 1953, 1954, and 1956 (Grace Kelly led the pack in 1955). Monroe's stardom would last less than ten years (before going immortal), leaving a filmography with a number of middling efforts—the western adventure *River of No Return* (1954), with Robert Mitchum, and the garish musical *There's No Business Like Show Business* (1954), both of which look like setbacks after her 1953 trio; her performances are downright awkward. Later, there was another slight musical, George Cukor's *Let's Make Love* (1960), in which she's softly appealing but disappointingly secondary to Yves Montand. Among her more underrated achievements are her sparkling, effortlessly funny work in the flimsy bauble *The Prince and the Showgirl* (1957), trouncing her overemphatic co-star (and director) Laurence Olivier, and then her deeply touching (if erratic) dramatic acting with an even-better Clark Gable in John Huston's *The Misfits* (1961), her final film. She remains beloved for two Billy Wilder classics: the overrated comedy *The Seven Year Itch* (1955), in which she's charming in a fantasy-creature role, and the impossible-to-overrate *Some Like It Hot* (1959), her best movie, featuring her distinctive mix of comic twinkle, voluptuous beauty, and, perhaps most key of all, little-girl-lost vulnerability. Her finest performance? That would have to be her hilarious yet unbearably poignant turn as an Ozark beauty (with Hollywood dreams) in *Bus Stop* (1956), a triumph sinfully ignored at Oscar time.

Instead of dealing further with the aforementioned films, or her persona as a serious-actress sex symbol who studied with Lee Strasberg at the Actors Studio, I'm interested in the lead-up to the Monroe phenomenon, the dues-paying years, when there was no assurance of her success. Certainly, her legend is partially tied to her premature death at thirty-six (and the supposed mysteries surrounding it), leaving her always young and beautiful but also marked as one of the movies' great casualties, forever a figure for rescue fantasies. Let's begin in post-war Hollywood and track Norma Jeane Mortenson's rise from modeling and walk-ons to bit parts and supporting roles to full-fledged stardom. How does a lovely, ambitious young woman stand out among countless lovely, ambitious hopefuls? How is she able to reveal her potential, or even realize that she *has* potential? Monroe was not plucked for stardom; she had to climb every individual ladder rung. First glimpsed speaking about eight lines as a waitress at The Gopher Hole in the juvenile-delinquency drama *Dangerous Years* (1947), she was barely visible uttering her *one* line to June Haver in *Scudda Hoo! Scudda Hay!* (1948). There was a principal role in *Ladies of the Chorus* (1948), a B (or even C) black-and-white musical, which proved not to be her big break. A comic bit with Groucho Marx in *Love Happy* (1950) was followed by her stint as one of a foursome of chorus girls in the western musical comedy *A Ticket to Tomahawk* (1950) with Dan Dailey (later billed below Monroe in *There's No Business Like Show Business*). In the Clifton Webb comedy *For Heaven's Sake* (1950), she's merely a photo in a magazine, just another blonde starlet, someone not yet recognizable.

Beginning with supporting roles in two 1950 classics, Monroe began her tentative haul to stardom. It actually took just three years, but with no less than a dozen films. Call it a case of three steps forward and two steps back, with, naturally, no guarantees of an eventual breakout. The odds were against her, the likelihood being that, before long, her studio (Fox) would tire of her and shift their attention to the next pretty young thing. Monroe's pre-stardom years had her mostly playing the undemanding roles of secretaries and models, sometimes dumb, sometimes devious, sometimes not given enough time to be either. I've excluded two especially negligible efforts: *The Fireball* (1950), a B movie starring a roller-skating Mickey Rooney, with Monroe in a girlfriend role (not Rooney's); and *Home Town Story* (1951), an hour-long newspaper yarn in which she is Jeffrey Lynn's secretary. Also absent is an A (but ordinary) boxing movie, *Right Cross* (1950), starring June Allyson and Ricardo Montalban, in which Monroe has one scene (about five lines) as a model with the memorable name of Dusky Ledoux. Now here are the rest, from *The Asphalt Jungle* to *Niagara,* forming a step-by-step account of just how Marilyn Monroe became *Marilyn Monroe.*

Monkey Business (1952): Marilyn Monroe

The Asphalt Jungle (1950) – It was a significant leap to go from chorus cutie in Fox's *A Ticket to Tomahawk* to being tested for (and then landing) a supporting role in an MGM production directed (and co-written) by Oscar winner John Huston. Like the Huston classics *The Maltese Falcon* (1941) and *The Treasure of the Sierra Madre* (1948), *The Asphalt Jungle* is focused on greed; it's an intricately wrought crime picture with an outstanding jewel-heist sequence and a neat gallery of shady characters, all in crystalline black and white. Ex-con mastermind Sam Jaffe (Oscar-nominated and terrific) puts together his team, including Sterling Hayden, an ex-con stick-up artist. The scheme is to be bankrolled by Louis Calhern, a crooked lawyer who's actually broke and planning a double-cross. Calhern is superb as a loathsome weakling with a slick façade (and an invalid wife). Billed eleventh in the end credits, Monroe plays Calhern's mistress, though young enough to be his granddaughter. First seen asleep, she's curled up in a chair like a cat. A happy little materialist, she enjoys very nice digs courtesy of Calhern, whom she calls her "Uncle Lon." The role established a key duality in the Monroe persona, the mix of a perennially childlike quality with a ripened beauty and purring sexuality. Her girlish nature is stressed when she calls a cop a "big bananahead," but then she turns on the "Marilyn" factor, employing her potent sexual wiles to try to manipulate him. Though fairly green as an actress, especially in her emotional confession (of previous lies) to the police, Monroe is ideal playing such a limited personality, an amoral gold digger interested only in herself. Jean Hagen, as Hayden's doormat girl, has the largest female role, but, to borrow the movie's slang for gun, it's Monroe who's the real "heater."

All About Eve (1950) - Monroe is billed ninth in her only Oscar-winning Best Picture, one of the great films about, among other things, the theater. Though blessed with Joseph L. Mankiewicz's incomparably literate and eminently quotable dialogue, as well as his unceasingly astute direction, Fox's *All About Eve* is hardly cinematic, but who cares when what it offers feels so authentic? Bette Davis gives one of the towering portraits of stardom. As Margo Channing, she's glamorous and caustically funny, but also a hardworking thespian devoted to an eight-shows-a-week lifestyle, currently dealing with self-sabotaging insecurities about her age (forty), and especially fearful that it's too late for a real life with her thirty-two-year-old lover (Gary Merrill), a hotshot director. Davis constructs a prickly, complicated personality, alternately blurring and separating an actress' onstage and backstage worlds. (We know she's good at heart because Thelma Ritter, her no-nonsense maid-dresser, genuinely likes her.) The movie is so close to perfection that its three flaws stick out: Merrill's awful and phony speech about the theater, scheming Anne Baxter's overly emotional mishandling of her big confrontation with critic George Sanders, and the vanishing of Ritter after the famed party sequence. The wittily cutting Sanders and the warm, classy Celeste Holm (as Davis' best friend) are both sublime, while Monroe is just about flawless in her two scenes as Miss Caswell, who, in Sanders' words, is "a graduate of the Copacabana School of Dramatic Arts." She's an absolute delight as a no-talent looker with acting aspirations. Fully aware of her sexual magnetism—which she can turn on like a switch—she's apparently sleeping with Sanders for the doors he can open. (This casting-couch element explains why Clifton Webb, seemingly perfect for Sanders' role, actually *wasn't*.) Davis sarcastically introduces the blatantly va-va-va-voom Monroe as an old friend of Sanders' mother. Later, when confronted with Monroe's possible casting in the ante-bellum *Aged in Wood*, Davis responds, "She looks like she might burn down a plantation." Watch Monroe readying herself to overwhelm producer Gregory Ratoff, beaming as she exits in bare-shouldered pursuit. In a cast of heavyweights, she not only holds her own but exhibits a gift for comedy as well as being an enjoyable contrast with the jaded Sanders, her sparkly eagerness offset by his dry superiority. How amusing to hear his reference to the Oscars being "questionable," unaware that the film itself would win Best Picture (and Best Supporting Actor for Sanders).

As Young as You Feel (1951) – After having been signed and dropped by Fox once before, Monroe was re-signed on the strength of her showings in *Asphalt Jungle* and *Eve*. Unfortunately, the studio carelessly cast her in forgettable light comedies, in those minor roles of secretaries or models. Based on a Paddy Chayefsky story, *As Young as You Feel* is a mild sitcom, only passably entertaining but blessedly short. In a role that appears to be a Clifton Webb cast-off, Monty Woolley stars as a printer forcibly retired at 65. He fights back by dying his hair and impersonating his company's big New York president, intending to change the policy of mandatory retirement. Sixth-billed Monroe is secretary to Albert Dekker, Woolley's print-factory boss. She's a skillful employee, not a dummy, and she sports a great haircut and wardrobe, not really permitted to showcase much more. The film's fine ensemble resorts to pushing, fighting for attention, including Thelma Ritter, Jean Peters, David Wayne, Constance Bennett, and Russ Tamblyn.

Love Nest (1951) – June Haver, once considered a possible threat to Betty Grable's status as Fox's top blonde, was clearly on her way out, relegated to this black-and-white sitcom opposite an equally bland William Lundigan as her husband. It was fourth-billed Monroe who would soon become Grable's successor, if she could just pry herself from the sitcom rut into which she had been dumped. A tenant in the NYC residence owned by the central couple, Monroe is a model and former WAC once stationed in Paris with Lundigan. She's his "old war buddy" Bobbie (as in Roberta), which Haver has obvious trouble getting past. Written by I.A.L. Diamond (later the co-writer of Monroe's *Some Like It Hot*), this comedy, like *As Young as You Feel*, doesn't present a Monroe who is breathy or stupid: she's a low-voiced, savvy young woman. However, her storyline, such as it is, fades away; there's no sense that Fox is grooming her for stardom. She's used as a bathing-suit-wearing, homewrecking threat, a heavenly face matched to a wicked body, a mere contract player meant for cliché roles.

Let's Make It Legal (1951) – The trend continued with a third TV-style comedy, one that turned out to be the final rom-com of Claudette Colbert, a key star of the genre, having kept it churning blithely for nearly two decades. (The fact that she's playing a grandmother was a tip-off that her end was near.) No surprise, it's not one of Colbert's best, an overly familiar comedy of remarriage (also co-written by I.A.L. Diamond) that arrived too late in the cycle, though she certainly gives it a touch of class. After twenty years of marriage to publicity man Macdonald Carey, her divorce (brought on by his gambling) becomes final at midnight. (Carey is no Cary Grant, nor is he Fred MacMurray or Ray Milland.) The arrival of Zachary Scott recreates their high-school triangle, only now Scott is a millionaire bachelor. As a client of Carey's, Monroe is a model, a recent "Miss Cucamonga" beauty-contest winner, seen, of course, in a bathing suit. She's also a gold digger who sets her sights on Scott even though he shows no interest in her, preferring the fifty-ish Colbert. Monroe has four scenes, again playing a devastating man-trap more conniving than dumb. Her contact with Colbert makes up for not working with her in *All About Eve*: Colbert was forced to relinquish playing Margo Channing because of a back injury.

Clash by Night (1952) – Thank goodness Monroe got loaned to RKO for this Fritz Lang-directed version of Clifford Odets' play, a noir-ish soap. Lang gives it a visual vibrancy, an atmospheric detailing of a California fishing community, before the script devolves into lustily overblown melodrama and hysterics. This was Monroe's best gig since *All About Eve,* freeing her from the tedium of disposably piffling comedies, again allowing her to share the screen with a major movie queen: Barbara Stanwyck. Monroe is billed fourth, above the title, after Stanwyck, Paul Douglas, and Robert Ryan. As a cannery girl, she's sometimes dressed in jeans, loosened from her usual glamour-puss costuming. Unleashed is a fresh and spirited young actress, especially playful with boyfriend Keith Andes (as Stanwyck's brother). Monroe and Andes share a mildly violent relationship—she bites his ear and punches his chin; he mock-strangles her—all in the name of foreplay. She is likably feisty with Andes, then genuinely sisterly and non-judgmental with Stanwyck. At forty-five, Stanwyck is about ten years too old for her role, but she clearly understands her knocked-around character, who returns home after the death of a married lover. She's hardboiled, alright: "Home is where you come when you run out of places." After marrying nice-guy fisherman Douglas, Stanwyck begins a torrid affair with film-projectionist Ryan, a one-note creep who seems like a film-noir fabrication. (The movie fails to make the case for him as an irresistible bad boy.) Of the three stars, Stanwyck comes off best, but even she can't surmount some impossible emotional transitions, while the usually excellent Douglas resorts to full-tilt overacting. Yet Monroe shines at every turn, including her happy-sloppy drunk scene. Kept separate from the main love triangle, she and Andes are presented as the couple who fit together and like each other. Coincidentally, Ryan appeared in the original Broadway production, in the Andes role, with Joseph Schildkraut in Ryan's screen role and Tallulah Bankhead in Stanwyck's part.

We're Not Married! (1952) – Back at Fox, Monroe was inserted into another sitcom, a dated and square comedy designed to be risqué (in a screen era in which married couples slept in twin beds). It boasts an A-list director, Edmund Goulding, and an all-star cast, yet there are few chances for anyone to excel. The plot hinges on something that happened two-and-a-half years ago: a Justice of the Peace (Victor Moore) married several couples the week *before* he was legally allowed. The movie shows five couples reacting to the news that they are unwed: Fred Allen and Ginger Rogers; David Wayne and Monroe; Paul Douglas and Eve Arden; Louis Calhern and Zsa Zsa Gabor; Eddie Bracken and Mitzi Gaynor. Most viewers will be miles ahead of the writing, and much of what happens is simply too lame to bother about. The Monroe-Wayne sequence is the best, though Monroe is used primarily as a mannequin (in a *two*-bathing-suits role). She's on the beauty-queen circuit but in the "Mrs." category, married to Wayne (and mother of their baby boy). While she's off being "Mrs. Mississippi" (no accent), Wayne plays Mr. Mom. In the film's only good joke, the living-in-sin revelation positively thrills Monroe. Now, as a "Miss," she'll be eligible for all the better pageants, with her goal to be Miss America (and keep Wayne as her "fiancé"). Isn't it pleasing that Nunnally Johnson's script doesn't retire her to the kitchen? Monroe and Wayne would soon be paired in another Johnson screenplay, *How to Marry a Millionaire,* further developing their wonderful odd-couple chemistry, the regular guy and the goddess he beguiles. By the way, *We're Not Married!* is the only Monroe movie in which she plays somebody's mother.

Don't Bother to Knock (1952) – Her career might have crumbled with this truly bad vehicle for the "dramatic" Marilyn Monroe. She is clearly not up to the task, but, in fairness, the material is crummy, sketchy melodrama, no more than pulpy junk. Plus she's miscast, too much in bombshell mode for her mentally fragile, once-suicidal character. Her pilot boyfriend died in a crash, and so she confuses pilot Richard Widmark (top-billed) with the dead lover. Showing occasional intimations of acting potential, Monroe mostly seems stilted and closed-off, in no way unbound enough to play an all-out crazy. Set in a NYC hotel, the plot has her hired as babysitter to little Donna Corcoran. There's a threadbare romantic subplot between Widmark and Anne Bancroft (in her film debut, as the hotel's lounge singer). With one character hiding in a bathroom, another locked in a closet, and someone else tied up in a bedroom, the film verges on outright comedy, a bedroom farce played as high melodrama. Nobody comes off well, with Bancroft, a decade before her Oscar win, showing as little dramatic oomph as Monroe. There's certainly no sense that the Marilyn Monroe breakthrough is a mere year away. What does come through is her terror (not the character's), an actress clenched (while trying her damnedest). Instead of director Roy Baker, she needed a George Cukor to guide her, to inspire her to relax, connect, and express. There's an actress in there, but she can't get out!

Monkey Business (1952) – This was to be no inane sitcom, not with Howard Hawks (*Bringing up Baby*) directing, not with Cary Grant and Ginger Rogers in the leads. And yet it's incredibly feeble and unfunny. Both stars, two comic giants, come off poorly, mugging their way to an embarrassing loss of dignity. The set-up, and a few of the early scenes, show promise, but it all falls apart once the actual plot kicks in. Chemist Grant, an absent-minded-professor type, is working on a youth-restoring formula. However, a lab chimpanzee mixes a formula of her own and tosses it into the water cooler. First, Grant drinks it, then Rogers, then both. It cures Grant's bad eyesight, bursitis, and makes him his 20-year-old self (of the 1920s), driving fast, roller-skating, and diving, none of it funny. Rogers dances, plays pranks, and is suddenly virginal, none of it funny. (She offers a tiring variation of her splendid 1942 *Major and the Minor* performance as a "12-year-old.") Being young again apparently does nothing more than make people act like idiots. Grant's boss is Charles Coburn whose secretary is, you guessed it, Monroe, the film's one bright spot. Because of Coburn's complaints about her "punctuation," she's "careful to get here before nine." After her briskly efficient secretaries in *Home Town Story* and *As Young as You Feel*, here she is hired for her looks but hopelessly craving to do well. Of her curvaceous incompetence, Coburn tells Grant, "Anybody can type." She has a swell scene with Grant, displaying a shapely gam and asking, "Isn't it wonderful?" She's referring to her non-rip plastic stockings (which he invented), while imbuing the film with her lovely joyous spirit. She shares a good deal of one-on-one screen time with Grant, which had to have been a thrill (as well as intimidating) for an up-and-comer. As for Rogers, she twice shoots rubber bands at Monroe's posterior. *Monkey Business* is another Monroe comedy co-written by I.A.L. Diamond; the fourth one, *Some Like It Hot*, was the charm. She would soon reteam with Hawks and Coburn for her career-altering *Gentlemen Prefer Blondes*.

Niagara (1953) – As part of the all-star anthology *O. Henry's Full House* (1952), Monroe has a six-line cameo as a streetwalker (of Old New York), opposite a homeless (and marvelous) Charles Laughton. In this first and best of the film's five episodes, she makes a firm connection with Laughton in their few moments together, adding him to her list of Golden Age co-stars (Davis, Colbert, Stanwyck, Grant, and Rogers). Again, no breathy voice, and just a touch of bruised toughness. You might say she was warming up for Rose Loomis in *Niagara,* an all-out "bad girl" who lifted Monroe into stardom (yet she never again played anything like her). This thriller is mostly perfunctory, yet Monroe's luscious glossiness singes the screen, enhanced by a saturated color scheme usually associated with Fox musicals (like *Gentlemen Prefer Blondes*). With competition only from the stunning titular locale and a dazzling bell-tower murder, *Niagara* is all hers. She's first seen smoking in bed, topless (covered by a sheet), in full makeup. What fun she is playing trash, even though her acting really isn't very good, a case of presence over nuances, offering more of a visually volatile impact than a delineation of character. (Director Henry Hathaway positively leers.) She seals the deal with her oozing rendition of a ballad titled "Kiss." Billed below Monroe, the estimable Joseph Cotten plays her jealous, unbalanced husband suffering from Korean War fatigue and going over the edge (like the Falls themselves). It's an underwritten role to which he tries to bring weight, but, alas, he remains a device. Meanwhile, Monroe and her lover (Richard Allan) plot to kill him. There's a dull inspector (Denis O'Dea) and a dull, nice woman (Jean Peters), but then *everybody* seems dull compared with Monroe, even though she isn't fully in command of her movie-star confidence, as she soon would be in *Gentlemen Prefer Blondes* and *How to Marry a Millionaire*. There would be future kinks in her onscreen confidence levels, in those shaky performances in *River of No Return* and *There's No Business Like Show Business,* but, when you take stock of her witty comic charisma in *The Seven Year Itch, The Prince and the Showgirl,* and *Some Like It Hot,* and her mature, searching depths within *The Misfits,* and her gorgeously exposed humanity in *Bus Stop,* you should feel some gratitude toward her sometimes frustrating trial period of the early '50s. While much of it might appear to have wasted her time, she was also identifying her strengths and weaknesses, nurturing her obvious comic instincts, learning to connect with the camera and her fellow actors, all in the name of combining sex, humor, and vulnerability into one of the more enrapturing onscreen forces of mid-century Hollywood (and ever after).

I Feel a Song (of Woe) Comin' On: Unvarnishing the Musical Biopic (1950-1957)

A hybrid genre, the musical biography conflated two popular forms, the Hollywood musical and the biographical drama, resulting in the kind of musical in which characters usually did *not* break impulsively into song or dance, instead saving their musical moments for the rehearsal hall and opening night. Attempting to depict the nuts and bolts of show business, musical biopics offered the so-called real lives of renowned singers, dancers, vaudevillians, and musicians, whether they be individuals or teams. Going back to their inception in the 1930s, musical biopics were conceived primarily as excuses for entertainment, leaning more heavily on the musical rather than the biographical aspects. What you got was a connect-the-dots approach, the dots being the musical numbers and the storyline just enough to make audiences feel they got something more than a variety show. Take *The Great Ziegfeld* (1936), the decade's biggest musical biopic and a monumentally undeserving winner of the Best Picture Oscar. Despite its three hours, did anyone learn anything about the titular impresario? Kinda, sorta, no, not really. William Powell is charming and remote as Ziegfeld, as is Myrna Loy as wife Billie Burke, with the self-consciously "radiant" Luise Rainer, as stage performer Anna Held, over-emoting her way to an Oscar. Aside from the spectacular "A Pretty Girl is Like a Melody" production number and musical performances by Ray Bolger and Fanny Brice, the whole affair is utterly impersonal and respectfully embalmed. Its success set the standard for the form.

The 1940s popularized a few different strains of musical biopics, though all of them stuck firmly to the convention that only the flimsiest of actual biographical detail was required. If you somehow felt that you had actually learned something about the films' subjects, chances were that little of it was true anyway. Manageably fictionalized accounts were always preferable to messy reality. It was nostalgia that was being peddled, and nothing said the good old days like songs of yesteryear, which is why we got Alice Faye as *Lillian Russell* (1940), Ann Sheridan as Nora Bayes in *Shine On Harvest Moon* (1944), and Betty Grable and June Haver as *The Dolly Sisters* (1946). The subjects themselves were already largely forgotten, so it was up to the stars to generate the necessary excitement. The decade's two colossal successes built around this format were *Yankee Doodle Dandy* (1942) and *The Jolson Story* (1946). Despite their enormous popularity and acclaim, this duo didn't reach any deeper than the aforementioned works, but they had two dynamos to carry them. *Yankee Doodle*'s James Cagney, in his Oscar-winning performance as George M. Cohan, is a case of one larger-than-life figure aptly cast as another, with the wiry Cagney owning this movie by virtue of his magnetic personality and eccentric dancing, putting on such a grand show that you forget the movie's biographical elements are no more than agreeably superficial. *The Jolson Story* brought Larry Parks an Oscar nomination for mastering Al Jolson's flamboyant (or slobbering) performing style, lip-synching to perfection, with the rest of the movie a colorful but facile showbiz saga, tepid whenever the music stops. The nutty, pointless sequel, *Jolson Sings Again* (1949), with Mr. Parks back for more, has so little to tackle that the making of the first film becomes a major plot point, with Parks ludicrously playing both Jolson and himself: Parks' Jolson says of Parks, "Kid's great!" Audiences clearly liked their musical biopics to be easily digestible and musically generous, heavy on the show-must-go-on blather, light on just about everything else.

The '40s musical biopics about individual performers look like multifaceted psychological portraits compared to the ones centered on Broadway composers. The biggest of these to come out of Warner Brothers was the splashy (and awful) *Night and Day* (1946) about Cole Porter, as played by Cary Grant (at his most uncomfortable, even embarrassed-looking). Of course, Porter's homosexuality is nonexistent, though wife Alexis Smith does confront him about treating her like an afterthought, but that's just a temporary wrinkle on the way to their happy ending. It was at MGM that the composer biopic really flourished, simply by reconceiving (and overwhelming) the formula into all-star extravaganzas. *Till the Clouds Roll By* (1946), supposedly about Robert Walker as Jerome Kern, has so little to say about Kern that it shifts its focus to his pal, Van Heflin, and Heflin's troublesome daughter, Lucille Bremer. Is that really the best they could come up with? The film's bad ideas and vapid dialogue are the price one pays for numbers by the likes of Judy Garland, Lena Horne, and Tony Martin. If MGM's *Words and Music* (1948), featuring a ridiculously droopy Tom Drake as Richard Rodgers alongside Mickey Rooney's Lorenz Hart, had just been an uninterrupted musical program they might really have had something. No, this time our gay subject, Mr. Hart, has an unfulfilled personal life because he's apparently too short to find happiness! Thank goodness for Gene Kelly and Vera-Ellen in the great "Slaughter on 10th Avenue" ballet and other special moments from Garland and June Allyson, but as a biopic it's brain-numbing nonsense. Were lame fictions, or no story at all, the only options?

Though the 1950s produced throwbacks to the bare-bones plotting and shut-up-and-get-to-the-songs approach to musical biopics—Fred Astaire and Red Skelton as Kalmar and Ruby in *Three Little Words* (1950), Mario Lanza in *The Great Caruso* (1951), Mitzi Gaynor as Eva Tanguay in *The I Don't Care Girl* (1952)—something new was also happening, or at least *trying* to happen. Musicals in general were getting better, less like disposable distractions and more like musical plays, with Vincente Minnelli's *Meet Me in St. Louis* (1944) exerting a major influence on the genre's artistic future. At the same time, post-war Hollywood was dealing with new issues, things like alcoholism (*The Lost Weekend*) and mental illness (*The Snake Pit*), which meant that audiences were being primed to accept more grown-up fare. The following musical biopics show a willingness to separate from the previous decades' antiseptic ways, a desire (sometimes failed) to go beyond featherweight excuses to hear beloved songs again. A sheen of superficiality and obvious compromise often remained, meaning that you could hardly refer to these films as warts and all, but at least they weren't *no* warts at all. The popularity of many of them was so significant that some of their subjects became more famous for their biopics than for their actual careers. These dramatic musicals essentially kept the drama and the music separate—unlike, say, *Gypsy* and *Funny Girl,* two "integrated" biopics conceived for Broadway—while hoping that the drama and the music would become emotionally entangled, infusing and intensifying each other, especially in the films about tragic artists. Though the cycle petered out by the decade's end with lesser pictures like Sal Mineo in *The Gene Krupa Story* (1959), the high-drama musical biopic has remained the model. Countless examples include Diana Ross as Billie Holiday in *Lady Sings the Blues* (1972), Sissy Spacek as Loretta Lynn in *Coal Miner's Daughter* (1980), Jamie Foxx as Ray Charles in *Ray* (2004), and Chadwick Boseman as James Brown in *Get on Up* (2014).

I'll Cry Tomorrow (1955): Susan Hayward

Young Man with a Horn (1950) – I'm cheating: this story of jazz cornetist Bix Beiderbecke (1903-1931) is technically not a biopic, based as it is on a 1938 novel inspired by him (with the names changed). Even so, and despite its flaws, it feels like a breakthrough for the musical biopic, delving into its central character's downfall. As "Rick," Kirk Douglas eventually goes to pieces, smashes his trumpet, and is briefly in the gutter, all of which implies that the movie succeeded at digging deeper. Yet Michael Curtiz's direction and even Douglas' performance seem only to hint at a willingness to explore beneath the surfaces, making the film feel beholden to old-fashioned story conventions rehashed from musical melodramas like *The Man I Love* (1946). However, there is something interesting here involving Lauren Bacall as Douglas' wealthy intellectual wife. She's the film's discordant element, the artist in search of an art, a frustrated person filled with spite and self-loathing. Jealous of her husband's gift, she tries to steal him from his art, to destroy what she can never have. (She even plainly, for the time, dabbles in lesbianism.) None of this is as fleshed out as it might've been, but it's still the film's best dramatic component. Doris Day is the nice girl on hand to sing the vocals, and as a musical program *Young Man with a Horn* is sublime. Its partial dramatic success doesn't negate the fact that Bacall's conflict retains a stinging force more riveting than anything in Douglas' downward spiral.

With a Song in My Heart (1952) – Here's the official kick-off of the 1950s brand of musical biography, even though in many ways it's just as glossy and conventional as its '40s counterparts. By splitting its attention between showbiz clichés and a story of genuine pain and courage, it feels like the transition to the better, richer biopics to come mid-decade. A vibrant Susan Hayward stars as vocalist Jane Froman (1907-1980), though you might say that Froman's glorious singing voice is the real star here, so clear and full, and with a sensational songbook to sing, notably Rodgers and Hart's gorgeous title tune. During Froman's swift and glitzy rise, Hayward glides smoothly through the musical stagings and proves to be an expert lip-syncher. Then we arrive at the reason Froman's story is being told: her agonizing comeback after surviving the 1943 plane crash that left her unable to walk. Hayward, mostly asked to be chipper and good-humored throughout her ordeal, is allowed only one real scene of despair. The film can't resist emphasizing soapy romance, with Hayward torn between husband-manager David Wayne and handsome pilot (and fellow crash survivor) Rory Calhoun. Thelma Ritter adds her patented comic warmth as Hayward's devoted nurse (from Flatbush, of course). Though the Oscar-nominated Hayward clearly has the stuff to penetrate the depths of this story, the film prefers glamour over guts (though it's positively stark compared to *Night and Day*'s short-shrift handling of Cole Porter's riding accident). Director Walter Lang delivered an entertaining, uplifting drama, a skin-deep and colorfully palatable look at a dark situation. It remains refreshing that *With a Song in My Heart* is a 1952 musical biopic about something other than pendulum career swings or a new show with second-act trouble.

Million Dollar Mermaid (1952) – After eight years of plush lightly-comic swim-sicals, MGM gave box-office princess Esther Williams her most ambitious opportunity, a musical drama about Australian swimmer/performer Annette Kellerman (1886-1975). Not just an ideal vehicle, it's one of Williams' better pictures, charting Kellerman's climb from a girl in leg braces to a swimming champ and eventual headliner at New York's Hippodrome. A major episode involves a scandal caused by her one-piece bathing suit, resulting in an arrest for the indecent exposure of bare legs. Victor Mature is her slick manager/love interest, and, as she rises, he sinks, making this an *A Star Is Born* for the pool set. The first half is actually more like the same year's *Pat and Mike,* with Mature devoted to the success of a female athlete, but then, unlike *Pat and Mike,* its male character sours and grows drearily insecure. *Million Dollar Mermaid* is best when fueled by feminism, celebrating Kellerman's courage, grit, and talent, with Williams coming through with a likably relaxed performance. Mature tells her, "Wet, you're terrific. Dry, you're just a nice girl who ought to settle down and get married." Williams' confident ease on dry land belies that assessment. Her Busby Berkeley water ballets (for the Hippodrome) are fantasies of color, smoke, and spray, followed by a Hollywood section in which she survives a spinal injury caused when a glass water tank cracks during the filming of her silent movie. This is a scary, well-done sequence from director Mervyn LeRoy, but the movie conveniently ends before having to deal with her recovery. Despite the central romance becoming a triangle (thanks to Hippodrome boss David Brian), the focus of *Million Dollar Mermaid* remains its inspiring female role model, portrayed by the only woman in the world qualified to play her.

The Glenn Miller Story (1954) – It's another biopic about a plane crash, but most of the audience knew the ending, making this particular biopic part of the nation's mourning process (like a musical *Pride of the Yankees*), a ten-years-later moment of respect for a man, his music, and the war that took them both. These factors necessitated a screenplay that was standard and unchallenging, sustaining a sentimental approach to the audience's shared memories of the recent past. Though it has a great director (Anthony Mann) and a great star (James Stewart), it's a slim, indistinct work with Miller (1904-1944) not much of an entity in Stewart's pleasantly bland interpretation. As Miller's wife, June Allyson, such a bright and spirited musical-comedy performer of the '40s, is an insufferable presence with a by-now sandpaper voice. Though the film clearly wants us to see her as an unyielding supporter of (and inspiration to) her husband, she comes off as an irritating, passive-aggressive Lady Macbeth, iron-willed about Stewart finding his "sound." Wouldn't a singular artist like Miller already have something he yearns to express, without all this moping around and the attendant nagging from his wife? The soundtrack, however, is consistently marvelous, as Miller makes his ascent from trombonist and arranger to bandleader, including appearances by Louis Armstrong and Gene Krupa in a Harlem speakeasy. With WWII, Miller gets a war-department commission, entertains the troops, and gets on that fateful plane. Maybe you can forgive the pandering pablum of *The Glenn Miller Story* by telling yourself that it was never intended to be anything more than the musical equivalent of removing one's hat in honor of a great deceased music maker.

Interrupted Melody (1955) – The story of opera star Marjorie Lawrence (1907-1979) covers both her career and her fight with polio, all the way to her thrilling comeback as Isolde at the Metropolitan Opera. Like *With a Song in My Heart,* this handsome biopic offers formulaic showbiz gloss "interrupted" by the physical adversity of trying to walk again. The opera sequences are beautifully staged, designed, and costumed, making them the highlights of a film never quite as penetrating off-stage, despite the crisis at its center. Superbly synchronized to recordings by Eileen Farrell, Eleanor Parker creates vivid onstage characterizations for seven opera roles. Rarely will you see these famous arias acted as fully or as luminously as they are here. Parker really did her homework (though her speaking voice is so scratchy you have to wonder how such a magnificent voice could be produced by a seemingly laryngitic character). Director Curtis Bernhardt's film opens excellently with atmospheric scenes set in Australia, with Parker a farm girl, but then it "goes Hollywood" with her nonexistent transition from farm girl to diva and her movie-ish romance with American obstetrician Glenn Ford. In his mushy, saintly role, Ford appears extremely ill at ease. As Parker's brother-manager,

Roger Moore is no better (and he looks twelve years old). When polio strikes, it comes directly after the only scene in which Parker is a bitch, making it look like divine punishment. The road to recovery moves from bleak to uplifting, including her wheelchair-bound rendition of "Over the Rainbow" for wounded soldiers. (Like too many musical biopics set in the recent past, there's no period flavor, no mention of dates, then suddenly it's WWII!) Alternately exceptional and banal, *Interrupted Melody* provided a showy Oscar-nominated field day for Parker, complete with debilitating illness and the hard fight back, but it's never truer as biography than when she's onstage, convincing you that Ms. Lawrence had the soul of an artist.

Love Me or Leave Me (1955) – In *I'll See You in My Dreams* (1951), the biopic about lyricist Gus Kahn, Patrice Wymore introduces "Love Me or Leave Me" over the phone to Doris Day (as Kahn's wife). Day's expression seems to say, "When I get the chance, I'm going to sing it way better," which she did in this Ruth Etting (1897-1978) biopic. Day got the MGM glamour treatment here, becoming a sexy, beautiful, mature star, a solid actress in a complicated role. One of the best of all musical biopics, *Love Me or Leave Me* tackles risky subject matter, though the times wouldn't allow it to be as honest as it was clearly capable of being. Day's insinuatingly expressive vocals of a cavalcade of standards made the soundtrack album a must, but between the songs lies an adult movie about sexual opportunism. To further her career from dime-a-dance gal to headliner, Day's Ruth uses James Cagney's Marty, a much-older mobster madly infatuated with her. It's a relationship built on calculation (hers) and lust (his) and was daring for the mid-'50s, even though Day couldn't be shown sleeping her way to the top. The compromise—her leading him on, while seemingly retaining her virtue (at least until they marry)—was meant to keep Day sympathetic and admirable—but it inadvertently makes Cagney the more likable character. He's a brutal mug but at least he plays fair; she's an ungrateful spoilsport, an ambitious passive-aggressive taker, and a tease. As in *Young Man with a Horn,* the spouse of the central subject dominates the movie. Funny, touching, and frightening, Cagney is at his greatest, unsparingly baring the pain and insecurity of loving someone in vain. It's a tremendous Oscar-nominated performance, as subtle as it is electrifying. His acting and Day's singing surmount the movie's bouts of timidity. There's saturated color, great costumes, but, again, little period flavor, and no help from Cameron Mitchell, the zero who makes it a love triangle. Very well-made by Charles

Vidor, *Love Me or Leave Me,* despite its shortcomings, has much to savor, but why, oh why, is there no close-up of Day when she finally sings the title tune?

I'll Cry Tomorrow (1955) – This is the big one from this era of musical biopics, the one that got closest to an uncompromised down-and-dirty approach to a rise-and-fall saga, an alcoholic drama conceived to make *The Lost Weekend* look like a pretty good time. Susan Hayward was back in the genre, but this was no *With a Song in My Heart,* no Technicolor entertainment with a softening prettiness. The life of singer-actress Lillian Roth (1910-1980), based on her autobiography, resulted in the performance of Hayward's career, a ferocious go-for-broke descent into alcoholism. Hayward is so available, illuminating both the hunger and agony of addiction, the heartbreaking *need,* as well as bravely doing her own singing, acquitting herself quite ably. (Incidentally, both Jane Froman and Lillian Roth outlived Hayward by five years.) *I'll Cry Tomorrow* is also an all-out mother-daughter movie, with a classic let's-blame-Mommy-for-everything scenario. Jo Van Fleet gives one of the great stage-mother performances, manipulating Hayward selfishly, ignoring the warning signs, though to her credit she's not an entirely unsympathetic horror. (Van Fleet and Hayward were just a few years apart, yet the casting works.) Unfortunately, the movie isn't as strong as its two actresses, with not a trace of period detail anywhere—you might think that Roth's entire life happened in 1955. Consider Hayward's big soundstage number, "Sing You Sinners," which looks like a contemporary MGM musical production, not at all evoking the early days of talkies. When she finally arrives at Alcoholics Anonymous, the film becomes little more than a promotion for the organization, securing a too-easy-feeling happy ending that includes an implausible tacked-on romance with sponsor Eddie Albert. The director, Daniel Mann, also guided 1955's other great female performance: Anna Magnani in *The Rose Tattoo* (which beat Hayward for the Oscar). Mann's work excels in the details of Hayward's harrowing drunken binges, but visually his movie isn't much. And the men, aside from Richard Conte as Hayward's sadistic husband, are a dull lot. *I'll Cry Tomorrow*—promoted as being "filmed on location…inside a woman's soul!"—is the kind of real-life showbiz tale that sends shivers down moviegoers' spines, yet the 1955 audience could handle it. It was a huge box-office hit.

The Eddy Duchin Story (1956) – Another box-office smash (but without critical acclaim), this film has much to commend, including a refreshing embrace of the 1920s, plus an abundance of New York locations, lush wide-screen color cinematography, and, of course, the music, with star Tyrone Power doing an outstanding job of looking like a virtuoso at the piano. Power does an all-around nice job as Duchin (1909-1951), beginning as an eager young musician whose musical success comes quickly and whose love life seems blessed, meeting and marrying stunning socialite Kim Novak. The best sequence is incidental, a ravishing montage of Power and Novak enjoying Central Park to the swoony strains of "I'll Take Romance," including their rainy stroll with a red umbrella. This kind of creamy filmmaking from director George Sidney is more affecting and persuasive than the more emotionally ambitious scenes to come. Too often what's intended as drama comes off as soap opera. Novak gives birth to their son and promptly dies, plunging Power into a grief so deep that he goes on a five-year tour and then enlists in the navy to fight WWII, finally returning home to repair his relationship with the son he abandoned and to take a second chance on love (with Victoria Shaw). Just when it looks like it's all going to work out, Power is stricken with leukemia. In true old-movie fashion, viewers are shielded from the severity of his illness, seeing only the occasional hand tremor. The Eddy Duchin Story is both polished and pedestrian, unlikely to produce any pesky tears. More poignant than anything dramatized here is the sad fact that Power, who carries this film so gracefully, would himself be dead in two years.

The Joker Is Wild (1957) – Frank Sinatra was riding high as an Oscar-winning dramatic actor thanks to *From Here to Eternity* (1953), followed by his even more piercing (also Oscar-nominated) turn in *The Man with the Golden Arm* (1955). He continued in this vein with the story of Joe E. Lewis (1902-1971), a singer whose vocal cords were slashed because he defied a mobster. The attack happens out of view, followed by a chilling scene in which Sinatra's bloody hand emerges, then the man himself, covered in blood as he crawls into a hallway. Though the role and the screenplay aren't up to Sinatra's former dramatic peaks, at least the movie is aiming for some of the black-and-white grittiness achieved by *I'll Cry Tomorrow*. Providing the charisma and verve sorely lacking elsewhere, Sinatra begins with a persona very much like his brash Pal Joey (a role he played that same year), until his throat is cut. The movie crams most of the singing into the first twenty minutes, while his voice is intact, including "All the Way," the film's Oscar-winning tune. Out of necessity, and in response to his effortless ease with audiences, he becomes a comic. And because he's a mug, the love of a slumming society girl (Jeanne

Crain) arouses feelings of inadequacy and self-loathing. Eddie Albert, in a part as thankless as his *I'll Cry Tomorrow* role, plays Sinatra's masochistically devoted pianist-pal, and Mitzi Gaynor is the chorine Sinatra marries on the rebound. Director Charles Vidor, apparently aiming for unadorned realism, shows little of the visual skills he brought to *Love Me or Leave Me*. The weak, hopeful ending copies a scene from Vidor's own *Cover Girl* (1944), with two Sinatras (instead of two Gene Kellys), one of them a chatty phantom. Is this the same movie that began with a slashing?

The Helen Morgan Story (1957) – We're back to Michael Curtiz (*Young Man with a Horn*) and a blatant attempt to imitate *I'll Cry Tomorrow,* focused as it is on another alcoholic female singer, in this case a casualty rather than a survivor. Helen Morgan (1900-1941) was best-known as the original Julie in Broadway's *Show Boat* (1927), a performance preserved in James Whale's celebrated 1936 film version. Earlier in 1957, there had been an acclaimed teleplay about Morgan that brought Emmy-winning attention to Polly Bergen, but Bergen wasn't a big enough movie name to headline a feature-film version of Morgan's life. Curtiz, who had given Ann Blyth her Oscar-nominated breakthrough as the despicable daughter in *Mildred Pierce* (1945), would now direct Blyth's swan song, one of the least convincing of all '50s musical biopics. Blyth had recently been one of MGM's soprano ingénues, in flops like *Rose Marie* (1954) and *Kismet* (1955), and she was certainly not a torch singer. Her Helen Morgan vocals were dubbed by Gogi Grant, who had a more appropriate singing voice. Trying for new acting depths, Blyth is all shiny surfaces. It's an emotionally inaccessible performance, possibly the screen's dullest alcoholic. If she can't sing it or act it, why in the world is she *in* it? Paul Newman gives the movie what little vim and vigor it possesses, despite his shallow character, a fast-talking Cagney-ish bootlegger. (It's yet another love triangle, thanks to married lawyer Richard Carlson.) Blyth rises from speakeasies to supper clubs to Broadway, but is soon down and out and hospitalized. Though Morgan's story did not end well, the movie opts for a happy ending, a surprise party! She can't be as surprised as any moviegoer who arrived expecting to see *The Helen Morgan Story.*

Westward Woe: The Civil War Western (1950-1959)

After *Gone With the Wind* (1939) achieved its phenomenal popularity and acclaim, every studio in town must have been trying to figure out how to duplicate, or at least come anywhere *near,* that kind of success. Would Civil War epics become all the rage? Not exactly, but it's still easy to identify the movies hoping for some residual shine off the glow of David O. Selznick's super-production, whether directly or indirectly.

Three black-and-white Civil War-themed westerns of 1940 stressed high-speed action over drama, each crafted with questionable levels of seriousness. Raoul Walsh's Kansas-set *Dark Command* generates some excitement but is mostly a shallow, insufficiently motivated conflict between a good guy (John Wayne) and a bad guy (Walter Pidgeon). The 1864-1865-set *Virginia City* and the pre-war *Santa Fe Trail,* both directed by Michael Curtiz and starring Errol Flynn, are lavish, geographically nimble melodramas frequently too foolish to be taken with a straight face (especially when Humphrey Bogart enters *Virginia City* as a Mexican bandito, complete with terrible accent, a villain North and South can briefly fight *together*). Apparently seeking not to offend anyone, Flynn is a Yankee in *Virginia City* and a Confederate in *Santa Fe Trail.* Though both these Warner Brothers films employ the same mixing of jarringly assorted elements, *Santa Fe Trail* is an especially patience-testing and unappetizing stew of rom-com love triangle, low-comedy hijinks, and, oh yeah, the John Brown story (which has to fight for screen time). These were all-you-can-eat entertainments merely tinged with historical detail and not my idea of true Civil War westerns, a legitimate sub-genre whose time hadn't quite come.

Irving Cummings' *Belle Starr* (1941), in Technicolor, was a more direct response to *Gone With the Wind* with Gene Tierney as a Scarlett O'Hara turned bandit, but it was a shamelessly derivative film for which Tierney provided an overanimated (and underwhelming) Vivien Leigh imitation. Universal-International's *Tap Roots* (1948), directed by George Marshall, is another colorful *GWTW* poser, with fiery, redheaded Susan Hayward, a former Scarlett contender in her very own Scarlett-like vehicle, and Van Heflin as her tepid, unsexy Rhett stand-in. The plot has a Southern county claiming neutrality so that life can go on as usual (with slaves), seceding from Mississippi rather than the Union, and soon in bloody battle with Confederate soldiers! Though *Tap Roots* plays like the screwiest, most puzzling of all Civil War movies, it's a fictionalized account of the Newton Knight story (told more accurately in the underappreciated *Free State of Jones,* a 2016 Matthew McConaughey vehicle). Devoid of Southern accents, *Tap Roots* is a flagrant muddle.

There were slyer copycats, movies set on either end of the Civil War but close enough to try for some *GWTW* atmosphere and accessories. Cecil B. DeMille's *Reap the Wild Wind* (1942), a moldy mediocrity from Paramount, has one-time Scarlett front-runner Paulette Goddard in a consolation-prize role. Hers is a tediously feisty and flirty performance that will make you deeply grateful she didn't actually play Scarlett. Ray Milland is her less than thrilling "Rhett," while a pre-*Tap Roots* Susan Hayward, like Goddard, gets to re-audition for *GWTW,* with both actresses flaunting Southern accents and their prettiness in period dress. Set in the South in 1840, and mighty colorful, *Reap the Wild Wind* has a giant squid at its climax. Take that, *GWTW*! Other poor *GWTW* wannabes include John M. Stahl's black-and-white production *The Foxes of Harrow* (1947) at Fox, set down south beginning in 1827, with Rex Harrison ridiculous as a Rhett-like character and Maureen O'Hara in the Scarlett slot; and Michael Curtiz's black-and-white *Bright Leaf* (1950) from Warner Brothers, a tobacco saga that starts as late as 1894 yet does everything it can to evoke *GWTW,* with Gary Cooper too old for his "Rhett Butler meets Kirk Douglas" kind of role, plus Patricia Neal as its overblown Scarlett, and even Lauren Bacall as Belle Watling! These blatant *GWTW* knock-offs not only couldn't compare with the original but were simply hopeless, overwrought movies.

The 1950s brought several high-profile Civil War movies: John Huston's black-and-white labor of love *The Red Badge of Courage* (1951), truncated and uneven, yet authentic-feeling and visually extraordinary; William Wyler's highly overrated and labored *Friendly Persuasion* (1956), centered on Indiana Quakers who very much resemble a 1950s sitcom family; Raoul Walsh's plodding *Band of Angels (1957),* which not even the actual Rhett Butler— Gable himself—could elevate, with his presence merely a reminder of how much he had aged in eighteen years and how little he connected with the passable Yvonne De Carlo as compared to Ms. Leigh; Edward Dmytryk's *Raintree County* (1957), an overlong and dramatically hollow epic, with hugely disappointing performances from Montgomery Clift and Elizabeth Taylor; and *The Horse Soldiers* (1959), a minor John Ford work with two major stars, John Wayne and William Holden, engaging in forced adversarial sparring on their vague and unexciting Union Army mission, including an amputation scene, one of its several shout-outs to *GWTW.*

But there were two great 1950s Civil War movies that most people missed, and, even today, are virtually unknown: Anthony Mann's *The Tall Target* (1951), an 1861-set train thriller starring Dick Powell, all about a pre-war assassination attempt on Lincoln (on his way to his inauguration); and Hugo Fregonese's *The Raid* (1954), in which Van Heflin and five other escaped Confederate officers infiltrate a Vermont town on a secret mission of theft and destruction.

And yet the bulk of really interesting post-*GWTW* Civil War movies are, in fact, westerns. No, not the aforementioned ones of 1940-41, which didn't bring any insight to the conflict and were merely popcorn movies most concerned with keeping pulse rates high. At their best, the Civil War westerns of the '50s make us look at the war in unexpected ways, intersecting the North and South with the West, a collision that offers fresh and fascinating perspectives. Until I saw these movies, I never thought about the seemingly far-off West as a vitally important place in the war effort. When these two genres mesh, the results expand one's perception of history, as well as the scope of both westerns and war movies. These are not, however, part of the celebrated sub-genre of psychological westerns of the '50s, movies that intensely explore character over big historical topics like the Civil War.

If westerns could be musicals (*The Harvey Girls*), comedies (*The Paleface*), even film noir (*Pursued*), then it's no surprise that they could be "pardners" with war movies. Even when the following films fall short, each is defined by an offbeat and compelling take on history, helping us to imagine all kinds of *other* things occurring while Miss Scarlett was trying to hold Tara together.

Escape from Fort Bravo (1953): Eleanor Parker and William Holden

Two Flags West (1950) – It begins in the autumn of 1864 at an Illinois POW camp for Confederate captives. An intriguing premise ignites when the prisoners, including a colonel (Joseph Cotten), are offered their freedom if they'll agree to join the Union Army in New Mexico and help defend Fort Thorn against Indians. Cornel Wilde is the Union captain who leads Cotten and his men westward, where they'll go so far as to change into Union uniforms. At the fort is a Union major (Jeff Chandler) and his brother's Spanish widow (Linda Darnell). She wants to leave the fort but a possessive Chandler won't let her go. His obsessive, unspoken desire for her provides an unexpected touch, a lusty psychosexual subplot. Chandler has the best role, stung with bitterness and resentment, though he isn't up to fulfilling its potential. Cotten gives one of his fine understated performances and Darnell is quite pleasing, too, while Wilde has little to do but be fair and nice. Director Robert Wise (later of *The Sound of Music*) unfolds a thoughtful, interesting drama, aided by Leon Shamroy's beautifully smoky and depth-filled black-and-white photography. The climax is, of course, an Indian siege, a visual stunner. An unfortunate aspect of many examples within this sub-genre is how Northerners and Southerners can come together to kill Indians. *Two Flags West* is also one of those Civil War westerns that can't quite live up to the promise of its singular set-up, and yet, with its simmering character subtexts, vast expanses, and Wise's artful staging, it remains a haunting example within this hybrid genre.

Rocky Mountain (1950) – One of the finest (and most underrated) of all Civil War westerns, this black-and-white beauty has Robert E. Lee himself sending a Confederate captain (Errol Flynn) and seven other soldiers out west to find outlaws to fight for the South. Clearly these are the war's waning days when such desperate action might be taken. The men rescue a stagecoach from an Indian attack, saving Patrice Wymore, a Yankee on her way to meet her Union fiancé Scott Forbes, who will soon come looking for her. Like *Two Flags West*, this movie derives much of its interest from the personal interactions between Confederates and Yankees forced to see each other as people, not just enemies. The film stresses their shared humanity, culminating with an impact both hopeful and deeply sad. With not one scene set indoors, *Rocky Mountain* was shot on gorgeously scenic locations (and some rather fine studio mock-ups). Directed by a peak-form William Keighley, a Warner Brothers regular, the film is bookended by two outstanding large-scale action sequences: Flynn and company racing (but failing) to stop the aforementioned stagecoach attack;

and a climactic sacrificial scene, a brutal massacre in which some characters play decoy in order to save others, an intensely moving and upsetting episode. Once again, Native Americans are the device that puts opposing forces temporarily on the same side. There's an especially elegiac ending, with one side paying tribute to the other in a flag-planting gesture, a grateful, respectful act while the war ironically still rages. Ms. Wymore (soon to be real-life Mrs. Flynn) is adequate here, while Flynn, in his best and final western, is rock-solid. It's funny how comfortable everyone's favorite Tasmanian seemed to be whenever he was set loose in the West.

Best of the Badmen (1951) – In just about all these movies, it's the high value of their initial hooks that reel you in and keep you watching. In this case, we have a post-war western in which the war isn't *really* over. Union Major Robert Ryan, a good guy, makes peace with Southern raiders led by Bruce Cabot, getting them to surrender, take loyalty oaths, and attain freedom, all of this angering carpetbagger Robert Preston (who wanted the reward money for these guys). The twist is that Ryan had just received his army-release papers, technically rendering him a civilian when he took action, including shooting dead one of Preston's men. Ryan is arrested for murder, convicted, and set to hang, all engineered by Preston. With the help of a mysterious, extremely blonde Claire Trevor, Ryan escapes and joins Cabot and his outlaw crew, all of them determined to bring down Preston. From there, the plot grows increasingly familiar and less complicated, without entirely losing the zing of where it started, when it depicted the post-war situation as something chaotic and distressingly unresolved. Also in Cabot's crew are old coot Walter Brennan and Lawrence Tierney (as Jesse James). Never as visually poetic or as emotionally probing as *Two Flags West* or *Rocky Mountain, Best of the Badmen* is a brightly colored and admittedly unnuanced entertainment with some hokey, square dialogue. Directed by William D. Russell, it has a fine cast *well* cast, including Trevor who does one of her all-purpose goodhearted dames.

Thunder over the Plains (1953) – This one really stretches the definition of a Civil War western, set as it is in 1869, and yet it is completely about the lingering impact of the war, its refusal to end. Again, the subject matter is superior to the storytelling, but director Andre de Toth and his cinematographer Bert Glennon offer striking visuals, highlighting their discerning flair for color and an arresting use of close-ups. Four years after defeat, Texas still hasn't been reinstated into the Union. There's a federal army of occupation in place, a state of martial law, but even harder on the citizens are the carpetbaggers and ever-increasing taxation. Randolph Scott is a federal officer, a captain who fought for the Union but is also a Texan pulled in two directions. Scott performs, of course, with his standard no-frills stoicism, even when forced to go rogue. Lex Barker is another captain, from the East and very unimpressed with Texas, though mightily impressed with Scott's wife, pretty Phyllis Kirk, to the point of assault. Both the good guy and the bad guy are Union soldiers while the rebel leader (Charles McGraw) is treated with respect and sympathy. It's always nice to see the lines blurred in terms of heroes and villains, with no one side claiming unambiguous purity or evil. Before Texas rejoins the Union in 1870, *Thunder over the Plains* provokes sensible thought about how a war's end doesn't automatically terminate the hurts and anger it engendered, sometimes leading to worse miseries.

Escape from Fort Bravo (1953) – Akin to *Two Flags West,* this western has Confederates in a Union POW camp in 1863 Arizona. There are two wars here, the other (no surprise) between the whites and the Mescalero Indians. With its rich, deep compositions from director John Sturges, and all that glorious outdoor scenery (despite some bad, fake "exteriors"), this is a compact, handsome MGM production. William Holden is a tough Union captain; John Forsythe is a captured Confederate captain. A stunningly beautiful Eleanor Parker arrives for the wedding of pal Polly Bergen, daughter of the Union colonel, but there's more to Parker than meets the eye. Whatever her secret agenda is, she surely brought enough gowns for a trip to rustic Arizona, including a very 1950s ball gown. Holden, soon after his Oscar-winning performance in *Stalag 17,* is now on the *other* side of a POW camp (though he'd be back inside one for *The Bridge on the River Kwai* in 1957). Parker manipulates Holden into falling in love with her, but then, damn, she falls for him, too. Their roles are choice, deserving of major stars, with true love making both of them more human and vulnerable. There is, of course, the titular escape, a subsequent capture, and a climactic encounter with those Mescaleros (in a strong extended action sequence in which the whites are trapped out in the open). *Escape from Fort Bravo* is an all-around above-average effort, though, yet again, the advantage of seeing the war from a far-off vantage point is undercut when it's used as an opportunity to kill more Indians.

Border River **(1954)** – It's South of the Border for this respectable, if less than distinguished, picture set during the last days of the war, in a Mexican free zone ruled by a greedy general (Pedro Armendariz). Into this safe haven (for both Yankees and Rebs) comes Confederate Major Joel McCrea. In need of supplies, he hopes to make a deal with Armendariz, selling two million dollars of Union gold bullion that he and his men stole in Colorado. No one loves McCrea's work more than I do, but he's more subdued here than necessary and without even a hint of a Southern accent. Meanwhile, luscious Yvonne De Carlo, as Armendariz's seemingly chaste, teasing mistress, is more animated than usual (as well as exquisitely costumed and photographed in ravishing color). McCrea and De Carlo, previously in *The San Francisco Story* (1952), fall in love, expectedly, while Armendariz and Alfonso Bedoya conduct themselves as the life of the supporting cast. The Confederates are the good guys, with the Mexicans (instead of the Indians) the bad guys, though there are "good" Mexicans here, too. You can give the Confederates a happy ending, but we still remember where all this is headed. Directed by George Sherman, *Border River* is better than routine, better than another McCrea Civil War western, *South of St. Louis* (1949), but it's not all it might've been.

Quantrill's Raiders **(1958)** – Here's an unexpected high-quality Civil War western, only seventy-one minutes long. Set in the Union town of Lawrence, Kansas, it's good-looking (in color), employing the wide screen imaginatively. The title character (Leo Gordon) fights for the South, but he's also a mad killer who uses the war as an excuse to loot and pillage. The real star is Steve Cochran as a Confederate captain posing as an honorably discharged Union army officer who now sells horses. His infiltration scheme remarkably resembles what Van Heflin does in *The Raid* (1954), though this movie is never quite as complex or as challenging as Heflin's film. In both, a Confederate immerses himself within a Union town, moves into a boardinghouse run by a woman, and bonds with a little boy who idolizes him. Most importantly, both main characters develop a conscience. Though the films differ in their final destinations, their initial set-ups are similarly engrossing. Cochran's mission is to help to destroy the Union arsenal, while of course falling in love, rather quickly, with landlady Diane Brewster. Yes, there's a "bad girl" (lusty, redheaded Gale Robbins) to offset Brewster's "good girl." The famously hairy-chested Cochran necessarily finds time to get his shirt badly torn, allowing him to expose some brawn for the final "hunk" of the movie. In addition to being beefcake, Cochran was an underrated actor always worth watching. Directed by Edward Bernds, who made the Zsa Zsa Gabor camp classic *Queen of Outer Space* that same year, *Quantrill's Raiders* remains a robust, forgotten little sleeper.

The Proud Rebel (1958) – This thoroughly winning, emotionally absorbing family picture is post-war and Illinois-set, yet it's very much a Civil War western, at least in spirit. Real-life father and son Alan Ladd and David Ladd (about ten or eleven years old) play Georgians in search of a doctor who can restore the boy's voice. He's been silent for a year due to the war trauma of seeing his mother killed and his home burned down. With the boy's essential attachment to his dog, this becomes one of the all-time best boy-and-his-dog movies (with a sensational canine acting job). The elder Ladd, a war veteran and formerly rich, goes to work for lone farmwoman Olivia de Havilland, a sturdily independent, unmarried lady. De Havilland impresses here, submersing herself in the role's physicality, believable as a capable frontier woman who touchingly softens through her contact with the Ladds. You'll immediately want them to become a family, but de Havilland and Ladd take their time, coming together in an affectingly restrained fashion. The villains are one-armed Dean Jagger and his two sons—they want de Havilland's land. Amid this western-like turf war, there's the suspense of waiting for the comparably traumatic situation that will allow the boy to find his voice. Cannily directed by Michael Curtiz, in one of his finest later efforts, *The Proud Rebel* is imbued with honest warmth and tenderness, almost never cloying. It was shot by Ted McCord in dark-hued colors and noir-ish shadows and is also enlivened by a stirring Jerome Moross score. Add excellent performances not only from de Havilland (in her ninth Curtiz film) and Jagger but from both Ladds, with pop especially attuned to bringing out the best in his boy.

Escort West (1959) – It's Nevada and the war's been over for three months, not nearly enough time for the emotional wounds to heal. This basic but pretty good western is lean and clean and just seventy-five minutes. Victor Mature is a Confederate captain on his way to Oregon to start a new life with his ten-year-old daughter Reba Waters. As a Reb-despising Bostonian, Faith Domergue is the film's personification of passionate post-war hatred. She's accompanying her much pleasanter sister, Elaine Stewart, who's on her way to marry Union Captain William Ching. Unbeknownst to them, Ching and his men are currently surrounded by Indians. Yes, again, Indians are an enemy both sides can rally against, which is exactly where the movie is headed. The straightforward plot is a simple quest to get through Indian territory safely. Mature rescues Domergue and Stewart, forcing all of them to become uncomfortable travel companions. While Domergue remains a consistent pain, Mature and Stewart grow close. The stalwart Mature is used primarily as an action star, which is no excuse for his semi-conscious personality when he's not in motion. Yet he's the "A" attraction in an otherwise "B" cast. I especially like the refreshing way the movie handles its resolution of the love triangle between Mature, Stewart, and Ching, not resorting to the obvious solution. Directed by Francis D. Lyon, *Escort West* is a low-budget wide-screen black-and-white movie that's worth a look for telling its spare story with genuine simplicity, and, like other Civil War westerns, for reminding us that enmity doesn't end with a peace treaty. Incidentally, one of its writers, Leo Gordon, played Quantrill in *Quantrill's Raiders*.

Westbound (1959) – Not one of the very best of the seven justly revered Randolph Scott westerns directed by Budd Boetticher, *Westbound* lacks back-story textures and mysterious character depths. It is nevertheless a fast-moving Civil War western with a good story complemented by good complications. In 1864, the Union is trying to move California gold into their treasury. Scott, in a typically resolute performance, is a Union captain who formerly ran a stage line; he's assigned to move the gold on his old line. The setting is the Colorado Territory, in a town of Southern sympathizers unwelcoming to Scott. But there are Union sympathizers, too, who come to Scott's aid. (We never see any gold.) The villain, Andrew Duggan, is married to Virginia Mayo, Scott's old flame. She opted for Duggan's money, and Scott seems to have gotten over her. Mayo is on hand to lend a little A-picture glamour to a mostly lackluster ensemble (spouting some sub-par dialogue). Also in the mix is the pointily buxom Karen Steele, a Jayne Mansfield on the range. Boetticher delivers his usual sweeping outdoor compositions and a tight running time of only sixty-nine minutes. There are two violent shockers here, both extremely well executed, leading to startling deaths. And there's another villain, a gunslinger (Michael Pate), someone both sides can hate. I'm happy to report that he's neither an Indian nor a Mexican. (Mr. Pate was coincidentally one of the writers of *Escape from Fort Bravo*.) Never as intimate or as penetrating as a Boetticher/Scott classic like *Ride Lonesome* (1959) or *Comanche Station* (1960), *Westbound* nonetheless has unmistakable integrity and is decidedly unpretentious, just like its leading man.

Shooting Scripts: The Western at Its Apex (1950-1959)

Beyond the specificity of the 1950s Civil War western, what about the overall state of the western genre at the mid-century? Rest assured, the '50s proved to be its greatest decade, a time of abundant riches. You will *never* run out of high-quality westerns from 1950s Hollywood. Even the most devout aficionados will continue to stumble upon neglected oaters previously missed (or never even heard of), unassuming little efforts with no reputation, buried by the era's overflow of excellence. You may have seen *Hondo* (1953) and *Vera Cruz* (1954), but how about *Three Hours to Kill* (1954) or *Saddle the Wind* (1958)? More to the point, just why did everything congeal for the western at this particular moment? It helped that movies were mostly finished telling those forging-a-nation stories, such as *Wells Fargo* (1937), allowing subtler, more complex stories to emerge. And there's no doubt that the genre had been gaining respect ever since John Ford's *Stagecoach* (1939), followed by *The Ox-Bow Incident* (1943), *My Darling Clementine* (1946), and *Red River* (1948). The '50s western also coincided with the general movie craze for psychology, leading logically to the "psychological western," a category noted for its intricate gray areas, including works such as *The Naked Spur* (1953). The new permissiveness of the late 1960s would introduce explicit realism to western violence (primarily in the form of all that blood we'd been spared for decades), just happening to accompany the demise of the genre. Had too much reality killed all the fun? Or maybe it was modern sensitivities toward history, a rising discomfort with the stereotypes of warpath Indians and the "civilizing" forces of whites. Though there had been notable exceptions—Anthony Mann's *Devil's Doorway* (1950) is as powerful an indictment of white ruthlessness, and the subsequent cruel treatment of Native Americans, as has ever been made—the western seemed to have become too much of a mine field. There would continue to be occasional high points, from *The Wild Bunch* (1969) to *Unforgiven* (1992), but the genre would never again be a movie (or television) staple. After the often mythologizing works of the '20s, '30s, and '40s, and *before* the revisionist sensibilities (and the gore) of the late '60s and beyond, the 1950s were the genre's peak years: great storytelling tied to complicated characters and themes; raw and edgy brutality, yet still more suggestive than graphic; and old conventions steered in fascinating directions, including indirect commentary on contemporary America. The

1950s western was equally at home with personal character-driven struggles and thematically expansive takes on the values and terrors of community.

Though the silent era had produced western epics, including *The Covered Wagon* (1923), *The Iron Horse* (1924), and *The Vanishing American* (1925), and talkies had brought forth Gary Cooper in *The Virginian* (1929) and John Wayne in *The Big Trail* (1930), the genre wasn't especially respected, primarily the domain of B pictures for Saturday-morning audiences, usually starring fellows you'd balk at calling actors. Westerns of the '30s had big stars and big budgets only when they told "the story of America," those tales of progress involving the trek westward. For many in the audience, it wasn't *that* long ago, and so sometimes it was the nostalgia of recent history, notably as Richard Dix led the Oscar-winning *Cimarron* (1931). Such flag-waving sagas of nation-building, including *Union Pacific* (1939), used broad strokes, pumped with pandering about U.S. exceptionalism, peopled with stick figures comfortable in melodramatic plots. Other mega-westerns gazed upon legends: Barbara Stanwyck in *Annie Oakley* (1935), Gary Cooper (as Bill Hickok) and Jean Arthur (as Calamity Jane) in *The Plainsman* (1936), and Tyrone Power in *Jesse James* (1939). These were more about charismatic stars suitably matched to larger-than-life personages than they were about insightful biography. Superficial, action-packed, and sentimentalized, such westerns were not the stuff of great movies.

Thank goodness for *Stagecoach* (1939). Its characters and situations were hardly revolutionary, but their treatment—in terms of depth of feeling, a burrowing empathy—has rarely been equaled, with John Ford bringing lyricism and delicacy to tried-and-true elements. Without the ambiguities the genre would embrace in the '50s, *Stagecoach* is a perfect distillation of western essences, with indelible black-and-white images and scenery, an archetypal Indian attack and iconic climactic shoot-out, plus a few heroic outcasts irresistibly finding redemption, such as innocent (in every way) prison escapee John Wayne discovering love with whore-with-a-heart-of-gold Claire Trevor. It's a film of overwhelming goodness, unafraid of emotion, a promising harbinger for the western of the 1940s.

Fritz Lang brought striking color and tactile beauty to *The Return of Frank James* (1940), while William Wyler guided Walter Brennan's outstanding Oscar-winning performance as Judge Roy Bean in *The Westerner* (1940), an acting turn of cagey dexterity, alternately scary and sympathetic. William A. Wellman's *The Ox-Bow Incident* (1943) was a message-picture downer, a warning about mob violence, too self-conscious and heavy-handed but properly upsetting, a prestigious box-office loser. At the other extreme was a trashy commercial winner: King Vidor's overscaled *Duel in the Sun* (1946), an empty but campy spectacle, short on taste but mighty colorful, mainly preoccupied with sex (between Jennifer Jones and Gregory Peck). Howard Hawks' *Red River* (1948) is a major '40s western, with a fiercely intense John Wayne at dramatic odds with an easy, relaxed Montgomery Clift (who anticipates Hollywood's more modern acting style of the '50s). Though it's flawed—witness every scene in which Joanne Dru appears—this cattle-drive *Mutiny on the Bounty* gets points for its pseudo father-son conflict and a bold tackling of leadership and its burdens, despite too much talk about "good beef."

Lesser-known worthwhile '40s westerns include Jacques Tourneur's *Canyon Passage* (1946), with Dana Andrews and Susan Hayward, a visually crisp, startlingly brutal Oregon-set picture; *Yellow Sky* (1948), William Wellman's moody reworking of *The Tempest,* starring Gregory Peck and Anne Baxter; Raoul Walsh's terrifically entertaining *Colorado Territory* (1949), a richly scenic revamp of Walsh's own *High Sierra* (1941), with Joel McCrea assuming Bogart's role; and Mark Robson's stylish yet grounded *Roughshod* (1949), with an especially good Gloria Grahame performance as a savvy yet vulnerable prostitute, while killer John Ireland seeks revenge on good-guy Robert Sterling. Each of these did their part in moving closer to the shadings, the deep-seated turbulences, soon to come.

But before we consider the '50s, a few words about the greatest of '40s westerns, Ford's *My Darling Clementine* (1946), a true work of art, impeccably fine in its dialogue and relationships, deftly balancing humor and poignancy, enriched by palpably atmospheric details and its blasts of violence. Yet nothing about it feels studied; it just breathes. Led by Henry Fonda's laconic Wyatt Earp, a deceptively funny and inventive piece of screen acting with a uniquely individualized physicality and lovely grace notes of vanity, *My Darling Clementine* is a spectacular black-and-white achievement, mixing beauty and pain, feeling both soulful and folkloric, while compositionally a most blissful cinematic experience.

You know what's to come in the '50s, first and foremost the Big Three—Fred Zinnemann's *High Noon* (1952), George Stevens' *Shane* (1953), and Ford's *The Searchers* (1956)—but also many other first-rate works by directors Anthony Mann and Budd Boetticher, plus Delmer Daves' *Broken Arrow* (1950) and *3:10 to Yuma* (1957), Henry King's masterwork *The Gunfighter* (1950), Nicholas Ray's gloriously outrageous *Johnny Guitar* (1954), Jacques

Tourneur's unjustly unknown *Wichita* (1955), William Wyler's popular yet underappreciated extra-large production *The Big Country* (1958), and Hawks' overrated *Rio Bravo* (1959). The age of stodgy accounts of America's frontier-forging was essentially over, as well as most of the self-congratulation that went with it, allowing for more variety in western stories than ever before, whether allegorical, psychologically fraught, or even noir-like in their darkness and suspense. Westerns of the '50s often seem elementally primal, playing like gripping morality plays. Any story, basically, could be told as a western, stripped to a simplicity of recognizable human experience. With so much genre activity throughout the decade, many westerns, beyond providing thrills, grabbed hold of hearts and minds. Here are ten that often get lost amid such Grade-A competition.

The Man from Laramie (1955): James Stewart

Rio Grande (1950) – Number three in the John Ford-John Wayne cavalry trilogy, following *Fort Apache* (1948) and *She Wore a Yellow Ribbon* (1949), *Rio Grande* is the least regarded yet by far the best, most sustained, most cohesive. *Fort Apache* is overlong, misshapen, and unaffecting, while *Yellow Ribbon* is indeed memorable (despite too many endings) and is certainly the most visually rapturous of the trio (in color, looking like a western *Red Shoes*), also the occasion for an especially moving Wayne performance. *Rio Grande* is a black-and-white beauty built on the power of emotional restraint: a family's pent-up wells of feeling and their meaningful silences. The military aspect of the plot—Wayne leading an undermanned unit against Apaches—is generic, merely a framework for the familial story at the center. Maureen O'Hara, in her first film opposite Wayne, plays his estranged wife; they haven't seen each other in fifteen years. She arrives at his fort to retrieve their son (Claude Jarman, Jr.), a West Point failure and recent enlistee sent to the unit of his father (with whom he has no relationship). O'Hara wants Jarman to go home with her but he refuses, and Wayne won't assist O'Hara in her mission. Despite their differences and the passage of time, deep love is always apparent among the three. Dashing behind a mustache, Wayne gives an admirably sensitive performance, and O'Hara, a bit too young for her role, gives what is arguably her finest performance, if only for the look on her face at seeing Wayne for the first time after all these years. *Rio Grande* is about letting your children grow up, as well as forgiveness, and the enduring strength of a true love. As often was the case, Ford incorporates plenty of music, mostly in the pleasing form of vocals by the Sons of the Pioneers. He also wisely keeps Victor McLaglen's comic relief in check, which he didn't do in *Fort Apache* and *Yellow Ribbon,* with their screamingly unfunny McLaglen antics. Oh, *Rio Grande* has the usual brawling, boozing, and Irish-isms intended to amuse, but they don't wear out their welcome as they so often do in Ford westerns. Also beneficial is the absence of the first two films' young-lovers subplot, instead keeping the focus tightened on the family. Yet there's no stinting on action, including Ben Johnson's remarkable horsemanship, plus an exciting rescue of children from an Apache camp. From its lovely start—women lined up as their men return, each waiting to see if her man is among the living—to its finish, *Rio Grande* is a lean and graceful work with Ford in firm control, a film as precise as a military salute.

Westward the Women (1951) – Though this is actually the kind of "making America" western I said Hollywood was finished with by the '50s (only to return for *How the West Was Won* in 1963), it certainly offers a fresh twist, a feminist slant which acknowledges it wasn't just cowboys and sheriffs who expanded America. Like *Rio Grande,* it derives its oomph more from its stewing emotional components than its well-staged action sequences. In 1851, Californian John McIntire hires guide Robert Taylor to lead a wagon train of about 140 mail-order brides from Chicago to McIntire's valley. Because "good women" are sought, whores Denise Darcel and Julie Bishop restyle themselves. It's the women who do the mate-choosing, based on photographs presented. These brave females immediately inspire awe, sympathy, and good will. Channeling Clark Gable, Taylor is their hard, ruggedly handsome taskmaster. After some early troubles involving the men he hires (one of whom commits a rape), Taylor sees all but two of them bolt, leaving arduous tasks to fall to the women. This is a big movie, superbly shot in black and white by William C. Mellor, impressively directed by William A. Wellman, and with a generously big-hearted story by Frank Capra. Though a romance develops between Taylor and Darcel, the movie never loses its toughness or its dignity, by turns rousing and touching, filled with such formidable presences as Hope Emerson. With the French Darcel, plus an Italian mother and son, and a Japanese boy, the melting pot is captured in action. Among the quieter but more wrenching episodes occurs when the women are forced to lighten their loads before entering the desert, abandoning some of the treasures of their pasts, then embarking on the merciless trek, an astonishing visual sequence. It's wholly satisfying to watch the women gain Taylor's respect, but *Westward the Women* delivers on all counts. This film earns its more sentimental moments as rewards to those characters who survive the grueling ordeal. Viewers share in those rewards, ready to embrace, overwhelmingly, all the good that comes from this adventure.

The Man from the Alamo **(1953)** – Before making his celebrated septet of westerns with Randolph Scott, director Budd Boetticher made this fleet, concise entry, an Alamo movie in which the battle serves as opener rather than climax, similar to how the later *Hour of the Gun* (1967) begins with the O.K. Corral shoot-out. The Alamo massacre is the set-up for an involving plotline of revenge and purification. Already having proven himself heroic mid-Alamo, Glenn Ford engages secretly (during a lull in the fight) with four fellow ranchers, electing one of them to leave the doomed situation to secure the safety of their families. Ford, the "winner," finds nothing but destruction, including his own ranch burned to the ground along with his wife and son murdered. But the villains are not Mexicans, as expected; they are Americans *disguised* as Mexicans, led by a Texas-hating Victor Jory. Because of his survival from the massacre, Ford is vilified, nearly lynched by supposedly good people. His only friend is a Mexican boy (Marc Cavell), which gives the film a soothing air of brotherhood amid much prejudice and volatility. After a brief infiltration into Jory's gang, Ford becomes a protector of those who recently turned against him, leading their wagon train away from Jory's pursuit, thus on his way to public redemption. Also aboard is conveniently single Julia Adams (who is caring for young Cavell) and one-armed Chill Wills, later Oscar-nominated for *The Alamo* (1960). With spare direction and some gorgeous color expanses, *The Man from the Alamo* is a real sleeper, examining the conflict between war duty and personal angst. The movie makes a resonant connection between Ford and Hugh O'Brian, a lieutenant who witnessed Ford's Alamo departure and has been badmouthing him. Coincidentally together on the wagon train, O'Brian, too, faces a choice between his family's safety and his military responsibility, which forges an unforeseen understanding between the two men. This is hardly an actor's movie, with Ford impressing most for his riding skills, but he does convey a lingering survivors' guilt regarding the Alamo, adding some welcome bristles of dimension.

Silver Lode (1954) – From Allan Dwan, a movie director since 1911, here's a terrific little picture, an allegory about a witch hunt, with a villain named McCarty. And how bitingly ironic that it's set on the Fourth of July, with America tested on its most patriotic day. Cattleman John Payne, in Silver Lode just two years, is about to wed Lizabeth Scott, the richest girl in town. (The film shares with *High Noon* a similarly real-time approach, as well as being set on the wedding day of its main character.) The ceremony is interrupted by so-called U.S. marshal Dan Duryea and his three deputies, here to arrest Payne for the murder of Duryea's brother. It's clear that Payne is a good guy and black-hatted Duryea is a louse, and so the movie pleasurably establishes a worrisome premise, growing ever more unsettling as the town—purportedly so in love with Payne—begins to turn against him. (He admits to killing Duryea's brother, but it wasn't murder!) The film hinges on Payne's granted request of two hours to prove his innocence, but when people start dying, Payne surely seems guilty. With its unerring tension, Karen De Wolf's screenplay becomes increasingly chilling and paranoiac as a civilized community unravels, making an all-too-easy transition to disintegrating loyalties and mob violence. It's a jolting work, escalated by severed telegraph wires and the fact that Payne is a former gunslinger. The most potent turn comes when Payne, just about abandoned, reverts to gunman, forced into self-defense mode, a good man pushed too far. It's difficult to watch good-guy Payne, compelled to act recklessly, fighting other good guys. This is a challenging dramatic curve, shaking up simple notions of good and bad, evoking fear as to what Payne might inflict. There's an extraordinary tracking shot (by cinematographer John Alton) as Payne wends his way through town, avoiding capture, but also obvious flaws, like the *Blazing Saddles*-type ensemble, almost a parody of western folk. Despite this supporting lineup from central casting, the writing and the direction almost never falter. As for Payne, he's primarily stoic but makes a good action star, while Duryea is at-home in his usual sleazy-scummy mode. How interesting that it's two ladies—good-girl Scott and likable floozie Dolores Moran—who remain loyal to Payne, helping him by any means necessary. For all the palpitations engendered by its climax, *Silver Lode* bravely maintains its embittered tone, holding contempt for those too unquestioningly susceptible to smooth-talking evil.

The Bounty Hunter (1954) – Randolph Scott spent much of the later '50s making standout westerns for Budd Boetticher, but his first half of the decade was kept busy with a sextet for director Andre de Toth, none better than this one, a solidly built, thoroughly absorbing western mystery. With de Toth's astute handling and an economically trim script, *The Bounty Hunter* presents a relentless and friendless Scott in the title role, a man seemingly in it for the money (though we eventually learn his deep-down motive). Projecting his patented mix of strength and decency, Scott is hired by a detective agency to locate three murdering train robbers who escaped with a hundred grand of government money. He arrives at the suspected location, a copper town, finding plenty of shady characters, including hotelier Ernest Borgnine (who walks with a limp) and saloon gal Marie Windsor. (This film was shot in 3-D, as was de Toth's big 1953 hit *House of Wax*.) What's neat about *The Bounty Hunter* is that once the townspeople learn Scott's true identity, they freak out. Those with guilty consciences start bolting, fearing exposure and capture, or worse, making this another prime paranoia-fueled western, inciting unrest in a West often sought for reinvention. As the town becomes a pressure cooker, *The Bounty Hunter* also plays as an enjoyably twisting mystery, with the "wanted" trio slowly becoming known to us. A variation on this plot appears in the also-good *No Name on the Bullet* (1959), in which assassin

Audie Murphy comes to town to kill somebody, and, again, the place erupts, with too many citizens believing they are the bullet's intended victim. (Unlike Scott, Murphy knows exactly who he has come to get, but both films operate as mysteries for their audiences, with *The Bounty Hunter* the trickier one to crack.) Though Scott—charming when he chooses to be—has a thin romance with doctor's daughter Dolores Dorn (a Shirley Jones type), the main event is the systematic revelation of who it is he's hunting, and, even more so, all that unnerving McCarthy-era panic.

They Rode West (1954) – Such a generic title for an unexpectedly provocative color western directed by film-noir expert Phil Karlson (*Kansas City Confidential*), enhanced by his canny visual acumen, including battle scenes that look more realistically brutal than most from this era, all the more viscerally unpleasant by virtue of not really providing anyone to root *against*. This is decidedly offbeat western fare, with tall, nice-looking Robert Francis—a blondish newcomer who died at 25 in a 1955 plane crash—as the new and dedicated young doctor at a cavalry outpost, a lieutenant who thinks that all people, including Indians, have the same value. He's strong but peaceful, green but skilled, and yet made highly unwelcome by Phil Carey, an anti-Indian captain who also happens to hate doctors. Wanting to fight disease rather than Indians, Francis is soon perceived as a traitor, going against orders to help the Kiowas' malaria epidemic. But his best intentions go awry, with Francis' anti-reservation stance inadvertently leading to the aforementioned battles. The movie's good guy happens to be a juvenile-looking radical, a defiantly honorable man without prejudice or bias, compelled to bend the rules. Donna Reed, as the colonel's habitually flirtatious niece, matures conveniently enough to tell Francis, "Your 'own kind' is the human race." The third part of a rather subdued love triangle is May Wynn as a white girl (raised by Indians) with whom Francis bonds. (He and Wynn had been paired in *The Caine Mutiny* earlier that year.) The film sustains its yearning sympathies for the mistreated Kiowas, caged by reservation life, further ennobled by their contrast with the more aggressive Comanches. Bravely dispensing his color-blind humanity, Francis extols the necessity of people simply taking care of each other. Though the film showcases his fine-boned leading-man potential, there would be only two more films for Francis before his untimely death. *They Rode West* deserves recognition for the way it upturns expectations, as well as its unusually sensitive aims and the extent of its hopeful liberalism.

The Man from Laramie (1955) – No chapter on '50s westerns would be complete without an Anthony Mann work, especially one starring James Stewart. Here's the last of their western quintet, which began with *Winchester '73* (1950), though the two best are *The Naked Spur* (1953) and *The Far Country* (1955), both featuring brilliantly thorny Stewart performances. Filmed in CinemaScope in New Mexico, *The Man from Laramie* is no slouch, most memorable for the shocking stabs of violence suffered by Stewart, including being lassoed and dragged through a campfire, and, much later, viciously shot through the hand. Stewart is an ex-army captain whose brother died in an Apache massacre of a cavalry patrol. The Indians used repeater rifles: how did they get them? It's a solid set-up, spawning several good threads, though Stewart's quest for revenge feels driven more by plot than character. The film's emotional center is Donald Crisp as the cattle rancher who owns everything, who loves his despicable son (Alex Nicol), and is also going blind; his is a sad, proud, and dignified performance. And good old Aline MacMahon adds some likable grit as a rival rancher and former flame of Crisp's. (They share a touching reunion once he's blind.) Arthur Kennedy, as Crisp's indispensable employee (*almost* another son), and Mr. Nicol have a Cain-and-Abel dynamic. However, Kennedy is fairly standard in an ill-defined part, and Nicol isn't up to his hothead role. Despite a laughably bad title tune, *The Man from Laramie* has the immediacy, the voltage, and the smarts you expect from an Anthony Mann western. Seek out other treasures from his western filmography: *The Furies* (1950), *Devil's Doorway* (1950), *The Tin Star* (1957), and *Man of the West* (1958).

Trooper Hook (1957) – As essential to '50s westerns as Anthony Mann or Randolph Scott is Joel McCrea, a versatile actor who pretty much devoted himself to the genre ever since the end of WWII. Consider *The Outriders* (1950), *The Tall Stranger* (1957), *Fort Massacre* (1958), and two musts, his Wyatt Earp in *Wichita* (1955) and his astonishingly affecting performance in Sam Peckinpah's truly great *Ride the High Country* (1962), among the handful of best-ever westerns. *Trooper Hook* explores the subject of women abducted by Indians, sometimes living so long among them that they belong to both worlds (and therefore neither). Think Natalie Wood in *The Searchers* (1956) or, later, Mary McDonnell in *Dances with Wolves* (1990). In this instance, it's Barbara Stanwyck, in her sixth and final film with McCrea. Even with a cheap budget, some drab black and white, and rather lukewarm moviemaking from Charles Marquis Warren, this is a worthy effort, an absorbing scenario that treats its characters humanely, its verve heightened by the two old pros in the leads. McCrea is the decent, fair-minded title character, an army sergeant who finds Stanwyck among his Apache prisoners and is assigned to return her to her husband (John Dehner) outside Tucson. Though previously childless, Stanwyck gave birth to the chief's son, now about five years old. Reviled by whites for not having killed herself, she is treated respectfully by McCrea. Both are strong and quiet, signifying they are a good match (just in case). With her son in tow, she and McCrea travel by horse, stagecoach, and wagon, with others along for the ride (none of whom add much). And there's another of those awful title tunes, with Tex Ritter chiming in for some occasional musical narration. *Trooper Hook* is about survival, bolstered by its pleasing coming together of the two leads, though even the warring Indian chief (Rodolfo Acosta) is humanized as a father. The movie combines suspense with restraint, but it's marred by overly convenient plotting at the climax. At fifty, Stanwyck was one film away from the end of twenty-seven years of solid stardom, mostly focusing on television thereafter, while McCrea had his singular triumph in *Ride the High Country* still ahead of him.

Ride Lonesome (1959) – Here's one of the best of the seven Budd Boetticher-Randolph Scott westerns, a series that started and ended with the two *other* best, *Seven Men from Now* (1956) and *Comanche Station* (1960). Boetticher's westerns thrive on authenticity, both in their physical surroundings and emotional layers (slowly revealed). The screenplay for *Ride Lonesome*, by Burt Kennedy, is both riling and thoughtful, with several remarkably natural sounding conversations. Boetticher's breathtaking wide-screen compositions feature his favored gnarled landscapes, which serve as disturbing complements to the script's emotionally jagged content. *Ride Lonesome* is brief yet still leisurely: I love the purity of watching people on horseback, the beauty of a journey in motion, and the physical exertion of what these characters actually *do*. There are no towns, just nature and a few outposts. Scott, as another bounty hunter, gets his man, a murderer (James Best), early on. Of course, Scott is plain and reserved, while Best is a sexy, charming rascal, a good ol' boy. Best is also confident that he'll soon be rescued by his brother (Lee Van Cleef). At a swing station, add two wanted outlaws (Pernell Roberts and dim, playful James Coburn in his film debut), plus the newly widowed Karen Steele. Roberts and Coburn want Best for themselves because their reward would be amnesty. When Roberts, lusting for the well-built Steele, says that she gives him "a way-down shiver," it's a rare old-movie reference to an erection. The only inauthenticity here is Steele's flawless hair and makeup as the days drag on, plus too much (and too repetitive) music. *Ride Lonesome* is mostly a tense expedition of five, featuring a masterfully staged Indian assault that begins with a stunning far-off introduction to the Indians' approach. Kennedy's script brings dimension to characters you expect to be mere types, notably Roberts who is especially intriguing for his desire to go straight. And there's more to Scott and his mission than meets the eye, courtesy of his haunting backstory, which culminates in one of the more powerful final images of the genre, an ending of cleansing but also isolation, both cathartic and aching.

Last Train from Gun Hill **(1959)** – Director John Sturges, maker of dueling Wyatt Earp westerns—the commercial *Gunfight at the O.K. Corral* (1957) and the artful (and sorely neglected) *Hour of the Gun* (1967)—also made this exceptional movie, a perfect balance of consummate film technique and taut story control. Its super-charged opening features a chase, a rape and murder, and a boy's escape. Kirk Douglas (Sturges' Doc Holliday in *O.K. Corral*) is the marshal whose Indian wife is the victim. One of her killers (Earl Holliman) is the son of Douglas' onetime best friend (Anthony Quinn), which provides the central conflict, with Quinn a powerful man determined to protect his rotten weakling son. Moral dilemmas abound: Quinn torn between sympathy for his pal and his own flesh and blood; Douglas wanting to capture Holliman but fearful that such an action risks orphaning his *own* son (plus there's the fact that Quinn once saved Douglas' life); and Quinn's mistress (Carolyn Jones) caught between her abusive lover and her concerns for good-man Douglas. The movie has it all: a ferociously good suspense yarn, superlative camerawork, wide-open vistas, and rich colors. So many of the western jewels of the '50s are cleverly concentrated B works, but this one is purely an A affair, including a top Dimitri Tiomkin score. Quinn's twang may come and go, but he's a weighty presence, as is Douglas, as a lawman and husband committed to what must be done. The acting honors belong entirely to Ms. Jones' smart, sarcastic turn as a bruised woman with a good heart, amusing and no-nonsense, flashing her Bette Davis eyes. (I wish she had played Davis' daughter in *something*.) Though Douglas and Quinn are better remembered together in *Lust for Life* (1956), *Last Train* is one of the last treasures of a genre's hallowed heyday, part of its figurative ride into the sunset.

What's Dunne is Done (Again): Remaking the 1930s (1951-1959)

G lorious Technicolor, breathtaking CinemaScope, and stereophonic sound!" So goes Cole Porter's ditty about what it took to get moviegoers to the box office in 1950s America, as sung by Janis Paige in *Silk Stockings* (1957), which, incidentally, is an example of one of the industry's key marketing ploys of that decade: to remake beloved movies of the past, with a special emphasis on classics of the 1930s. (*Silk Stockings* is a Broadway-based musical version of 1939's *Ninotchka*.) Hollywood is always working overtime at getting people into seats, always trying to second-guess the public's taste and moods. But panic was running especially high in the 1950s because the movies were facing their biggest competition and most colossal threat—television. The new medium's popularity had been widening since the late 1940s, moving quickly past novelty status to become an institution with series such as *I Love Lucy* creating the concept of "must-see TV." The notion of remakes—accessorized with those perks of color, wide-screen photography, and enhanced sound—made good business sense, right? But could movies prevail against *free* visual entertainment in the comfort and privacy of the American home?

Hollywood was already famous for recycling its former hits, modifying them for new generations, with certain vehicles, such as *The Three Musketeers,* refurbished more frequently than others. Up against small-screen competition, the studios' quest for sure things gained heightened fervor in the 1950s, with the film output of the '30s treated as a cookbook of favorite recipes ripe for reseasoning. Black-and-white, square-shaped classics could be gussied up with not only vibrant colors and rectangular shapes (which arrived in 1953), but international locations! Movies in 3-D were a more blatant (and desperate) salvo in the battle with television, but the onslaught of remakes was every bit as concerted an effort to entice moviegoers, mixing tried-and-true and state-of-the-art.

It was hoped that young audiences, unfamiliar with these properties, would fall for them just as their parents and grandparents had. Contemporary '30s plots were updated, striving for relevance despite their used storylines, some of them adapting easily, others lost without their Depression-based foundations. For the film fans who remembered the '30s versions, there might be some surprises, such as a happy ending where there had previously been tears, or a comedy favorite transformed into an original musical, or, less drastically, a drama finding new sparks when entwined with an irresistible (and possibly incessant) title tune. Sometimes the '50s remakes proved even more popular than their '30s counterparts, and occasionally they got increased Oscar attention, too. Of course, color and a wider screen don't automatically produce superior movies; sometimes they inflict a garishness which overwhelms simpler virtues. The most poorly received of the '50s remakes have been mercifully forgotten; it's as if they never happened.

There were certainly 1940s movies remade for the '50s—*The Philadelphia Story* (1940) became *High Society* (1956); *Tom, Dick and Harry* (1941) became *The Girl Most Likely* (1958)—and '30s movies continued to be remade beyond the '50s, with 1960s versions of *Mutiny on the Bounty, Stagecoach,* and *Goodbye, Mr. Chips,* but there surely seemed to be a special pilfering of the 1930s throughout the 1950s. The patron saint of this phenomenon was Irene Dunne, who saw just about every one of her major hits redone, even into the '60s.

Among the 1930s pictures given a '50s overhaul are those that became musicals—*Daddy Long Legs* (1931) as a 1955 Fred Astaire vehicle; *The Farmer Takes a Wife* (1935) as a 1953 Betty Grable colorfest; *Bachelor Mother* (1939) as *Bundle of Joy* (1956)—while some '30s musicals remained musical—*The Merry Widow* (1934), revived for a non-triple-threat Lana Turner in 1952; *Rose-Marie* (1936), losing her hyphen in 1954. Among non-musicals, *An American Tragedy* (1931) found greater acclaim as *A Place in the Sun* (1951), while *The Rains Came* (1939) was far inferior as *The Rains of Ranchipur* (1955). Jennifer Jones failed to ignite either of her 1957 versions of *A Farewell to Arms* (1932) and *The Barretts of Wimpole Street* (1934), and *Stage Struck* (1958) didn't do for Susan Strasberg what it had done for Katharine Hepburn as *Morning Glory* (1933). Carole Lombard's role in *Nothing Sacred* (1937) acquired a 1954 gender change for Jerry Lewis in *Living It Up*. (He would subsequently take Ginger Rogers' 1942 role in *The Major and the Minor* for 1955's *You're Never Too Young*.) Paramount made money putting Bob Hope into *Fancy Pants* (1950), a remodeling of *Ruggles of Red Gap* (1935), while Fox flopped with Tyrone Power in *I'll Never Forget You* (1951), their post-war update of *Berkeley Square* (1933). The exact-replica approach was deployed by MGM for a satisfactory 1952 redo of *The Prisoner of Zenda*, which, despite the addition of color, was a virtual shot-for-shot, line-by-line retread of the wondrous 1937 version, dipping even further into the past by featuring old-timer Lewis Stone (who had played the title role in the 1922 silent version).

In considering the following ten remakes, I must warn of spoilers. It's sometimes necessary to compare the endings of the '30s films with their '50s offspring, demonstrating how moviemakers fiddled with the formulas and altered the ingredients, presumably for changing times. Most of these movies, and the '50s remakes in general, were not improvements over their '30s inspirations, but that's no surprise considering the caliber of the works being repackaged. Witness the meshing and the entangling of the sensibilities of two different decades.

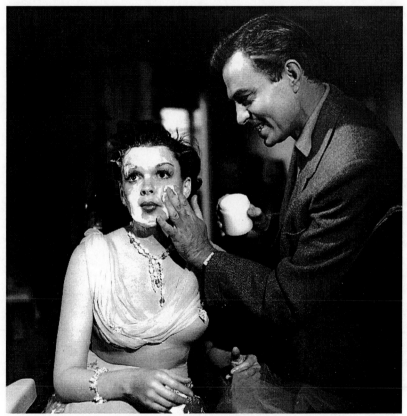

A Star Is Born (1954): Judy Garland and James Mason

Show Boat (1951) – If MGM had brought Jerome Kern and Oscar Hammerstein's legendary 1927 musical to the screen in 1936 it no doubt would have starred Jeanette MacDonald and Nelson Eddy. Instead, it was Universal (and director James Whale) who made that year's adored, visually splendid black-and-white version starring Irene Dunne, Allan Jones, and Helen Morgan (who had created her role of Julie onstage). MGM got their turn fifteen years later, teaming Kathryn Grayson and Howard Keel as the central singing duo (ingénue Magnolia and gambler Gaylord), with Ava Gardner as tragic mixed-race Julie. The film wasn't as acclaimed as its predecessor, but it was a massive popular success. Directed by MGM-musical stalwart George Sidney, it's a rather uneven Technicolor production, yet it managed to improve the material in a few significant ways. *Show Boat* has always had "book" trouble in its final chunk (after the couple splits, as they grow old, all the way to their daughter becoming a star). MGM wisely slowed the maniacally rapid plotting, deleting Magnolia's own rise to stardom and her highly unsatisfying geriatric reunion with Gaylord. After separating, Grayson and Keel are reunited just a few years later, with their little girl still a tot, allowing for a real chance at a future. The 1951 script also permits Julie (long gone in the original) to return as the happy ending's catalyst. Ms. Gardner, too whispery and tentative in her early scenes, cuts loose and is deeply touching in a new down-and-out scene, a drunken confrontation with Keel. Unfortunately, she wasn't allowed to do her own singing (which recordings prove was preferable to the mismatched voice with which she was dubbed), but she was given a haunting *Stella Dallas*-style finish. Overall, the characters seem less cardboard than they did in 1936, with Keel an ideal Gaylord, a singing Gable in decidedly "Rhett Butler" attire (thanks to *GWTW*'s costume designer Walter Plunkett). Keel far surpasses lightweight Allan Jones, also exuding more chemistry with Grayson than Jones ever did with Dunne. (Jones had looked too young for his role, while Dunne looked too old.) Grayson's singing is rather shrill, with muddy diction, though isn't it nice that she doesn't repeat Dunne's blackface number? Based on Edna Ferber's novel, which also became a 1929 partial talkie, *Show Boat* is essentially a masochistic soap opera elevated by a magnificent score. Grayson and Keel reteamed for *Lovely to Look At* (1952), a remake of *Roberta* (1935), another Irene Dunne '30s musical with Kern melodies, but box-office lightning didn't strike twice, nor should it have.

Let's Do It Again (1953) – It was futile to try to remake the great screwball comedy *The Awful Truth* (1937). With its ingenious Leo McCarey direction and peerless work from Irene Dunne and Cary Grant, *The Awful Truth* is a sophisticated treatment of divorce as the ultimate foreplay, a sexy, subtle, and slapsticky game of cat and mouse. Perfect opponents, Dunne and Grant bust up each other's new romances, all on the road to getting back together. If you subtract all the wit and all the fun, you have *Let's Do It Again,* a flat, pointless exercise that vanished without a trace. Neither the addition of bright colors, nor turning it into a musical, did it any service. Reset in a showbiz milieu, it stars Jane Wyman as a retired theater star and Ray Milland as a Broadway composer. Previously paired in *The Lost Weekend* (1945), Wyman and Milland do not make musical-comedy magic. Once a dapper light comedian, Milland is forced and charmless, while Wyman, who comes off better, is simply no Irene Dunne in the laugh-making department. Offering her own twist on Dunne's memorably tacky, uncouth (and hilarious) sister "Lola" (created to sabotage Grant's engagement), Wyman is sister "Phyllis," a husky-voiced vamp in a fringed gown, wielding a cigarette holder. Wyman certainly is game, but faring best is Aldo Ray in the old Ralph Bellamy role, a wealthy Oklahoma oilman, now an Alaskan uranium miner. The script offers a lame *Lost Weekend* crack when Wyman says of Milland that he "used to drink like a fish," and there's also an in-joke about an unseen star named Lucy Warriner, which was Dunne's *Awful Truth* name. But without any zip in Alexander Hall's direction, this is no *Awful Truth;* it's just plain awful.

Mogambo **(1953)** – Remaking the pre-Code *Red Dust* (1932) also meant cleaning it up. Jean Harlow's "Vantine" was an unapologetic prostitute, whereas Ava Gardner's "Honey Bear" is a WWII widow who became a playgirl only to forget her sorrows. You'll miss the racy carnal openness of *Red Dust,* but *Mogambo* is a surprisingly satisfying and enjoyable jungle picture, changing the setting from a Southeast Asian rubber plantation to the world of African big-game hunting. Still reigning as Hollywood's "King," Clark Gable was deemed macho enough to repeat his original role, even though, looking worn out, he doesn't really radiate sufficient heat anymore. He's now in the safari business, also selling animals to zoos and circuses. Directed by John Ford—though I can't detect his presence—*Mogambo* feels padded (33 minutes longer than *Red Dust*), overdoing its Technicolor travelogue aspects, including all that footage of natives and animals, adding more clutter than texture. But this is part of what the movie was selling: filmed on location! The African locale and safari scenes make it seem more like *Red Dust* meets *King Solomon's Mines* than a straight remake. It's really Gardner's show, resulting in her sole Oscar nomination. She's beautiful and brassy and likable, though somewhat mild when compared with Harlow (who had better one-liners). In this Code-era softening of such a character, Gardner, stumbling upon a Catholic priest, has him hear her confession. We also see her praying. (It's hard to imagine

Harlow going this route.) To Gardner's freewheeling credit, she still manages to be a slinky, smart-mouthed delight. Eventually, a British couple, Donald Sinden and Grace Kelly, arrive for safari. Unlike Mary Astor's fire-and-ice cheating wife of 1932, Kelly is clearly better at ice than fire, though she and Gable do begin an affair (with Kelly also getting an Oscar nomination). At the end, Gardner gets a proposal from Gable; Harlow just got back into his bed. Though *Mogambo* was a hit, and remains a lushly colorful adventure, I prefer the trashier humanity and studio exotica of *Red Dust*.

Magnificent Obsession **(1954)** – The financial success of this color-saturated remake helped launch a decade of high-gloss soaps, as well as establishing Douglas Sirk as the key director of '50s melodrama. Based on Lloyd C. Douglas' novel, the 1935 version had starred Irene Dunne (of course), with Jane Wyman now taking another crack at a Dunne role (after the *Let's Do It Again* fiasco). The male role—a spoiled bad-boy millionaire turned sensitive doctor—has had quite a success rate, making Robert Taylor a star in 1935 and doing the same for Rock Hudson nineteen years later, with two generations of soap audiences swooning at such selfless transitions. Wyman is widowed, though her surgeon husband might have been saved had his resuscitator not been borrowed to revive playboy Hudson after his foolishly daredevil accident in a speedboat. Otto Kruger, as an insufferable painter, smugly preaches to Hudson the title's concept, a pay-it-forward philosophy of doing good deeds (but always in secret). *Magnificent Obsession* is high-minded treacle (complete with heavenly choirs), with Kruger its stand-in for God… if God is a pretentious windbag. Trying to escape Hudson's attention, Wyman is hit by a car as she exits a cab. (Is Rock *trying* to kill the whole family?) She's blinded, prompting the movie to shift gears, focusing on Hudson's redemption, including eventual love between the stars. Off he goes to medical school, so he can operate on her eyes, becoming a neurosurgeon (with gray temples, which proves he's serious). Like Robert Taylor before him, Hudson is unconvincing throughout, especially in the guise of brilliant surgeon. Wyman snagged an Oscar nomination for her sincere (though skin-deep) acting, unassisted by the radio-serial quality of the dialogue. It's entirely ludicrous, though the earlier version, directed by John M. Stahl, offered *some* restraint. Sirk's version, though faithful to the 1935 plot and its masochistic religiosity, feels more artificial and drained of feeling. In subsequent soaps, such as *There's Always Tomorrow* (1956)—movies about more than jerking tears at glamorous suffering—Sirk would locate interesting subtexts and apply more delicate shadings.

A Star Is Born (1954) – Someone was bound to improve upon a '30s classic. Director George Cukor used the 1937 *A Star Is Born* as a blueprint for emotions to be dissected and expanded in 1954. (Cukor had already made the 1932 *What Price Hollywood?* whose plot was a virtual sketch for the first *A Star Is Born*.) Janet Gaynor and especially Fredric March had been effective (and Oscar-nominated) in 1937, but Judy Garland and James Mason (also both Oscar-nominated) turned a soap opera into a surging drama. Another musicalization of a famous movie, this isn't a true musical, more a drama about a singer (who generously displays her wares). Cukor's version is indeed overlong, but it's a moving and authentic-feeling Hollywood story. Its first half hour, at the Shrine Auditorium—outside and inside, onstage and off—is as good as any movie's first act, a seamless collage of swirling colors, charged emotions, and some thrilling music making, a perfect set-up for the film's depiction of the highs and lows of show business. Mason, as a fading star, brings real ugliness and fury to his drunkenness. (In 1937, Mr. March was never as embarrassing or as dissipated as Mason, never as emotionally bare.) There's a lovely moment when Mason helps Garland see herself as something special, giving her permission to dream bigger than she dared. This is a great gift that he bestows, and it bonds them forever; the stars share an extraordinary rapport and intimacy. His superb Oscar-night meltdown, filled with shame and self-disgust, is poignantly climaxed with the tenderness she shows him. Musically and dramatically, Garland is electrifying. You believe she's "most alive when I'm singing," and her fifteen-minute "Born in a Trunk" sequence is the vocal equivalent of one of those showstopping ballets in '50s movie musicals. Even better are her performances of "The Man That Got Away" and "Someone at Last," two phenomenal displays of her interpretive musical genius. And her dressing-room breakdown astounds in its rawness and spontaneity. This remake also boasts some glorious wide-screen color from Sam Leavitt, a trunkful of great songs, and a first-rate script from Moss Hart (faithful to the 1937 plot but richer in its exploration of the characters). The earlier version is saddled with an unfortunately cloying theme, about success having to be paid for with heartbreak. And Ms. Gaynor, a huge star, is ironically implausible as star material, without any clear attributes for success, making her onscreen rise mystifying. In Garland's case, it's the reverse: why does her blatantly deserving ascension take so damned long?

Young at Heart (**1955**) – Another musical stab at a famed soap, *Young at Heart* brought songs to the absorbing, if contrived, *Four Daughters* (1938), which makes sense because the earlier picture is about a musical family. Such a *happy* family, and their happiness seems even more synthetic in 1955, with the addition of storybook color (which calls attention to the fact that they're living on a soundstage street). In 1938, a miscast Claude Rains (huffing and puffing in age makeup) played the music-dean father, a widower with that daughterly quartet (played by three Lane sisters and Gale Page). For 1955, it was only *three* daughters, a trio consisting of Doris Day, Dorothy Malone, and Elisabeth Fraser, with Robert Keith more appropriate than Rains as the all-American dad. In the Jeffrey Lynn role, affable Gig Young is the composer who moves in with them, causing a three-way crush among the sisters. Finally, enter Frank Sinatra (at 35 minutes) in the role that made John Garfield a star, the cynical, self-pitying music arranger, who, in 1938, seemed to be a Depression-era product, like a Clifford Odets character, a jolt of defeatist darkness thrust into this sunny world. Without a Depression context, Sinatra is less sympathetic, less tolerable in his bellyaching outlook. Another problem is the actors' ages. In 1938, the young leads were actually young, making it easier to digest the immaturity of their behavior. The young cast members of 1955 may be young at heart but not in years. The stars are obviously over thirty, which makes their foolish impulses and actions harder to accept. Following the original plot, Day sets out to prove Sinatra wrong about life, leading to his falling in love with her. She happens to be engaged to Mr. Young, who is pined over by Ms. Fraser, with Day opting to elope with Sinatra rather than hurt Fraser. Setting up the new happy ending, Day realizes she loves Sinatra, who survives the suicidal snowstorm car crash that killed Garfield. The consistent soapiness is tempered by the natural verve and easy chemistry of Sinatra and Day, both deserving of more demanding material. She may be top-billed but he wins the musical show. Day is saddled with four bummer songs, while Sinatra not only sings the title tune (over the opening credits) but croons three standards in ideal saloon settings: "Someone to Watch Over Me," "Just One of Those Things," and "One for My Baby." He's in prime form, which is why this movie, if nothing else, is a priceless record of his glory days as an aching balladeer. Without the bittersweet aftertaste of *Four Daughters, Young at Heart* ends with Sinatra, Day, and their baby boy a perfect '50s family, singing and gleaming on their soundstage street.

The Opposite Sex (1956) – George Cukor's high-comic/lowdown gem *The Women* (1939) famously features not a single man. The remake, besides adding color, a wide screen, and a few songs, includes male characters who, ironically, are less vivid than the men only talked about in 1939. And though Norma Shearer was the most inconsistently effective member of Cukor's ensemble, she was positively flawless compared to June Allyson, reliably unbearable in one of her good-wife roles. She'll soon have you rooting for the conniving and luscious Joan Collins (in the Joan Crawford role). Allyson's character, now a retired performer, is married to a Broadway producer (Leslie Nielsen), with Collins a chorus girl in one of his shows. As Sylvia, the catty horror played so fabulously by Rosalind Russell in '39, Dolores Gray provides the style, size, and crackle lacking everywhere else. A sensational singer, Gray is given only the nifty title tune, while the parched Allyson, barely able to talk, sings far too often (though she's necessarily dubbed for her ballad). Another semi-musical, *The Opposite Sex* bursts into song only when performer characters are in performance, though Ann Miller (in the Paulette Goddard role), a nightclub entertainer, surprisingly never sings or dances. Then there's Ann Sheridan as Allyson's playwright pal, a melding of the roles played in 1939 by Lucile Watson (Shearer's mother) and Florence Nash (the "old maid" authoress), plus Joan Blondell—who was previously married to Allyson's real-life husband Dick Powell—as the always-pregnant one. (The old Joan Fontaine role is reduced to a walk-on in Reno.) As the scene-stealing countess, done for Cukor so brilliantly by the inimitable Mary Boland, we have Agnes Moorehead, a huge disappointment, partially because the role is cut to shreds. Instead of the countess, it's Sylvia who hooks up with the cowboy (Jeff Richards), though she doesn't marry him (as Ms. Boland did). For all its clawing, *The Women* celebrates females, specifically in its strong friendships (which vanquish the bitchy characters) while also reveling in the awe-inspiring comedic prowess of its man-free cast. But the buoyant sparkle of *The Women,* in which even the bit players are memorable, is snuffed in *The Opposite Sex.* Under David Miller's sluggish direction and despite being filmed in color, there's nothing jungle-red about it.

An Affair to Remember (1957) – Director Leo McCarey was back at the helm, remaking his own Best Picture Oscar nominee *Love Affair* (1939) with the expected embellishments of color, CinemaScope, and a theme song (gorgeously sung by Vic Damone, with lyrics co-written by McCarey). But is there any reason for the remake to be twenty-seven minutes longer than the original? No, especially since this is nearly one of those shot-for-shot replications; somehow, it's both faithful and padded (with McCarey's pacing more leisurely and his touch heavier). In roles created by Irene Dunne (who else?) and Charles Boyer, here's equally entrancing Deborah Kerr and Cary Grant. If you've always wondered why Grant's character has a French grandmother and why the non-singing Kerr is playing a nightclub singer, these are details lazily retained from *Love Affair*, in which Frenchman Boyer logically has a French grandmother, and Dunne, an actual singer, *sings*, as she so often did onscreen. (Kerr utilizes her *King and I* voice: Marni Nixon). The appeal of the remake's first half, the shipboard romance, rests entirely on the bantering skills of its star duo, even if much of the writing is self-consciously glib. It's about nothing more than Grant and Kerr being charming movie stars, seeming to appear as themselves, practically floating above the material. He's an engaged playboy; she's a ladylike mistress set up in a penthouse. (The film is decidedly mute on her situation, though her lover wants to marry her.) The stars agree to clean up their acts, support themselves, and meet in six months atop the Empire State Building. The pull of the story lies in the fact that these aren't kids. They're mature people who have been sidetracked, now trying to replace their easy compromises with something real. An accident prevents her from meeting him, and she chooses not to burden him with her inability to walk. (In both versions, the light comedy of the first half outshines the sudsy manipulations of the second.) The low point finds Kerr coaching a children's chorus and band, complete with two sickening songs. As the goo and the masochism mount, the surefire final five minutes are beautifully handled by the stars. *Love Affair* is slightly superior overall, mostly because of its fleet running time, but it doesn't have the remake's beloved song to envelop it so snugly.

***My Man Godfrey* (1957)** – The impulse to remake screwball comedies was misguided. The genre was an outgrowth of the Depression, a format in which regular folks were often able to laugh at the foibles of the rich, who often seemed clueless about the *really* important things. Audiences could feel better about their own fates while gorging on sumptuous production values. Remaking *My Man Godfrey* (1936), one of the funniest screwball comedies and among the more Depression-oriented, was an atrocious idea, especially on the heels of a disastrous (and musicalized) remake of *It Happened One Night* (1934), a seismically bad venture known as *You Can't Run Away from It* (1956), starring June Allyson and Jack Lemmon. Allyson, having already trounced *The Women*, stars in the *Godfrey* remake, wrecking a third great '30s comedy. Tackling the memory of *Godfrey*'s divine Carole Lombard was a doomed prospect. Allyson's dizzy heiress lacks Lombard's joyous adolescent abandon; she's no fun at all. David Niven, a logical replacement for William Powell, is perfectly fine, but what a crazy makeover his character was given. When Powell played Godfrey, he was a forgotten man at a city dump; found by Lombard, he became her family's butler, though he was actually a rich guy who dropped out of society after a bad love affair. Niven is introduced in roughly the same way, but he's loaded down with a bizarre backstory: Romanian-born but Austrian by nationality; Oxford-educated, and London-dwelling for a decade (which explains the British accent); a WWII bomber pilot, as an Austrian; went to sea and jumped ship; now an illegal alien in America. Was Godfrey a Nazi soldier? Are you kidding me? Strenuously trying to justify itself, this contemporary *Godfrey* remains pointless and unforgivably mirthless (even though many of the 1936 episodes are repeated). Jessie Royce Landis, a swell comedienne, is miscast as the dotty mother; Landis is nobody's ninny. The only pleasure comes from Eva Gabor (in a role refashioned from the Alan Mowbray original); she has the abundant charm elsewhere absent. With Henry Koster (who had directed Niven in *The Bishop's Wife*) mostly at a loss, this *Godfrey* doesn't have a madcap bone in its body. Niven eventually surrenders to authorities and is deported, but Allyson follows, ready to secure his citizenship via marriage. Why bother to call this thing *My Man Godfrey*?

Imitation of Life **(1959)** – With its reputation as a Douglas Sirk masterpiece, this remake has certainly dwarfed the simpler 1934 version, an Oscar nominee for Best Picture directed by John M. Stahl. The 1934 plot has two single mothers joining forces, Claudette Colbert and African-American Louise Beavers, with Colbert turning Beavers' pancake recipe into an empire. Business-minded Colbert becomes the pancake queen, while Beavers, the source of all the money, is content in the background, so unthreateningly happy in her place, continuing to look after Colbert. (She rubs Colbert's tired feet, but who rubs hers?) The plot becomes a dual mother-daughter tract, with Beavers' light-skinned daughter determined to pass for white and Colbert's daughter falling for her mother's new love. Sirk's remake delivers a more compelling treatment of the black mother and daughter (Oscar nominees Juanita Moore and Susan Kohner) and their worthy plotline about race and self-loathing. Wisely dispensing with the Aunt Jemima aspects, Sirk has Lana Turner (in Colbert's role) as an aspiring actress who becomes a major star. You no longer have to feel uncomfortable about watching a white woman grow wealthy by running a business built on a black woman's talent, though selfless subservience remains integral to the plot. Ms. Moore is devoted to serving Ms. Turner, just minus the maple syrup. The remake's biggest hurdle is to make you believe Lana Turner as a great stage actress. The only time we see her "act" is at a bad audition (acknowledged as such); the rest is all dressing rooms and curtain calls. If we actually saw her onstage, the illusion might shatter. Casting her seems a sly joke: whenever Turner strives most to be genuine, she personifies falseness. Both Sandra Dee (as her daughter) and John Gavin (the mutual love interest), separately tell her to "stop acting!" Her stardom leads to weary dissatisfaction, but her talent, knowing no bounds, can't stop wowing everyone! She and Kohner (trying to pass for white) parallel each other, both wanting more from life than it first offers, yet the film punishes them both, sympathizing with the more conventional characters. Lavishly mounted and intensely colorful, this movie has trouble clarifying the difference between what's real and what's an imitation, promoting gloss while denouncing it. To his credit, Sirk intensifies the mother-daughter confrontations, including an all-out showdown between Turner and Dee, a scene denied us in 1934. The remake succeeds at being more than a copycat of its predecessor, mostly surpassing it, but it becomes moralizing and heavy-handed, a melodrama with lofty pretensions. Without an essential core of authenticity, this *Imitation of Life* is just another masquerade.

The Genre that Got Away: Final Bows for the Original Hollywood Musical (1955-1957)

The first bona fide movie musical, *The Broadway Melody* (1929), was an original property with new songs (by composer Nacio Herb Brown and lyricist Arthur Freed) attached to a new backstage story (old as the hills). It marked the dawn of a new age, alright, with both talkies and musicals here to stay. Despite a few rocky years in the early 1930s, musicals solidified their popularity by mid-decade, headed for a twenty-year heyday. During that happy time, movie-musical content alternated between Broadway-based and homegrown material. But even the movies' original musicals owed a debt to Broadway, the ongoing model for where musicals were headed, as well as a source for exciting talent, having fostered two fellas named Fred Astaire and Gene Kelly.

With one major exception—the team of Harry Warren and Al Dubin, responsible for those wonderful songs in the Busby Berkeley extravaganzas at Warner Brothers—most of the songwriters of the best original movie musicals of the 1930s were more identified with Broadway than Hollywood. Richard Rodgers and Lorenz Hart brought distinction to two of the decade's screen highlights, *Love Me Tonight* (1932), which introduced "Isn't it Romantic?" and *Hallelujah I'm a Bum* (1933). Later, Harold Arlen and E.Y. Harburg musicalized a little something called *The Wizard of Oz* (1939). If you want to appreciate the high-caliber breadth of the New York contribution to the Hollywood musical, look no further than the RKO pictures of Fred Astaire and Ginger Rogers. Yes, their first starring vehicle *The Gay Divorcee* (1934) was based on a 1932 Cole Porter Broadway show (starring Astaire himself) followed by *Roberta* (1935), an adaptation of a 1933 Jerome Kern stage success, but next came brand-new scores for most of the dance team's subsequent vehicles, providing an overflow of additions to the Great American Songbook, with Astaire the introducer of enduring popular-music standards: Irving Berlin's "Cheek to Cheek" and "Isn't This a Lovely Day?" in *Top Hat* (1935), Berlin's "Let's Face the Music and Dance" in *Follow the Fleet* (1936), Jerome Kern and Dorothy Fields' "The Way You Look Tonight" and "A Fine Romance" in *Swing Time* (1936), George and Ira Gershwin's "They Can't Take That Away from Me" and "Let's Call the Whole Thing Off" in *Shall We Dance* (1937), and Berlin's "Change Partners" in *Carefree* (1938).

This Broadway-to-Hollywood trend continued into the 1940s, beyond the Art Deco world of Fred and Ginger, with Mr. Kern summoning more gorgeous melodies for two splendid Rita Hayworth musicals at Columbia: *You Were Never Lovelier* (1942) with Astaire and *Cover Girl* (1944) with Gene Kelly. Mr. Berlin offered mostly new songs for Astaire and Bing Crosby in *Holiday Inn* (1942) and an even mix of old and new for Astaire and Judy Garland in *Easter Parade* (1948). For both Garland and Kelly, Cole Porter contributed the score for one of the decade's most inventive (and least popular) movie musicals, *The Pirate* (1948), just before having his greatest Broadway success—*Kiss Me Kate* (1948). Even Kurt Weill went Hollywood when he wrote the music for an ambitious, occasionally enchanting misfire, *Where Do We Go from Here?* (1945), while Jule Styne, *before* starting his Broadway career with *High Button Shoes* (1947), composed lovely ballads for Frank Sinatra in *Anchors Aweigh* (1945).

But the Hollywood musical was also highly influenced by the *kinds* of stories being musicalized on Broadway, and by the ways in which song and dance were used to *tell* those stories. Rodgers and Hammerstein's *Oklahoma!* (1943) was the great landmark for integration, with musical moments that moved the story forward and revealed character. Certainly, the most emotion-fused Fred-and-Ginger dances advance their films' love stories, and "Over the Rainbow" is the perfect establishing of a character through song, but, for the most part, movie musicals used singing and dancing as diverting interruptions. In Vincente Minnelli's *Meet Me in St. Louis* (1944), an MGM musical with a new score by Hugh Martin and Ralph Blane, the impact of *Oklahoma!* is apparent. It isn't entirely integrated, but it surely has its moments including Judy Garland's renditions of "The Boy Next Door" and "Have Yourself a Merry Little Christmas," both exquisitely integral to the plot and Garland's character. *The Harvey Girls* (1946), again with Garland at MGM, was no *Oklahoma!* as far as western musicals go, and its integration was in-and-out, but look at its central production number "On the Atchison, Topeka, and the Santa Fe," a superbly constructed musical episode that transmits more about its lead, supporting, and background characters—as well as the time, place, and social framework—than could be accomplished by twenty-five pages of dialogue.

The most celebrated movie musicals of the early 1950s attached old songs to original screenplays: the Gershwins' trunkful for Vincente Minnelli's *An American in Paris* (1951), the Arthur Freed-Nacio Herb Brown early-talkie favorites for Gene Kelly and Stanley Donen's *Singin' in the Rain* (1952), and Howard Dietz-Arthur Schwartz show tunes for Minnelli's *The Band Wagon* (1953). Each was made at the peerless MGM—the first two starring Kelly, the last starring Astaire. All three mixed sophisticated song-and-dance integration with more traditional razzmatazz, both old-school and state-of-the-art, including extended "ballet" sequences that remain innovative peaks of an art form at its apex. The multi-Oscar-winning *American in Paris* is the weakest, most uneven of the trio, but could movie musicals ever top *Singin' in the Rain* or *The Band Wagon*? Add one more, *Seven Brides for Seven Brothers* (1954), a Best Picture Oscar nominee with an original score by Gene de Paul and Johnny Mercer. It's a musical so emotionally rich, character-driven, and structurally sound that it's easy to assume (wrongly) it's an adaptation of a hit Broadway show. With MGM cranking out four consecutive classics, the first half of the 1950s was a new-musical golden age. How odd that it began tumbling down in 1955.

A number of colliding issues caused the demise. The increasing popularity of television variety series was a challenge to movie producers because audiences could now enjoy song and dance at home (for free). Then there was the rise of rock and roll, which suddenly meant that popular music was no longer reliant on Broadway and Hollywood output. (There was one great rock and roll film musical, *The Girl Can't Help It* [1956], but it didn't spawn any other good ones.) Finally, the studio system of moviemaking was dismantling, with even hallowed MGM letting go of most of its musical contract players, including Howard Keel and Jane Powell, stars of the recent smash-hit *Seven Brides*. (Instead of their success rewarded with another prime original property, Keel and Powell were gone from MGM musicals by the end of 1955.) Overall, musicals weren't going anywhere, but, with the confluence of these undeniable forces, the decision makers increasingly relied on safe transfers of Broadway hits, knowing it was far less risky to mount *South Pacific* (1958) than any new concoction (*Seven Brides* be damned). If you could get Marlon Brando to star in *Guys and Dolls* (1955) or have a dubbed Deborah Kerr in *The King and I* (1956), why worry about keeping a musical factory humming with contracted performers?

The age of the original movie musical officially ended on an ironically triumphant note with Lerner and Loewe's *Gigi* (1958) winning nine Oscars including Best Picture. Directed by Vincente Minnelli for MGM, *Gigi* is no *Band Wagon* or *Seven Brides,* nor is it anywhere near the quality of Lerner and Loewe's recent stage hit *My Fair Lady* (1956), which it steals from shamelessly. Despite its elegant beauty, *Gigi* is dramatically problematic (some might say creepy), and it's rarely as witty as it imagines. Its Oscar win now looks like the equivalent of being presented with a gold watch, a polite acknowledgement of the end of an era. However, within that post-*Seven Brides* and *pre-Gigi* period of change and doubt and panic, there was still marvelous stuff happening in original Hollywood musicals. Though dancing toward extinction, the genre was forging forward.

Daddy Long Legs (1955): Leslie Caron and Fred Astaire

Jupiter's Darling (**1955**) – Esther Williams thrived in a musical sub-genre all her own, the swimming musical, beginning with *Bathing Beauty* (1944). In 1949 and 1950, she was the screen's second most popular female star (behind Betty Grable) and continued her success into the new decade. George Sidney, her *Bathing Beauty* director, also helmed *Jupiter's Darling*, Williams' swimming-musical swan song. Though one of her better vehicles, it proved unpopular enough to drain the last drop from Williams' resident pool at MGM. Swimsicals could hardly be labeled integrated, with their usually trite plots pausing for guest-star specialty numbers and Williams' mandatory backstroke. They are stock rom-coms, only poolside, but, as '50s musicals were expected to try a little harder, even Williams was eventually affected, first with the dramatic biopic *Million Dollar Mermaid* (1952), then with *Jupiter's Darling*, based on a 1927 Robert E. Sherwood play (*The Road to Rome*). Williams plays an independent chariot-riding Greek woman living in 216 B.C. Rome, engaged for seven years to dictator George Sanders (a weak, mild fellow). He-man Howard Keel, in his third (and best) picture with Williams, is Hannibal, the bearded barbarian set to conquer Rome. *Jupiter's Darling* occasionally hits its mark—an amusing winking tone—though Williams is hardly a sparkling comedienne (too grounded for tongue-in-cheek frivolity), while Keel seems bored and unhappy. More silly than bright, it's often lively and lavish, and though its songs (by Burton Lane and Harold Adamson) are only average, one of them leads to a peak among all Williams' swimming numbers: "I Have a Dream," a fantasy of romantic yearning in which she frolics with six underwater male statues come to life. The sequence uses swimming to make a story point, to express her desire for something more erotically gratifying than Mr. Sanders. Her vocal may be dubbed but the number doesn't really take off until she submerges for her magical escapade. Keel, of course, handles the bulk of the singing, and Marge and Gower Champion, as slaves, enliven things with their dances. There's also an exciting underwater chase, deep into a cave, as three men pursue Williams; she out-breathes them and gets away, as strong as she is beautiful. *Jupiter's Darling* probably would have been a hit if it had been made even two years earlier, before the musical tides were turning.

Daddy Long Legs (**1955**) – After his triple-threat triumph in *The Band Wagon* (1953), Fred Astaire, in his mid-fifties, next starred in this musical adaptation of a well-worn story—a 1919 film success for Mary Pickford, ditto for Janet Gaynor in 1931—retooled for Leslie Caron, the enchanting gamine of *An American in Paris* (1951) and *Lili* (1953). With a 32-year age difference, Astaire and Caron had the challenge of convincing moviegoers not only that they could dance together but be linked romantically, one of several questionable May-December pairings of the decade (usually involving Audrey Hepburn). Astaire is attractively cast as a New York millionaire bachelor who sets up an anonymous U.S. college scholarship for French orphan Caron. The school scenes are hopelessly phony, but Caron is reliably radiant and charming throughout. And director Jean Negulesco, unaccustomed to musicals, keeps the festivities likable, even though the film is far too long (despite its underuse of Thelma Ritter as Astaire's secretary). Borrowing from *On the Town* (1949) and *An American in Paris,* the film has one of those numbers in which someone imagines what an unknown figure might be like, with Caron wondering about guardian Astaire, envisioning him as a sprightly Texan (in boots and cowboy hat), a monocled playboy, and a literal guardian angel (in a lovely pas de deux with her, the film's best matching of the stars' contrasting dance techniques). Later, in a red spaghetti-strapped dress, Caron deftly adapts to Astaire's rhythmically intricate style for the excellent "Sluefoot" at the college dance. It's the scene in which the characters truly connect; fittingly, it's dance that brings them together. Caron is also game for a direct evocation of Astaire's "Ginger" days, with Johnny Mercer's score providing a swooningly Ginger-worthy ballad, "Something's Gotta Give," leading to a romantic floater of a dance. Roland Petit choreographed Caron's large-scale dream ballet in which she searches for Astaire, allowing for her appearances as both a ballerina and a Cyd Charisse-like sex bomb. But while *Daddy Long Legs* is a generous showcase of Caron's dancing versatility, it's more at home in Astaireland than Petit's world. (Aside from the ballet sequences, the choreography is by Astaire and David Robel.) As for the age issue, well, at least it's a factor in the plot, rather than ignored (which would only make it worse). Astaire *does* question the appropriateness of his proposing to Caron, which makes it easier to adjust to their ending up together. Besides, he's literally swept her off her feet, which has to count for something. *Daddy Long Legs* is far from being one of Astaire's best musicals, but it's pleasing to watch him take command of his dapper older-man role and mesh with a winsome new partner. This "daddy" of movie musicals is still in tip-top top-hat form.

***The Girl Rush* (1955)** – Totally forgotten, it's of interest because of leading lady Rosalind Russell. In 1953, she won a Tony for the Broadway musical *Wonderful Town,* based on the 1940 stage comedy *My Sister Eileen* which was adapted into a 1942 screen hit for Russell, netting her an Oscar nomination.

With no film version of *Wonderful Town* in sight, Russell brandished her newly honed musical skills in this original project scored by the *Meet Me in St. Louis* team of Hugh Martin and Ralph Blane. The resulting songs aren't bad, just not good enough, leading to nothing-special numbers. From Paramount, *The Girl Rush* is flatly directed by Robert Pirosh, with a plot too thin to absorb much in the way of song integration. Russell inherits half of a ramshackle Las Vegas casino, bolting from Providence and her job at the historical museum. The men she'll encounter are casino owner Fernando Lamas and hotel heir Eddie Albert, while the other female is Gloria DeHaven, star of the revue at Lamas' joint. Dumb, blonde, and named Taffy, DeHaven makes too little of her role's comic potential, but Marion Lorne is a hoot as Russell's Aunt Clara (a decade before she was another Aunt Clara, on TV's *Bewitched*), and, look, there's George Chakiris as an extra in Rhode Island and a dancer in Vegas. Flimsy, sure, yet it still bares the push-pull of wanting to be both a new-fangled Broadway-type book musical and an old-time forget-your-troubles time-killer (where it's more at home). Russell is dauntless, whether croaking admirably or hoofing a soft shoe with the breezy Mr. Albert. For the onstage "Hillbilly Heart," she begins in a pink gown (with chorus boys in tuxes), then shifts to low-down duds for some raucous choreography. She and Lamas make a terrible romantic duo: she's too aggressive and energized for his studly, zombified nature. But even amid such musical-comedy nonsense, Russell is every inch a star, especially in a red and black suit, a wrap, and a large *flat* black hat worthy of Auntie Mame (a role that was soon to be hers).

It's Always Fair Weather (1955) – The best original Hollywood musical of the post-*Seven Brides* 1950s, it certainly boasts the best screenplay, the work of Betty Comden and Adolph Green, which winningly juggles cynicism and optimism. Directed and choreographed by Gene Kelly and Stanley Donen—who, with Comden and Green, had scored a big success with *On the Town* (1949)—MGM's *It's Always Fair Weather* is a sequel in spirit, a what-if in which a cheerful trio is made a lot less cheerful by the real world. Potentially sour and unpleasant, the result is, instead, a reaffirmation of hope and confidence. The 1945 prologue has victorious G.I.s Kelly, Dan Dailey, and Michael Kidd ready to tackle the future, until Kelly, slammed by a Dear John letter, triggers the boys' drunken spree, leading to the great garbage-can lid dance, which is not only a nighttime wide-screen "New York, New York" but also a thrilling release of steam and a virtuosic dance display (with those lids on the trio's left feet). Assuming their devotion will be unchanged, they agree to meet in ten years, but 1955 proves to be no V-E Day: Kelly is a shady small-time New York operator; once-aspiring painter Dailey is miserable in Chicago advertising; and Kidd has a burger joint in Schenectady. Personally, slick Kelly is a womanizer, stuffy Dailey is on the verge of divorce, and hick Kidd is married with five children. Kelly and Dailey take the focus, their acting filled with nuances of self-loathing and disappointment, while Kidd, in the benign Sinatra slot (the Italian runt), has less to do. Now strangers, the guys irritate each other as reminders of all they *didn't* do, of how far off course they veered. This isn't lightweight fare, but its honesty makes the ultimately rekindled positivity that much more satisfying. Cyd Charisse, however, is out of her depth as a brainy career gal, a television program-coordinator on hand for Kelly. (In the film's worst move, they never dance together; how else can we know they're right for each other?) But Dolores Gray is sensational as the glisteningly narcissistic TV star of a live variety show. One of the last best things to happen to the MGM musical, Gray offers her warm Broadway-belt singing voice and her comically grand extravagance, hijacking the film with "Thanks a Lot, But No Thanks," her slinky red-clad showstopper with worshipful chorus boys. Built upon a solid score of Andre Previn music and Comden-and-Green lyrics, *It's Always Fair Weather* is a rejuvenation musical, climaxing with Kelly's joyous roller-skated "I Like Myself," a skate-tapping "Singin' in the Rain" (again along city streets). Dailey gets a musical breakdown, "Situation-Wise," but the most emotionally affecting number is the three-way split-screen "Once Upon a Time," a rueful soft shoe that ingeniously both joins and separates the main trio on their shaky way to reconnecting. There's also enjoyable satire of television programs and on-air advertising (the pandering, condescension, and slobbering), but *It's Always Fair Weather* is about unwinding—physically but mostly mentally—and trying, before it's too late, to be the best, truest version of yourself.

My Sister Eileen (1955) – Columbia, which had made the 1942 *My Sister Eileen,* wanted to make a musical version without buying the rights to *Wonderful Town.* They commissioned a new, apparently legal version, not as sturdy as *Wonderful Town* (with its savvy Leonard Bernstein-Betty Comden-Adolph Green score) but an improvement on the 1942 film, even without Roz Russell. The 1955 *Eileen* is less pushed, more relaxed than the '42 version, which is strained and exaggerated, even tiring. The *Gentlemen Prefer Blondes* team, Jule Styne and Leo Robin, wrote the 1955 score, which is decent, but what elevates this musical is its "musical numbers and dances staged by Robert Fosse" (that's Bob, to you). Fosse is in it, too, cast as the sweet soda jerk, but it's his outstanding choreography that occasionally makes *My Sister Eileen* a major musical from a fading era. The ever-skillful Betty Garrett and top-billed Janet Leigh (in the title role) are the nice-girl Ohio sisters who move to Greenwich Village: ordinary-looking Garrett is an aspiring writer; and adorable Leigh is an aspiring actress whom most men can't resist. Much of the humor is meant to come from two ongoing sources: Garrett's self-deprecation in response to Leigh's surefire appeal; and their new apartment, a spacious basement studio which periodically shakes because of all that blasting for the new subway. While the comic elements are exceedingly familiar, the same can't be said of Fosse's dances, with the film's high point a theater-alley competition between Fosse and Tommy Rall (as a slick reporter), both men vying for Ms. Leigh. Reunited from the great "From This Moment On" number in *Kiss Me Kate* (1953), Fosse and Rall astonish in this faultlessly conceived and executed dance, filled with breathtaking leaps, spins, flips, slides, and some classic Fosse hat-work, a crackerjack number that was revived for the Broadway revue *Fosse* (1999). The next-best number is the nighttime "Give Me a Band and My Baby" with Garrett and Leigh joining Fosse and Rall on an empty park bandstand. (This foursome constitutes an old-home week of MGM graduates.) Dramatically, this sequence is pointless, but as a burst of pleasure it's playful, clever, and tricky in its choreography, all of it gleefully performed. Ms. Leigh does incredibly well in the dances, even partnering Fosse for a fresh, charming courtyard duet to "There's Nothin' Like Love." Unlike Leigh, newcomer Jack Lemmon, as a magazine publisher, *is* uncomfortable, especially in his musical-comedy seduction attempt on Garrett. Another up-and-comer, Blake Edwards, co-wrote the screenplay, while the director, Richard Quine, played Fosse's role onstage in 1940 and in the 1942 film. This 1955 version belongs to Fosse, all the way to his witty staging of the climactic conga, with the Brazilian fleet in the girls' apartment. But however much he raised its game, he couldn't singlehandedly make *My Sister Eileen* more than an above-average movie musical.

Artists and Models (1955) – The fourteenth of Paramount's sixteen Dean Martin and Jerry Lewis vehicles, this musical comedy benefits from having Frank Tashlin as its director, one year away from his masterwork *The Girl Can't Help It*. But aside from Tashlin's dazzling color sense, *Artists and Models* isn't much. (And it's unrelated to the same-titled movie musical of 1937.) More goofy than funny, it's also mired in coy '50s romancing (true of *My*

Sister Eileen too). Again, the central pair lives as roommates in Greenwich Village, with Dean an aspiring painter and Jerry an aspiring children's-story writer. Also in the building are roommates Dorothy Malone (a cartoonist) and Shirley MacLaine (a publisher's secretary and sometime-model for Malone). Tashlin co-wrote the screenplay, which is filled with good ideas unfulfilled, including worries about the impact of lurid comic books on kids' minds, like that of obsessed man-child Jerry. And the Cold War plot about commie spies (led by Eva Gabor) should be much more fun than it is. But *Artists and Models* is a good early showcase for MacLaine (in her second film), well-matched to Jerry's energy. She makes a bold romantic assault on him, reprising Dean's "Innamorata" (the film's "That's Amore" wannabe), singing it real loud on a flight of stairs and causing Jerry to drop (several times) all that he's carrying. She dances in this scene, too, using the banister as a balance beam, her spunk the film's chief asset. Meanwhile, Malone is her plasticized self, and the big title-tune benefit number feels like a '40s Betty Grable cast-off, with showgirls as paints on a palette. There's too much goo in the forgettable songs by Harry Warren and Jack Brooks, meaning that *Artists and Models* is only rarely as galvanizing as its primary colors, mostly when MacLaine takes hold of it.

Meet Me in Las Vegas (1956) – As fine a musical as *It's Always Fair Weather* is, it didn't serve Cyd Charisse whose one number, the gym-set "Baby, You Knock Me Out," didn't really suit her, nor did it have anything to do with the plot. But *Meet Me in Las Vegas*, a mere piffle compared with *Fair Weather*, gave Charisse one of the top sequences of her screen-dancing career. Among '50s movie-musical ballets, "Frankie and Johnny" ranks with the best, an onstage number set to a terrific Sammy Davis, Jr. vocal of the old song. Unlike Charisse's appearances in the ballets of *Singin' in the Rain* and *The Band Wagon,* this time she's the center, rather than Astaire or Kelly. And she sustains her sizzle throughout its sexy, slyly funny barroom plot, a tongue-in-cheek "Slaughter on 10th Avenue" brilliantly choreographed by Hermes Pan. With Charisse in an azure-colored costume of fringe and sparkles, her legs generously exposed and unleashed, "Frankie and Johnny" becomes one of the last major dances of the MGM musical, tucked too safely away in this oh-so minor movie. But for seven minutes it's a super musical, with Charisse formidably loving her man, John Brascia, until shooting him dead for doing her wrong with Liliane Montevecchi. (It's funny about single-threat Charisse, such a phenomenal dancer and so limited an actress: when dancing, she seems a gifted thespian, as she does as "Frankie," combining lust, comic glints, and a fierce presence.)

Despite "Frankie and Johnny," the demise of musicals like *Meet Me in Las Vegas* was not a bad thing. Its producer, Joe Pasternak, was, at this late date, still making his brand of '40s musicals, emphasizing specialty talent, mixing pop and classical arts. On those terms, this one is better than most, with Lena Horne caressing "If You Can Dream" and Charisse going "classical" for a modern-dress *Sleeping Beauty* (with lovely Eugene Loring choreography). But Frankie Laine's "Hell Hath No Fury," with four female dancing devils, and a cloying duet ("My Lucky Charm") between Dan Dailey and a female Japanese child (in a kimono) are inexcusable. There *is* a plot, about love and gambling, and it's actually not bad, just stretched beyond endurance, set over days but feeling like weeks. Charisse is a diva ballerina playing Vegas; Mr. Dailey is a gambling rancher. (It's almost *Grand Hotel*, with a sheltered ballerina learning about love.) The blah Nicholas Brodszky-Sammy Cahn score provides the stars with a *Seven Brides*-type hoe-down at the ranch, joined by ten guys. And their happy ending is refreshing, with Charisse not having to hang up her toe shoes simply because she's found her mate, even though the dearth of chemistry between them is unavoidable. There are also cameos from big stars, including Tony Martin, Charisse's real-life husband, and, look, George Chakiris, again, in a tiny role, with *West Side Story* still five years away.

High Society **(1956)** – A big fat hit because of its superstar trio, this Cole Porter musicalization of *The Philadelphia Story* is the movie-musical equivalent of a Rolls Royce with flat tires. Matching Porter to Philip Barry's 1939 play and George Cukor's 1940 film version sounds heaven-sent, but the result is painfully deficient in snap, crackle, and sophistication. Porter's score is inadequate, and the director, the talented Charles Walters (*Lili*), delivers one of his least attractive musicals, lacking any invigorating use of color or camera movement. Despite its Oscar-winning quartet—Bing Crosby, Grace Kelly, Frank Sinatra, Celeste Holm—the cast can't begin to compete with their 1940 predecessors. Crosby (in the Cary Grant slot) and Sinatra (in the Oscar-winning James Stewart role) walk through their parts, coming to life for their duet, "Well, Did You Evah?" an old (and good) Porter song interpolated into the score. The 1956 Crosby is such a dreary romantic lead; shouldn't Sinatra be playing Crosby's role? And though Ms. Kelly is actually from Philadelphia, the setting has been changed to the more music-friendly Newport (R.I.), with its jazz festival. Using Louis Armstrong as a Greek chorus is an inspired yet sadly under-utilized idea, though he rouses things with "Now You Has Jazz," his number with Crosby. Ms. Holm, previously with Sinatra in Mr. Walters'

The Tender Trap (1955), is a good sport here, fairly untaxed, and Kelly is certainly logically cast as Tracy Lord. But she's no Katharine Hepburn, lacking the range, comic instincts, and theatrical ease to pull off such a high-style role. Colder, more remote than Hepburn, Kelly is, ironically, closer than Hepburn to the Tracy described in both versions: the cool goddess. Far less likable (and a helluva lot less fun) than Hepburn, Kelly remains more irritating than fascinating. (When Hepburn's Tracy is being dumped on by her father and her ex-husband, you want to scream, "Stop blaming her for your weaknesses, she's worth ten of you!") The Crosby-Kelly snore of a duet, "True Love," got an Oscar nomination, but the best new song is Sinatra's "You're Sensational," a beautifully sung wooing of the perennially pedestaled Kelly.

Funny Face (1957) – In the tradition of *Singin' in the Rain* and *The Band Wagon, Funny Face* is a songbook musical, creating a new property from mostly old songs, in this case those by George and Ira Gershwin. *An American in Paris* (1951) had gotten there first, taking Gershwin oldies all the way to a Best Picture Oscar. Like *Band Wagon, Funny Face* borrows the title of a hit Broadway show that starred Fred Astaire (and his sister Adele), then places Astaire himself in a plot that bears no relation to the original show's storyline. After Leslie Caron, Astaire has another thirty-years-younger leading lady in Audrey Hepburn. Though Hepburn didn't click as well with him as Caron did on the dance floor, *Funny Face* is much superior to *Daddy Long Legs*. Directed by Stanley Donen, and choreographed by Astaire and Eugene Loring, *Funny Face* is a high-fashion musical set in New York and Paris, a devastatingly chic and visually resplendent work. Made for Paramount (Hepburn's studio), but indelibly the work of Donen and Astaire, *Funny Face* is the only Paramount "MGM musical," a blissful collision. As the editor of *Quality Magazine,* Kay Thompson opens the film with a master class in sheer fabulousness, launching into the whimsically instructive "Think Pink!" and dynamically declaring ownership of the movie. Astaire is a Richard Avedon-like fashion photographer (Avedon was the film's "special visual consultant"), and Hepburn becomes the magazine's unlikely new model, a Greenwich Village bookshop clerk obsessed with a beatnik philosophy based on empathy. (If screenwriter Leonard Gershe's satire of fashion is affectionate, his take on beatnik culture mostly feels like mockery.) By ignoring the age difference addressed in *Daddy Long Legs, Funny Face* fails romantically. Who can believe that Hepburn is agog after a casual kiss from a pushing-sixty Astaire? Her response, a poignant rendition of "How Long Has This Been Going On?" is really prompted by ol' Fred? Oh, there's a love affair at work here, but it's the valentine Hepburn receives from her director. Donen makes *Funny Face* a worship service to her charm, beauty, and versatility, and she revels in his ardor, especially during the fantastic photo-shoot medley, with Astaire taking her picture all over Paris (train station, opera house, the Louvre, etc.). The sequence is a rush of sensory saturation, enhanced by the gorgeously gauzy hues of Ray June's cinematography, with Hepburn iconically matched to her Hubert de Givenchy wardrobe. Though she also engages in a delightfully charged cool-cat dance with two hipster fellows in a smoky Parisian café, her best musical moment with Astaire comes early, in the all-red darkroom-set title tune, sung by him then danced by both in a light, easy manner. "Bonjour, Paris!" is another Donen variation on "New York, New York," with our entranced star trio taking in the sights. ("Think Pink!" and "Bonjour, Paris!" were composed by the film's producer, Roger Edens, with lyrics by Mr. Gershe.) Though there's plenty of third-act plot silliness, there's also the best number, "Clap Yo' Hands," with Astaire and Thompson posing as beatniks: he's goateed and strumming a guitar; she's enviably stylish in her beret. They overpower beatnik cool with impeccable showbiz pizzazz and fearless comic gusto, constituting the cherry on top of a sumptuous musical parfait.

Les Girls (1957) – Cole Porter again, still bereft of inspiration, unable to offer songs worthy of the film's ambitions. The concept is enticing, a musical *Rashomon*, with three divergent courtroom accounts of the same story. As musicals go, it's too script-heavy, bogging down in tedious complications, forgetting to get back to music-making. And then, when it does, it often disappoints. The occasion is a libel suit over a tell-all book about Gene Kelly's club act with three girls: British Kay Kendall, French Taina Elg, and American Mitzi Gaynor. (Elg is suing Kendall.) The courtroom is in London, but the flashbacks are in Paris, with *Les Girls* aiming for a zesty sophistication it rarely achieves, never quite funny or witty enough, though visually it can often be ravishingly colorful (including Oscar-winning costumes from Orry-Kelly). Director George Cukor, recently of the Judy Garland *A Star Is Born* (1954), can't surmount the roadblocks of John Patrick's wordy script and Porter's lesser score. And Kelly seems secondary to the trio, the way Astaire modestly played third fiddle to Hepburn and Thompson in *Funny Face*. But Kelly is downright muted, in need of a big solo number to establish his character. Meanwhile, Kendall, a marvel of a comedienne, is given material unworthy of her, including a lackluster comic duet with Kelly. There are only two good numbers, one at the beginning and one near the end, both onstage sequences, including the title tune in which the four leads, joined by other ladies, execute some typically exciting and eclectic Jack Cole choreography, an intoxicating mix of the exotic and the chic. But the best number—the reason to see this movie—is the *Wild One* spoof "Why Am I So Gone (About That Gal)?" with Kelly as a Brando-type toughie paired with waitress Gaynor. On a stunning red floor, against a red and white wall, with the stars dressed in black, the number suddenly turns *Les Girls* into a first-rate MGM musical, splashy and transporting and thrillingly danced. Elsewhere, Gaynor is ordinary, hopelessly trying to be another Eve Arden but too conscientiously workmanlike in her wisecracking delivery, never at all fun or funny. (She's the last person you expect to find alongside Ms. Kendall in a comedy.) *Les Girls* was Gene Kelly's final vehicle as an MGM musical star. Though his somewhat distracted onscreen presence seems to indicate his realization that his era, this *whole* era, was over, at least he got one appropriately great dance for his exit.

CODA: Who could have predicted Damien Chazelle's *La La Land* at the late date of 2016? As an original musical with a brand-new (and melodious) score, it defied six decades of Hollywood's general discomfort with musicals conceived directly for the screen. Chazelle and his charismatic, chemistry-stoked stars, Ryan Gosling and Emma Stone, honor the history and conventions of the genre while infusing it with contemporary sensibilities about love and relationships, success and art. Blessedly relaxed in his approach, Chazelle restores the Hollywood musical to its perch as the ultimate cinematic purveyor of beauty and enchantment, trusting its escapist, dream-inducing potential. He also incorporates, among other things, an *American in Paris*-like climax and, from France, the color-centric technique and amorous wistfulness of the Hollywood-inflected *Umbrellas of Cherbourg* (1964), plus the disillusionment of *It's Always Fair Weather* and the overriding optimism of many a showbiz saga. Gosling and Stone aren't top-flight singer-dancers, but their resonant acting and star presences buoy their musical adequacy; they quite comfortably inhabit Chazelle's vision. In *La La Land,* a 21st-century filmmaker displays the visual panache and the romantic soul to revitalize a golden-age genre's splendor.

The Men from the Boys: '30s Icons in the Age of Rebels (1956-1960)

You could say that everything changed in September of 1951 when *A Streetcar Named Desire* was released and Marlon Brando forever altered the course of movie acting. Male stars were no longer required to behave themselves onscreen, free to sweat and slouch and mumble, able to be more overtly sexual and prone to violence. This wasn't exactly new. The pre-Code era had depicted plenty of loose behavior, in terms both sexual and violent. Consider Clark Gable's open eroticism in *Red Dust* (1932), or James Cagney's white-hot unpredictability in *The Public Enemy* (1931). In the later '30s and 1940s, John Garfield, Brando's most prominent forerunner, made his name by projecting a moodiness, insolence, and inner turmoil that looked ahead not only to Brando but to other rebel stars of the '50s. The post-war era, from which this new breed had sprung, also marked the dawn of the Actors Studio whose training came to be known as the Method, a way for New York stage actors to dig deeply into characters, including the emotional recall of an actor's personal experiences. This striving for truth sometimes sacrificed audibility and diction, and could also encourage self-indulgence, leading to a kind of acting that feels good to the actor but communicates little. The Actors Studio had been an outgrowth of New York's Group Theatre of the 1930s, which had been inspired by the Moscow Art Theatre and the teachings of Konstantin Stanislavsky. Whether New Yorkers studied with Stella Adler (as Brando did), Sanford Meisner, or Lee Strasberg (the Method's standard bearer)—all of whom, in their different ways, followed the teachings of Stanislavsky—everyone was after the same thing: realism in acting. Styles come and go, but any player, in any era, onstage or on film, simply hopes to be believable.

After Garfield, before Brando, came Montgomery Clift in *Red River* and *The Search* (both from 1948). Clift was the first movie actor to introduce the post-war version of a super-naturalistic acting style, the fusing of an actor and his role by way of an "inside-out" perspective (built on psychological details and intense feeling) rather than "outside-in," the external unlocking of a character through, say, the fit of the right pair of shoes, or an application of facial hair. Clift and his peers were responding to the era's psychological awareness, with playwrights like Tennessee Williams and Arthur Miller writing characters whose rich intricacies were just waiting to be probed by eager actors.

It was Brando's Stanley Kowalski in Williams' *Streetcar* that marked a new age in screen acting, even though Brando had made his movie debut the year before, in *The Men* (1950), three years after creating the role of Stanley on Broadway (where his performance caused a similar sensation in theatrical circles). Early 1950s Hollywood quaked at Brando's exciting volatility, his combination of beauty and ugliness, sensitivity and cruelty, and, yes, sex and violence, but also his talent to surprise and illuminate. He surpassed himself with his Oscar-winning performance in *On the Waterfront* (1954), a far cry from his Stanley, noted for its agonizing poignancy and unashamed tenderness. Meanwhile, Mr. Clift had been keeping pace, scoring in both *A Place in the Sun* (1951) and *From Here to Eternity* (1953), displaying a scarred, throbbing vulnerability. And then, to make it a triumvirate of young and beautiful male talent, along came James Dean with the one-two-three punch of *East of Eden* (1955), *Rebel Without a Cause* (1955), and *Giant* (1956). In the first two, he turned teen angst into something far more complex and troubling than anything Andy Hardy had ever pondered, and, in the third, he moved rebelliousness into vengeful ambition. The gangsters of the early '30s, followed by John Garfield, qualified as anti-heroes, and they had often been sympathetic, but never quite as intimately exposed as Brando, Clift, and Dean who were making brooding introspection a hallmark of their art, and their times.

Though these three actors appeared to have started an acting revolution—joined by up-and-comers Anthony Perkins and Paul Newman—their success did *not* send old-guard movie stars quivering behind the Hollywood sign. One of the great surprises of the 1950s is that, in this age often associated with the rebel trio, longtime screen actors weren't at all cowed, responding with some of the best, most nuanced acting of their careers. Though their "method," if they had one, was likely to be "learn your lines and don't bump into the furniture," they were clearly as dedicated to scrupulous truth-finding as any scene-study-obsessed New York stage actor. Whether they were reacting to the challenge of the new fellows or had simply aged like beefsteak, the major actors of the 1930s—some of them the prototypes of the talkies—managed not only to stay relevant but often pushed themselves creatively, resulting in some of the greatest performances in movie history. A noticeable exception was Cary Grant. Though absolutely sublime in *North by Northwest* (1959), a classic from this period, Grant chose to stick with giving audiences what they expected from him, turning down *A Star Is Born* (1954) and denying himself an artistic stretch that he might have pulled off brilliantly.

I wish I could make this a unisex chapter, but history won't allow it. Hollywood's female stars of the '30s were less fortunate than the men, succumbing to the sexism that still remains, with fifty-ish actresses rarely entrusted with star vehicles. Most of the prominent ladies of the '30s had retired from features by the late 1950s, or were accepting supporting roles, or moved into television (or were waiting for the crumbs of the grand-dame horror craze of the '60s). True, *Auntie Mame* (1958) had recharged the film career of 51-year-old Rosalind Russell, and Katharine Hepburn, never someone to be caught in a trend, continued to get plum parts into her fifties, doing stunning work in *Suddenly, Last Summer* (1959) and giving her best-ever screen performance in *Long Day's Journey into Night* (1962).

Apologies to a few performances that merit inclusion here, ineligible because I have dealt with them extensively in previous books, choosing not to repeat myself: Gary Cooper in *They Came to Cordura* (1959), Clark Gable in *The Misfits* (1961), Maurice Chevalier in *Fanny* (1961), and Joel McCrea in *Ride the High Country* (1962).

Middle of the Night (1959): Kim Novak and Fredric March

The Searchers (1956) – After giving his arguably worst performance, as Genghis Khan in *The Conqueror* (1956), John Wayne next did his finest work, as openly racist anti-hero Ethan Edwards in John Ford's extraordinary western, an emotionally overwhelming experience with a huge heart and a dark soul. It was a long way from the Wayne of the '30s, primarily a star of B westerns, until Ford proved he was an A-lister by casting him as the true-blue Ringo Kid in *Stagecoach* (1939), heralding the arrival of America's favorite movie hero of the next three decades. Wayne spent the war years fighting onscreen in titles like *The Fighting Seabees* (1944) and *Back to Bataan* (1945), but began showing acting chops in the post-war era, in Howard Hawks' *Red River* (1948) and Ford's *She Wore a Yellow Ribbon* (1949). Though his relentlessly driven *Red River* character was certainly a warm-up, Wayne revealed a new capacity for rumbling complexity in *The Searchers,* a major reason for this classic's ever-soaring reputation. Wayne embodies a man apart, a characteristic touchingly expressed in the unspoken (yet unmistakable) love he feels for his brother's wife (Dorothy Jordan). The eventual search involves his niece, the only survivor of a Comanche attack on the brother's family. Wayne's seething performance unsettlingly combines grief with vengeance, becoming downright scary as the search reaches five years. At what point will he consider the girl a Comanche and no longer his niece? Observing some recaptured girls, he says, "They ain't white...anymore," exiting with a chilling look of pity overshadowed by revulsion. Wayne's acting, in his transition from rescuer to threat, is remarkably vanity-free; he's not afraid to make us squirm. But the film's walloping impact lies in Ethan's rediscovery of his humanity. Through every repressed and unleashed emotion along the way, Wayne builds to one of the more moving and cathartic moments of movie history, its power augmented by his unsentimental simplicity. *The Searchers* is often magnificent, thanks to Ford's exquisite filmmaking, his breathtaking compositions (kudos to the color cinematography of Winton C. Hoch), but, unfortunately, there's also a good bit of patience-testing comic relief (never Ford's forte). Wayne's performance, however, feels ageless, as modern and complicatedly disruptive as that of any rebel.

The Harder They Fall (1956) – Despite an occasional prime opportunity in something like *Black Legion* (1937), Humphrey Bogart spent much of the '30s as a bad guy getting shot by bigger stars. But superstar status was eventually his reward with classics such as *The Maltese Falcon* (1941) and *Casablanca* (1942). Before his premature death in 1957, the 1950s brought Bogart his only Oscar for his grizzled yet endearingly funny and surprisingly tender work in *The African Queen* (1951), beating Brando in *Streetcar*. He received another Oscar nomination as Captain Queeg in *The Caine Mutiny* (1954), a risky change of pace, playing weak, and only partially effective. He was better-suited to *The Barefoot Contessa* (1954) but too old for *Sabrina* (1954) and *The Desperate Hours* (1955). How nice that his final picture, *The Harder They Fall,* was a worthy swan song, a fitting showcase for his brand of cynicism mixed with redemptive idealism. With a stinging screenplay, perhaps too cynical and then too hopeful, it's one of the more vicious and brutal of boxing movies, delving into the abuse of fighters. (Even the fans are horrors here.) As an unemployed sports writer hired as a press agent by a crooked promoter (Rod Steiger), Bogart is seduced by the money. Steiger, at his slimiest, showily enacts pure villainy, positively Satanic but fun to hate. Though her role is fairly thankless, Jan Sterling is a good no-nonsense match for Bogart, sensibly cast as his smart, honest wife. As he gives the build-up to Steiger's latest find—a sweet (and gigantic) no-talent fighter who's to be exploited and then discarded—Bogart incrementally accumulates guilt over his actions. The movie builds to his crisis of conscience, putting his life at risk to cleanse his soul. Overoptimistic at its conclusion, and occasionally heavy-handed, this black-and-white drama is nonetheless grittily authentic-feeling. Directed by Mark Robson, who had already scored in the ring with *Champion* (1949), *The Harder They Fall* gave Bogart his final opportunity to reveal inner strife with the savvy and openness to make us feel it right along with him.

***These Wilder Years* (1956)** – James Cagney had a swell 1955: *Love Me or Leave Me* contained his greatest performance since *White Heat* (1949); and he was a lively bright spot in *Mister Roberts,* a popular (if highly overrated) success. *These Wilder Years* grabbed no comparable attention, and why should it have? It would appear to be a pat, forgettable television-style drama, or might have been without Cagney at its center. He brings depth, brains, and sensitivity to his role as a lonely, single Detroit steel tycoon who returns to his hometown to find the son he gave up twenty years ago. Without the star's immediacy and emotional weight, the character would be a caricature: the ruthless businessman who has everything but love, now ready to claim the humanity he sacrificed on his way to the top. Barbara Stanwyck runs the maternity home that handled the adoption, firmly protecting her records from outsiders. She's an unmarried, tirelessly good person; hers is a smooth, sincere performance of a paper-thin role. No middle-aged romance blooms (in the stars' only film together), but Cagney bonds, in a fatherly way, with a sweet pregnant teen (Betty Lou Keim). It's just a melodrama, however satisfyingly feel-good, but Cagney elevates it, making it seem better than it is (even though he's at least a dozen years too old for his role). Not at all flashy, Cagney is remarkably delicate in his effects, surmounting the inherent soapiness, taking his time, allowing his character breathing room. Roy Rowland's direction is as colorless as the production values, while Stanwyck and Walter Pidgeon (as a hotshot lawyer) remain decidedly secondary. Here's an unfairly neglected Cagney performance, a far cry from the razzle-dazzle of his Oscar win for *Yankee Doodle Dandy* (1942), and coming a full quarter century after *The Public Enemy* first catapulted him to stardom.

12 Angry Men (1957) – Speaking of *Mister Roberts*, Henry Fonda restored his dormant film stardom when he brought his Tony-winning stage triumph to the screen, giving moviegoers a chance to admire his likably low-key star turn. He next made two prestigious but not altogether satisfying movies—King Vidor's *War and Peace* (1956) and Alfred Hitchcock's *The Wrong Man* (1957)—but then nabbed what would become one of his signature roles, in the film version of the 1954 teleplay *12 Angry Men* (the first film directed by Sidney Lumet). It's a masterful handling of a tricky prospect, a movie almost entirely set in one drab little room, as jurors deliberate a death-penalty murder case after six days of testimony. Within these confines, the film was superbly shot by Boris Kaufman in black and white, using subtly interesting camera movement and powerfully employed close-ups. (The overall craftsmanship is so beautifully unobtrusive.) Reginald Rose's real-time script is tightly constructed, a well-oiled machine, which means it's also simplistic and schematic. Leading the ensemble, and co-producing as well, Fonda is outstanding in what is really a non-role, more a symbol of heroic liberalism, an urban shining knight. On paper, Juror 8 is an architect, married with three kids, an upper-middle-class Everyman, but Fonda makes him a living-breathing fully-dimensional person. As one against eleven, he systematically attempts to bring the others to his "not guilty" stance. Fonda's eyes are extremely penetrating, making his impact on the others entirely plausible, without any undue exertion. The two bully jurors are Lee J. Cobb and Ed Begley, overacting in overripe roles (and the only two who actually seem "angry"). Lumet's one mistake is unnecessarily showing us the scared-looking teenage defendant: we should get all of our perceptions about the case directly from the twelve. Juror 8 was never intended to be as multifaceted as Fonda's *Young Mr. Lincoln* (1939), or as full of surprises as his

Wyatt Earp in *My Darling Clementine* (1946), yet he joins Fonda's gallery of indelibly etched, intensely concentrated portraits.

***Witness for the Prosecution* (1957)** – Considering it was just five years since Charles Laughton had co-starred in *Abbott and Costello Meet Captain Kidd*, it was especially restorative when Hollywood offered him a career-crowning role in this juicily entertaining Agatha Christie courtroom mystery (based on her 1953 play, from her 1925 story). As the barrister defending Tyrone Power on a murder charge, Laughton dominates; his performance is both a crafty courtroom showstopper and a comic tour de force. The script is an enjoyable puzzle, though it's mostly surface trickery, not really credible but still good fun (if you don't think too hard). Billy Wilder doesn't seem to buy it wholly either, with spotty, unpersuasive direction. However, you can't fault a moment of Laughton's work, making this his most impressive turn since his phenomenal 1930s run, including his definitive Oscar-winning title role in *The Private Life of Henry VIII* (1933), a delightful *Ruggles of Red Gap* (1935), and the iconically evil Captain Bligh of *Mutiny on the Bounty* (1935). Making a Henry VIII-sized meal of Christie's mystery, he endows a soulful center to a plot inhabited more by devices than characters. Home from the hospital, having survived a heart attack, he's sparked by the prospect of a big trial. The film's propulsive charge derives from his reinvigoration, spurred by the challenge, making a vibrant return to the living. Laughton is formidably alert in the courtroom, often witty and ingeniously unpredictable in his line readings (as in the way he bellows the word "Liar!" as the capper of a quiet sentence). He and real-life wife Elsa Lanchester make a flawless comic duo; she's his pushy nurse, so cheerfully efficient and driving him mad. Hilariously ornery whenever in her presence, he revels in defying her, sneaking cigars and brandy. Their amusing interplay is the tasty counterpoint to an elaborate mystery; Lanchester's character was created by Wilder and co-writer Harry Kurnitz. Mr. Power and Marlene Dietrich (as Power's wife), two other '30s stars, are both seen to advantage, but there's never any doubt whose show this is, even though Laughton is third-billed. In a late-life Oscar-nominated performance that engaged all his prodigious resources, Laughton took command not only of the courtroom but the entire proceedings.

***Vertigo* (1958)** – Achieving major stardom in 1939, as the all-American boy of *Mr. Smith Goes to Washington* and *Destry Rides Again*, James Stewart won an Oscar for his expert sarcasm (and drunken romancing) in *The Philadelphia*

Story (1940). The post-war era saw a darkening of his persona, memorably conveying the desperation at the heart of *It's a Wonderful Life* (1946) and continuing into the 1950s, his greatest decade in film. Stewart reached new levels of bristling emotional turbulence in his five westerns for Anthony Mann, most notably *The Naked Spur* (1953) and *The Far Country* (1955), and he directly addressed sexual insecurity opposite Grace Kelly in Alfred Hitchcock's invaluable *Rear Window* (1954). But he was to be greater than ever, again working with Hitchcock, in *Vertigo,* delivering the kind of nakedly intimate, nothing-withheld performance that any Method actor would envy. As a man who quits the police force because of his acrophobia, Stewart accepts a private-detective job to follow an old chum's wife (Kim Novak), a woman seemingly possessed by a dead relative. Hitchcock utilizes a pulpy, extravagant plot as a trigger for a more probing and mysterious exploration of desire and obsession, guilt and fear. *Vertigo* plays like a fever dream, an entanglement of facts contradicted by feelings. The story is crazy-brilliant, a tale of romantic resurrection informed by Stewart's intense longing: falling for Novak, haunted by her, adjusting reality to try to claim her, chasing the unreal. Raw in his mental fragility, with love alternately devastating and reviving him, Stewart wholeheartedly embarks on a creepy path to correcting a guilty past. As an actor, he is fearlessly game, diving into a bottomless pit of heartbreaking need and yearning. Ms. Novak was never more aptly cast, quite touching as a beautiful woman, a gorgeous object, aching to be loved for her real self. With cinematographer Robert Burks' gauzily rapturous color and Bernard Herrmann's all-enveloping score, *Vertigo* is Hitchcock's strangest, most provocative film. It feels remarkably uncompromised by 1958 standards, perhaps too perplexing to have attracted much Code interference. After all, *Vertigo* is beyond logic or plausibility, residing in a realm of the purely sensory. It's a great, emotionally searching work of art, decades ahead of its time (without ever being equaled). *Vertigo* announced that 50-year-old Jimmy Stewart was a strong contender for recognition as the freest, boldest, and most inventive movie actor of this Method-infused era.

Separate Tables (1958) – In a year in which James Stewart's performance in *Vertigo* wasn't even nominated, the Best Actor Oscar went to David Niven in *Separate Tables,* not as deserving as Stewart but a worthy choice. Niven managed one of those startling cast-against-type victories, challenging people's fixed perceptions of him as witty, charming, and ever-dapper. In the late 1930s, he had been spiffy support in costume pictures like *The Prisoner* *of Zenda* (1937) and then achieved light-comedy stardom opposite Ginger Rogers in the enchanting *Bachelor Mother* (1939). Effortless comedy was his forte, continuing in the '40s (*The Bishop's Wife*) and the '50s (with the mega-smash *Around the World in Eighty Days*). No one could have expected Niven to show up as the sexually troubled major in *Separate Tables,* a screen adaptation of Terence Rattigan's 1954 play. The character, arrested for being a movie-theater masher, is someone who can only handle sexual matters with strangers in dark settings. The film hasn't aged well; it's just a soap opera with a "classy" British veneer, its stiff-upper-lip superficiality substituting for actual weight. And, with its hotel setting and ensemble cast, it's merely a low-grade *Grand Hotel.* Yet Niven's work remains alive and intriguing, the film's freshest aspect. As his character spins tales of military exploits (even though he never saw any action), Niven carries a puffed-up posture, artfully deploying military mannerisms as part of his clenched persona. The fidgety physicality tries to mask his terror, yet the frightened man within is always apparent. In this Niven performance unlike any other, he is shatteringly poignant when exposed. The toll of his life is streaked painfully across his face. Central to the plot is his friendship with a mousy virgin (Deborah Kerr), a coming together of two sexually frustrated people. Kerr is quite skillful, too, but her role is more cliché than Niven's, browbeaten by a dragon mother (a wickedly good Gladys Cooper, back in her *Now, Voyager* mode). Niven's character also serves as a gay metaphor, an opportunity for the gay Rattigan to explore someone whose sexuality is deemed criminal and must be expressed surreptitiously. Delbert Mann (*Marty*) directed dully, succumbing to staginess, despite a cast that includes Burt Lancaster, Rita Hayworth, and an Oscar-winning Wendy Hiller. (Seeing a homely Kerr alongside Lancaster offers no reminders of their lusty beach frolic in 1953's *From Here to Eternity*). *Separate Tables* is packed with drama, most of it thin, but Niven, especially when stripped of his subterfuge, is the real deal. He has no need of sparkling banter.

Middle of the Night (1959) – Fredric March got a Best Actor Oscar in the '30s (for *Dr. Jekyll and Mr. Hyde*) and another in the '40s (for *The Best Years of Our Lives*), but, by the mid-'50s, he was proving to be a terrific character actor, doing stellar work in *Executive Suite* (1954) and *The Man in the Gray Flannel Suit* (1956). He capped the decade, by now in his sixties, with a lead role in the screen version of Paddy Chayefsky's 1954 teleplay (and 1956 stage play) *Middle of the Night* (which had starred Edward G. Robinson on Broadway). Though quite obviously a play, the movie (also written by Chayefsky) is solid and compelling, working best as a portrait of middle age, a strong character study of a widowed 56-year-old grandfather embarking on a May-December romance with his 24-year-old receptionist (top-billed Kim Novak). As so often was the case, Chayefsky's writing tends toward the overexplicit and self-consciously engineered, but this piece has a potent positive message: choose a messy, risky life over staid peace and comfort. Against a milieu of New York's garment district, March is the film's grounding force. With his leading-man beauty long behind him, he proved to be a talent ripening with age, delivering an honest, shrewdly perceptive piece of acting attuned to his character's every glimmer of feeling. His complications include a son, a daddy-fixated daughter, and an older sister who lives with him. What March so plainly bares, on his way to rejuvenation, is pure need. Novak, in a role more down-to-earth (yet neurotic) than the one she played in *Vertigo,* fares less well, not only shaky in her acting but too much of a knockout for the part. (Pretty is fine, but does she have to be a goddess?) Delbert Mann (*Separate Tables*) directed, working alongside Chayefsky with whom he had collaborated on *Marty,* the 1955 Best Picture Oscar winner. *Middle of the Night* holds up better than *Marty,* both dramatically and as a finer-looking black-and-white film. Amplified by Fredric March's churning spells of jealousy and doubt, *Middle of the Night* lingers as a substantial mid-life-crisis picture.

The Devil's Disciple (1959) – You have to applaud Burt Lancaster and Kirk Douglas for lending their big names to this adaptation of George Bernard Shaw's 1897 Revolutionary War comedy, especially considering that neither one of them is well cast: Burt's too youthful for his minister role; Kirk's too mature for the rascally title role. But Laurence Olivier was going to steal it no matter who played their parts. He is sheer perfection as the British general, lifting the movie whenever he arrives, then, upon exiting, leaving you to pine for his return. After attaining U.S. stardom with three instant Hollywood classics—*Wuthering Heights* (1939), *Rebecca* (1940), and *Pride and Prejudice* (1940)—Olivier returned to England and brought Shakespeare to the screen as star-director of *Henry V* (1944) and *Hamlet,* the 1948 Best Picture Oscar winner. Back in Hollywood for *Carrie* (1952), directed by William Wyler (*Wuthering Heights*), he gave perhaps his greatest non-Shakespearean screen performance. (It went unnoticed.) *Richard III* (1956) made him three-for-three with the Bard, but Marilyn Monroe's spontaneity dwarfed his more studied technique in the comedy *The Prince and the Showgirl* (1957). Olivier was infinitely funnier in *The Devil's Disciple,* a pleasing little adaptation, short and fast and made modestly in black and white, though somewhat marred by the minor discomforts of its macho star duo. Even so, Shaw's ideas about history, war, and sex continue to vibrate, keeping the film enlivened, lighthearted, and unpretentious. Director Guy Hamilton, best-known for *Goldfinger* (1964), shouldn't have employed realistic locations, or added battle scenes, which only heighten an awkward contrast between the dialogue's rich theatricality and actual warfare. Olivier, with his deftly elegant delivery, is a model of dry subtlety; his is the kind of performance from which you cannot look away (or you might miss a perfectly arched eyebrow). And his wit perfectly aligns with Shaw's (which can't be said of our hardworking headliners). Olivier would embrace a more modern cinema with *The Entertainer* (1960), but in *The Devil's Disciple* he proved that understatement, precision, and a cutting way with words never go out of style.

Inherit the Wind **(1960)** – Probably the most revered of American movie actors, going back to his consecutive Oscar wins in 1937 (*Captains Courageous*) and 1938 (*Boys Town*), Spencer Tracy is best remembered for his 25-year partnership with Katharine Hepburn, an astonishing nine-film display of teamwork and chemistry (even when their vehicles were unworthy). Tracy's acting was venerated for its economy, intelligence, and restraint, from *The Power and the Glory* (1933) to *Test Pilot* (1938), *The Seventh Cross* (1944) to *Bad Day at Black Rock* (1955), *Father of the Bride* (1950) to *The Actress* (1953). The final phase of his career belonged to director Stanley Kramer, who used the actor's cumulative gravitas for roles in which he could be a wise-old mouthpiece for progressive ideas, ultimately garnering Tracy his seventh, eighth, and ninth Oscar nominations for *Inherit the Wind, Judgment at Nuremburg* (1961), and *Guess Who's Coming to Dinner* (1967). Based on the 1955 play by Jerome Lawrence and Robert E. Lee (a fictionalized account of the 1925 Scopes trial), *Inherit the Wind* is a heavy piece of machinery that delivers message-movie heft, mixing theatrical proficiency, self-satisfied smugness, and pure hokum. (The only surprise is that it's more relevant now than it was in 1960, with the evolution debate unexpectedly resurfacing in recent years.) In an unnamed Southern state, Dick York is a teacher arrested for teaching evolution. He's defended by Tracy, the liberal lawyer and presumed atheist (based on Clarence Darrow) from Chicago. Tracy was once good friends with Fredric March, the conservative prosecutor (based on William Jennings Bryan). The big scene comes when Tracy puts March on the stand, challenging him on his literal reading of the Bible. After all the nice things I've said about

March, I must accuse him of big-time overacting in this role. His real-life wife, Florence Eldridge, plays his spouse (for the millionth time, even more ubiquitous in March's career than Elsa Lanchester was in Charles Laughton's). One of the best elements here is the warm rapport between Tracy and Eldridge as reminiscing old friends. However, Tracy's character, like Fonda's in *12 Angry Men*, feels more constructed than humanized by its authors, conceived as a sane balance between church and state, a respectful progressive, almost a checklist of worthy attributes. Add Kramer's predilection for being obvious and oppressive, and it's clear why Tracy's casting was necessary. Bringing plain-talking truth and individuality to whatever he did, Tracy overcomes the director's and the writers' need to hit us over the head. He wasn't the grand old man of movie acting for nothing. He's exceptionally fine here, so sharp, wily, and impassioned, bringing authenticity to whatever words he utters, planting himself and telling it like it is. There's no better method than that.

Sex, Sin, and Sable: The Trashtacular (1959-1966)

Melodrama has always been a staple of feature films. The first version of *Madame X* was released as far back as 1916. Tastes change but audiences have never lost interest in juicy yarns well told, continually compelled by that irresistible need to know what happens *next*. Though melodrama—anything driven by plot rather than character—can be the basis for screenplays in any genre, the term soap opera is allied with purely female-driven melodramas, with Hollywood's Golden Age the heyday of "women's pictures." Love stories were the basic fodder of soaps, specifically the stuff that gets in love's way, anything from a third party to a world war. A soap's final destination may be tears, or it may be happiness, or, in combination, tears of happiness.

Each movie decade has produced soaps wholeheartedly embraced by the public. In the 1920s, the recent World War became the background for the decade's quintessential romance, *7ᵗʰ Heaven* (1927), director Frank Borzage's beautiful film about a war-threatened love between Janet Gaynor and Charles Farrell. The 1930s brought a string of classic soaps defined by the great ladies of the screen: Claudette Colbert in *Imitation of Life* (1934), Marlene Dietrich in *The Garden of Allah* (1936), Barbara Stanwyck in *Stella Dallas* (1937), Irene Dunne in *Love Affair* (1939), and Bette Davis in *Dark Victory* (1939).

Soaps of the 1940s brought Oscars to Ginger Rogers for *Kitty Foyle* (1940), Joan Crawford for *Mildred Pierce* (1945), and Olivia de Havilland for *To Each His Own* (1946). And who could forget Vivien Leigh in *Waterloo Bridge* (1940), Bette Davis in *Now, Voyager* (1942), or Greer Garson in *Random Harvest* (1942)? The 1950s began with some old-school examples, like Jane Wyman in *The Blue Veil* (1951), but the formulas were about to change because of the influence of a few fantastically popular pictures. At their core, though, these soaps were still peddling the same old Production Code values and "cautionary" characters, not to mention the pristine good taste of married couples in twin beds.

Three Coins in the Fountain (1954) took one of Hollywood's oldest plots—three females looking for husbands—and convinced moviegoers that it was something new, thanks to the perks of a wide-screen Italian travelogue and an instantly beloved title tune. Though dribbling dross, *Three Coins* was a smash. In travelogue terms, *Love Is a Many-Splendored Thing* (1955) did for Hong Kong what *Three Coins* did for Italy, and it, too, was set to an Oscar-winning song of which audiences couldn't get enough. As long as screen soaps were sumptuously wrapped packages, audiences apparently didn't care if they were empty inside.

At this same time, Douglas Sirk directed a series of melodramas that have made him a critics' darling, lauded for his piercing commentaries on middle-class America and his deconstructions of Hollywood artifice. However ambitious Sirk's intentions, ticket buyers lined up because of his movies' soapy excesses. There isn't a plausible second in his 1954 remake of *Magnificent Obsession*, with its wheezy pay-it-forward blather, and it was followed by his equally heavy-going *All That Heaven Allows* (1955). But *Written on the Wind* (1956), probably Sirk's most fully realized melodrama, is a film in which glossy trappings (color, décor, fashion) genuinely enliven and heighten the drama, sometimes to dazzling effect. It's also got an exceptional performance from Robert Stack as a self-destructing character, worth mentioning because this era of soaps is not noted for the recognizable humanity of its casts. Sirk's celebrated 1959 remake of *Imitation of Life*, a mostly plasticized denunciation of plasticity, is half-good (Susan Kohner's half) and half-bad (Lana Turner's half). Sirk's films have managed the remarkable feat of being both underrated and overrated.

The most influential soap of the late '50s was *Peyton Place* (1957), based on the bestseller, which gave the genre a new raciness. Like the more discreet *Kings Row* (1942), *Peyton Place* was about all the nasty things going on behind closed doors in an idyllic community. Its popularity brought more blatant sexual content into screen soaps, and it set a standard for the genre's ensemble casts, spreading its alarmingly efficient pile-on of plot threads over a cross section of characters. Directed by Mark Robson, *Peyton Place* is far superior to all the movies it spawned, notably in its atmospheric New England setting and the poignancy in its performances from Russ Tamblyn and Diane Varsi. Even so, what made the picture a must-see was its deep-dark family secrets, physical and mental abuse, murder in self-defense, premarital sex, suicide, skinny-dipping, and lines such as, "Girls want to do the same things as boys."

A Summer Place (1959), like *Three Coins* or *Love Is a Many-Splendored Thing*, is unimaginable without its famous theme. It's also got Arthur Kennedy (*Peyton Place*), Dorothy McGuire (*Three Coins*), Troy Donahue and Sandra Dee (both of *Imitation of Life*), and dual plots of love and lust: one youthful; one middle-aged. Its focus on sex follows the *Peyton Place* template, and it champions both true love and really good sex. All these movies' forces—the travelogue and title-tune embellishments of *Three Coins,* the hyper-intense visual vitality of the Sirk movies, the emphasis on sex and ensemble casts in *Peyton Place* and *A Summer Place*—yielded what I'll call trashtaculars, those big-budget soaps so prevalent in the early '60s, usually good to look at, lurid yet tame, and intense but hollow. If soaps, no matter how tawdry, are romantic fantasies, then these were invitations to be sent far away, where the scandalous woes of others could be enjoyed alongside high-fashion wardrobes, exotic locations, and impossibly attractive people. These are not good movies, yet they form a fascinating sub-genre of soaps that often seemed bold but were decidedly timid, inching toward permissiveness but chained to old morals. They're part of the end of Old Hollywood's gloss and glamour, both of which were essential to the trashtacular, where even the sleaze is brightly colored and none too shabby. Why, after the glory days of soaps when great actresses got great-performance opportunities, did moviegoers settle for these indifferently acted, two-dimensionally overwrought pictures? Maybe it was a reaction to what was going on elsewhere on movie screens, where dramas had become so blisteringly real with films such as *On the Waterfront, Blackboard Jungle, The Man with the Golden Arm, The Defiant Ones,* and *Anatomy of a Murder*. Maybe audiences liked trashtaculars *because* they were free of insight, disturbing emotion, and honest depths. They were so comfortingly false.

From *Rome Adventure* (1962) to *The Pleasure Seekers* (1965), *Claudelle Inglish* (1961) to *Youngblood Hawke* (1964), *Walk on the Wild Side* (1962) to *Love Has Many Faces* (1965), trashtaculars offered the last gasp of sin on the screen, all the way to *Valley of the Dolls* (1967), the genre's final box-office hit and the zenith of everything terrible about it. By then, there was nowhere for the genre to go. Like the '60s sex farces to be examined later, there was simply no longer any reason for the trashtacular to exist. Suddenly, it was the age of the sexual revolution, the women's movement, and, in the industry, the start of the ratings system and unparalleled onscreen sex and nudity. The genre's audience, like its major stars, retired from the screen too, unconnected to an *Easy Rider* cinema in which a western was *The Wild Bunch,* a comedy was *MASH,* and a musical was *Cabaret*. There would still be an occasional big-screen adaptation of a book by Jacqueline Susann or Sidney Sheldon, but these were anomalies. Trashtacular sensibilities found refuge on television, with the format ruling prime-time in the *Dynasty*-loving 1980s. This makes sense because network TV still had boundaries regarding language, nudity, and violence, allowing good old-fashioned (and expensive) trash to thrive.

But, for now, sit back and enter a world of mindless escapism, complete with guilt-free vicarious indulgences, all intended to make you appreciate your comparatively humdrum life. In overall quality, these movies make *Peyton Place* seem like Ibsen. Naughty as they hoped to be, they more accurately represent the waning days of the Production Code, a last stand of stereotypical gender roles. In their shiny desire to please, trashtaculars were part of the end of American movies' innocence.

Madame X (1966): John Forsythe and Lana Turner

The Best of Everything (**1959**) – Expanding the *Three Coins* format from a trio of females to a quintet, this high-sheened adaptation of Rona Jaffe's novel was directed by *Three Coins'* own Jean Negulesco. Set inside a New York publishing house, it's got the usual round-up of cautionary characters, just in case you're a young woman considering a move to the big bad city. Though we've got secretaries (Diane Baker, Suzy Parker), editors (Joan Crawford, Martha Hyer), and a Radcliffe graduate (Hope Lange) rising from secretary *to* editor, no woman in this movie seems to *want* a career. It's just something to do until *he* comes along. By mixing youthful yearnings with adultery, divorce, unwed pregnancy, and break-up hysteria, it plays like *Three Coins* meets *Valley of the Dolls*. Within an ensemble of relative newcomers, Crawford steals the show by sheer force of presence. She's the cliché of the hard career woman who discovers that it's too late for personal happiness. She's meant to be pitied, but she's also a bitch. Whatever you think of her, she's got more life than any of the young pathetic bores around her. The movie is mostly about women loving deeply and men behaving badly (not just as people, but as actors, too). If only Stephen Boyd, paired with Ms. Lange, could match the sexual heat he cranked up for Charlton Heston in *Ben-Hur*. *The Best of Everything* entrusts juicy plotlines to vapid, pretty people, nullifying any potential impact. Aside from Crawford's panache and Johnny Mathis' silky rendering of the title tune, the movie's peak of soapy glamour arrives when a woman falls from a fire escape because her high heel catches in the grating. But it's Ms. Baker, as a nice girl who makes a mistake, who gets to say, "Now I'm just somebody who's had an affair."

Go Naked in the World (**1961**) – The colossal gorgeousness of Gina Lollobrigida, enhanced by an endless array of Helen Rose wardrobe creations, is a welcome distraction from the moldiness of this outdated nonsense. She's a high-priced call girl, just a variation on the whore with a heart of gold. Tony Franciosa seems rather mature to be playing the army serviceman too naive to realize what she is. Of course, his father, wealthy contractor Ernest Borgnine, has also slept with Gina. Aside from admiring her beauty and enjoying the Acapulco weather, why exactly are we here? Certainly not to endure Borgnine's "acting," a performance almost entirely yelled, nor to care about the charmless, vacant Franciosa. It's supposedly true love between Gina and Tony, but naturally he's devastated by the truth about her. When he asks her how many men she's had, she replies, "Why count waves in the ocean?" Ouch! And there's the obligatory scene, right out of *Camille,* of him throwing cash at her. Even worse is the ludicrous father-son confrontation atop a twenty-floor-high construction beam. Not finished pillaging *Camille,* the script has Gina trying to drive Tony away for his own good, even though it's killing her inside. As late as 1961, men still had to be "saved" from loving "bad" women.

Return to Peyton Place (1961) – It's one of those pointless sequels, the kind that merely repackages everything that happened the first time around. Franz Waxman's lovely score is back, but now it has unfortunate lyrics sung by Rosemary Clooney (coincidentally, wife of José Ferrer, the film's useless director). Isn't it interesting that none of the original cast returned? The "new" plot centers on Allison (Carol Lynley) and the publication of her bombshell book about Peyton Place. Like her mother (Eleanor Parker) before her, Lynley falls for a married man, her publisher (Jeff Chandler), and they begin an affair as she becomes the toast of Manhattan. Its phonier moments include Chandler coaxing book revisions out of Lynley in what look like therapy sessions, getting at *the truth!* Without the textures and tenderness of the previous film, the result is a shallow shambles. A climactic town meeting substitutes for the former picture's courtroom drama, with Ms. Parker giving the same public apology to her daughter that Lana Turner delivered in 1957. Typically, the men are cardboard, just objects to obsess over. It is nice to see Tuesday Weld as Selena, but, as with Crawford in *The Best of Everything,* it's an old-timer who stands out. As the film's villain, the calculating, clinging mother of Brett Halsey (in the old David Nelson role), Mary Astor provides genuine smarts and dimension, making it plain how enjoyable this kind of trash can be when acted with relish and humanity. Yet the trashtaculars increasingly strayed from real life, preferring to be rituals of suffering in which any actual pain was conveniently numbed, quickly classifying them as high camp.

Back Street (1961) – The third and worst version of Fannie Hurst's novel, with Susan Hayward following Irene Dunne (1932) and Margaret Sullavan (1941). Producer Ross Hunter reveled in the materialistic trappings of the trashtacular, allowing Hayward, as a fashion designer, a high-price-tagged variety of anguish. This isn't Hayward the Oscar winner, it's Hayward the movie star leading her fans into a completely manufactured world where there's no discernible connection between celluloid emotion and real emotion, the most comforting aspect of trashtaculars. No matter how bad things get, nothing *really* hurts. *Back Street*'s adulterous romance feels impersonal, worsened by awful dialogue and a slurpy score. Costume designer Jean Louis is the real star here, while leading man John Gavin is a motorized eight-by-ten glossy. Opposite the pretty, empty Gavin, Hayward has to act like crazy, essentially acting for two. Both stars play relentlessly good, unselfish people, leaving Vera Miles (as Gavin's wife) to have all the fun as a boozy cheater and rotten mother. (Miles and Gavin had recently appeared together in *Psycho*.) Despite her ripe opportunity, Miles offers a strained attempt at a Claire Trevor-style bad girl. David Miller directed, but it looks like Mr. Hunter called all the shots. Though the '41 version is equally mechanical in its plotting, it's truly affecting, thanks to delicate, restrained performances from Ms. Sullavan and Charles Boyer. Twenty years later, there's no delicacy, no restraint. All that can be commended is Hunter's self-control in not commissioning a title tune.

Susan Slade (1961) – The *Summer Place* gang—writer-director Delmer Daves, Dorothy McGuire, Troy Donahue—are at it again. It's visually more accomplished than most '60s soaps (kudos to cinematographer Lucien Ballard), but dramatically it's hopelessly emblematic of the era's penchant for dated theatrics and unnuanced characters. Instead of Sandra Dee, it's sweet, earnest Connie Stevens in the title role, though you'll soon be wishing that the more personable Dee had been available. But Stevens' bland competence fits right into the well-trod framework, with a plot that borrows from old chestnuts such as *Way Down East* and *The Old Maid*. Sheltered, innocent Stevens has shipboard sex with rich mountain-climbing hunk Grant Williams. You guessed it, she's impregnated! Mr. Donahue plays a sensitive social outcast and aspiring novelist, mostly on hand to look blond and cute, enhanced by all the red in his wardrobe. Stevens' parents are Ms. McGuire and Lloyd Nolan (reunited sixteen years after *A Tree Grows in Brooklyn*). McGuire is in her arch, genteel mode, while Nolan, by now the Lewis Stone of the wide screen, is his windbag self. Not having to admit she's a grandmother, McGuire pretends that Stevens' baby is hers, that *she's* its mother. If there's anything nice to be said about the plot of *Susan Slade,* it's that Stevens gets a happy ending, free from lifelong punishment for her *sin*.

The Chapman Report (1962) – It's about a Kinsey-like study of female sexuality, and there was every reason to expect something good, with George Cukor directing a stellar quartet of actresses. But the outcome is a familiar mix of sensationalism and hokum, with surprisingly little depth or feeling. Dr. Andrew Duggan and his assistant, Efrem Zimbalist, Jr., come to L.A. to conduct anonymous interviews with women, including frigid Jane Fonda, adulterous Shelley Winters, drunken nympho Claire Bloom, and beach-boy-chasing Glynis Johns. Local doctor Henry Daniell condemns Duggan's work, which neglects love in the sexual equation. Imagine what he'd have to say about all the male eye candy on display, from the likes of Chad Everett, Corey Allen, and Ty Hardin. Tonally, the film is all over the place, with Bloom's scenes playing like third-rate Blanche DuBois imitations, and Johns' silly comic relief simply in the wrong movie. (John Dehner, as Johns' tasteful, cultured husband, is clearly gay, though the movie ignores the obvious.) Mr. Zimbalist, the most boring of actors, unethically pursues widow/virgin Fonda (who wears the greatest white picture hat in movie history). It's Shelley Winters who gives the simplest, truest performance; it helps that she's got the most plausible plotline. (Cukor gave Winters her big break in *A Double Life* in 1947.) Though Cukor makes fine use of long takes in the interview sessions, this is a long and lumpy movie built on a foundation of skimpy character studies.

The Carpetbaggers (1964) – Audiences loved Hollywood trashing itself, which is why this critically trounced adaptation of Harold Robbins' novel was such a big hit. Set in the '20s and '30s, it's all plot with nobody home. George Peppard stars as a loosely disguised Howard Hughes, an entrepreneur of business, aviation, and movies, but he doesn't have the necessary star quality to make this dour, ruthless creep charismatic. He walks through the movie, monotone and lifeless for 150 minutes. This expensively mounted dreck has a big-name supporting cast, including a brown-haired Alan Ladd (in his final role) as an eventual cowboy star. Ladd looks awful and is even more inanimate than Peppard, a sad finish to a sterling career. Carroll Baker is the gold-digging tart who finds stardom and a slutty, alcoholic demise. Trying to outdo Baker, Martha Hyer, as a prostitute turned star, is clearly hoping for a Shirley Jones-type Oscar for her efforts. Finally, there's Elizabeth Ashley, the good wife Peppard ignores and turns into a whiny scold. Aside from Ashley, is every woman in this movie a whore? Then we've got lawyer Lew Ayres, agent Bob Cummings, studio head Martin Balsam, and, yes, hooker Audrey Totter. The same scenes keep being repeated: Ayres quitting; Ashley finding Peppard with another woman; Baker throwing herself at someone, etc. There's not a fleeting moment of humanity on the premises. More schlock than shock, it's a shameful piece of filmmaking from director Edward Dmytryk, and, for all its raciness, it features more begging for sex, and refusing of sex, than actual sex!

Where Love Has Gone (1964) – If Susan Hayward and Lana Turner were the queens of the trashtacular—two superstars extending their reigns into middle age—then what could be more of a soap-opera orgasm than Hayward *playing* Turner? Here we have a fictionalized account of the 1958 Turner scandal when her gangster lover, Johnny Stompanato, was stabbed to death by her daughter Cheryl. Based on another Harold Robbins potboiler, and rejoining Robbins with *Carpetbaggers* director Edward Dmytryk (a partnership that had already inflicted ample damage), this is a gaudy, claptrap reworking of the actual event. Instead of a film star, Hayward is a society woman, also a great sculptor with an appetite for the fellas. And she's not convincing as either the lady or the tramp (though she looks sensational, assisted by Edith Head). Joey Heatherton is the daughter, and Hayward's sculpting chisel is the murder weapon. It's surprisingly drawn-out, even numbingly dull, while most of us are here only to see Hayward confront Bette Davis (as Hayward's white-haired society-matron mother). When Davis' proper, powerful dowager clashes with Hayward's hard, growlingly sarcastic dame, it injects the movie with flashes of real star power, even though the roles aren't well-drawn. (Davis was probably still seething over Hayward's recent temerity in remaking *Dark Victory,* as *Stolen Hours.*) Mike Connors is a could-be-anybody male, the war hero Hayward marries. Davis' attempts to control everything lead to Hayward's promiscuity and Connors' boozing. Then you've got the *Mildred Pierce* love triangle with mother and daughter loving the same guy (and the daughter killing him). Because Dmytryk's direction is devoid of any zest, *Where Love Has Gone* rarely achieves the status of vulgar fun. Although there is a title tune sung by Jack Jones, the only thing you'll remember is when Hayward finally takes a poker to Davis' portrait.

Madame X (1966) – Here's Ross Hunter doing for Lana Turner what he did for Susan Hayward with *Back Street,* dusting off and updating a tried-and-true soap warhorse (from a 1908 play). It's the last of Turner's star vehicles, and perhaps the last "old movie" ever made. Everything about it feels on the verge of extinction. Because *Madame X,* at its best, is a screwy melodrama, it requires a fast pace (so we don't ask too many questions) and an actress with vast emotional reserves (to fill in the lapses of logic). In 1937, Gladys George devoured the role, infusing it with intimacy and guts. The material remained hoary and crude, but Ms. George was heart-wrenching. No such luck in 1966. No matter how low this Madame X falls, there's never anything bruised about Turner. She may be looser than usual, and she is sincere, but she was never the kind of star who tore into a role. Here she's merely part of the film's overall preference for surfaces. In this version, she's a shopgirl who marries wealthy (and dopey) John Forsythe. Feeling neglected, she starts having fun with Ricardo Montalban (until his accidental death). Turner, fearing scandal, is somehow convinced by mother-in-law Constance Bennett to fake her own death and start anew in Europe, which means leaving behind Forsythe and their little boy. This seems a tad drastic, despite Forsythe's political ambitions. From here, it's mostly watching Turner change hair color, all the while turning into a lush. When back in America, she shoots blackmailer Burgess Meredith dead and, in a crazily classic coincidence, will be defended by her grown son (Keir Dullea), with neither of them knowing the other's identity. If the son had a line in which he introduced himself (and simply said his *name*), there would be no climax! *Madame X* is the essential vehicle of masochism, but it cannot work when a producer and a star present it at such a glacial remove.

The Oscar (1966) – The popularity of *The Carpetbaggers* encouraged more sleaze about the movie industry, and what *screams* back-stabbing ambition and career-climbing mania better than the Academy Awards? Though based on a novel by a Hollywood insider (writer-director Richard Sale), there's nothing authentic-feeling about *The Oscar*. Cast as a star-monster, Stephen Boyd gives a stiff-jawed, fire-breathing performance: all ham but no meat. The script steals from *All About Eve* and *The Bad and the Beautiful,* but it's so dreadful you'll hardly notice. Opening on Oscar night, it flashes back to nominee Boyd's early days. Mom was a tramp, Dad a suicide. Boyd becomes a star quickly and, just as quickly, box-office poison. He's horrid to everybody, and they'll all eventually get a chance to tell him off. Tony Bennett, proving that not all great singers are born actors, is embarrassingly inept as Boyd's doormat sidekick. As for the women, Eleanor Parker is "glam" and over the top as the talent scout who discovers (and beds) Boyd, and Elke Sommer is the virgin costume designer he marries and makes miserable. The most restrained acting comes from Milton Berle as Boyd's agent—he retains his dignity. We're spared scenes from Boyd's Oscar-nominated work in *Breakthrough,* or scenes from *any* of his movies, but we do get to see Merle Oberon present the Best Actor award. With *The Oscar* and *Valley of the Dolls* (1967), the laughably overheated hysterics of glitzy trashtaculars had just about run their course. In the new cinema, the genre was passé and made itself scarce. From then on, if you wanted to go naked in the world, you could actually take off your clothes.

Muscling In: The Mega-Macho Mission Movies (1960-1969)

There have always been motion pictures aimed directly at male audiences, with whole genres—westerns, gangster movies, war films—assumed to be men's domain. Some examples from the late 1950s—the great WWII spectacle *The Bridge on the River Kwai* (1957), the lavish but ham-fisted saga *The Vikings* (1958)—were part of the movies' general move toward grander-scaled male-oriented fare, which came to 1960s fruition with the sub-genre of mission movies. Take a group of guys, usually some kind of cross section, bring them together for a virtually impossible task and then build to an action-packed climax, a culmination of all that was promised at the start. The idea was nothing new and is typical of heist films such as *The Asphalt Jungle* (1950) and *The Killing* (1956). Now add all the bells and whistles of '60s filmmaking—the far-off locations splashed across a vast screen, the majestic scores amplifying the danger and the courage, plus the intermingling of big stars and striking newcomers—and watch some fairly basic plots become memorable epics. From *The Magnificent Seven* (1960) to *The Wild Bunch* (1969), man-centric output pervaded the decade, producing pop classics that became outright rituals for male fans, the kinds of movies not just to be quoted but memorized. Paeans to teamwork and brotherhood or just plain-old blasts of testosterone, these films were also tests of endurance, allowing men to imagine how they might fare amid such challenges. Could they, too, meet the required level of masculinity? Or honor? In addition to being rousing and inspiring, these missions often dramatized conflicts (external and internal) between cynicism and idealism. After all, a tough guy without humanity is just a villain. Hollywood offered timeless instructions as to how a boy (of any age), dreaming of heroics, could be fearless and feared without sacrificing moral principles.

Not all of the butch extravaganzas clicked: *Battle of the Bulge* (1965), which hoped to be another *Longest Day,* bulged in all the wrong places, as did the later *Midway* (1976) and *A Bridge Too Far* (1977); *The Heroes of Telemark* (1966) failed in its emulation of *The Guns of Navarone;* and *Kelly's Heroes* (1970) didn't meet its *Dirty Dozen* expectations. As for projects less derivative, *Grand Prix* (1966) is a bore beyond belief, three hours of filler in search of a movie. (Who knew that speeding cars could induce narcolepsy?) Although *Cool Hand Luke* (1967) is a beloved piece of anti-hero rebellion, it is an utterly empty film about nothing except Paul Newman's blue-eyed magnetism.

After the profligate '60s—the decade that brought us *Cleopatra* (1963) and *Hello, Dolly!* (1969)—movie budgets appeared to scale back in the '70s, with the male domination continuing in the more modestly mounted vehicles of Charles Bronson and Clint Eastwood, modeled more on *Point Blank* (1967) than *The Great Escape* (1963). *The Longest Yard* (1974), with Burt Reynolds, was another medium-sized addition to the for-men-only canon, while the larger-scale all-star productions had mostly become the province of the '70s disaster-movie craze, which was male-driven, too, but at least women actually appeared and even spoke lines (which wasn't always the case in the '60s mission movies).

This brings me to an unfortunate sidebar of such a *man*-datory era. In the late '60s, while male blockbusters were doing well, female-driven fare, notably the soap-opera staple, was on the wane, creating a perilous moment for feminine stars. The 1968 ratings system, allowing for more blood and violence, more sex and nudity, seemed to coincide with, or perhaps even induced, a significant drop-off in quality female roles. Many of the '60s prominent ladies quickly retired or faded away, including, no surprise, those past or nearing forty, such as Doris Day, Leslie Caron, Debbie Reynolds, Joanne Woodward, Audrey Hepburn, Janet Leigh, Elizabeth Taylor, and Anne Bancroft, but also younger stars like Natalie Wood, Shirley MacLaine, Lee Remick, and Julie Andrews. Some of them (like MacLaine) would make comebacks, but the early '70s was mostly unfriendly to female stories, with prostitution offering some of the best parts in American movies: Jane Fonda in *Klute* (1971) and Julie Christie in *McCabe and Mrs. Miller* (1971). Neither the magnificent seven nor the wild bunch intended, in some parallel mission, to remove women from the screen, but they didn't help any.

The '60s male mania had a usual-suspects employment policy. The main directors were John Sturges and Robert Aldrich, and likely to be on the men-u were James Coburn, Charles Bronson, Robert Ryan, Ernest Borgnine, and, the two kings of the era, Lee Marvin and Steve McQueen, both icons of rugged cool. Whether the plan was a gunfight, a wartime operation, a complicated escape, a mechanical procedure, a desert rescue, or a train robbery, the manpowered plots of '60s commercial moviemaking continue to enthrall their target audience, never having been topped in their displays of macho men *being* macho, providing lessons in manliness for fifty years and counting.

The Great Escape (1963): Richard Attenborough and Steve McQueen

The Magnificent Seven (**1960**) – The kickoff movie of the mega-macho decade is a remake of a foreign-language film mostly unknown to the American version's core audience. Akira Kurosawa's *Seven Samurai* (1954), set in 16th-century Japan, adapted to the western genre perfectly, and, though John Sturges' westernization is nowhere near the masterpiece level of Kurosawa's achievement, it's still a solid, surefire entertainment. Like the Kurosawa original, its plot is simple but the execution is exemplary, further bolstered by the surging thrills of Elmer Bernstein's Oscar-nominated score. The seven are hired by Mexican farmers to protect their village from a Mexican bandit (Eli Wallach, overacting, starting with his accent) and his crew of forty. Yul Brynner, all in black, leads the seven, making him the most unlikely western star since Marlene Dietrich, or, among men, Errol Flynn. Maybe this is why Brynner chose to underplay, erasing any reminder of his King-of-Siam flashiness. Not yet a leading man, Steve McQueen is charming and unusually good-looking comic relief, becoming Brynner's sidekick, firmly hitching his onscreen future to the company of men. The other five are brawny Charles Bronson, natty and neurotic Robert Vaughn, gold-hungry Brad Dexter, knife-wielding James Coburn, and young hothead Horst Buchholz. To give the story an emotional charge to match the action, the seven are, to varying degrees, feeling down about their gunslinging lives: lonely, or broke, or on the run, or simply with nothing to show for their careers. The mission effectively provides purpose and perhaps meaning, allowing the audience to care as the seven themselves begin to care, working as a unit, teaching the villagers, becoming genuinely involved. Yes, they're macho, but with heart and soul, knowing what's right, dusting off their ideals. Don't get me wrong: *The Magnificent Seven* is no probing psychological western; it's a broad-canvassed epic driven by a primal premise. Mixing toughness and tenderness, its tests of masculinity are tempered by sentimentality. With canny use of the wide screen and the know-how of putting on a good show, John Sturges presented *The Magnificent Seven* with the sure hand of a practiced and dexterous gunman.

The Guns of Navarone (1961) – From the West to WWII, here's another life-or-death objective assigned to talented specialists, another polished crowd-pleasing adventure rather than a great movie. Without the character complexity of a *Bridge on the River Kwai*, it's closer to a comic-book war tale, especially when its half-dozen unit (a magnificent *six*?) a bit too easily outwits countless Nazis, which includes dressing up in their uniforms. The setting is 1943 Greece; the mission is to destroy two massive radar-controlled guns. Anthony Quayle leads the Allied team: Gregory Peck (world's greatest mountain climber), David Niven (explosives genius), Stanley Baker (mechanical marvel), and Anthony Quinn and James Darren (both Greeks). Director J. Lee Thompson has a knack for suspense, and, once more, here's an action movie that tries (with moderate success) to humanize its characters, thus heightening our interest in their cause and each man's survival. Along the way, there are ongoing tensions between Peck and Quinn, plus Quayle breaks his leg, and also the addition of two females, Irene Papas and Gia Scala (both of the Greek Resistance), with Papas serving as a love interest for Quinn. Peck is disappointing (just one year away from *To Kill a Mockingbird*), dull and unconvincing, while Niven, comic relief for a while, suddenly starts making big speeches. The best acting comes from an earthy, full-bodied Quinn, warming up for *Zorba the Greek* (1964), especially good in a showy scene in which he, putting on an act, grovels before the Nazis. Again, it's hard to overestimate the persuasive impact of an all-encasing score, with Dimitri Tiomkin's music rightfully claiming one of the film's seven Oscar nominations, including one for Best Picture, winning only for its volcanic special effects.

The Longest Day (1962) – It was intended to be the last word on D-Day, a painstaking reenactment from every perceivable angle, manned by producer Darryl F. Zanuck, with three credited directors and just about every name actor alive making a cameo appearance, the result being a nearly all-male *Around the World in Eighty Days*. (Oh look, Roddy McDowall, Robert Ryan, Edmond O'Brien…) *The Longest Day* tries to do too much, which was actually the point, to do *everything*. And, unsurprisingly, it's better at action than it is at dialogue or character. Not all of its mini-dramas land, or even establish themselves properly, with many characters dispensed with unsatisfyingly, sometimes simply dropped. (Oh look, Rod Steiger, Richard Burton, Mel Ferrer…) A movie at war with itself, its staggering visual authenticity is at odds with its panorama of movie stars (the dramatic equivalent of name-dropping). Once those famous faces start arriving fast and furiously, the star-sighting game borders on the comical, damaging all that impeccable verisimilitude. It does help that everyone speaks his/her own language, rather than the cheat of English only (with assorted accents), but the real star is the astounding Oscar-winning black-and-white camerawork (of two cinematographers), which includes nighttime paratrooper landings into France, aerial coverage of the beach invasion, and a shootout across a port town. (Oh look, Peter Lawford, Jeffrey Hunter, Sal Mineo…) Unlike *Magnificent Seven* or *Guns of Navarone*, *The Longest Day* can't engage audiences emotionally through its characters because no one is around long enough, with the stars present merely to offer their respect for the real-life heroes. (Oh look, Richard Todd, Sean Connery, Robert Mitchum…) You will remember Red Buttons because his parachute leaves him dangling from a church tower, and also Curt Jürgens, the most three-dimensional Nazi. John Wayne, milking his persona, breaks an ankle but won't be stopped! And the one-scene Eisenhower is a dubbed non-actor lookalike named Henry Grace, better-known as the Oscar-winning set decorator of *Gigi* (1958). Nominated for five Oscars including Best Picture, *The Longest Day* doesn't really have an ending because the battle keeps on going. What's memorable is the scope and immediacy of its you-are-there approach, a D-Day not to be topped until *Saving Private Ryan* (1998). (Did I mention Robert Wagner, Eddie Albert, Henry Fonda…?)

The Great Escape (1963) – Possibly the best American movie of its year, it's not only a terrifically entertaining WWII action picture but also a thinking man's drama, as smart as it is exciting. It's long, alright, but John Sturges, emboldened by his *Magnificent Seven* prowess, paces it beautifully. He and his screenwriters (James Clavell and W.R. Burnett) build concern and sympathy for these men and their friendships, as well as arousing admiration. A true story fictionalized, the plot is right there in the title, yet the results are far more intricate, a quietly stirring celebration of skill and ingenuity, of organization and teamwork. The location is a new Nazi P.O.W. camp designed specifically for Allied officers with reputations as escape artists. Steve McQueen, no longer Yul Brynner's sidekick and now a full-blown movie star, is a U.S. captain, a pilot. Exploiting his bad-boy comic edge (and appeal), McQueen amusingly spends much of the movie in isolation (for, yes, trying to escape). James Garner is another American, an R.A.F. member known as "The Scrounger" because he can procure anything, even from behind prison walls. But, to the Nazis, the most notorious prisoner is Richard Attenborough, a British squadron leader. It is he who will lead this great escape, a plan to free 250 men by constructing three tunnels. In contrast to the drive-by males of *The Longest Day*, here's an ensemble that shines, led by its top-notch trio. Joining McQueen for a *Magnificent Seven* reunion are an Australian James Coburn and a Polish Charles Bronson (the main tunnel digger). For all its masculinity, *The Great Escape* is a surprisingly sensitive movie, with men helping each other in unexpected ways. The muscular Bronson turns out to suffer from crippling claustrophobia, thus assisted every step of the way by fellow tunnel-digger John Leyton who patiently (some might say lovingly) deals with his friend's panic. And Donald Pleasence, as "The Forger," goes blind, thereafter taken care of by Garner. These vulnerabilities, and the attentive responses they receive, bring considerable emotional weight to such a slam-bang operation, unshowily declaring that it isn't just brute strength that qualifies as manliness. Despite this refreshing gentleness, *The Great Escape* famously provides the arguably greatest macho movie moment of all time, when McQueen steals a motorcycle and rides it—in a great leap—over a fence. Mixing muscle, brains, and intimacy, and accompanied by Elmer Bernstein's enjoyably jaunty, staccato score, *The Great Escape* received only one Oscar nomination (for film editing) when it should have seen acknowledgement for more of its individuals who, like the characters themselves, came together so triumphantly for the sake of a team.

The Hill (1965) – Another POW camp, but *The Hill* is an entirely different kind of survival movie. Instead of incarcerating enemies, its British prison— situated in a blazing nowhere within North Africa—confines offending British soldiers. *The Hill* can be searing in its brutality, raw in its realism, yet much of it feels over the top, pitched too hysterically. There's marvelously fluid black and white from Oswald Morris, his camera roving and roaming with a documentarian's hungry eye, his backgrounds often filled with men drilling and marching. But the overall effect is too self-conscious, too flashy, with Sidney Lumet's direction, at first startlingly impressive, soon undone by relentless overkill. Like the hill on its prison grounds—a pyramid-like mound—the movie itself is a sadistic endurance test. The subject is British militarism run amok, with the hill a rather obnoxious metaphor for, well, you name it—war, survival, *life*—as we watch men ordered up and down it. Elsewhere, *The Hill* operates like most prison movies, but has there ever been one so virtuosically overwrought? Or with a cast who screams as much? Harry Andrews is the sergeant major running the joint, a performance crafted entirely of crescendos, a blaring case of please-make-it-stop overacting. His evil guard is Ian Hendry, clearly from the same acting school. The good guys are Michael Redgrave, too typically cast as a weak, wispy medical officer, and voice-of-reason guard Ian Bannen. One prison cell is occupied by five fellows, including our star, Sean Connery, taking a break from martinis and Bond girls and probably reconsidering his choice, especially when undergoing a beating by three guards who bust his foot. (In terms of its macho-movie credentials, *The Hill* asks men to ponder how long they might last in such a harrowing place.) Connery is here for assaulting his commanding officer over orders he deemed stupid. A military rebel, he feels that "by the book" no longer makes any sense. The film's second half is stronger, once the plot becomes fueled by revenge (over an inmate's death), but, at its worst, *The Hill* plays like a gruesome cartoon, as punitive to its audience as it is to its characters, all the way to its ironic downer of an ending. To his everlasting credit, Connery never pushes. His acting is solid, strong, hyper-masculine but *true*, unlike just about everything else around him.

The Flight of the Phoenix (1965) – It's not the West, nor is it WWII, but it is about men banding together to meet a daunting, perhaps insurmountable, challenge. Soon to helm *The Dirty Dozen* (1967), director Robert Aldrich here spruces his male-ensemble skills, and, though it feels dragged out, *The Flight of the Phoenix* is a generally good, reasonably absorbing effort, delivering when it counts, incurring the necessary tension. A group of fourteen—primarily oil and army men—are aboard a plane headed for Benghazi when a sandstorm forces pilot James Stewart to land. What ensues—in the middle of the Sahara—is a battle of wills between old-timer Stewart and young Hardy Kruger, a German aircraft designer who believes they have the materials to repair the plane. For survival, they have water and pressed dates, with the repair operation providing vital hope and purpose. Kruger, blond and serious, tireless and practical, comes off like a master-race Nazi, which is quite effective. Stewart, however, is merely competent, too reliant on his (by 1965) overly familiar bag of tricks. Though it's shameful that Peter Finch, as a British army captain, is underused, at least there's the perk of Ernest Borgnine dying early. It's *The Great Escape*'s Richard Attenborough who's the standout as Stewart's alcoholic navigator and sidekick, yet it was Ian Bannen (of *The Hill*) who got the cast's sole Oscar nomination, undeserved for his slight role as a grinning wise guy. But then most of the actors, including Dan Duryea and George Kennedy, are attached to half-drawn characters, with too little revealed about why they were on the plane. That's why it's easy to remember the action climax and not much else.

The Professionals (1966) – Writer-director Richard Brooks was better-known for *Blackboard Jungle* (1955) and *Elmer Gantry* (1960) than for action-adventure fare, yet he did a neat dual Oscar-nominated writing-directing job on this WWI-era western. Like *The Magnificent Seven*, it's a scenic below-the-border affair. Wealthy American Ralph Bellamy, whose Mexican wife Claudia Cardinale was kidnapped by Mexican rebel Jack Palance, hand-picks a team for her rescue: weapons expert/tactician Lee Marvin; dynamite expert Burt Lancaster (Brooks' Elmer Gantry); ace horseman Robert Ryan; and scout/archer/tracker Woody Strode. Marvin, a year away from *The Dirty Dozen* (as was Mr. Ryan), leads the team with a low-key force. In contrast, Lancaster positively gleams as a charismatic womanizer, executing his physical stunts with his usual glee. The two are old pals who rode six years with Palance for Pancho Villa! It's a classic set-up for redemption, with two middle-aged guys, past their idealistic days and heading for a big score (ten grand apiece), about to reconnect with their youthful consciences. World-weary cynicism is a launching pad for reclaimed values, an appealing romantic notion when applied to tough guys, from Rhett Butler to Rick of *Casablanca* to *The Magnificent Seven*. It's always fun to watch someone sell out for a while, before doing the right thing, experiencing the best of both worlds. *The Professionals* is hardly morally challenging or psychologically intricate, simply an enjoyable action picture, albeit a bit more grown-up than most. As in *The Hill* and *Flight of the Phoenix,* the desert adds significantly to the burdens and the beauty; Conrad Hall's Oscar-nominated cinematography is often stunning, especially amid blowing sands. (But Maurice Jarre's score is intrusively upbeat, a real mismatch.) The feisty Cardinale has the best female role within the films of this chapter, even though she is, of course, more than partly cast for her robust sensuality. Lancaster makes up for letting Marvin play head man by claiming the climactic action sequence for himself, singlehandedly besting about a half-dozen foes in a rocky-landscape shootout, proving himself, in tip-top form at age 52, the poster boy for mid-life virility.

The Dirty Dozen (1967) – Many would probably cite this Robert Aldrich WWII behemoth as the quintessential man-mission movie, but I don't think it rates even close to *The Great Escape.* Pandering in its forced machismo and comic relief, *The Dirty Dozen* feels aimed more at boys than men, set against a make-believe WWII free of any urgency. It starts in 1944 London with Lee Marvin, a major assigned to train a unit of death-row soldiers for a plot to kill Nazi officers inside a French chateau. If they are successful, their sentences will be commuted. It's a great hook for a war movie, but what follows is dramatically paper-thin and conventional, lopsided in its structure and pacing, and ultimately feeling longer than it is. The mission doesn't start until an hour and forty-five minutes into a 150-minute movie. (Funny that Aldrich made this straight-man '60s favorite as well as the gay-man '60s favorite *What Ever Happened to Baby Jane?*) *The Dirty Dozen* is a coldly manufactured product with its uninteresting visuals, inauthentic grit, and trumped-up suspense, plus Marvin's "comic" one-upmanship of Robert Ryan, his stuffy superior officer (the actors reunited from last year's *The Professionals*). Of the titular twelve, five are nonentities barely glimpsed, while the more conspicuous seven are Jim Brown, Trini Lopez, stoic German-speaking Charles Bronson, goofy Donald Sutherland, beefy Clint Walker, Southern religious zealot and convicted rapist Telly Savalas, and tough-guy troublemaker John Cassavetes (who received the film's only acting Oscar nomination). Enough isn't seen of their valuable training—the learning to work as a team—which seems essential if the movie is to have any emotional power. Also around are Ernest Borgnine, as a general, and George Kennedy, as a major, both recently of Aldrich's *Flight of the Phoenix.* (Kennedy beat Cassavetes for that Oscar for *Cool Hand Luke.*) Typifying the falseness of *The Dirty Dozen* is the scene in which Marvin treats the men to prostitutes, which is played and directed coyly, like a school-prom sequence. Macho slop is the worst kind of all.

Bullitt (1968) – Noticeably underpopulated when measured against the bulk of '60s mega-macho flicks, *Bullitt* belongs here as the culmination of Steve McQueen's status as the genre's kingpin, graduating from *The Magnificent Seven*'s funny-sexy sidekick to *The Great Escape*'s dude-hero to *Bullitt*'s super-cool, super-cop superstar. Who needs a magnificent septet or a dirty twelve-pack when you can have the 1968 McQueen? He's a one-man show of man's-man moviegoing. *Bullitt* also belongs here for topping McQueen's motorcycle leap—previously the most testosterone-fueled moment of the decade—with what is still regarded as the screen's greatest car chase, an extended set piece in which McQueen masterfully maneuvers his green Mustang, pursuing two villains through San Francisco and beyond, memorably soaring above (and slamming down on) the city's sloping roads. (A reward was the Oscar for film editing.) *Bullitt* has no big mission, no ragtag crew becoming a well-oiled machine, not even a piece of history to examine, but it plays potently with male fantasies, with a character and a star who invite hero worship, who inhabit "cool," assisted by a jazzy Lalo Schifrin score. Underneath his '60s hipster confidence, McQueen is playing an old-fashioned hero, the incorruptible police lieutenant. He dominates the movie with old-school presence, a Gable-sized star quality, and his intense (blue-eyed) concentration. I like the humanizing touch of his buying seven TV dinners, the kind of small detail that speaks volumes about a character's daily life (more real-world, say, than James Bond's). For contrast, there's Robert Vaughn, fellow *Magnificent Seven* alumnus, as a sleazy, arrogant politician, while poor Jacqueline Bisset, as McQueen's beautiful girlfriend, must rattle off an unnecessary yawn of a speech, all about his ugly work and what it must be doing to him. The plot is nothing special, but its propulsion constitutes an adrenaline rush with several good chases of varying kinds including a nifty climax, a chase on foot atop an airport runway. *Bullitt* is the rare '60s movie that still looks modern. Its impact influenced the look, feel, and attitudes of decades' worth of crime pictures, and yet it's really more about male movie stardom than anything else (the way *Gilda,* in the form of Rita Hayworth, is about female stardom). With tight-knit direction from Englishman Peter Yates, *Bullitt* is the movie, more than any other, that still makes boys and men want to grow up to be Steve McQueen.

The Wild Bunch (1969) – Emboldened by the screen's new permissiveness, director Sam Peckinpah confronted gunslinging lives with fresh eyes. Incorporating sprays of blood and slow-motion violence, *The Wild Bunch* allowed audiences to see, unsanitized, what they had been spared from westerns during four decades of Production Code-enforced good taste. To some this was a deglorification, to others merely sensationalism, but can Peckinpah's enhancements really be dismissed as gratuitous in such an obviously serious work? Even though it's epic, and an ensemble piece, *The Wild Bunch* is thematically akin to Peckinpah's other great '60s western, *Ride the High Country* (1962), his first masterpiece of western elegy, of aging in general, with both films taking stock of gun-toting lives that don't have much to show for them. Instead of the earlier movie's good-guy Joel McCrea contemplating his lonely lawman's existence, now it's outlaw William Holden doing the same sort of thing. Both men are committed to a last-hurrah job, a chance to test his late-life mettle and perhaps silence those nagging questions, any pesky thoughts about his life's overall pointlessness. Both actors are extraordinary, imbuing their dramas with contained complexities, enriched by their similarly economical acting styles. They are the credibly seasoned lynchpins of Peckinpah bookends, the two best westerns of the decade. As for Holden, his is a hard, effortlessly tough performance unlike any he ever gave. No longer trying to look like a leading man, he looks better than he had in years, handsome in a leathery way, with blue eyes that singe the screen. The rest of the bunch are Ernest Borgnine, brothers Warren Oates and Ben Johnson, Mexican Jaime Sanchez, and mangy old geezer Edmond O'Brien. Set in Texas and Mexico in 1913, the film is built upon three major set pieces: the bunch's opening robbery of a railroad office, which includes the law's ambush, leading to a street-side massacre involving innocent bystanders; the bunch's mid-picture train robbery of an arms shipment; and the famed blood-spattering blaze-of-glory finale. Similar to the way *Ride the High Country* plays as a battle of wits and wills between McCrea and Randolph Scott—old pals currently at odds—*The Wild Bunch* has Holden (and company) chased by former bunch member Robert Ryan (pulled from prison to aid the law in nabbing his friends). In both films, these are matches of equals: two men who know each other extremely well and respect each other highly. *The Wild Bunch* is essentially a chase with interruptions of criminal and violent activity, especially disturbing for the fact that children always seem to be observing and absorbing, never seeing anything that might do them any good, so impressionably susceptible to an ugly world, destined to emulate it. If that sounds heavy, *The Wild Bunch* also has the most unforgettable bridge explosion since *The Bridge on the River Kwai* (which had also been made possible by Holden). Entering a new, confusing age of automobiles and machine guns, *The Wild Bunch* isn't just about the end of the bunch but the end of the West, the West as it was known in the classic Hollywood western. With Peckinpah's phenomenal craft and cohesively sustained vision plus Lucien Ballard's magnificent cinematography, *The Wild Bunch* caps the decade of macho with its biggest and loudest bang, a last-stand acknowledgement of loyalty and friendship, a bad-ass outburst that can't quite conceal the encroaching sadness.

"For Immature Audiences Only": The Heavy-Breathing Sex Comedy (1961-1966)

Romantic comedies and screwball comedies of the 1930s and '40s were often quite sexy—consider Clark Gable and Claudette Colbert in *It Happened One Night* (1934), or Henry Fonda and Barbara Stanwyck in *The Lady Eve* (1941)—but something less suggestive and much more overt, a *blatant* sexual preoccupation, started appearing in the 1950s, in direct contrast with the middle-class American values and "good clean fun" being espoused on television sitcoms of the Eisenhower era. The flip side of such "decency" was an erotic repression, which found cinematic expression in the form of sex comedies. You can start by blaming Broadway, which was usually ahead of Hollywood in terms of sexual content, free from being reined in by any Production Code. Based on F. Hugh Herbert's 1951 Broadway play, director Otto Preminger's *The Moon Is Blue* (1953) was the official kickoff of the screen's mid-century affair with sex comedies, simply because it caused such a furor. Casually tossing around such words as virgin, mistress, seduce, and pregnant, it was released without Code approval and condemned by the Catholic Legion of Decency. Maggie McNamara, as its childlike kook, shocks the other characters with her bluntness yet comes off like an overgrown Margaret O'Brien. Not even co-stars William Holden and David Niven could make this numbingly tame material seem like anything but a piffling trifle, inconceivable today (or ever) as anyone's idea of a dirty movie. But the controversy sold lots of tickets, ushering in the next fifteen years of carnal-minded comedies, most of which were devoid of wit and scintillation and, oh yeah, *sexiness*.

In addition to Broadway's frisky influence, Hollywood increased its libidinous profile when a new, unabashedly sexual star, Marilyn Monroe, emerged in 1953, the same year as *The Moon Is Blue*. In 1955, the forces of Monroe and the Broadway sex comedy converged for *The Seven Year Itch*, another mild and minor sex-themed amusement. Based on George Axelrod's 1952 play, Billy Wilder's film version is better remembered for its swoony image of Monroe and her billowing white dress than it is for its plot. Alone for the summer, a husband (Tom Ewell, repeating his expert Tony Award-winning performance) indulges an active but harmless fantasy life, which includes the nameless bombshell (guess who) upstairs. In the vicarious thrills it stokes and tickles, *The Seven Year Itch*, like most of the films addressed in this chapter, panders to straight men, sympathizing with any festering convention-breaking desires they might be harboring. (You can feel the beginnings of Wilder's unfortunate penchant for labored smarminess, but more on that later.) There's rarely any actual sex to be had in these movies, and nice-guy Ewell gets none from Monroe (so irresistibly sweet and charming in her disappointingly undemanding sex-object role).

Many sex comedies of the '50s (and beyond) continued to be properties adapted from Broadway plays. Though often arriving with patinas of class and integrity (mostly unearned), they usually resulted in stagy movies in which big stars spouted brittle pseudo-sophisticated dialogue in coy situations. True, Hollywood usually expunged what little bite such vehicles had, thereby ensuring that nothing *actually* daring was going to happen. Take Ginger Rogers and Dan Dailey in *Oh, Men! Oh, Women!* (1957), or Ava Gardner and Stewart Granger in *The Little Hut* (1957), both of which co-starred David Niven, plus Doris Day and Richard Widmark in *The Tunnel of Love* (1958), all of them serving as evidence of the limp state of the adult sex comedy of the 1950s.

Starring Tony Curtis and Janet Leigh, Blake Edwards' *The Perfect Furlough* (1958) is a horny, contrived army-themed sex comedy, which, in almost textbook fashion, anticipates the all-out puerile nature of the '60s sex-com. (Incidentally, it was Edwards who would revamp the genre for a post-sexual-revolution age with the overrated, tiresomely unfunny *"10"* in 1979. Updating the form's usual components—the straight-male fantasies, the objectified females, the leering tone—he managed to revive its popularity.) But it wasn't just directors like Wilder and Edwards who were instigating the growing appetite for sex comedies. Voluptuous European screen goddesses, notably Sophia Loren and Brigitte Bardot, were upping the ante of what people wanted to see at the movies, not to mention home-grown ladies, such as Jayne Mansfield, who were trying to follow the Marilyn Monroe playbook.

In 1959, there were two major sex comedies—*Some Like It Hot* and *Pillow Talk*—a pair that seemed to signify that better days were ahead. Though they were both highly influential, their special charms were not easily duplicated, even by the talents involved. Billy Wilder's ingeniously constructed and playfully subversive *Some Like It Hot*, with its glorious trio of Marilyn Monroe, Tony Curtis, and Jack Lemmon, remains a reasonable candidate for the funniest comedy of the sound era, an enduringly (and endearingly) sexy, endlessly witty, and flat-out hilarious play on gender. It's never uptight or smutty, two qualities that would smother many an upcoming sex-com. Wilder's classic is a giddy '20s period piece, while *Pillow Talk* is a battle-of-the-sexes comedy of its particular moment, a bright, colorful romp boosted by the snap-crackle chemistry of Doris Day and Rock Hudson, with her crisp, deliberate style complementing his easygoing temperament. It's a play on *The Shop Around the Corner* (1940), with Day loving one guy and hating another, not knowing that they're both Hudson, the hated "Rock" a disembodied voice at the other end of her party line. *Pillow Talk* retains a buoyant spirit and an unforced sex appeal, exemplified by its seemingly shared split-screen bathtub, in which Day's exposed foot "touches" Hudson's. It's far superior to all the '60s comedies these two stars made, together and apart.

After these two promising high points, things went wrong and steadily worsened. By the late '60s, the drooling "fun" of sex comedies would become culturally obsolete. In a newly uncensored movie world, with a ratings system that could accommodate onscreen sex and nudity, the genre, as it had evolved, had run its course. How could movies, in such an increasingly uninhibited climate, continue to promote the old rules of courtship, the "saving yourself for marriage" guidelines that had controlled amorous comedies for decades? Mike Nichols' *The Graduate* (1967) and Paul Mazursky's *Bob & Carol & Ted & Alice* (1969), two flawed but invigorating sex-fueled satires (both set in LA), were major gusts of fresh air, completely representative of changing times. Who would ever again want to sit through a musty, downright stupid yawn such as *Promise Her Anything* (1966) or *Not with My Wife, You Don't!* (1966)? For the most part, the beast was dead, even on Broadway, though there would still be occasional stage-based screen adaptations, such as *Lovers and Other Strangers* (1970), which combined older-fashioned sitcom-like sex comedy with some of the screen's new permissiveness, and *The Owl and the Pussycat* (1971), which embraced the new freedoms in an abrasively overboard manner.

The ten films highlighted are part of the movies' embarrassingly fumbling foreplay, its excited yet anxious path toward the sexual revolution. Nervously "risqué," hyperactive and adolescent, these farces might be labeled as premature ejaculations. To be kind, perhaps their relentless, lip-smacking tastelessness helped accelerate the movies' arrival at a new maturity. But, at their cores, they are a startlingly innocent collection of wet-dream experiences, something to grow out of as soon as possible.

Sunday in New York (1963): Jane Fonda and Rod Taylor

The Marriage-Go-Round (1961) – Based on Leslie Stevens' 1958 Broadway hit, it stars Susan Hayward and James Mason (in roles played onstage by Claudette Colbert and Charles Boyer), continuing the *Moon Is Blue* trend of racy-yet-toothless sex comedies. It's a typical straight-male sitcom fantasy, this time with a college setting. Mason is a cultural anthropology professor; Hayward is the dean of women. Married sixteen years, and with two kids away at school, they are a happy twin-bed duo. The stars address us directly throughout, as if we were their students. The subject: monogamy. Enter Julie Newmar, repeating her Tony Award-winning performance as what used to be called "a magnificent specimen," a blonde Swede, daughter of their Nobel Prize-winning friend. Not only their houseguest, she's a gal with a mission: to convince Mason, whom she greatly admires, to make a baby with her. However, the plot's shock factor feels hedged because the young woman is a foreigner, someone ostensibly from another world. No American girl would be as brazen as this ardent seductress! But Hayward needn't feel left out; she has an admirer too, though hers is a married middle-aged professor. Our star trio is polished, with Hayward flaunting her smiling sarcasm, Mason offering pleasurable flashes of wit, and Newmar providing a vibrant presence. But the film doesn't move much beyond the tee-hee nature of its premise. Among its few amusements is Mason dancing a living-room mambo with Newmar and maracas. She also gives him a gold statuette of her naked body, which Hayward calls the "Swedish Oscar," striking a match on its ass to light her cigarette. Directed perfunctorily by Walter Lang, who had made *With a Song in My Heart* (1952), one of Hayward's biggest hits, *The Marriage-Go-Round* is a lukewarm sex comedy, mere child's play in terms of what was to come.

Boys' Night Out **(1962)** – Call it *The Apartment* (1960) meets the Doris-and-Rock formula, with the result another safe and remarkably innocuous sex comedy, wasting a talented ensemble. Divorced James Garner and his three married pals (Howard Duff, Tony Randall, Howard Morris), all of them commuters between NYC and Connecticut, rent a fabulous Manhattan pad (complete with a mirrored bedroom ceiling) for presumed sexcapades. They hire Kim Novak as their resident plaything, not knowing she's actually doing post-graduate work in sociology ("Adolescent Sexual Fantasies in the Adult Suburban Male"). And she's a virgin. While distracting the married trio away from any sexual activity, Novak, in the film's most diverting notion, provides the men with what their wives won't. And it has nothing to do with sex: she listens to Randall talk, allows Duff to fix things, and lets Morris eat whatever he wants. Of course, things proceed differently with handsome Garner, with whom she fights from the start, instantly indicating that they're meant for each other. Despite being directed by *Pillow Talk*'s own Michael Gordon, it's all too squeaky clean, with even the usually impeccable Garner stranded in a confused tangle of a role. (Why, for instance, is he hanging out with these guys?) Novak deploys her soft sensuality but she's no comedienne, lacking the necessary charm and twinkle that might have lifted *Boys' Night Out* a few notches.

Come Blow Your Horn **(1963)** – Neil Simon's first Broadway hit (in 1961) became this Frank Sinatra vehicle, with a screenplay by Norman Lear and direction by Bud Yorkin (the team later responsible for television's *All in the Family*). But it's such an ordinary sitcom that not even Rat Pack-era Sinatra can make it seem even slightly cool. (Oddly, he breaks into the title tune mid-picture, as if this were suddenly a musical.) He's back in *Tender Trap* mode, cast as a swinging bachelor, this time living in a lavish red-walled NYC apartment that looks like a bordello's waiting room. The plot is the usual push-pull of naughtiness and conventionality. Tony Bill (a George Hamilton lookalike) is the 21-year-old who idolizes big-brother Sinatra. Bill runs away from Yonkers, and from parents Lee J. Cobb and Molly Picon, to move into Sinatra's place in the big bad city. The set-up appears to be Simon's early try at an *Odd Couple*-type situation. It's supposedly hilarious that Cobb—overacting, even for him—is in the artificial fruit trade, and quite unbelievable that Sinatra is working in the family business. To his credit, Sinatra seems more engaged than he does in most of his bad films of the '60s. (Playing thirty-nine, he was pushing fifty, with Cobb only four years his senior.) Picon is a cartoon of a Jewish mother, but Jill St. John is a bright spot, even though her role (a dumb sexpot) is, for its time, typically demeaning. The "good" girl is Barbara Rush, dating Sinatra for six months but without any hanky-panky. Naturally, she's rewarded with marriage. The kid brother will evolve into the older brother, complete with a sleazy capper: Sinatra, who has kept his great apartment by servicing the building's lady owner, encourages his brother to continue the tradition. The "ick" quotient of the genre appears to be gaining some steam. However, Lear and Yorkin went on to make one of the best sex comedies of the decade, *Divorce American Style* (1967), a lucid pre-*Bob & Carol* movie with an eye toward the shifting landscape.

Irma la Douce **(1963)** – It plays like a kids' movie about hookers. After the triumphs of *Some Like It Hot* and *The Apartment,* Billy Wilder and Jack Lemmon failed miserably with this vulgar, garishly broad display of wink-wink prurience. It's a Paris-set monstrosity, with Shirley MacLaine (in the title role) as a dedicated prostitute and Lemmon an honest policeman. He's also a sexual innocent, but why does he have to be so juvenile? More than any other star, the unthreateningly asexual Lemmon is the poster child for the decade's sex-crazed comedies and their overriding timidity. He's the perennial teenage boy, which was somewhat true even in *The Apartment,* already a far cry from his delicious lustiness and fearless abandon in *Some Like It Hot.* And Wilder's bludgeoning *Irma* direction belies the fact that he once directed a comedy as nimbly paced and sexually sophisticated as *Some Like It Hot.* After being fired as a policeman, Lemmon "acquires" MacLaine following a fight with her pimp, leading to a reversal of standard gender roles, with her committed to supporting him through prostitution, proud that no man of hers has to work. But, to keep her from other men, Lemmon creates an alter ego, Lord X, who will pay for her services, which means he must accept manual labor to afford her (for sessions of no more than double solitaire). The set-up is similar to what Tony Curtis does in *Some Like It Hot,* when he becomes Mr. Shell Oil, including the phony wealth and the impotence. And, in a nod to Lemmon's own *Some Like It Hot* character, he gets lost in his own charade. Yet none of this is funny this time around, partially because Lemmon's Lord X is such an over-the-top British caricature, partially because the film is stretched to a punishing 147 minutes. Almost everything about this box-office blockbuster weighs a ton, including the idiocy revolving around Lemmon's "murder" of his alter ego. The exception is MacLaine. In a big black wig (with a green bow), she underplays so defiantly that you're sure she's figured out how crude and just plain awful this movie is and that her only recourse is to pull inward. (Her generous reward was an Oscar nomination.) Like *Fanny* (1961), *Irma la Douce* is based on a musical but uses its score merely as background music. (The stage musical was a hit in Paris in 1956, in London in 1958, on Broadway in 1960.) The melodies are sublime, too good to be drowned out by such unrelenting noise.

Under the Yum Yum Tree (1963) – Jack Lemmon actually made a worse movie than *Irma la Douce* in 1963, a project in which he isn't even part of the main plot. Based on a Broadway play by Lawrence Roman, it's about an experiment between California collegemates Carol Lynley and Dean Jones. It's Lynley's idea that she and Jones live together platonically before risking marriage, to see if they have "character compatibility." This actually puts the movie a bit ahead of its time, before "living together" became an inescapable cultural concept. They move into Centaur Apartments, where a wealthy Lemmon is the lecherous landlord; his tenants are all attractive females. In one sense he couldn't possibly be more miscast, so utterly unconvincing, and yet he's exactly what this kind of comedy craves, a neutered lech, a randy buffoon who couldn't possibly be any more harmless. Despite the requisite red-walled bachelor pad and a red car, he's just Jack Lemmon, America's boy sweetheart playing dress-up. (Gig Young, who created the role onstage, must have had some genuine oomph.) Lynley is lovely, but, oh, that toneless voice of hers, while Jones, repeating his stage role, seems appropriately like a young Jimmy Stewart. There are welcome sightings of Paul Lynde (the super) and Imogene Coca (the housekeeper) as a married couple: Lynde idolizes Lemmon; Coca disapproves of him. I guess it's refreshing that Lemmon isn't "tamed" at the end, but, really, who'd want him? Directed by David Swift, who co-wrote the script with the playwright, *Under the Yum Yum Tree* squanders the potential in Lynley's forward-thinking impulse, too foolish to give its premise a fair shake. And Lemmon wasn't finished, continuing his sex-com dominance with *Good Neighbor Sam* (1964) and *How to Murder Your Wife* (1965), the latter a particularly misogynistic marriage-bashing travesty. Though Lemmon appeared to be smearing his good name, he was actually gaining in box-office popularity. The crassness of mid-'60s sex comedies was apparently in tune with a pre-sexual-revolution mood of agitated confusion.

***Sunday in New York* (1963)** – Another movie inching its way toward sexual upheaval, this is a rather pleasant mix of the old-fashioned and the now, with Norman Krasna adapting his own 1961 Broadway hit (under Peter Tewksbury's somewhat stagy direction). Krasna had written more romantic comedies than just about anyone, for both stage and screen, including two of my favorite movies, *Bachelor Mother* (1939) and *It Started with Eve* (1941). Though this is lesser Krasna, it puts most of its era's sex comedies to shame, lifted further by its appealing quartet: Jane Fonda, Rod Taylor, Cliff Robertson, and Robert Culp (later of *Bob & Carol & Ted & Alice*). Plus there's nifty Peter Nero music (including a title tune sung by Mel Tormé), beautiful Orry-Kelly clothes for Fonda, and NYC locations. A 22-year-old virgin from Albany, Fonda comes to town to see her airline-pilot brother (Robertson). She's just been dumped by boyfriend Culp and wants to know if a girl going steady is expected to sleep with her beau. Robertson claims his own purity to help ensure hers, when he's actually sleeping with Jo Morrow. Fonda learns the truth, then sets about seducing Rod Taylor, a guy she "met cute" on a city bus; they got caught on each other. But Taylor won't deflower a virgin. Culp's arrival leads to mounting mistaken-identity complications, the kind of thing on which Krasna's writing thrived. With Fonda ensconced in his apartment, Robertson and girlfriend Morrow spend most of the movie trying to find a place to have sex, which seems seismically modern for a 1963 comedy. He eventually proposes to her, and, in refreshing proof of progress, the non-virgin goes unpunished, winning the guy despite her sexual activity. Robertson's subtle, effortlessly funny performance makes *Sunday in New York* more his movie than anyone else's. As for Fonda, she has an animated sparkle that made her one of the decade's deftest screen comediennes, notably in two other Broadway-based vehicles, *Period of Adjustment* (1962) and *Barefoot in the Park* (1967). And

Taylor, a reliably charming light comedian, does his best Cary Grant, though his role feels like a slapped-together construct: a sports-writing music critic about to become a foreign correspondent after he finishes his book!

Sex and the Single Girl (1964) – A riff on Helen Gurley Brown's book title, this smash-hit fiasco, pitched to the balcony, stars Natalie Wood as a fictional "Helen Brown." Trite yet still offensive, it's one of the more lame-brained of '60s sex comedies, which grew more frantic and desperate the more popular they became, with all their pent-up lust near to bursting. In this world, a woman can only be one of three things: a wife, a virgin, or a slut. Wood may be a best-selling psychologist, but mostly she's a beautiful 23-year-old virgin. The movie mocks her professional life, depicting her as silly, frustrated, and needy, all of which plays to sexist fantasies of cutting women down to size, making this a sorry update of the boss-lady comedies of the '40s, in which, somehow, Rosalind Russell had to be taught *not* to make men feel inferior. Tony Curtis, as managing editor of a filthy rag, sets out to prove that Wood is a sex-expert fraud by exposing her virginity. He comes to her as a patient but pretends to be Henry Fonda, a pal of his. Fonda and Lauren Bacall play a battling married couple, with Curtis co-opting their story for his sessions with Wood. The plot shamelessly steals from *Some Like It Hot,* with Curtis himself *again* feigning impotence, *again* getting a woman to attempt arousing him. When he puts on a woman's robe, he says, "I look just like Jack Lemmon did in that movie where he dressed up like a girl." There are four more references to Lemmon, which is fitting, since he was the patron saint of moronic sex farces. Wood's acting is frenzied and amateurish, evoking a flailing marionette, with very little of the rom-com charm and skill she had displayed in *Love with the Proper Stranger* (1963), a palpably sexy movie. Curtis coasts and Fonda barely registers, but Bacall is sharp and likable (especially when calling Wood "Kid"), with the right comic energy (just the wrong material). Co-written by Joseph Heller (*Catch-22*), this stinker was directed by Richard Quine who botches everything, including a berserk drawn-out freeway chase featuring the entire cast. Not only does Wood give up her practice for marriage to Curtis, but she wins him by cranking phony tears. It's hard to believe that the overactive goofery of *Sex and the Single Girl* predates Wood's appearance in *Bob & Carol & Ted & Alice* by only five years; it feels more like fifty.

What's New Pussycat (1965) – How bad can a comedy be when it stars Peter Sellers, Peter O'Toole, and Woody Allen (who also wrote the original screenplay)? *This* bad. Set in Paris, it aims to be brisk and titillating, but it's more exhausting than anything else, with a plotline that quickly becomes dull (even though it never takes a breath). O'Toole is a redheaded editor of a French fashion magazine, a womanizer with a marriage-minded girlfriend (Romy Schneider). His problem is that he can't say no to all the women throwing themselves at him. But O'Toole isn't very believable in his lust, and, with material this feeble, he soon becomes tedious. His psychoanalyst is German-accented Sellers (with long hair and glasses), a lascivious fellow with a fat wife. He's in love with his married nymphomaniac patient (Capucine, reteamed with Sellers after *The Pink Panther*). Has Woody Allen's writing ever been this witless? He plays O'Toole's pal, in love with Ms. Schneider. Who thought it was funny for Paula Prentiss, as a stripper chasing O'Toole, to overdose on pills, and not once but three times? Such a terrible role for the quirky Prentiss, but then nobody comes off well. The best bit involves a cameo from Richard Burton, which ends with O'Toole telling him to "give my regards to what's-her-name." The film's other laugh comes when Sellers refers to Ursula Andress, who inexplicably parachutes into O'Toole's car, as a "personal friend of James Bond." Frenetic and ugly-looking, *What's New Pussycat* climaxes with a farcical hotel sequence in which the entire cast races about, executing mirthless slapstick, which continues with a pointless go-cart chase, all of it wretchedly directed by Clive Donner. It's another very bad yet very popular sex comedy, with enough of the audience still getting their jollies from such panty-raid shenanigans. The best thing here is Tom Jones' assertive handling of the Burt Bacharach-Hal David title tune. Now that's sexy.

A Very Special Favor (1965) – After the gruesome box-office peaks of *Sex and the Single Girl, How to Murder Your Wife,* and *What's New Pussycat,* the '60s sex comedy was finally running out of gas, growing more dated by the minute, haplessly imitating itself, and even starting to lose the conviction of its mollifying messages, the ones about the cure-all sanctity of marriage and holding on to one's virginity until the wedding night. Rock Hudson, who helped get the genre rolling with *Pillow Talk* and who had continued with far weaker comedies, whether with Doris Day (*Lover Come Back* – 1961, *Send Me No Flowers* – 1964) or Gina Lollobrigida (*Come September* – 1961, *Strange Bedfellows* – 1965), was beginning to seem bored, on remote control despite his professionalism. Enter Leslie Caron, game and gifted, but no Day as a Hudson teammate, ultimately appearing unsure of herself. Even with other *Pillow Talk* contributors—director Michael Gordon and co-writer Stanley

Shapiro—*A Very Special Favor* is uninspired, fusing the too-familiar plots of *Pillow Talk* and *Sex and the Single Girl*. Caron is a screwed-up virginal psychologist; Hudson is a ladies' man pretending to have a problem so he can woo her. Why? In an especially distasteful move, Caron's father (Charles Boyer) asks virile Hudson to deflower her ("a 30-year-old spinster") and make her "a woman" before she weds wimpy Dick Shawn. Much is made of her advanced age! Like Natalie Wood in 1964, Caron is a female doctor treated as a punchline. Hudson's made-up issue is the burden of his irresistibility to women: he just can't say no (like O'Toole in *What's New Pussycat*). In reality, he loves his lifestyle of women constantly throwing themselves at him; they're also grateful to cook for him and do his laundry. At the climax, Hudson tries to make Caron think he's turned gay, but it's hardly worth the set-up, mostly of interest as one of Hudson's occasional onscreen winks at his own sexuality. Earlier, in an unrelated scene, Caron tells him, "Hiding in closets isn't going to cure you." (You can't make this stuff up.) Gone is the *Pillow Talk* snap in Gordon's direction, with the whole venture steadily deflating, part of the death throes of the '60s sex comedy.

The Swinger (**1966**) – With a screenplay by Lawrence Roman (*Under the Yum Yum Tree*), it's a horror, but also a fascinating time capsule of an era at the point of extinction. Here's a scrubbed-clean almost-musical about depravity. In spite of the peeping and the smirking, it's another "virgin" comedy, this one taking its inspiration from a way-back charmer, *Theodora Goes Wild* (1936). Following Irene Dunne's lead, Ann-Margret writes a salacious novel yet she's really just a good girl. And she pretends to be bad for a nudie-magazine editor, the ever-charmless Tony Franciosa. A stunning physical presence, Ann-Margret has absolutely no energy whenever she's not gyrating to music. Her line readings are lifeless, her acting vapid. Only when singing and dancing does she spring to life and seem like a star. There's no indication that she would transform herself into a fine actress, even though *Carnal Knowledge* was just five years away. *The Swinger* is simply another all-talk-and-no-action gyp. Even Franciosa's boss, dirty old man Robert Coote, turns out to be a cuddly fraud. Filled with irritating late-'60s visual tricks, *The Swinger* is a sad late work of director George Sidney, maker of many noteworthy MGM movies, from *Anchors Aweigh* (1945) to *Scaramouche* (1952). He had directed two Ann-Margret hits, *Bye Bye Birdie* (1963) and *Viva Las Vegas* (1964), but nobody cared about *The Swinger*. It was further proof that this particular brand of sex comedy, with its manic hormone-fueled stamina tied to outmoded social conventions, was mercifully over. Maybe it was time to try to treat sex in comedies in a more grown-up fashion, not just in *Divorce American Style* and *Bob & Carol & Ted & Alice,* but later in *MASH* (1970), *Everything You Always Wanted to Know About Sex* But Were Afraid to Ask* (1972), *The Heartbreak Kid* (1972), and, even later, *Shampoo* (1975). The laughs could be raucous and outrageous without being sophomoric (at least until Blake Edwards returned to the scene). But let's leave the '60s sex-com behind with the full force of kittenish, uncontained Ann-Margret. Singing the title tune at the beginning and end of *The Swinger,* first all in black, then all in yellow, she's a fitting final image, for better or worse, of the era's perspiring purity.

With Songs They Have Sung: Broadway's Takeover of the Hollywood Musical (1961-1969)

From the moment that movies learned to sing, the industry's most convenient outside supplier of musical material was the Broadway stage. In 1929 and 1930, there were film adaptations of hit shows such as *Sally, The Cocoanuts, Rio Rita, Sunny, Spring Is Here, Hit the Deck, Good News, Follow Thru, Whoopee,* and *No, No, Nanette.* Stage operettas also arrived on screens, including *The Vagabond King* and *New Moon,* both in 1930. Most of these movies were frivolous affairs based on frivolous shows, the kind of lightweight fare that could be adapted without serious concerns over fidelity to the source materials. In 1936, there was a more prestigious Broadway-based movie musical—the James Whale production of *Show Boat*—but most of the mid-'30s musicals derived from stage shows continued to be diverting larks, including *Roberta* (1935), *Naughty Marietta* (1935), and *Anything Goes* (1936). Despite the rare landmark Broadway musical, whether *Show Boat* in 1927 or *Porgy and Bess* in 1935, the stature of the art form didn't shift decisively until Rodgers and Hammerstein's *Oklahoma!* (1943), which signaled the reign of the integrated musical, the kind in which songs revealed character and moved the story forward. As never before, the Broadway musical became a major artistic and cultural force in America, no longer dismissible as mere escapism designed to make people forget their troubles.

Hollywood had always treated Broadway as a place to buy vehicles for movie stars, rarely allowing New York players to repeat their roles onscreen. Give *Babes in Arms* to Mickey and Judy, *I Married an Angel* to Jeanette and Nelson, *Panama Hattie* to Ann Sothern, and *Lady in the Dark* to Ginger Rogers. Throughout the 1940s and early '50s, Hollywood continued to adapt Broadway fare freely—no genuflecting required. When Gene Kelly and Frank Sinatra headlined *On the Town* (1949), it was more MGM musical than sacrosanct recreation of the 1944 hit. The studio's artisans and craftspeople, its stars and directors, tailored other stage musicals, stamping the MGM imprint upon *Annie Get Your Gun* (1950), *Kiss Me Kate* (1953), *Brigadoon* (1954), and *Kismet* (1955). However, Ray Bolger got to repeat his 1948 *Where's Charley?* success for Warner Brothers in 1952, and Ethel Merman belted her way through the 1953 Fox version of her 1950 hit *Call Me Madam,* but these were exceptions. Usually, a Broadway star like Alfred Drake was, to Hollywood's way of thinking, simply refining material for MGM's Howard Keel. And Fox could ignore Carol Channing when they bought *Gentlemen Prefer Blondes* (1949), reconceiving it as a 1953 launching pad for an entirely different kind of blonde, Marilyn Monroe.

The more serious-minded Broadway musicals started arriving on movie screens in the mid-'50s at precisely the moment when the studios were losing their nerve regarding original Hollywood musicals, caving to the competition of television variety and rock and roll, despite a recent smash-hit original called *Seven Brides for Seven Brothers* (1954). Adaptations of stage hits were deemed surer prospects because Broadway continued to make steady contributions to the era's popular music. You might not have seen *South Pacific* onstage, but you knew "Some Enchanted Evening," which might be enough incentive to make you want to see the movie. Just as *Oklahoma!* had altered Broadway in 1943, its 1955 screen version announced a similar shift in Hollywood. The days of contract players such as Jane Powell, Donald O'Connor, and Betty Grable were definitely over. Broadway pedigree assumed firm command of the movie musical.

After twelve years of anticipation, *Oklahoma!* couldn't be just any movie musical. The property, a star in its own right, couldn't be treated casually, or, more to the point, like a musical. It was directed by Fred Zinnemann, recent Oscar winner for *From Here to Eternity* (1953), a man who had never gone near a movie musical, thus setting a trend. Such illustrious endeavors couldn't be entrusted to mere makers of musicals. Only the finest serious artists need apply. No one admires Zinnemann more than I do, but his *Oklahoma!* is an unsurprisingly flawed effort, with casting both perfect (Gordon MacRae and Gene Nelson) and bizarre (Rod Steiger and Gloria Grahame). Mounted like an epic, it proved to be both faithful to its source and enormously popular. Mission accomplished. Also that year, another film musical bolstered the kickoff of Broadway-based super productions: Joseph L. Mankiewicz's entertaining but visually stagnant version of Frank Loesser's 1950 *Guys and Dolls*. Mankiewicz, another great Oscar-winning director (*All About Eve*) without movie-musical credentials, made another faithful (reasonably) box-office biggie, solidifying another element of these Broadway-to-Hollywood transfers: the casting of major stars who couldn't really sing, leaving them to muddle through as best they could, all in the cause of lessening the financial risk. The usually nonsinging Jean Simmons fared well, better than Marlon Brando did. Meanwhile, Frank Sinatra, perfect for Brando's role, is standing right next to him. But *Guys and Dolls* was no ordinary musical comedy, and Brando, whether he belonged in it or not, was simply the hottest name in movies.

After *Oklahoma!* Rodgers and Hammerstein continued to raise the prestige level of the movie musical. *The King and I* (1956) not only won an Oscar for Yul Brynner (the original-cast king of 1951) but also found a leading lady (Deborah Kerr) so perfect that no one cared it was Marni Nixon singing for her (in the most seamlessly convincing example of vocal dubbing in film-musical history). Luckily, *The King and I* was made before Hollywood became entrenched in strenuously overproducing their Broadway adaptations. Unintrusively directed by Walter Lang (a reliable old movie-musical hand at Fox), *King and I* was faithful, admirable, and, best of all, had a star duo with a crackling chemistry. *Carousel,* from earlier in 1956, was a less felicitous Rodgers and Hammerstein movie, reteaming the *Oklahoma!* pair, Gordon MacRae and Shirley Jones (both less comfortably cast), with another A-list director not known for musicals (Henry King); the results were drearily uninspiring. *South Pacific* (1958), a major box-office success, was another Rodgers and Hammerstein disappointment, with lackluster stars, crazy color effects, and director Joshua Logan (from the 1949 stage production) clearly overwhelmed. *Carousel* and *South Pacific* proved that great scores weren't enough to ensure great movie musicals.

The old-style adaptations hadn't yet completely vanished. There was *Pal Joey* (1957), a reworking of the 1940 show into a Frank Sinatra vehicle, and *Silk Stockings* (1957), which treated its 1955 source as fodder for a last-gasp old-school MGM musical, primed for Hollywood greats Fred Astaire and Cyd Charisse. These served as almost a kind of closure on the original point of movie musicals: to showcase great singers and dancers, while providing just enough plot to connect the musical numbers. During the 1960s, musical talent often seemed beside the point, secondary to the distinction of the properties, tertiary to famous (but miscast) personalities. (Remember Janet Leigh in Chita Rivera's role in the 1963 *Bye Bye Birdie*?) And, for a while, it seemed to pay off. Suddenly, after the heyday of Astaire, Kelly, and Garland, the genre was having its most lauded decade. Four of the ten Oscar-winning Best Pictures of the '60s were musicals! In the quest for bigger, longer, and splashier, the studios gave audiences their money's worth to the point of bludgeoning. But why couldn't there have been more movies like *The Pajama Game* (1957)? Based on a 1954 show, it boasted nearly its entire original cast, but with the smart enhancements of an ideal Hollywood star (Doris Day) and a superb movie-musical director (Stanley Donen). True, the show is no masterwork, but the movie—unpretentious and inventive and stylish—remains one of the finest screen musicals based on a Broadway show.

The 1960s began with two Broadway-based musicals that don't fit the decade's mold of mega-productions. *Can-Can,* based on Cole Porter's 1953 show, has two sets of stars—Maurice Chevalier and Louis Jourdan; Frank Sinatra and Shirley MacLaine—and is essentially *Gigi Meets the Rat Pack,* a free-for-all travesty. The more modest *Bells Are Ringing,* with its Jule Styne melodies, is more significant by virtue of preserving Judy Holliday's winning stage performance. Otherwise, it's an extremely slight and static MGM musical, directed by an uncharacteristically lazy Vincente Minnelli. Then, in 1961, a virtual parade of mammoth adaptations began. Dim the lights, cue the overture, and sing out, Louise!

The Sound of Music (1965): Julie Andrews

West Side Story (1961) – It became a beloved movie because of Leonard Bernstein's music, Jerome Robbins' choreography, and its contemporary take on *Romeo and Juliet,* winning ten Oscars including Best Picture and surpassing the original 1957 show's popularity. But, despite the highly charged energy of tensions between rival gangs in NYC, much of its dialogue creaks and much of the drama is superficial. When Gene Kelly led "New York, New York" on location in *On the Town,* it was easy to accept as an uncontained burst of joy. However, when the tough guys of *West Side Story* break into balletic choreography on actual city streets, it's not only pretentious but downright silly. (The film's mixing of locations with obviously fake sets produces jarring effects.) As Tony, Richard Beymer is too boy-next-door to be cast as an ex-gang leader, a character whose transition from former delinquent to ardent lover should be touching. But how can it be when Beymer is never anything but a wide-eyed juvenile? Not a singer, not a star, and miscast, what's he doing here? Natalie Wood, dubbed by Marni Nixon, fares better, lovely and innocent as Puerto Rican Maria. Even better are Oscar winners George Chakiris and Rita Moreno, an exciting team: he's slick, sly, and sharp; she's funny, passionate, and strong. I applaud the decision to have them face-off in "America," leading the ensemble in a friendly battle of genders (instead of the show's all-female rendition). Best of all is unheralded Russ Tamblyn who is not only believable as a young hoodlum but is able to individualize the choreography with his bad-boy physicality. Minus any of the principal players, the one spectacularly executed sequence is the garage-set "Cool" performed by the gang of Jets, thrillingly danced and photographed. The frustration-fueled propulsion in the "Cool" choreography explodes from the dancers, an organic physical expression of intense feeling. The movie's finale—with characters making too-precisely timed exits to the music—marks the other extreme, a formally controlled staginess. For their stylistically erratic work, Mr. Robbins and Robert Wise—paired to combine the know-hows of stage and screen—shared the Best Director Oscar, even though Robbins was fired midway because his perfectionism put the film behind schedule and over budget. However, Robbins was responsible for the filming of "Cool," the movie's most Oscar-worthy moment.

The Music Man (1962) – As a 1957 show, it beat *West Side Story* for the Best Musical Tony Award. As a movie, it was a Best Picture Oscar nominee directed by Morton DaCosta (who had guided it onstage). DaCosta never got the hang of movies, having already made a stubbornly theatrical *Auntie Mame*

(1958), which he had also directed onstage; both movies weigh a ton, too often telegraphing the pieces' stage origins. Onscreen, *The Music Man* revels in its overly worked-out professionalism, its meticulous mechanization. It feels like a '60s Disney movie, stressing the material's wholesomeness over its wit, coming off more cartoonish than satiric; it's pleasant and sturdy but hardly transporting. The Meredith Willson score is a treat, so why don't any of the numbers make an impact? As Harold Hill, a flimflam artist out to scam River City, Iowa, in 1912, Robert Preston repeats his Tony-winning stage triumph, and he's mightily impressive rattling off his rapid-paced patter. But he looks too old for the part and has no sex appeal in what is, basically, a romantic lead. There's something remote about his polished presence; the camera never warms up to his performance. Since his con-man antics don't meet much resistance, Preston starts to seem repetitive fairly quickly. As Marian the librarian (and piano teacher), Shirley Jones actually has the better role; it's really the story of her blossoming, the "old maid" who opens herself to love (with Preston). Unfortunately, Jones, an undeserving Oscar winner for *Elmer Gantry* (1960), is too bland, not nearly as interesting as her character. But there's top-notch support from Paul Ford (the mayor), Hermione Gingold (the mayor's wife), and, from the Broadway cast, Pert Kelton (Jones' mother). And who can forget little Ronny Howard as Jones' lisping kid brother? Typical of the '60s Broadway-musical adaptations, *The Music Man* feels much too long, with a plot that occasionally just stops moving. Not even Preston's virtuosic wordplay can keep the darned thing's motor revved.

Gypsy **(1962)** – Mervyn LeRoy was historically bad at directing stage material for the screen, recently doing especially leaden work on *Mister Roberts* (1955), *The Bad Seed* (1956), and, with his future *Gypsy* star Rosalind Russell, *A Majority of One* (1961). Tackling the 1959 Jule Styne-Stephen Sondheim show—an essential showbiz musical, with a downbeat death-of-vaudeville perspective—LeRoy made another effortful and visually unimaginative movie. Because the story is so compelling, it's never boring. I bemoan the film's rejection of the show's original star, Ethel Merman, for the role of Rose, the King Lear of musical theater, the steamroller of stage mothers. (If not Merman, why not Judy Garland?) Coming off the fairly recent box-office success of *Auntie Mame*, Rosalind Russell was the biggest middle-aged female name in pictures, the one most likely to bring sizable audiences to *Gypsy*. (She had also won a Tony for the 1953 musical *Wonderful Town*.) Russell properly dominates, but she seems to be giving a best-of performance, incorporating favorite previous roles, notably her desperate Rosemary in *Picnic* (1955), and, of course, Mame, from which she borrows a glamorous panache that seems a bit much for lowdown Rose. Even though Russell never played Rose onstage, she appears to be recreating a stage performance, with a pronounced theatricality more tiring than mesmerizing. She's also diminished by dubbing from Lisa Kirk, whose refined vocals don't always match the star's interpretation or energy. Russell herself sings occasionally, notably in the up-tempo "Mr. Goldstone." (An ongoing conundrum of this era was whether to cast big stars and allow them to sing for themselves, however inadequately, *or* to dub them with trained voices that might prove disconcerting when emanating from such well-known faces.) Rose may have most of the songs, but the movie's best numbers are without Russell: the beguiling soft-shoed "All I Need Is the Girl," performed by chorus boy Paul Wallace (from the original cast); "You Gotta Have a Gimmick," from a hilarious trio of vulgar but goodhearted strippers; and the strip montage, once Natalie Wood emerges as Gypsy Rose Lee. Before that, she's plain, untalented Louise, in the shadow of her talented kid sister (Ann Jillian). Ironically, after Wood makes the transition to Gypsy, her acting becomes awkward and self-conscious, just when she ought to be at her most confident. *Gypsy* was Wood's second musical based on a show directed and choreographed by Jerome Robbins, and it was another hit, but it didn't receive the Oscar love afforded *West Side Story*.

The Unsinkable Molly Brown (1964) – With a real movie-musical director— Charles Walters, of *Easter Parade* (1948) and *Lili* (1953)—and a bona fide movie-musical star—Debbie Reynolds—*Molly Brown* had both Hollywood and Broadway clout in spades. And yet this MGM musical is no better than the adaptations being made by inexperienced directors and underqualified stars. *Molly Brown* is lavish but lumbering, sold in an off-putting, garish style that won't quit. Despite a lively score from *The Music Man*'s Meredith Willson, the show isn't first-rate, yet it deserved better than this draining movie. As the illiterate orphan who hits it rich, Ms. Reynolds somehow got an Oscar nomination, even though she squandered her triple-threat opportunity. Her singing is pushed and unpleasant, her acting strained and phony; it's enough to make Betty Hutton avert her eyes. Where, oh where, did Reynolds mislay her previously undeniable comic skills? Only her hoofing is impressive, the high point being "He's My Friend," in which she, assisted by two chorus boys at a posh party, terrifically executes Peter Gennaro's stamina-testing choreography. From the 1960 stage production (which starred Tammy Grimes), Harve

Presnell plays Reynolds' husband, sometimes seeming a Howard Keel clone in looks and voice. (Though he teaches her to read and write, he's primarily a dumb fool.) *Molly Brown* feels like a mishmash of other (better) properties, including *Annie Get Your Gun, Ruggles of Red Gap, Auntie Mame,* even *Stella Dallas* (with its party to which no one comes). Reynolds and Presnell strike gold in the Colorado wilderness and move to a Denver mansion, but they're social outcasts until they return from Europe with a few crowned heads in tow. There isn't one simple plausible moment, certainly not Reynolds valiantly surviving the Titanic and taking charge of her lifeboat, and especially not the bizarre ending, with Presnell creepily hiding, like Boo Radley, behind an open door. Walters' direction consistently lacks his usual good taste; this is a movie musical committed to shaking you by the shoulders.

My Fair Lady (**1964**) – A quintessential example of the overly reverential museum-piece approach, this long-awaited film of the 1956 classic never comes to life, seemingly terrified of spontaneity. Some pruning might've helped; instead, it appears that every song, verse, and reprise of the masterful Alan Jay Lerner-Frederick Loewe score is intact. *My Fair Lady* won director George Cukor his only Oscar, despite being one of his wobblier efforts. In his lifetime of bringing theater pieces to the screen, this must be his stagiest movie, deadly paced and punishingly long. In its maddening quest to be true to its stage origins, claustrophobia sets in; you're always aware of being on a soundstage, even in the exterior scenes. Who wants to watch Covent Garden wake up inside an obviously airless Warner Brothers complex? And the Ascot sequence looks to be taking place within a 1960s variety special. I don't mean to advocate for the real Covent Garden or the real Ascot, just substitutions with more visual vitality and attractiveness. Presented as if it were under glass, or, at its worst, just about embalmed, *My Fair Lady* managed to win eight Oscars including Best Picture. Oscar winner Rex Harrison repeats his stage role, and he's formidably definitive as sharp-tongued phoneticist Henry Higgins, wisely opting to sing his wordy songs "live" rather than lip-sync. In spite of his piercing inflections and dazzling vocal power, he has no chemistry with Audrey Hepburn's Eliza, the Cockney flower girl he bets he can turn into a lady in six months. Controversially cast in the role that made Julie Andrews a stage star, Hepburn brought the desired box-office prowess but required Marni Nixon's soprano. (Was there really no one else?) It's not a convincing match-up, with Nixon's tones having no credible connection to Hepburn's speaking voice. (Like Rosalind Russell in *Gypsy,* Hepburn does some of her own singing.) Overall, Hepburn's performance was underrated, considered the movie's weak link but often its freshest element. Though forced as the flower girl, she's quite at home as the lady, and has lovely moments of humor and vulnerability sprinkled throughout. Harrison's climactic "I've Grown Accustomed to Her Face" is indeed candid, but the growth of the central relationship has to be taken on faith, an invisible necessity of the plot. Repeating his stage role, Stanley Holloway is raucously wonderful as Hepburn's father, but his scenes tend to bog things down further, making a long movie *longer*. How come no one notices that Eliza's incessant suitor, Freddy (Jeremy Brett), is a stalker? And why doesn't anyone ever wonder about Higgins and Col. Pickering (Wilfrid Hyde-White), two middle-aged confirmed bachelors living together?

The Sound of Music (1965) – Here's the big one, the most adored screen adaptation of a Broadway musical, another Best Picture Oscar winner from *West Side Story*'s Robert Wise. Going the opposite route of *My Fair Lady*, it luxuriates in being outside, making Salzburg itself an essential component. Wise reworked his *West Side Story* opening, hovering high above the location, with Alps replacing New York skyscrapers. This time his use of the real outdoors for musical numbers is true to his gleeful characters, in a way it wasn't for street hoods. Its most treasured open-air moment, novice Julie Andrews' title-tune communion with an Alp, remains an iconically infectious display of pure pleasure. (How could any stage production compete with *that*?) Because the 1959 show is one of Rodgers and Hammerstein's lesser works, the film was able to make smart improvements, rearranging the songs' order and finding inspired ways to stage them. How clever to take an icky song like "The Lonely Goatherd" and make it a marionette performance; how exhilarating to scatter "Do-Re-Mi" all over Salzburg. Unlike most of the era's Broadway-based film musicals, *The Sound of Music* actually feels like a movie, carried by a star you can enjoy without reservations. Andrews may have missed playing *My Fair Lady*'s Eliza onscreen, but thank goodness she was cast as Maria, succeeding Mary Martin (the role's creator). It's hard to overestimate Andrews' enveloping impact, her ingratiating mix of spunk and warmth. Those who label her performance as saccharine forget how funny she can be, how adept she is at physical comedy, and how affecting she is when trying to resist falling in love. It's wishful thinking to believe that she, as the new governess, could make happy the whole *un*happy Von Trapp family—all seven children and their widowed naval-captain father (Christopher Plummer)—

and yet Andrews is a believable life force. Plummer's performance, however, is misjudged; he's too arch and glib, not *really* brooding or intimidating. But Eleanor Parker is just right as the baroness, so chic, so wittily urbane. It was savvy to cut her character's songs, separating her from Maria's world of music-making, which helps to make the captain's choice between them even clearer. *The Sound of Music* has no conflicts that last very long; its power lies in its soothing conviction that everything will work out, that anything can be accomplished by the triple-threatening Julie Andrews.

Camelot (1967) – Julie Andrews and Richard Burton starred in this Lerner-and-Loewe musical in 1960, yet somehow, in 1967, when both stars were among the biggest in movies, the Joshua Logan-directed screen version starred Vanessa Redgrave and Richard Harris. Maybe it was doomed from that moment on. It's certainly one of the ugliest of movie musicals, with hideous color choices, but more damaging is its dearth of wit, charm, humor, and any emotional rewards. Despite flashy editing, Logan's pacing is abysmal. It's one of those mystifying productions that alternates between defiantly fake-looking sets and the natural world. (At least *My Fair Lady* committed to its frustrating artifice.) Even with a few songs deleted, *Camelot* is interminable, attached to three uninteresting leads. As King Arthur, Mr. Harris is consistently self-indulgent and occasionally prissy, acting in a deliberate, declamatory style, and he's so damned slow, stretching his lines while the running time escalates. Redgrave begins charmingly, and she looks sensational in a white hooded cape. Her "Simple Joys of Maidenhood" is enchanting and unpredictable, but her charms quickly wear thin. She has the wrong energy, too low-key and offbeat for an epic musical, with singing that's too light and reedy. It's acceptable for one star to talk-sing, but not both of them! Someone with a real voice should sing these lovely melodies, no? Third lead Franco Nero, as Lancelot, is thankfully dubbed; he's exceedingly attractive but such a stiff. *Camelot* was Warner Brothers' expensive follow-up to their Lerner-and-Loewe blockbuster *My Fair Lady*, but it's a debacle, a tuneful guidebook for how *not* to bring a stage musical to the movies.

Funny Girl (1968) – *Oliver!* was the Best Picture Oscar winner of 1968, a British adaptation of a British stage musical and one of the few good, sane, and entirely unembarrassing musical adaptations of the '60s. On the American front, the big stage-to-screen musical that year was William Wyler's version of the 1964 Jule Styne-Bob Merrill musical *Funny Girl*, a biopic about singer-comedienne Fanny Brice and another Best Picture Oscar nominee. *Funny Girl* was never much of a show, and it isn't much of a movie, but it remains a glorious showcase for Barbra Streisand, its original stage star. Comparable to what Judy Garland achieved in *A Star Is Born,* this is a full-throttle display of a remarkable talent. Solely because of Streisand's Oscar-winning performance— as hilarious and touching as it is vocally astonishing—*Funny Girl* stands as one of the more enduring of '60s musicals derived from the stage. Her joke-armored vulnerability (an irresistible component) helps disguise the fact that *Funny Girl* is pretty old-fashioned, with a script full of clichés: the rags-to-riches arc; the star who finds happiness only onstage; the *Star Is Born*-style marriage; a woman bravely giving up the man she loves. It's also a musical without a second act. After Fanny becomes a star and marries Nicky (Omar Sharif), the plot sputters, stagnating in weepy soap opera, though the script works overtime at keeping Fanny lovable, retaining her sweet innocence after years of stardom. Sharif, as an elegant gambler, is a blank playing a blank, a handsome cipher. But Kay Medford, repeating her stage role as Fanny's deadpan, saloon-owning mother, is excellent, with good lines and even better delivery. As for the benefits of having a great dramatic director, the influence of Mr. Wyler is scarce, though the movie is certainly a classy affair, and it does offer his usual restraint. Streisand's "Don't Rain on My Parade" is the most cinematic sequence, traveling by train, car, and boat, while her scorching rendition of "My Man," Brice's signature song (which wasn't used in the show), provides the emotionally bare finale. *Funny Girl* is a conventional musical biopic, not so different from a standard '30s or '40s variation, but that's easy to forget any time Streisand is center stage.

Finian's Rainbow (1968) – Upholding the trend of non-musical directors helming musical transfers, a young Francis Ford Coppola was assigned this challenging 1947 Burton Lane-E.Y. Harburg musical, which also turned out to be a Fred Astaire movie! It's not the disaster reasonably expected, but it's typically overlong and misshapen (thanks to too much going on). Here's a case of a first-rate score serving a less than first-rate "book," with Irish immigrants Astaire and daughter Petula Clark arriving in Rainbow Valley (near Fort Knox). Astaire has a crock of gold that he stole from a leprechaun (Tommy Steele) who wants it back. Coppola gets off to a good start, with spectacular national scenery as our father-daughter duo roams the U.S.A., accompanied by Ms. Clark's voiceover vocal of "Look to the Rainbow." But the movie soon falls into stylistic clashes: actual rolling hills *and* obvious soundstage exteriors; realistic plotting uncomfortably alongside fantasy elements; too many intersecting (but not intersecting *enough*) storylines, including a rather tricky subplot about a racist senator (Keenan Wynn) who turns black. Coppola employs quick cuts within numbers; his work is showy yet unsure, overcompensating for obvious unease in the genre. The numbers are hampered by a wearying sameness of setting and staging, though "Something Sort of Grandish," between Ms. Clark and Mr. Steele, set among white sheets and a clothesline, is a standout. But what could anyone do with the laughable device of the mute girl who communicates solely through dance? As for Astaire, he does a pleasing jig with Ms. Clark, but, pushing seventy, and in his final film-musical role, his dancing is limited. (Who wants to be the one to say that the incomparable Astaire is great "for his age"?) He uses a brogue and gives it his all, but he's too mild and gentle in a role that demands a shameless old comedian. Ms. Clark is fresh and unforced, though no Julie Andrews in terms of screen presence, and Steele, an energized performer, is not the scene-stealing delight he ought to be. At one point, he spouts lyrics from "Night and Day" to Astaire, the man who introduced the song on Broadway in *Gay Divorce* in 1932!

Sweet Charity (1969) – Adapted from the 1966 Cy Coleman-Dorothy Fields-Neil Simon musical of Federico Fellini's 1957 masterwork *Nights of Cabiria* (a foreign-film Oscar winner), *Sweet Charity* retained its director-choreographer, Bob Fosse, making his debut as a movie director. Like Coppola, Fosse tends to overdo, utilizing every cinematic trick in the book. He certainly shakes things up, even if his invention often feels like gimmickry. (With such boundless enthusiasm, Fosse appears to be readying himself, consciously or not, to direct his staggeringly brilliant 1972 *Cabaret*.) Assuming Gwen Verdon's stage role, Shirley MacLaine is properly effective as the optimistic Charity, a NYC dance-hall hostess. But perhaps she's too well cast, having already played her share of doormats, by now almost imitating herself. The MacLaine of *Some Came Running* (1958) would have been perfect, more unprotected; the 1969 MacLaine seems too knowing, too shielded by a superstar's armor. She's reunited with Fosse from *The Pajama Game* (1954), the show in which she, as an understudy, was discovered by Hollywood. John McMartin, from *Charity*'s Broadway cast, is the insurance man who wants to marry MacLaine, okay with her past, until he isn't. (They evoke Blanche and Mitch from *A Streetcar Named Desire,* ready for happiness if he can just "forgive" her.) And, as MacLaine's co-workers, Chita Rivera and Paula Kelly join her in cutting loose for "There's Gotta Be Something Better Than This," a sizzling rooftop trio. The MacLaine-led "I'm a Brass Band" is another of several showstoppers, but the film is much too long and overproduced for its essentially small story. *Sweet Charity* is finally a masochistic musical with a condescending look at "tramps," but you can't knock its fabulous score and ingenious choreography (dig that "Frug"). And it surely glistens when compared with two other 1969 musical adaptations, both atrocities: Joshua Logan's *Paint Your Wagon* and Gene Kelly's *Hello, Dolly!* Though *Cabaret* restored faith in the form's potential, and *Grease* (1978) provided a wildly popular mediocrity, *Man of La Mancha* (1972) and *Mame* (1974) were new lows, doing their part to secure the demise of Broadway-to-Hollywood transfers for the remainder of the century. Then, in 2002, *Chicago* quite unexpectedly revived the genre, winning its own Best Picture Oscar, the fifth for a musical with a Broadway lineage.

Fade to Color: The Glorious Demise of Black and White (1962-1967)

Even after the technical advance of three-strip Technicolor in feature films, which arrived with *Becky Sharp* (1935), black and white remained the preferred choice for "serious" movies. The saturated hues of Technicolor seemed intended for more fanciful projects, primarily the escapist worlds of historical adventure and lavish musicals, *not* for adult-minded dramas or any movie aiming for what might be called realism. Though black and white remained the domain of low-budget movies, it was also, in the hands of great filmmakers, the palette for most of the best movies of the Golden Age, even after color became an available option. Think of Orson Welles' *Citizen Kane* (1941) and *The Magnificent Ambersons* (1942), or Alfred Hitchcock's *Shadow of a Doubt* (1943) and *Notorious* (1946). How about *The Maltese Falcon* (1941), *Casablanca* (1942), *Laura* (1944), *Double Indemnity* (1944), *The Best Years of Our Lives* (1946), and *The Treasure of the Sierra Madre* (1948)? Care to imagine any of them in color?

In the late 1930s, producer David O. Selznick was unusual in taking color rather seriously, not only when he capped the decade with his state-of-the-art *Gone With the Wind,* but even earlier with his voluptuously colorful romantic melodrama *The Garden of Allah* (1936), soon followed by unexpected color projects: his Hollywood tearjerker, *A Star Is Born* (1937), and his screwball comedy, *Nothing Sacred* (1937). A seemingly more sensible and appropriate use of Technicolor occurred over at Warner Brothers when they mounted *The Adventures of Robin Hood* (1938) in all its fairy-tale splendor, still a candidate for the most rapturously beautiful use of Technicolor *ever*. MGM's *The Wizard of Oz* (1939) was certainly no slouch, but, despite both films' glories, they inhabited storybook worlds, perhaps further proving that grown-up movies belonged in black and white. The actual world may exist in color, but black-and-white movies *seemed* more realistic, with Technicolor's heightened beauty applying an otherworldly sheen to nature. *Gone With the Wind* gave color a legitimacy, securing it as the logical realm of the historical epic, but it didn't lead to many Technicolor prestige projects. Though embraced by the public, color remained black and white's flashy (and usually frivolous) younger sibling.

In the 1940s, color continued to provide the rainbow for escapist fare, the more fantastic the better. Technicolor was where you could find Maureen O'Hara as exotic (yet redheaded) princesses, Maria Montez as good-and-evil twins, and Alice Faye and Betty Grable inhabiting Rio, Havana, Miami, Frisco, and Coney Island. It was where Tyrone Power was a swashbuckler, Danny Kaye cavorted with Virginia Mayo, and Gene Kelly danced with a mouse and played with musketeers. Occasionally, it was the canvas upon which big-budget westerns sprawled. Most major stars of the 1930s and early '40s never (or rarely) got anywhere near Technicolor because they didn't appear in *those* kinds of movies. The best example of a serious color drama of the '40s is *For Whom the Bell Tolls* (1943), like *Gone With the Wind* another sweeping war-torn romantic spectacle. Another (if lesser) Technicolor dramatic success, *Blossoms in the Dust* (1941) dealt with the subject of illegitimacy and gave Greer Garson (of the flaming red hair) her one big color vehicle during her peak years. It was as if MGM were saying, "Okay, remember what she looks like in color because she's going right back to black and white where you'll have to remind yourself just how red her hair really is." While there were disappointing attempts at prestigious Technicolor dramas, including *Wilson* (1944), *An American Romance* (1944), and *Joan of Arc* (1948), color found warm favor in a few outstanding family pictures at MGM: *Meet Me in St. Louis* (1944), *National Velvet* (1944), and *The Yearling* (1946). There were some successful color surprises, too, like the pulpy melodrama *Leave Her to Heaven* (1945) and the post-war comedy *Apartment for Peggy* (1948). Color was branching out in all directions.

Between *Gone With the Wind* in 1939 and *An American in Paris* in 1951, not a single Academy Award-winning Best Picture was in color, and it wasn't until 1956 that all five nominees were in color (which didn't happen again until 1967). Color steadily gained respect in the 1950s, with Technicolor not quite as Crayola-looking as it had been, finding rich new subtleties in major achievements such as *The African Queen* (1951), *The Searchers* (1956), *Vertigo* (1958), and *The Nun's Story* (1959). Great films, great color, with not one of them looking like a garish Grable musical. Then consider just a few of the '50s classics made in black and white, namely *Sunset Blvd.* (1950), *On the Waterfront* (1954), *The Night of the Hunter* (1955), and *Some Like It Hot* (1959). Here was a heyday of virtual equality between color and black and white, when either was perfectly viable, depending on a director's (or a studio's) preference. But it wouldn't be too long before one of these options was off the table.

Black and white started losing ground as color continued its trend toward looking more life-like. Didn't the color in *Elmer Gantry* (1960) or *Splendor in the Grass* (1961) look more real, less lusciously vibrant, than the color in

Cover Girl (1944) or *King Solomon's Mines* (1950)? Certainly. Had "Glorious Technicolor" simply been an adolescent phase of extravagant wonderment? Was it now time for color to grow up and be as mature as black and white? Television had, in a way, prolonged black and white's reign, influencing movies when black-and-white kitchen-sink teleplays were successfully adapted for the screen, including *Marty* (1955) and *Days of Wine and Roses* (1962), all in the name of so-called greater realism. But it would also seem that television was the final nail in the coffin of black and white's dramatic dominance. By the mid-to-late '60s, all the black-and-white television series were making the transition to color, knowing full well that Americans were increasingly buying color sets, implicitly demanding color programming. With *free* color entertainment at home, how many people were going to go out and spend money to see something in black and white?

Black-and-white movies were essentially finished in 1967, but the first two-thirds of the decade were a glorious last stand, giving us the following notable black-and-white works: *The Apartment* (1960), *Psycho* (1960), *The Hustler* (1961), *The Manchurian Candidate* (1962), *To Kill a Mockingbird* (1962), *Hud* (1963), *Dr. Strangelove* (1964), *The Americanization of Emily* (1964), *The Spy Who Came in from the Cold* (1965), and *Who's Afraid of Virginia Woolf?* (1966), which was the final film to win an Oscar specifically for black-and-white cinematography. (By the next year, there was no need for such a category.) Here are ten more worthy farewells to a visual art thereafter used only sparingly, by directors aiming for a certain mood or evocation of a period. Black and white already seemed long-gone—a daring novelty and a financial risk—when Peter Bogdanovich resurrected it for *The Last Picture Show* (1971), where it worked beautifully, as it later did in Woody Allen's *Manhattan* (1979), Steven Spielberg's *Schindler's List* (1993), and George Clooney's *Good Night, and Good Luck* (2005), among other examples, of which I wish there were many more.

Seven Days in May (1964): Burt Lancaster and Kirk Douglas

Lolita (1962) – The film's tag line—"How did they ever make a movie of *Lolita*?"—suggests how much Vladimir Nabokov's novel was ahead of its time. The same is true of this superlative screen version, which isn't just bold and adult but able to balance comedy, tragedy, and satire, with director Stanley Kubrick making it all feel cohesive and inevitable. James Mason is all one could hope for as Humbert Humbert, an Englishman in America, hired as a college lecturer in French Literature. He's wryly funny, subtle, and devious, marrying widow Shelley Winters while lusting after her thoughtless, bratty teen daughter (Sue Lyon, in the title role). After making Lyon his conquest, Mason becomes miserable and possessive, consumed with the terror of losing her. He's not a nice guy, yet his need is sympathetic, his desperation compelling, and he's finally heartbreaking. Mason gives a bravely bare, emotionally unshackled performance, possibly his greatest. This may be Winters' finest hour, too; she's wonderfully vulgar and tacky yet also startlingly poignant. There's also the bonus of an ingenious Peter Sellers as Mason's nemesis, a dazzling question mark who appears in a series of guises intended to manipulate Mason. (Sellers even mentions *Spartacus,* Kubrick's previous film.) Few movies mix hilarity, dark subject matter, and the inexplicable desires of the heart as piercingly as *Lolita*. The first half is one of the wittier and more sophisticated comedies of manners, while the second half squirms in pain and paranoia, a transition that proves remarkably moving. *Lolita* is also enhanced by Bob Harris' lushly aching "love theme," which at first seems a spoof of Hollywood soundtracks but soon encompasses all the turmoil in Mason's yearnings. With Kubrick so confidently in control, and three stars surpassing themselves, *Lolita* is a black-and-white masterpiece, superbly photographed by Oswald Morris who perfectly etched all the grays in which these characters lurk.

Birdman of Alcatraz (1962) – In the same year he made his great (also black-and-white) thriller *The Manchurian Candidate,* John Frankenheimer directed this biopic about Robert Stroud (Burt Lancaster, in the title role). It's an impressive movie, enriched by Burnett Guffey's Oscar-nominated black-and-white photography, with Lancaster's subdued (quiet yet full) performance an inspired contrast with his recent Oscar-winning bravado in *Elmer Gantry* (1960). An unusually thoughtful, grounded piece of acting, Lancaster's performance begins in a familiar mode, streaked with anger and a flair for violence. He's sent up for murder and then kills a guard. He'll spend the next fifty-three years in prison, in solitary most of his life, with the bulk of the film set not at Alcatraz but at Leavenworth (Kansas). It should be called *Birdman of Leavenworth,* which admittedly doesn't have the same zing as *Alcatraz.* (The real Stroud died in 1963.) The strongest section is its middle, centering on Stroud's birdman years, which start with the baby sparrow he finds in the exercise yard, nested in a fallen branch. Birds humanize him, make him gentle, give him purpose. He trains them, makes cages for them, kills insects to feed them, even cares for their babies. He'll create an aviary, publish articles, and sell his remedies. By the time he writes a book on bird diseases, he's become a self-taught authority. Of course, the power of the story derives from the contrast between his past and his present, the convicted murderer's transition into a peaceful life-saving giant. The movie is commendably low-key, but it's simply too long. Despite a fine cast to support Lancaster (mother Thelma Ritter, wife Betty Field, fellow inmate Telly Savalas, friendly guard Neville Brand, no-nonsense warden Karl Malden), the movie dampens any time Lancaster is without his birds, instantly losing its footing, its core, its powerful simplicity. The birds are his most essential co-stars, with Lancaster's concentrated intensity tenderly focused on their fragile needs.

Lilies of the Field **(1963)** – Most famous as the movie that nabbed an Oscar for Sidney Poitier, this is nice, unpretentious whimsy anchored by two performances, not just Poitier's engaging one as a drifter but also Lilia Skala's as a formidable nun. Because the movie is slight and agreeable, it feels like an update of a '40s religious comedy such as *Come to the Stable* (1949), a Southwestern fairy tale selling feel-good virtues. When Poitier's car needs water, he stops at a farmhouse where five escaped East German nuns happen to be living. Mother Superior (Skala) believes he is heaven-sent (and the movie appears to prove her right). She wants him to build a chapel for them. For free! It's implausible that he finds it so difficult to tear himself away, but that's part of the fun. While building the chapel, he gets paying work elsewhere, operating heavy machinery. Speaking of bulldozers, Skala is a stern, proud presence, a potent mix of firmness and abundant faith, always certain that God will somehow provide. She is grandly entertaining as she bosses Poitier around; they are pleasing comic sparring partners. The movie works rather well when focused on their relationship, including the amusing English lessons he gives the nuns, but it loses steam when too many other characters join the plot. Despite his thinly conceived role, Poitier has never seemed so relaxed onscreen. It's more of a charismatic star turn than a brilliant characterization, but it is enormously satisfying to watch his gains in self-esteem as he strives to build the chapel and accomplish something great. My favorite Poitier moment is his anticipatory ecstasy as he orders a gigantic breakfast at a trading-post counter, literally growling "melted butter" and "maple syrup." (That's about as lusty as this picture ever gets.) The excellent Oscar-nominated black and white is the work of Ernest Haller (who shot *Gone With the Wind*). Cleanly directed by Ralph Nelson, *Lilies* mostly keeps its sentimentality in check, but, instead of THE END, we get an AMEN.

***Love with the Proper Stranger* (1963)** – An uneven but ingratiating hybrid of stark drama and sitcom, this love story is from producer Alan J. Pakula and director Robert Mulligan, the team who had recently made *To Kill a Mockingbird*. It takes the risk of injecting the subject of abortion into a big-star vehicle but then devolves into something safe and comfy, becoming an overcompensating apology for its daring, unconventional first half. It begins with a great hook: a Macy's employee (Natalie Wood) tracks down an underemployed musician (Steve McQueen) to tell him that their one-night-stand has left her pregnant. Does he know a good abortion doctor? One of the best sections involves the time they spend together raising the money for this back-alley procedure, including the waiting for the appointment. They start to connect, if awkwardly, their cynical veneers beginning to fade. The scene with the abortionists is unsettlingly powerful, leading to a deepening in the Wood-McQueen relationship. Smothered by an overprotective Italian family, Wood makes the girl's actions believable, a heartfelt (and stop-start) striving for independence. And McQueen, also playing Italian-American, and seeming a bit Sinatra-esque, has an appealing comic energy. You can admire the mixing of tones but also feel betrayed by the final third, a soothing and formulaic rom-com featuring playing-hard-to-get tactics. After raising real grown-up problems, Arnold Schulman's screenplay succumbs to the forces of an irresistible Hollywood ending, which is partially why so many people love this admittedly winning movie. Another virtue/flaw is the film's Italian-American flavor, which is warmly affectionate but rather broadly served. The textured Oscar-nominated black and white (of cinematographer Milton Krasner) and the gritty NYC locations give the film an ordinary-people ambiance, in the *Marty* tradition, though who could ever think of Wood or McQueen as *regular*? Face it: they are an impossibly attractive couple with a sizzling chemistry. And Mr. Mulligan, their clearly enamored director, next made *Baby the Rain Must Fall* (1965) with McQueen and *Inside Daisy Clover* (1965) with Wood.

Seven Days in May (1964) – Not through with Cold War paranoia after making *The Manchurian Candidate* (1962), John Frankenheimer came back for more. It may not be as good as his former film, but *Seven Days in May* is nonetheless a riveting and concise drama with a bristling Rod Serling script (adapted from a novel). Frankenheimer's work is extremely precise, with impeccable editing and gorgeously framed compositions shot by Ellsworth Fredricks in deep-focus black and white. President Fredric March has divided the country with regard to his nuclear disarmament treaty with the Russians. Burt Lancaster is the Chairman of the Joint Chiefs of Staff (and a four-star general), a right-winger plotting a military takeover of the government, already having built a secret army base in El Paso. Kirk Douglas, as a colonel who works for Lancaster, figures it all out and goes to March. As actors, Lancaster and Douglas complement each other, with Lancaster contained but electric as a megalomaniac villain, while Douglas sustains an intelligent reserve. Best of all is March, who continued to get better and better the older he got. Fully dimensional as a man of morals and integrity, he carries the weight of the presidency; he's so caring, so damned smart, altogether extraordinary. A typically bruised Ava Gardner is lovely and touching as Lancaster's ex-mistress (though her scenes are with Douglas). And a likable (but hammy) Oscar-nominated Edmond O'Brien plays a boozy Georgia senator. *Seven Days in May* is an all-around winner, delivering thought-provoking themes as well as crackerjack suspense.

The Best Man (1964) – Based on Gore Vidal's 1960 Broadway play, it's a still-relevant political tract with pungent dialogue, solid structure, and an all-star cast. Well-made by director Franklin J. Schaffner and graced with vivid black-and-white imagery from cinematographer Haskell Wexler, *The Best Man* takes place at a 1964 presidential convention in LA. With no mention of either Democrat or Republican, the party remains unnamed. But how could liberal intellectual atheist Henry Fonda and religious commie-hating conservative Cliff Robertson be in the same party? They're nothing alike: Fonda is rich, Robertson grew up poor; Fonda is a womanizer, Robertson isn't; Fonda's marriage to Margaret Leighton is hanging by a thread, while Robertson and wife Edie Adams are hot for each other. But is either one of them suited to be a president? Though a Secretary of State, Fonda is an indecisive man, plus he had a secret nervous breakdown. Robertson is a Mafia-fighting U.S. senator who may have a gay past. Both men seek the endorsement of ex-president Lee Tracy (repeating his stage role), who's dying of cancer. Tracy, the great 1930s speed-talking wisecracker, is sensational here in a dramatic vein, a wily and charismatic old codger, in pain but still a fighter. He was Oscar-nominated for this movie, his first screen appearance since 1947. In addition to Tracy, the cast features other old-timers such as Richard Arlen, Gene Raymond, and Ann Sothern. The steely performance from Cliff Robertson is perhaps the best of his career, a scary, unblinking turn as a ruthless political tiger. Fonda, of course, is impeccably natural, ideally cast as a brainy, measured fellow. Straightforward in its approach, *The Best Man* doesn't seem to have aged, with Vidal nailing our political climate for the last fifty years and counting.

***Hush...Hush, Sweet Charlotte* (1964)** – Obviously it's a stab at repeating the success of *What Ever Happened to Baby Jane?* (1962), but this time the decay is of a Southern, rather than Hollywood, variety. The tone, however, remains Gothic. (Both films were based on stories by Henry Farrell.) As in *Baby Jane,* Bette Davis has ruined her life over what she *thinks* happened in the long-ago past, with this film also copying *Baby Jane*'s violent extended-flashback prologue (this one set in 1927 but looking a lot like 1964). *Baby Jane*'s director, Robert Aldrich, is back, and so is actor Victor Buono, now as Davis' father. It's not as good as *Baby Jane*, which is far from great, but it's another entertaining movie with an intriguing mystery plot and some juicy theatrics, a swell showcase for celebrated veterans. However, it's much too long and it doesn't always play fair. Wealthy Davis lives in a Louisiana mansion that's going to be razed to accommodate a bridge, and yet she refuses to leave. Surprisingly, Davis is the picture's weakest link, outacted by a trio of great ladies: Olivia de Havilland (in the Joan Crawford role), Davis' seemingly sweet cousin, a deliciously nasty twist on Melanie Hamilton; Agnes Moorehead, Davis' grouchy, mumbling, but loyal servant, a scene-stealing comic hoot of a characterization; and Mary Astor, in her final role, in two smartly restrained scenes as an old widow. Davis is effective only when quiet, otherwise detached from the role's potential to move us, shrieking her big scenes, overdoing her Southern accent, utterly undone by the role's incessant victimization. (De Havilland slaps her six times!) As a doctor, Joseph Cotten does his share of scenery-chewing, too. I realize that the Oscar-nominated Moorehead is also over the top, but she's a wonderfully outrageous white-trash delight with her frightful hair, heavy drawl, and those high-pitched line readings. It's called playing it to the hilt, while Davis just strains herself. The movie benefits enormously from Joseph Biroc's moody Oscar-nominated black-and-white photography, as well as the overall rotting-splendor ambiance. Despite its plot holes, *Hush…Hush* revels in its company of black-and-white stars still gloriously black and white.

36 Hours (1964) – This highly absorbing WWII picture is actually closer to the comic-book movies made during the war than it is to the more realistic WWII movies made in the ensuing decades. It's a D-Day fantasia, gleefully outlandish but intensely suspenseful. Based on a Roald Dahl story, it was written and directed by George Seaton, who neatly balances an elaborate plot with an atmospheric realism, assisted by three top stars: James Garner, Eva Marie Saint, and Rod Taylor. (After *The Americanization of Emily,* this was Garner's second D-Day movie of 1964.) On May 31, 1944, a U.S. major (Garner) goes to Lisbon to find out if the Germans know the plan for D-Day. He's drugged and sent to Germany where, still unconscious, his hair is grayed and his vision weakened, an attempt to age him six years. When he soon wakes, he's told it's 1950 and that he's convalescing in Occupied Germany after the Allied victory. It's an extravagant Nazi ruse to get Garner to reveal the details of the upcoming invasion, casually trying to convince him that D-Day is *so* six years ago. The scheme is crazily intricate and farfetched, but it leads to nail-biting fun. Its play-acted construct, in which scores of people are employed to convince one man of an unreal reality, may remind you of *The Truman Show* (1998). Here, Nazis play Americans on a military hospital "set," a fantastically complex operation in an isolated location. Taylor is Garner's doctor; Saint is his nurse. They have thirty-six hours to extract the information. Taylor is a good guy on the wrong side, hoping to use his Garner-related experiments to help actual amnesia and battle-fatigue victims. Will Garner reveal the D-Day details, or will he figure out what's going on, or both? The movie sets up an intellectual battle between two sharp, evenly matched men. And it works as well as it does because Garner and Taylor are unusually intelligent and personable actors with natural tendencies for subtlety, which goes a long way in making this clever humdinger of a plot almost plausible. This is one of the last of the big black-and-white movies, with cinematographer Philip H. Lathrop's work giving the film both wartime veracity and kinetic thrills, including a pulse-racing climactic chase. *36 Hours* is a thriller of mind *and* body, both a brain twister and a physical workout.

Bunny Lake Is Missing (1965) – Otto Preminger, after years of nudging Hollywood toward more controversial fare with films such as *The Man with the Golden Arm* (1955) and *Anatomy of a Murder* (1959), here returned to where he started, in stylish mysteries (like *Laura* and *Fallen Angel*), updating his noir-ish credentials for the mid-'60s. The gripping set-up has American journalist Keir Dullea and his "unwed mother" sister, Carol Lynley, setting up home in swinging London. Lynley's four-year-old daughter Bunny has gone missing from her first day of school, and, adding to the horror, no one can recall having seen the child. Dullea and Lynley can't seem to prove Bunny's existence, leaving everyone (including us) to wonder if there really is a Bunny. Laurence Olivier is brilliant as the inspector, underplaying masterfully yet getting the most out of every line. It's a mesmerizingly economical performance, of a caliber that rewards the utmost scrutiny. Unfortunately, the film resorts to some cheap psychology, overblown theatrics, and a number of red herrings. But there's also some fascinating intimations of incest regarding the siblings (who seem to be living as a couple), plus the paranoiac unease of foreigners living abroad. And the climax, though drawn-out and not especially credible, surely delivers some good scare effects. A gorgeous score by Paul Glass is another key asset. The cast features some great British reliables, such as the crisply efficient Anna Massey, eccentrically amusing Martita Hunt, and an outrageous Noel Coward who has a high old time playing against type as a kinky lech. The limpest link is Lynley, with her flat voice and amateur technique. As for Preminger, he excels visually, amplifying the considerable tension with long takes, assisted by Denys Coop's sensual wide-screen camera moves. With Hitchcock having left black and white behind after *Psycho* (1960), *Bunny Lake* is one of the last of the luxuriously dark and shadowy Grade-A mystery-thrillers.

***In Cold Blood* (1967)** – Call it the final major American film of the black-and-white era. Hereafter, filmmakers predominantly opted for color, denying moviegoers a form of cinematic expression that had captivated them for many decades. (Black and white was not outdated, nor was it inferior to color, but, culturally speaking, it was *over*.) Based on Truman Capote's non-fiction account of a Kansas family's brutal murder in 1959, *In Cold Blood* is one of writer-director Richard Brooks' most accomplished works, a searing and disturbing drama. With its documentary style, small-name cast, and actual locations, its immersion into its story feels authentic. The first half hour sets up the events with exceeding care, as ex-prison mates Scott Wilson and Robert Blake plot the robbery, while the Clutter family goes about its business, unaware it's their final day. When the duo arrives at the Clutter home, the movie cuts to the morning after and the discovery of the deaths; we don't see the murders till the very end. Blake is both the saner and crazier of the two, definitely smarter but more prone to snapping. He and Wilson are indeed well cast as sociopathic dreamers. They have a *Midnight Cowboy* kind of partnership, practically seeming to be auditioning for the Voight/Hoffman roles of 1969. (At one point, Blake says, "Remember Bogart in *Treasure of Sierra Madre?*" Blake was the kid in that!) The film's language is awfully colorful for 1967 but would soon be the typical jargon of the New Hollywood. *In Cold Blood* is a chilling, tightly controlled work, a top film of its innovative year, joining *Bonnie and Clyde* and *The Graduate* among the more striking achievements of '67. It's probing and it's provocative, exploring violence and its formative seeds, but, though forward-looking in style and content, it's the last gasp of the golden age of black and white, thanks to the tactile magnificence of Conrad Hall's haunting Oscar-nominated cinematography.

Side Effects Include Bloating: The Mad, Mad, Chitty, Chitty Productions (1963-1970)

Competition from television was never going away, and it was going to take more than Technicolor, CinemaScope, and stereophonic sound to keep ticket buyers returning to movie theaters, especially as the audience was becoming ever more acclimated to the joys of being entertained in one's own living room. Spectacles had long been part of the American movie landscape going back as far as D.W. Griffith's *The Birth of a Nation* (1915) and *Intolerance* (1916), but television prompted an era in which blockbuster productions seemed more prevalent than ever, offering extended running times as well as all-around extravagance. Whatever your reaction to *The Robe* (1953) or *War and Peace* (1956), you couldn't say you hadn't gotten your money's worth, or that you hadn't really seen something! Producer Mike Todd's *Around the World in Eighty Days* (1956), filmed in Todd-AO, the latest advancement in wide-screen splendor (upping the ante on plain-old CinemaScope), was not only a phenomenal box-office success but it convinced Academy voters that it was enough of a singular affair to warrant a Best Picture Oscar, as if big-deal showmanship equaled wondrous achievement. Memorably goosed with non-stop star cameos, *Around the World* is a perfectly agreeable venture, but it's lopsided by a glaring unevenness and is ultimately as mediocre as it is whimsical, stranding director Michael Anderson as a mere functionary within Todd's amusing folly. With the public unable to resist the film's aura of being a one-of-a-kind entertainment, *Around the World* solidified Hollywood's commitment to making a certain kind of no-expense-spared "event" fare, the kind that could in no way be found at home.

Everyone could expect that Cecil B. DeMille's *The Ten Commandments* (1956), William Wyler's *Ben-Hur* (1959), and Stanley Kubrick's *Spartacus* (1960) would be scaled on colossal terms and make moviegoers deliriously happy, including feeling ennobled by history and/or religion (helped along by varying amounts of sex and violence). David Lean's *Lawrence of Arabia* (1962), perhaps the most pictorially brilliant epic of them all, was a more dramatically challenging (or, rather, dramatically cryptic) work, but it shared with the aforementioned titles a visual grandeur, a surging score, dynamic relationships, all churning with historical heft. But as the 1960s wore on, a curious circumstance developed, with an increasing number of films inexplicably given an epic stature entirely unrelated to their material. *Pepe* (1960), complete with Cantinflas from *Around the World in Eighty Days*, took the former film's star-cameo template and ran amok, inflating a silly movie-business comedy into witless interminability, looking like a shapeless rough cut desperately in search of an editor. *The Alamo* (1960), starring and directed by John Wayne, might have lived up to its epic-worthy subject (and running time of 200 minutes) if it had included a single penetrating scene, instead consisting of flabby filler waiting for a climactic battle lasting only nine minutes! Too often "epic" connoted excessive length and cost, regardless of content, with an awful lot of fancy packaging disguising dispiritingly puny objects. If a movie was *sold* as an event, wouldn't the public be convinced that they had to see it? It was the old "If you see only one movie this year, make it…" Adding to the misery was Hollywood's insatiable need to try to outdo its own hits, usually without the essential ingredients which had accounted for those initial successes, spending all kinds of money to top *Mary Poppins* or *Doctor Zhivago*.

Did audiences feel better about themselves—more culturally sophisticated, perhaps—whenever the next big dumb spectacle featured an overture and an intermission? These frills were intended to give a patina of class and prestige, particularly when a costly effort was in no other way classy *or* prestigious. Many would probably cite *Mutiny on the Bounty* (1962), a much-maligned remake of a 1935 Best Picture Oscar winner, as a quintessential example of how far astray a '60s epic could be led (including being 45 minutes longer than the previous version), and yet I feel it is in many ways superior to its predecessor, including its more multi-dimensional leads. Despite its ample merits, *Mutiny* became a benchmark of uncontrolled Hollywood profligacy, including a misbehaving star (Marlon Brando). But it was immediately outshone by the uncontested poster child of '60s overindulgence: Joseph L. Mankiewicz's *Cleopatra* (1963), a movie inadvertently designed to make you miss Cecil B. DeMille (who never would have made anything so dull). *Cleopatra* sold lots of tickets, driven by its real-life romantic scandal—the love affair between Elizabeth Taylor and Richard Burton—but, like *Mutiny*, it finally cost too much to be feasibly profitable. If you assumed that *Cleopatra* put an end to the era's reckless overspending, you'd be wrong. The remainder of the decade is filled with gambles that didn't pay off, including a number of those Broadway-musical adaptations previously addressed, notably *Paint Your Wagon* and *Hello, Dolly!* (both from 1969). Some box-office successes, such as *The Blue Max* and *Grand Prix* (both from 1966), were nearly as punishingly long (and just as enervating) as *Cleopatra,* and served as proof that, by the later '60s, the mega-productions were becoming ever more stultifying and lifeless, lumbering like dinosaurs nearing extinction. As these so-called bloaters gorged on lavish settings, countless locations, and cumbersome screenplays, they increasingly left audiences without anything or anyone to care about, as hollow as balloons yet weighing far too much to take flight.

The movies featured here share a type of bloating that is out of proportion with the stories they were trying to tell, mostly unable to justify their epic approach and smothering production values. Such bloating could affect any genre, with an assortment of projects falling prey to the notion that "bigger" automatically meant better, that the nth degree was the desired degree. Throwing dollars at something would increase the odds of *more* dollars being flung in return, right? The following movies, not entirely without their charms, may have left you too exhausted to get out of your seat, but that was okay: most bloaters provided "exit music" to help with your transition back to the land of the living.

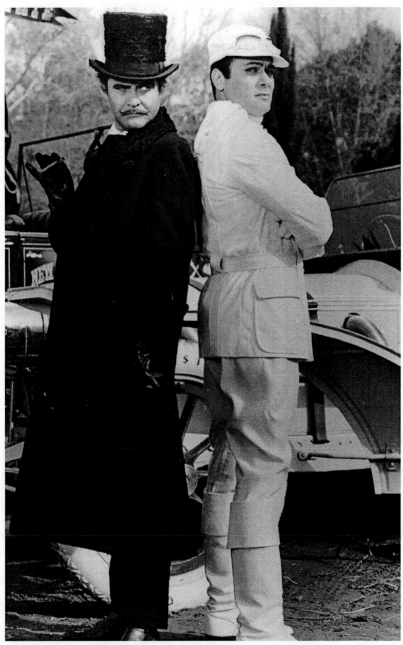

The Great Race (1965): Jack Lemmon vs. Tony Curtis

How the West Was Won **(1963)** – Released a few months before *Cleopatra,* the title says it all. It wasn't just going to be a big western; it was going to be the western to end all westerns. Shot in the rarely used Cinerama—the last word in wide-screen enveloping—it employed no less than three A-list western directors: George Marshall (*Destry Rides Again*), Henry Hathaway (*Rawhide*), and, of course, John Ford. You have to hand it to them for creating a seamless piece of work: all its dramatic scenes, regardless of who directed them, are equally conventional and forgettable. Here's an epic with everything except content, unaccountably garnering an Oscar for its screenplay—its undeniably worst component. Following the *Around the World* model, *everyone* is in it! Yet it still manages to be a generic yawn. Its popularity and Best Picture Oscar nomination can only be attributed to two things: the number of big stars wafting through and the width of its image (especially during a buffalo stampede, the one impressive sequence). There's no narrative drive, just trivial plot threads putting too much emphasis, considering the title, on bland romances. How depressing to watch all that money and star power misused on something so emotionally barren. Debbie Reynolds is asked to carry the first half, and George Peppard (as her nephew) is meant to haul the rest. Reynolds' musical numbers don't help, especially "Raise a Ruckus Tonight," her apparent audition to play Molly Brown. Gregory Peck does offer some amusement as an opportunistic gambler (who marries Reynolds), while Carroll Baker (as Reynolds' sister) uncomfortably chases an old-looking James Stewart, which leads to Peppard, their son. Richard Widmark and Eli Wallach give drearily familiar performances as bad guys, and, hey, there's John Wayne as Sherman, Harry Morgan as Grant, and a silent Raymond Massey as Lincoln! None other than Spencer Tracy was called upon to narrate, unfortunately beginning with something about wandering mountain men "in search of beaver."

It's a Mad, Mad, Mad, Mad World **(1963)** – If *How the West Was Won* was scaled to be the culmination of an entire genre, then this comedy was intended to be nothing less than the funniest movie ever made. Oddly, at the helm was message-movie director Stanley Kramer, recently of *Judgment at Nuremburg* (1961), a man who had never directed a comedy and was apparently unfamiliar with the concept of "less is more." The end result is an often nitwit farce more frantic than hilarious, just as much about stunt people as it is about comedians. For a movie that's overlong by about an hour, it was certainly mad to include an overture and an intermission, particularly in something seemingly aimed at kids (and childlike adults). The cast is an all-star assemblage of comedy names, each of them wildly overqualified for what they're asked to do. The funniest aspect may be the now-piddling amount of money that the characters are greedily chasing: $350,000, hidden beneath a big "W," the details revealed in the dying words of car-crash victim Jimmy Durante. Top-billed Spencer Tracy (Kramer's favorite actor) is the police captain following the money, which means he's tracking the four cars of treasure hunters, the witnesses to Durante's demise: second-honeymooners Sid Caesar and Edie Adams; trucker Jonathan Winters; pals Buddy Hackett and Mickey Rooney, headed to Vegas; and Milton Berle, wife Dorothy Provine, and battle-axe mother-in-law Ethel Merman. Added along the way are Dick Shawn, Phil Silvers, and Terry-Thomas. It's no joke that equal time is not afforded to funny ladies. Even Merman, the most prominent female, is mostly used as the butt of mean-spirited laughs. Among the few highlights are Jonathan Winters destroying a gas station, and Sid Caesar and Edie Adams trapped in a hardware-store basement. Winters, Caesar, and Mr. Shawn come off best, but no one could save the screamingly unfunny climax involving a loose fire escape and a fire truck's ladder. Continually operating on the notion that louder and more manic will automatically register as funnier, the movie was a sizable hit, a fact that justifies calling our world *mad* no less than four times.

The Hallelujah Trail (1965) – Its poster proclaimed, "See How the West Was Fun!" I'm sorry, but the actual West had to have been more fun than this ghastly comic western. Coming off his Grade-A success *The Great Escape* (1963), director John Sturges, another fellow not known for his funny bone, took a thin script and expanded it, in true '60s fashion, to irrationally overconfident proportions (yep, including an overture and an intermission). Though set in 1867, it's in line with the era's smirking sex comedies, but devoid of any comic flair; Sturges' ponderous pacing borders on directorial derangement. (An intermission was a real risk: would anyone return?) The plot follows the transport of forty wagons of whiskey to Denver with the journey's challenges including Indians and temperance ladies. Burt Lancaster is the army colonel leading the escort, and Lee Remick is the emancipated temperance leader. The wonderful Remick got a big-picture opportunity here, but it couldn't have been a worse waste of her gifts. An effortless actress and a sparkling presence, she's assigned nothing worth doing (and she and Lancaster have no chemistry). Recently an Oscar-nominated alcoholic in *Days of Wine and Roses* (1962), Remick is firmly anti-alcohol here (providing something of a lame inside joke). The climax is, of course, endless, a "comic" action sequence involving quicksand and Indians (drunk on champagne). *The Hallelujah Trail* was a staggering miscalculation, attaching mindless spending to rampant inanity.

***The Great Race* (1965)** – Though occasionally funny, this ungainly comedy isn't helped by director Blake Edwards' sledgehammer touch; it's also rather grandly overproduced and sorely in need of cutting. How ironic that *The Great Race* is dedicated to Laurel and Hardy, the legendary duo whose feature films were modestly budgeted and briskly timed. Set at the dawn of the age of automobiles, it swells all the way to 160 minutes. And yet kids love it, mostly because it's so cartoonish, with Tony Curtis the all-in-white good guy and Jack Lemmon the black-clad villain, reteamed from *Some Like It Hot* (1959). In his mustache-twirling, maniacally laughing burlesque of evil, Lemmon delivers the best of his over-the-top comic turns of the mid-'60s. (His sidekick is put-upon Peter Falk, commendable for being low-key *and* funny.) This movie's emancipated female is Natalie Wood, an aspiring reporter. There's a good running gag of her endless parade of Edith Head fashions; she changes costumes at an alarming rate. The car race goes from New York to Paris, giving the film some *Around the World* splash. All three stars are in the race, with Curtis mostly functioning as straight man, though he and Wood engage in battle-of-the-sexes rants (not unlike scenes in their *Sex and the Single Girl,* with Wood again a forced comic player—game and spirited but shrill). Intermission arrives when our stars are stranded on a melting iceberg, but, following the entr'acte, comes the best section, a *Prisoner of Zenda* spoof with Lemmon in the additional role of the villain's lookalike, a dizzy crown prince (with his own made-to-order Lemmon cackle). If *Mad, Mad World* wanted to be the funniest movie of all time, then *The Great Race* merely hoped to have the biggest, longest, and most colorful of pie fights, with Wood positively demolished by whipped cream as Curtis moves about unscathed, while Lemmon's delighted prince shouts, "Throw more brandy!" Where does a comedy go after this? Only one place: toppling the Eiffel Tower. The bloat of *The Great Race* is everywhere evident; it's just easy to forgive in light of intermittent pleasures.

***Inside Daisy Clover* (1965)** – A tale of big, bad Hollywood, it got a curious handling, turning the usual clichés into a pretentious and perplexing drag. Here the bloat seeps into an intellectual realm, with ordinary Hollywood fare turned into some kind of icy deconstruction, meaning that there's little of what might be called "recognizable humanity." God forbid it should make sense, like *Sunset Blvd.* (1950) or *A Star Is Born* (1954). Or were those classics too annoyingly straightforward and psychologically true for some? *Daisy Clover* doesn't feel like the work of insiders; it's more like a horror hybrid in which an industry appears to have been overtaken by vampires. Natalie Wood stars as a 15-year-old wildcat, a California beach urchin who wants to sing, right up until the moment she signs a movie contract and becomes "America's Little Valentine." The studio head is Christopher Plummer; he and his wife (Katharine Bard) seem to be trying to keep Wood in a cult, assisted by Roddy McDowall, their ghoulish lackey. Set in 1936, it consists of one bizarre scene after another, with Gavin Lambert's screenplay (based on his novel) insistently uninvolving and mystifying. And why cast a post-25 Wood in a role that ages only to sixteen? (Wood and her director, Robert Mulligan, had recently done great work together on *Love with the Proper Stranger,* but Wood's role here is just too vapid and monotonous.) Thank goodness for Robert Redford who provides some actual life and humanoid charm as an Errol Flynn-ish star, soon sleeping with underage Wood. (This explains her casting: a real teenager, such as Patty Duke, would have seemed too uncomfortably accurate). Redford's not around when it's revealed that he likes boys, too, and you even have to wonder if anyone ever told the actor this important detail. Wood's two big movie-musical numbers are both anachronistically "1965," as well as extremely tacky. And she has the expected breakdown, leading to a terrible climax involving a "comically" interrupted suicide attempt, one of many head-scratching moments. The one thing we never come close to doing is getting inside Daisy Clover, though the movie might have been less bad if mounted more intimately, rather than as a sterile star vehicle. Striving to say something (but not sure what), while suggesting a scalding "importance," *Inside Daisy Clover* offers nothing but maddening question marks, all dressed and decorated but with no one to inhabit it and nothing but blanks in its arsenal.

Khartoum (1966) – Based on a true story of 1880s Africa, this is epic historical filmmaking, the kind dying to emulate *Lawrence of Arabia.* Its British general does have the makings of a Lawrence, vain and visionary, but Charlton Heston, unyieldingly hardworking and earnest, has no touch of madness, no turbulent complexity. With gray temples and a studious British accent, he makes an honorable try; he's just out of his depth. It should have been Trevor Howard in the role, but you don't mount an epic (at least not the kind with an overture) without a Heston-sized star to ensure some return on your investment. *Khartoum* opens with a gorgeous travelogue of Egypt and the Sudan, the Nile and the desert, then continues to flaunt its wide-screen splendor. However, it is dramatically wanting, unable to deliver the intended Oscar-caliber gravity. Heston's character, already a hero to the Sudanese for having ended the slave trade, accepts the request of his Prime Minister (crustily good Ralph Richardson) to evacuate Egyptians from Khartoum. They are in danger from the Mahdi (Laurence Olivier), a Muslim leader forging a holy war. With a deepened voice and dark makeup, Olivier is doing a slight variation on his recent stage and screen performances as Othello, while also trying to outdo Alec Guinness' Prince Feisal in *Lawrence*. Mostly confined to his tent, a majestic Olivier is quite striking all in white (including his turban). But *Khartoum* is never enough of a real duel between him and Heston. They share only two scenes, one early and one late, totaling about fifteen minutes, leaving two hours of screen time without any comparable interaction. Whether or not that's historically accurate, it mars the storytelling and the direction (by Basil Dearden), keeping things more flaccid than taut. Despite beautiful locations, well-executed battles, and an air of integrity, *Khartoum* bogs down in talkiness. There's never enough at stake (for the audience) in a film that sometimes uncomfortably evokes those old-fashioned British-Empire adventures of the '30s. *Khartoum* isn't bad, it just falls considerably short of its ambitions.

Thoroughly Modern Millie **(1967)** – I have enormous affection for this musical, the first one Julie Andrews made after *The Sound of Music*, having done two 1966 dramas in between: Alfred Hitchcock's *Torn Curtain* and George Roy Hill's *Hawaii*. She and Mr. Hill reteamed for *Millie*, a madcap '20s spoof, a chance for the star to honor the spirit of *The Boy Friend*, her 1954 Broadway debut vehicle. There is much to savor here, despite its status as an obvious bloater, enlarging a charmingly light and giddy plot rather gargantuanly, as if it had to live up to *The Sound of Music* in size and length. At 138 minutes, it's crazily overlong. And why an intermission for such fluff? Andrews, however, is unerringly relaxed, confident, and generous with her co-stars, all the while dancing up a storm. *Millie* begins with some terrific stuff: the title tune, in which Andrews transitions from hick to flapper; the number inside a hotel elevator powered by tap-dancing feet (courtesy of Andrews and Mary Tyler Moore); and "The Tapioca," a group tap number, a clever riff on

"The Carioca" and other novelty dances. Andrews may become "modern" but her agenda is old-fashioned: to marry her boss (handsome, straight-arrowed John Gavin). She and Ms. Moore live in a NYC hotel for "single young ladies" run by Beatrice Lillie (who's running a white-slavery operation on the side). As the screen's most amusing racist, the great Lillie is a treat, as is a delightful Ms. Moore as a wealthy airhead (who gets to say "bitch"). Englishman James Fox makes a captivatingly energized juvenile, an all-American dancing fool. And arriving late is Oscar-nominated Carol Channing as a millionaire ex-chorus girl, a swell dame and a font of effervescent fun. Alas, the script's brightness deteriorates steadily and frenetically wears you out with fireworks, acrobatics, and a chase through Chinatown. Mr. Hill's direction shows no feel for sophisticated silliness nor stylish attractiveness; visually, the movie is as flat as Andrews' post-makeover bosom. But the knockout ensemble is always at-the-ready with a dollop of wit or a genuine laugh, plus there's all that snappy choreography from Joe Layton. You can both celebrate and feel depressed about *Millie,* which might have been truly wonderful had it not opted to overstuff itself. The movie made money, but poor Julie Andrews: her next two films, *Star!* (1968) and *Darling Lili* (1970), bloated their way to failure. Between 1964 and 1970, she skyrocketed to superstardom and plunged into box-office oblivion.

Ice Station Zebra (1968) – After *The Hallelujah Trail,* John Sturges directed the superb but neglected western *Hour of the Gun* (1967), then continued in his macho vein with this all-male submarine drama. Lacking the action-movie oomph of Sturges' *The Great Escape,* it is absurdly embellished with an overture, intermission, entr'acte, and exit music. Was there a point in taking a routine Cold War plot and mounting it like a prestige project? Based on Alistair MacLean's novel, *Ice Station Zebra* seems not only delusional but just plain bad—long and tedious, of course, but also muddled and trite. And quite phony-looking with all that snow and ice which appears to be Styrofoam. (It's no wonder that this movie lost the Special Visual Effects Oscar to *2001: A Space Odyssey.*) Rock Hudson is a US nuclear-sub captain on a mysterious mission to the North Pole, involving rescues at a British weather station. Along for the ride are Patrick McGoohan, a spy of some sort, and Ernest Borgnine, a gregarious Russian (on our side, while struggling with his poor accent). Sturges is defeated by a script that's too slow in revealing information, resulting in an exceedingly boring opening hour. There's one memorable sequence in which the submerged vessel tries to crash through the ice on the surface, but the rest is unsuspenseful, including the climactic standoff between Hudson's crew and Soviet paratroopers. It's hokey, conventional nonsense, the kind of top-secret pulp found in comic books, including much ado about a roll of film wanted by both sides. As for Hudson, he's drab and stolid, too aware of his career in decline.

Chitty Chitty Bang Bang **(1968)** – As a moviegoing child of the late '60s, I'm here to tell you it was not a good time for children's musicals. After two synthetic horrors from 1967, *The Happiest Millionaire* and *Doctor Dolittle*, along came *Chitty Chitty Bang Bang* starring Dick Van Dyke who had to take some of the blame. It was *Mary Poppins* (1964), in which he starred, that all these films were trying so desperately to replicate. At age four, I loved *The Great Race*, and at six I loved *Thoroughly Modern Millie*, but, at seven, even I knew that *Chitty* was dreadful, despite Van Dyke and a score by *Mary Poppins'* Sherman Brothers. Van Dyke looks as if he knows this undertaking is hopeless, appearing distracted and woefully uninspired (aside from some nifty hoofing). And clearly cast to be Julie Andrews, Sally Ann Howes is simply not major-star material. Her big ballad is the movie's blatant go-for-popcorn moment. While she is trying to emulate Andrews, Van Dyke seems to be trying to emulate himself, the guy everybody loved in *Mary Poppins*. As in *Poppins,* there are two kids, a girl and a boy, both so British they can barely talk, while Van Dyke, as their father, has no British accent at all. He plays an eccentric inventor, circa 1910, while Ms. Howes is "Truly Scrumptious," the daughter of a candy maker. Here's a kids' movie that's sickly sweet, with no feeling or basic longing to ground it. The second half has Van Dyke telling the kids an elaborate fairy tale in which they appear (as does the title-role car); it includes a trip to Vulgaria (where at least Robert Helpmann offers some sinister flash as a child catcher). Who can believe that Roald Dahl wrote the script, or that it's based on an Ian Fleming story? Also below par are the Sherman Brothers, unable to compete with their *Poppins* score, with a title tune begging to be another "Supercalifragilistic…" Taking overproduction to an elephantine level, *Chitty* was yet another clunker that dared to include an intermission, a chance for entire families to run screaming from the theater.

Ryan's Daughter **(1970)** – The 1960s had been smashing for David Lean, all those Oscars for *Lawrence of Arabia* followed by the box-office bonanza *Doctor Zhivago* (1965). Though deeply flawed as drama, *Zhivago* at least was good enough to justify its literary-epic length and vast size. The same couldn't be said for Lean's *Ryan's Daughter,* which seemed to use *Zhivago* as an inappropriate model. The *Ryan's* plot, an original by Robert Bolt, had the makings of an old-style woman's picture with some historical color. However, scaled by Lean to *Zhivago* proportions and inflated past three hours, it became a confounding artistic disaster. Basically, it's an Irish *Madame Bovary* set during World War I, with young Sarah Miles smitten with widowed schoolteacher Robert Mitchum, seeing him as worldly until she's disillusioned by their unexciting wedding night. She pursues erotic passion with an ossified Christopher Jones, a British major (who's married *and* shell-shocked). With the Irish rooting for the Germans, Miles is sleeping with the enemy and headed for destruction. It's rather nice, though, to see Mitchum cast against type, so mild and modest, and with a good brogue. There are showier roles for Leo McKern (Miles' pub-owning father), Trevor Howard (the tough priest trying to hold the village together), and John Mills (an Irish Quasimodo). Offering an occasional grunt, Mills was inexplicably awarded an Oscar for what is a stunt performance. Meanwhile, hoping to be another "Lara's Theme," Maurice Jarre's score is not only irritating but irritatingly incessant. Overall, Ms. Miles manages to behave brazenly without being terribly exciting; she's not exactly a young Jean Simmons. When the intermission comes, it only highlights the fact that this is an epic production in search of an epic story. Lean's pacing is deadly, and, despite an excellent storm sequence and the gorgeously photographed beach and cliffs, the usual Lean visual inventiveness escapes him. In response to the film's clobbering critical reaction, he didn't make another movie until he redeemed himself with *A Passage to India* (1984). By then, the heyday of overtures and intermissions was a distant memory, with the bloaters having been killed off not just by this movie but by other mummifying losers as disparate as *Nicholas and Alexandra* (1971) and *Mame* (1974).

Bonnie & Clyde & Ted & Alice: Approaching the 1970s (1968-1970)

It was perhaps the most seismic shift in American movies since the transition to sound: the onscreen freedoms of the late 1960s. Bigger than any sound-era technological innovation, such as CinemaScope in 1953, here was a final unshackling from three decades of choke-holding enforcement of the Production Code. It had been a long time coming, encouraged by the openness of European cinema, certainly, but also by an accelerating cultural shift in America, a time of questioning, including a new outspokenness on such brewing concepts as free love, women's liberation, gay identity, and the anti-war movement regarding U.S. involvement in Vietnam. By the mid-'60s, Hollywood was in the process of saying goodbye to one audience—the generation who still wanted to see *Madame X* (1966)—and hello to an audience ready for *Who's Afraid of Virginia Woolf?* (1966). In the Code's place came the film-rating system, christened by the Motion Picture Association of America on November 1, 1968, making possible the occasionally naked, bloody, and foul-mouthed Hollywood we've known ever since. As never before, movies were essentially able to do anything they wanted. Film content quickly went way beyond what previous generations could have imagined; it was pre-Code cinema times ten. Without interference from Code censorship, adults could make their own decisions about what they wanted to see. In 1969, when the low-budget *Easy Rider* made easy money and the spendthrift *Hello, Dolly!* couldn't turn a profit, the deal seemed sealed. Among the casualties were "virgin" rom-coms, *Peyton Place*-type soaps, tee-hee sex farces, as well as Julie Andrews and Elvis Presley.

If it appears that I've been pretty hard on the 1960s, it has to do with the exhausting of outmoded conventions, the bloating of longstanding genres, and the cowardice about sex, all of which prompted an artistic revolution. Even so, there was much great work along the way—1962 and 1964 are two exemplary years in American film—and yet an increasing amount of tired-out fare helped spark the revitalizing housecleaning of the later '60s. Between the Code's mid-'60s crumbling and the rating-system's 1968 arrival, it appears that 1967 was the cusp year, the marker between old and new Hollywood, both a last gasp and a brave leap, with some films qualifying as a bit of each. Among westerns there was *Hombre,* which might be called *Stagecoach* with a heightened social conscience, starring Paul Newman as an Apache-raised white man, and the great *Hour of the Gun,* yet another Wyatt Earp movie but one filled with ambiguities, with Earp (James Garner) a scary, revenge-twisted good guy. In the world of romantic comedy, the breezy *Barefoot in the Park* brought some raging honeymoon hormones to familiar newlywed fluff, while two commercial marriage comedies had unusually mature agendas: *Two for the Road* retained the high fashion and glamorous locations expected from an Audrey Hepburn comedy, while dissecting the decline of her relationship with Albert Finney; *Divorce American Style* explored two splits—that of Dick Van Dyke and Debbie Reynolds, and Jason Robards and Jean Simmons—with adult humor and recognizable situations rather than moronic sex-comedy antics. Then came *Guess Who's Coming to Dinner*, the year's most clear-cut case of old meets new, with legends Spencer Tracy and Katharine Hepburn, first teamed in 1942, headlining a hot-button interracial-marriage comedy alongside Sidney Poitier as the "who" brought home by the stars' daughter. Catering to both Tracy-Hepburn fans *and* the now generation, the film is a self-congratulatory sitcom with the accomplished stars making high-concept pandering sometimes *seem* like witty contemporary comedy.

Point Blank, also of 1967, took a typical film-noir plot and restyled it with late '60s visual tricks, jazzy editing, flashes of nudity, and eruptions of violence, the effect being that of an art-house noir. But two biggies of 1967 defined the year and the new era, both of them overrated but with an impact that can't be overestimated. Arthur Penn's *Bonnie and Clyde,* starring Warren Beatty as impotent Clyde and Faye Dunaway as thrill-seeking Bonnie, came out in August and rattled the crime genre. With its startling approach to violence—a jolting swerve between comedy and gunplay—*Bonnie and Clyde* still has the power to surprise, unnerve, and get a laugh. Later, in December, came Mike Nichols' *The Graduate,* a new-generation exploration of the gap between parents and young adults, a *Rebel Without a Cause* with an emphasis on sex and comedy. During Andy Hardy's days, parents were wise and young people were overdramatizing, but, ever since James Dean, the grownups were more likely to behave foolishly. In *The Graduate,* Mrs. Robinson (Anne Bancroft) isn't given a fair shake; she's an unhappy, unfulfilled woman conceived as the evil queen. America responded to Dustin Hoffman's comic deadpan, as well as his indecision within confusing times. *Bonnie and Clyde* and *The Graduate,* the main events of 1967, lost the Best Picture Oscar to the lesser *In the Heat of the Night,* which, starring Sidney Poitier as a great police detective, had the patina of being a socially conscious film about racism, which it *was* to an extent. But it was also a standard murder mystery, finally deemed a more palatable pick for the famously safe-minded Academy.

Old-guard Hollywood's uncomfortable reaction to changing times was reflected in other late-'60s choices for the Best Picture Oscar. For 1966, the blisteringly provocative and emotionally scalding *Who's Afraid of Virginia Woolf?* lost to the reassuringly high-minded historical wheezer *A Man for All Seasons,* a literate and tasteful prestige picture unlikely to scare anybody the way *Virginia Woolf* could. The 1968 race honored a nicely done adaptation of the musical *Oliver!* but the film event of that year, love it or hate it, was Stanley Kubrick's dramatically wanting but altogether visionary *2001: A Space Odyssey,* a visual and aural feast. Though the not nominated *2001* was about nothing less than humankind's existence, it apparently couldn't compete with Charles Dickens. By 1969, the Academy was seeing the writing on the wall, choosing the X-rated *Midnight Cowboy* over the bromantically charged *Butch Cassidy and the Sundance Kid.* I'm not wild about either movie, much preferring *The Wild Bunch* (not nominated), but *Midnight Cowboy* is certainly superior to *Butch Cassidy,* and its win augured a step in the right direction, an acknowledgement of modern subject matter. The 1970 Oscar lineup, however, perfectly reflected Academy discomfort, with two retrograde nominees—the tearjerking *Love Story* and the *High and the Mighty*-ish *Airport*—and two groundbreaking nominees—*MASH* and *Five Easy Pieces*—all four losing to the middle-of-the-road *Patton,* which, somehow, could be interpreted as reactionary *or* liberal, even though it's really just George C. Scott's one-man show.

When the new freedoms really took off, what followed was a so-called Second Golden Age of Hollywood, specifically in the first half of the 1970s, the era of *The Last Picture Show, Cabaret,* both *Godfather* movies, *The Candidate, American Graffiti, Mean Streets, Conrack, The Conversation, Chinatown, Nashville, Dog Day Afternoon,* etc. On the way there were the films of 1968-1970, some of which were clearly influenced by the gains of 1967's cusp movies, signifying a brief period that was integral to a transition headed for gold.

Bob & Carol & Ted & Alice (1969): Natalie Wood

Planet of the Apes (1968) – Along with *2001* later in the year, this blockbuster was part of science fiction's legitimization from B pictures to A pictures, graduating from low-budget black and white, having served its time as a Cold War metaphor. *Planet of the Apes* was cautionary in new ways, with updated preoccupations that included racism, sensitivity toward the animal kingdom, and the future of humanity itself. Beyond the presumed excitement and suspense, it's a witty comedy of manners, satirizing evolution, religion, and polite society. Charlton Heston recharged a sagging career, showing off his non-sagging naked butt. Ideally cast as an astronaut, he gives a robustly physical performance. And his director, Franklin J. Schaffner, did an ace job in every respect, from the film's breathtaking visual scope to its even-keeled balance between humor and thrills. Powerful orangutan Maurice Evans and two smarty-pants chimpanzees—archaeologist Roddy McDowall and "animal" psychologist Kim Hunter—become vivid characters able to shine through the phenomenal ape makeup. (The script can't resist one-liners like "Human see, human do.") Based on Pierre Boulle's novel, but with a different (and great) twist ending, *Planet of the Apes* was designed to strike fear in the hearts of apathetic human beings; its message being that it may be later than you think.

The Detective (1968) – One of the issues given higher visibility and basic acknowledgement in the new landscape was homosexuality, even if the portrayals were bleak and pitiful. After all, nothing good could come from the same-sex desire of Marlon Brando in *Reflections in a Golden Eye* (1967) or Rod Steiger in *The Sergeant* (1968). The gay characters in *The Detective* aren't center stage, but the film still makes a decent, if limited, try at something up-to-date. Gordon Douglas, of studio-system Hollywood, seems the wrong director for material more suited to the grittiness of a Sidney Lumet. And though Frank Sinatra is solid in the title role of homicide cop, a tough (and fairly glum) man of integrity, Robert Mitchum would have been better. The plot hinges on the violent murder of a rich gay man, but *The Detective* is thrown off-balance by Sinatra's separation from wife Lee Remick, with two extended flashbacks embellishing their story. Remick, stuck with an undercooked character, shares Sinatra's blue-eyed intensity, but their whiny relationship drags the movie down. Regarding the case, Sinatra believes in live and let live, proving it when he punches homophobic cop Robert Duvall for being abusive to a gay guy. Sinatra's detective also feels modern in his overall disillusionment, so it's too bad that the movie becomes increasingly lumpy—a city corruption subplot is one too many—and overcomplicated. As for the gay content, there's a scene of men rounded up, caught fooling around (fully clothed) inside a truck, plus Tony Musante as a psychotic case. The main gay figure is tormented, self-loathing William Windom whose story dominates the film's final fifteen minutes. It's the climactic flashback to the night of the murder, which includes a gay-bar sequence ("Laura" on the soundtrack) with an encounter that leads to off-screen sex, followed by an argument and the killing. Though *The Detective* tries to do too much, it gave Frank Sinatra his most successful brush with the new cinema, two decades past his smiling sailor days with Gene Kelly.

The Lion in Winter (1968) – It would seem to belong to the "prestigious" theater-based adaptations of historical England—*Becket* (1964), *A Man for All Seasons* (1966), *Anne of the Thousand Days* (1969)—because that's exactly what it is. But *The Lion in Winter,* set in 1183, also left a firm mark on the medieval brand of such lavish fare: it would never be pretty again. Hereafter, no Robin Hood-era drama, including any *about* Robin Hood, would ever be a colorful storybook. The medieval castle of *The Lion in Winter* is damp, dirty, drafty, and depressing. And yet all that period-detail realism is ironically at odds with the source material—James Goldman's Broadway play—a high comedy in which a scheming royal family does horrible things to each other while spouting brittle dialogue, including witty zingers. Director Anthony Harvey repeats the mistake of Gabriel Pascal who helmed the 1945 film version of *Caesar and Cleopatra* (1945). Pascal brought monumental production values to George Bernard Shaw's delicate sophisticated comedy, turning a jewel into a boulder. Nonetheless, *The Lion in Winter* is indeed entertaining, graced with Peter O'Toole as English King Henry II (also his role in *Becket*) and an Oscar-winning Katharine Hepburn as Eleanor (Henry's imprisoned queen). Though the tensions between the script's theatricality and the film's physical veracity create a self-conscious discord, the royal intrigue is enticing enough to keep the movie chugging, spiked with showy acting on all fronts (though O'Toole yells too much). Set in France, it's a home-for-the-holidays family ordeal, with Hepburn out of her English prison for the festivities and O'Toole seeking an annulment so he can marry his mistress. The stars' three sons include Anthony Hopkins as a gay Richard the Lionheart (apparently closeted as played by Ian Hunter in *The Adventures of Robin Hood*). Hopkins is in love with Timothy Dalton (Philip II of France), meaning that *The Lion in Winter* brings the simmering gay subtexts of other O'Toole historical ventures, such as *Lawrence of Arabia* (1962) and, yes, *Becket,* out into the open. Hopkins and Dalton are actually about to have sex when O'Toole interrupts. (The script includes the cliché of Hopkins having been close to Mommy, distant from Daddy.) Though its incessant cleverness and gamesmanship can be wearying, *The Lion in Winter* was named Best Picture of 1968 by the New York Film Critics' Circle.

Take the Money and Run **(1969)** – Just as the career of comedy star-director Jerry Lewis was fading fast, along came a different kind of funnyman-director, a more adult and thinking-person's screen comedian—Woody Allen. By the late '70s, with his Oscar-winning *Annie Hall* (1977) and even-better *Manhattan* (1979), Allen was the supreme chronicler of complicated, therapy-assisted urban romance. Though he had written the awful, instantly dated *What's New Pussycat* (1965), he redeemed himself with *Take the Money and Run,* his first venture as star-director-writer, an impressively sustained spoof of crime and prison movies (co-written by Mickey Rose). It's a mockumentary ahead of its time, with Allen showing an easy flair for both verbal and visual humor. He's first glimpsed playing a cello in a marching band, a blissfully ridiculous sight. Allen's famed love of classic Hollywood (notably in his 1969 play/1972 film *Play it Again, Sam*) is apparent, as the film recalls *I Am a Fugitive from a Chain Gang, They Live By Night, The Killing,* etc. Janet Margolin is the first of Allen's pretty, fresh, and natural leading ladies, most memorable when she's talking about the unfair voting for the "Ten Most Wanted." (When Allen's embarrassed parents are interviewed, it's from behind Groucho glasses.) His best bits include his ticklish response to prison frisking and his soap gun turning into lather in the rain. And though it's a highlight when his gang has to compete with another crew of robbers showing up at the same bank, the most inspired scene involves Allen's bad penmanship on his stick-up note, leading to much discussion among bank employees ("gub" or "gun," "apt natural" or "act natural"?). Slight but consistently funny, *Take the Money and Run* was a happy harbinger for Allen's long reign as one of America's funniest men and finest post-Code filmmakers.

Bob & Carol & Ted & Alice **(1969)** – The two-coupled 1967 marriage comedy *Divorce American Style* was a significant step on the way to this more adventurous account of the sexual revolution as it was unfolding. Never mind the youth culture, what about the subculture of married swingers? Whether or not moviegoers themselves were experimenting, they had certainly heard about or were reading about the issues raised in writer-director Paul Mazursky's *Bob & Carol*. Had it really been just a half-decade since the adolescent prurience of Jack Lemmon's sex comedies? And here is Natalie Wood herself, just five years after that cringe-inducing farce known as *Sex and the Single Girl*. Set among the wealthy of Los Angeles, *Bob & Carol*, co-written by Mazursky and Larry Tucker, is highly amusing satire, with Ms. Wood and husband Robert Culp embarking on an emotional and physical odyssey after their interpersonal communications are transformed by only one weekend retreat. Of course, they talk ad nauseam about their *feelings,* and they do engage in sexual freedom: Culp has a one-night stand; Wood has sex with a tennis instructor. They attain a comic nonchalance regarding each other's flings, with Wood's tryst more of an eye-opener for 1969, a married woman's sexual exploration on equal terms with her husband's. Their married friends, Elliott Gould and Dyan Cannon (both Oscar-nominated), serve as a dose of reality as surrogates for the more conventional world beyond. Their extended bedroom conversation—he wants to have sex; she's not in the mood—is a boudoir classic. With Wood and Culp in their happy haze, Gould and Cannon steal the show, with Cannon especially funny in her nervous edginess. (Wood and Culp might have more dimension if we met them before the retreat and could better evaluate the change in them.) The foursome smokes some pot and will eventually end up in bed together. But will they go all the way? *Bob & Carol* is a smart, deliciously verbal comedy that is kind to its characters as they confront social and sexual boundaries, muddling through the best they can. Wood was thirty when she made this movie, a big fat hit in which she staked her claim on the new era. And yet she vanished from theater screens as decidedly as Doris Day. Yes, motherhood awaited Wood, but seen here, looking so beautiful and so primed for the next challenge, it seems a shame she didn't continue her onscreen growth into the new decade, especially after having been at the forefront of the screen's sexual mores with *Splendor in the Grass* (1961), *Love with the Proper Stranger* (1963), and, then, as "Carol," going further than she probably ever dreamed.

***The Sterile Cuckoo* (1969)** – If *Bob & Carol & Ted & Alice* was aimed at the adults, then *The Sterile Cuckoo* was designed for the thriving youth culture as an honest account of love and sex among college students. It's a simple, nicely observed drama of first love between freshmen—Liza Minnelli and Wendell Burton—at different schools. Like Barbra Streisand, Minnelli was a new star who didn't look like a star, despite her resemblance to her movie-star mother

Judy Garland. Streisand and Minnelli were offbeat-looking by Hollywood standards yet seemed suited to this burgeoning age of deglamorization. As Pookie, Minnelli is extraordinary, so remarkably assured for someone in her early twenties, giving an unblinkingly vivid and electrically alert performance. The character is a kook, a lonely, strange, unloved girl; she's childlike and heartbreakingly vulnerable. But she's also like a screwball-comedy heroine, a relentless pursuer barging ahead, spinning tales, and full of spunk. Similar to Shirley MacLaine in the 1958 *Some Came Running* (directed by Liza's father Vincente), Minnelli's acting is nakedly exposed, unafraid to be pathetic or embarrassing. She bares the sad, scared girl underneath the "show." Her famous phone-call scene—with Mr. Burton on the other end, beginning to pull away—is shot in one take, more than five minutes, with Minnelli hitting a you-name-it range of emotion without ever seeming self-indulgent. A perfect foil, Burton is sweet, mild, and natural. She opens him up; he lets her be herself. They lose their virginity together in a motel cottage, an awkward and appealing scene that takes its time, the kind of sequence that was a fairly new prospect in American movies (usually having happened off-screen). The director, Alan J. Pakula, later guided Jane Fonda in *Klute* (1971) and Meryl Streep in *Sophie's Choice* (1982), making him a major director of actresses, a latter-day George Cukor. Though Pakula includes too many montages of young love, and overuses the film's excellent theme, "Come Saturday Morning," *The Sterile Cuckoo* remains a special film. The promise of Minnelli's Oscar-nominated performance was fulfilled with her Oscar win for *Cabaret* (1972), but her movie career wasn't able to survive three high-profile flops of the mid-'70s: *Lucky Lady* (1975), *A Matter of Time* (1976), and *New York, New York* (1977).

***They Shoot Horses, Don't They?* (1969)** – Joining Liza Minnelli in the 1969 Best Actress Oscar race was Jane Fonda, another second-generation star. In movies since 1960, Fonda made her name in the kind of sex comedy that had recently gone kaput. After *Barbarella* (1968) had anointed her as a sex goddess, Fonda repositioned herself toward serious-actress territory (where she found her greatest success). If late '60s screen content recalled the openness of pre-Code Hollywood, *They Shoot Horses, Don't They?* feels like a direct descendant, a flavorful new-Hollywood look at Depression America, set in the pre-Code year of 1932. Evoking the young Barbara Stanwyck, Fonda plays a hard, angry, self-hating woman, a deftly wisecracking toughie with a protective outer shell. Looking terrific as a '30s dame, she's fiercely good here, despite the role's emotional limitations and its questionable final destination. Among the desperate hopefuls joining Fonda in the grim, tawdry world of marathon dancing are Red Buttons, Bonnie Bedelia, Bruce Dern, and a striking Susannah York as a Harlow-styled wannabe from London, heading toward madness. No one could miss the dance marathon as a metaphor for life's struggle, which makes sense, but this compelling drama weakens in its second half, the heavier and more "symbolic" it becomes. Michael Sarrazin is saddled with the Angel of Death role (a blank slate, like a sweet alien), while an Oscar-winning Gig Young is sensational as the M.C., a charismatic showman. Onstage, he's a rousing sentimentalist, cynically exploiting both the dancers and the audience, a representative of sleazy showbiz (akin to the also Oscar-winning Joel Grey in the 1972 *Cabaret*). But off-stage, with his mask down, Mr. Young is a clear-eyed realist. Directed by Sydney Pollack, *They Shoot Horses, Don't They?* is a mostly gripping piece of work, with Jane Fonda, the premier screen actress of her day, confidently on her way to her Oscar for *Klute* (1971).

MASH (1970) – Robert Altman became a major directorial force with this freewheeling comedy set during the Korean War. *MASH* remains a hilariously daring work that hasn't aged a bit, even though it's a 1970 act of counterculture rebellion set two decades earlier. The merry anarchy, not seen since the days of *Duck Soup* (1933), makes perfect sense: in war, why not have as much booze, sex, and laughs as possible? Loose and effortless, it all feels seamlessly juggled by Altman. Donald Sutherland and Elliott Gould are top surgeons who do their jobs impeccably and devotedly, while also poking fun at anyone rigid, priggish, humorless, hypocritical, or by-the-book, all of which is *very* 1970. And who can resist lovable rogues aiming at uptight targets? Without ever slacking off at their work, the guys turn the medical unit into a prank-filled camp/resort, swilling martinis and driving golf balls a few miles from the front. In Sutherland and Gould, *MASH* has two Grouchos, with plenty of Margaret Dumonts. Augmented by Altman's signature use of overlapping dialogue, *MASH* is an innovative comedy that brings a screwball zaniness into a horror situation; audiences of 1970 couldn't forget the Vietnam War raging off-screen. And reality is ever-present, whether or not commented upon, notably amid the bloodied operating tables. With a minimum of nudity and "language," *MASH* is subversively original: broadcasting a sex scene over a loudspeaker, reenacting *The Last Supper*, orchestrating the public display of a private shower, and climaxing with an ecstatically chaotic (and drug-tampered) football game. There are a few connections to the beloved TV series it spawned—Gary Burghoff as Radar; the theme song—but the film continues to stand apart, singular as both a comedy and a war movie.

***Five Easy Pieces* (1970)** – Jack Nicholson walked away with the acting honors in *Easy Rider* (1969), though there wasn't much in the way of competition. He then made the jump to full-blown stardom and anti-hero status as the center of this searching drama, a seminal work of America's new interest in self-actualization, in figuring out what the hell it all means. Directed by Bob Rafelson, it's an uneven work, marred by caricatured characters, yet it maintains its intimate feeling and genuine quest for answers. Nicholson, in the process of forming his iconic star persona, is superb: intelligent and concentrated but also restless, confused, and steeped in self-loathing. The classic diner scene (with waitress Lorna Thayer) is about "No Substitutions"— life's arbitrary, frustrating rules—and it was instantly embraced as being emblematic of that feeling of having had enough! Nicholson plays a talented pianist who bolted from his musical family three years ago, drifting aimlessly, free of ties and responsibilities, working on an oil rig, and trying to—in the jargon of the day—"find himself." He can't always articulate his emotions, which is reflected in his dissatisfaction and rebelliousness, his probing for more fulfilling ways to live. (It's *The Razor's Edge* for 1970.) With no easy answers, his running continues. Unfortunately, the movie isn't very kind to women, notably Nicholson's dimwitted doormat girlfriend (Karen Black). Ms. Black doesn't help things by playing down to her needy easy-target role and seems to laugh at her own character. But then most of the women here are caricatured or made to seem annoying, even though the screenplay was written by a woman (Carole Eastman). Nicholson has a moving climactic monologue—a spontaneous, richly felt expression of unguarded emotion— delivered to his stroke-victim father. *Five Easy Pieces* endures as a time capsule of early '70s angst, while also marking the turbulent emergence of Jack Nicholson.

***Little Big Man* (1970)** – Even before Sam Peckinpah's *The Wild Bunch* (1969), westerns such as John Ford's somber *Cheyenne Autumn* (1964) and John Sturges' dark-hued *Hour of the Gun* (1967) were moving closer to upending many of the genre's conventions. The revisionist *Little Big Man* joins forces from 1967's two touchstones—*Bonnie and Clyde* director Arthur Penn and *The Graduate* star Dustin Hoffman—making it a fitting movie upon which to end this chapter. Hoffman, as a 121-year-old man and the sole white survivor of Little Big Horn, recounts his life, starting at age ten when he survived an Indian attack. He was adopted by Cheyennes, then adopted by whites, a reverend and his wife (Faye Dunaway, another *Bonnie and Clyde* alumnus, but playing more of a nineteenth-century "Mrs. Robinson"). Throughout, Hoffman gives an amiably unforced performance, charming and funny in what amounts to a western Forrest Gump, always *there*. His life seesaws between the Indians and the whites, all that history coming together in one man. He shares a warm serious-minded relationship with Chief Dan George as his "grandfather," a man of touching dignity. As for Dunaway, only in the movie for about fifteen minutes, she's an animated Southern delight, a religious hypocrite and a cheating wife (who also inappropriately bathes Hoffman, dries him off, and kisses him). Episodic in nature, *Little Big Man* can be broadly comic, especially in its depiction of whites (like Dunaway), with Mr. Penn aiming for a *Bonnie and Clyde* mix of tones, keeping things riskily off-kilter as he creates another bloody farce. (As in *MASH*, the war content evokes Vietnam.) Geared for a skeptical audience, the film's depiction of Custer (Richard Mulligan) is that of an arrogant jerk and bloodthirsty madman, highly comical in his cartoonish buffoonery yet still scary. Mulligan is quite game for the over-the-top conception, which includes having an all-out mad scene during Little Big Horn. Though Penn's directorial touch is hardly subtle, he keeps this epic moving at a fast clip. *Little Big Man* may ultimately be a talent-heavy mishmash, not as affecting or as powerful as Anthony Mann's similarly themed *Devil's Doorway* (1950), but its assets and its flaws, taken together, are representative of its rule-breaking era. It's a quirky, anti-establishment film about turning history on its head at a time when movies and the industry itself were being turned on their collective heads.

Index